Controlling the Atom in the 21st Century

Controlling the Atom in the 21st Century

EDITED BY

David P. O'Very,
Christopher E. Paine,
and Dan W. Reicher

Westview Press
BOULDER • SAN FRANCISCO • OXFORD

Copyright © 1994 by Westview Press, Inc.

Published in 1994 in the United States of America by Westview Press, Inc., 5500 Central Avenue, Boulder, Colorado 80301-2877, and in the United Kingdom by Westview Press, 36 Lonsdale Road, Summertown, Oxford OX2 7EW

Library of Congress Cataloging-in-Publication Data
Controlling the atom in the 21st century / edited by David P. O'Very,
    Christopher E. Paine, and Dan W. Reicher.
        p.   cm.
    Includes bibliographical references and index.
    ISBN 0-8133-8816-3
    1. Nuclear energy—Law and legislation.   2. Nuclear power plants—
Licenses.   3. Nuclear nonproliferation.   I. O'Very, David P.
II. Paine, Christopher E.   III. Reicher, Dan W.
K3990.6.C66   1994
333.792'4—dc20   93-39042
                                                                                      CIP

Printed and bound in the United States of America

The paper used in this publication meets the requirements
of the American National Standard for Permanence of Paper
for Printed Library Materials Z39.48-1984.

10   9   8   7   6   5   4   3   2   1

Contents

Preface

The Natural Resources Defense Council (NRDC) is a nonprofit membership organization dedicated to protecting the planet's natural resources and to improving the quality of the human environment. With 170,000 members and a staff of lawyers, scientists, and environmental specialists, NRDC combines the power of law, science, and people in defense of the environment.

For over 20 years, NRDC has been a leader in efforts to: (1) halt commercial use and proliferation of nuclear weapons-usable materials; (2) phase out underground nuclear test explosions; (3) increase public knowledge of, and influence on, both civil and defense nuclear activities; (4) permanently dispose of nuclear waste in an environmentally sound manner; (5) cooperatively verify storage and dismantlement of U.S. and former Soviet nuclear weapons; and (6) ensure environmental compliance by, and clean-up of, the U.S. nuclear weapons complex. *Controlling the Atom in the 21st Century* represents NRDC's continued dedication to these and other important nuclear issues.

In December 1992, NRDC assembled a diverse group of professionals at the Graves Mountain Lodge in Syria, Virginia, for a three-day conference to examine solutions to the various problems posed by the civilian and defense uses of nuclear energy. NRDC commissioned a number of working papers that served as the basis for discussion at the conference. These papers were later revised for publication. The papers represent the views of the authors and do not necessarily reflect those of NRDC, the conference participants, or the editors.

David P. O'Very
Christopher E. Paine
Dan W. Reicher

Acknowledgments

Controlling the Atom in the 21st Century is the product of a diverse group of authors concerned with improving the ways in which the U.S. regulates both civil and defense nuclear activities and controls the dissemination of weapons-usable nuclear materials, technology, and information.

The editors would like to thank the conference participants for their comments on the papers that formed the basis for this publication and acknowledge the support of NRDC's nuclear program staff in Washington, D.C., with special thanks to program assistant Jean Reynolds, Scoville intern Karen Cramer, and visiting associate Eric Fersht for their able assistance during the various stages of this project.

We also want to express our appreciation for the generous support of the John D. and Catherine T. MacArthur Foundation and the Prospect Hill Foundation, which made the Graves Mountain conference and this publication possible. In addition, we gratefully acknowledge the grants provided by the W. Alton Jones Foundation, the Carnegie Corporation of New York, the Ford Foundation, the HKH Foundation, the Rockefeller Brothers Fund, and two anonymous donors in support of NRDC's overall Nuclear Program.

Finally, we thank the 170,000 members of NRDC, whose support makes all our work possible.

D.P.O.
C.E.P.
D.W.R.

Introduction

Five decades after splitting the atom, both defense and civilian applications of nuclear energy have reached a critical juncture. The demise of the Warsaw Pact and the disintegration of the Soviet Union have removed the longstanding rationale for maintaining a large nuclear arsenal. But the nuclear threat from the former Soviet Union has been replaced by a host of proliferation problems, exemplified by the disclosure of Iraq's clandestine nuclear weapons program and the splintering of the world's largest nuclear superpower, the USSR, into separate states. In addition, the U.S. and Russia are faced with the staggering environmental legacy of nearly fifty years of nuclear weapons production.

On the civilian side, nuclear power utilities have canceled or indefinitely deferred plans to construct more than 100 nuclear power plants since the early 1970s, and no new commercial U.S. reactors have been ordered since 1978. The future of the nuclear power industry is obscured by limited on-site waste storage capacity at some nuclear power plants, the absence of a permanent high-level radioactive waste repository, and the controversy over the siting of low-level waste facilities. At the same time, many utilities are developing alternative means for meeting energy needs, including increased energy efficiency and conservation.

Despite these problems and changes, both defense and civilian nuclear interests continue to plan for future operations. The Department of Energy (DOE) is evaluating a "reconfiguration" program that will consolidate and modernize its nuclear weapons complex. With rising concerns over global warming, dependence on foreign oil, and the safety of aging current reactors, the commercial nuclear industry is seeking to put on line a new generation of smaller, safer, and more efficient standardized reactors. The industry is also expected to seek relicensing of existing reactors whose 40-year licenses will begin to expire around the turn of the century.

The current conditions in the defense and civilian nuclear industries provide an unprecedented opportunity to re-examine underlying policies and regulatory mechanisms for fissile materials and nuclear power production. The upcoming 40th anniversary of the 1954 Atomic Energy Act, the extension conference of the Nuclear Non-Proliferation Treaty in 1995, a new administration, a new Congress, and a dramatically altered geopolitical landscape create the potential for achieving significant reforms in the way the U.S. controls defense and civilian uses of the atom for decades to come.

To this end, in December 1992 the Natural Resources Defense Council (NRDC) held a working conference entitled "Controlling the Atom in the 21st Century" in Syria, Virginia. The conference assembled experts from many fields, including law, physics, political science, engineering, and economics. The participants' institutional affiliations included Congress, federal and state agencies, environmental organizations, industry, and academia. A broad range of interrelated issues concerning nuclear energy and nuclear weapons was explored, with the goal of generating fresh perspectives for the new administration, Congress, the agencies, the courts, the nuclear industry, and the public. The tone of the conference was neither pronor anti-nuclear. Instead, the overall theme emerging from the conference was a general recognition of the need to "democratize" choices about nuclear energy. Within this broad theme, the common issues examined included the division of regulatory authority between the federal government and states, the role of the public in decision-making, and access to information for both improved public policy-making and more accurate market-based assessments of risk.

Prior to the conference, NRDC convened four working sessions to facilitate the development of the issues. The sessions were structured as follows:

Group One: Reforming the Legislative and Regulatory Framework
               Governing Nuclear Waste and Contamination;
Group Two: Reforming the Legislative and Regulatory Framework
               Governing Nuclear Power Operations;
Group Three: Restructuring DOE's Nuclear Weapons Complex and
               Nuclear Energy Research;
Group Four: Strengthening the U.S. Role in International Control of
               Nuclear Energy.

Based on the results of these preliminary meetings, NRDC commissioned a number of working papers that served as the foundation for discussions at the conference. Following the conference, authors revised their papers in light of the conference discussions and comments they received. These papers were then combined and reproduced for this publication. The papers represent the views of the authors and do not necessarily reflect those of NRDC, the conference participants, or the editors.

Although there is some overlap, the papers have been grouped into three parts: (1) nuclear weapons; (2) nuclear power; and (3) nuclear waste. The first part contains papers on development of a comprehensive international control system for nuclear weapons-usable materials and technology, the government's control of nuclear information, and the restructuring of the U.S. nuclear weapons production complex. The second part includes papers on the state role in regulating nuclear power; public participation in the licensing, oversight, and re-licensing of nuclear power plants; congressional oversight of nuclear activities; and the future of nuclear power from an investment perspective. The final part contains papers on the regulation of radioactive pollution, decommissioning of nuclear power plants, and the disposal of high-level nuclear waste.

The papers are neither pro- nor anti-nuclear and do not make broad conclusions on the viability or morality of nuclear energy. Instead, they discuss various problems posed by nuclear power and nuclear weapons and recommend likely approaches for achieving solutions.

Three common themes emerge from the papers. The first is access to information. Federal law restricts nuclear power and weapons information more severely than most other kinds of information. Domestically, this policy affects individuals and institutions seeking to make investment choices regarding utility companies that run nuclear power plants. The policy has also blocked public access to information concerning the environmental damage and safety risks resulting from extensive radioactive contamination at U.S. nuclear weapons facilities. Internationally, the policy has frustrated the inspection and verification efforts with the former Soviet Union that are needed to ensure reductions in nuclear weapons stockpiles and prevent proliferation of weapons information and materials.

A second recurring theme is public participation. There is a marked contrast between nuclear energy and other industries with respect to public participation and citizen enforcement. Federal law increasingly restricts public participation in the regulation and decommissioning of nuclear power plants and generally denies citizens the right to sue civilian and defense facilities for dangerous nuclear management practices.

The final theme is the balance of power between federal and state governments over the regulation of nuclear energy. Regulation of nuclear energy is unique in that state governments generally have little authority over nuclear activities affecting the health and safety of their citizens. For example, the federal government has the exclusive authority to regulate the construction and operation of nuclear power plants in order to control radiation hazards. In addition, states have limited authority under federal law to regulate the discharge of radioactive pollutants into the environment or the disposal of high-level nuclear waste.

Taken together, the papers indicate that decisions made in the U.S. regarding nuclear power and nuclear weapons production are all too often undemocratic. The basis for this policy stems from World War II and the Cold War, and today does not justify excluding state governments and citizens from the nuclear regulatory process. Further, restricting public access to broad categories of nuclear information does nothing to prevent concerted attempts to evade specialized controls on nuclear weapons materials and technology. Instead, this policy only serves to polarize citizens, industry, and government into militant pro- and anti-nuclear camps, and produce gridlock in key areas, such as the disposal of high-level nuclear waste.

The papers suggest that what is needed is a problem-solving approach that seeks to minimize the environmental and security risks imposed by nuclear energy while providing for more open consultative processes to evaluate the prospective benefits of further investments in both civilian and defense nuclear activities.

D.P.O.
C.E.P.
D.W.R.

PART ONE

Nuclear Weapons

1

Strengthening International Controls on the Military Applications of Nuclear Energy

Technical and Political Aspects of a Universal Nuclear Explosive Material Cutoff and Control (NEMC²) System

Christopher E. Paine
Thomas B. Cochran

The end of the Cold War and centralized authoritarian rule in the former Soviet Union (FSU) have brought about unprecedented opportunities, not only for deep reduction of U.S. nuclear arms and a reordering of government priorities here at home, but also for the realization of longstanding U.S. nuclear nonproliferation goals. The U.S. government can no longer claim an urgent need to subordinate nonproliferation objectives to the imperative of maintaining political-military alliances aimed at "containing" a hostile communist superpower. At the same time, disclosure of Iraq's secret nuclear weapons program has given developing countries and nuclear exporting nations greater appreciation of the need for a truly effective international inspection system to guarantee the peaceful uses of nuclear materials and technology.

In combination, these factors create the best political opportunity since the beginning of the nuclear era for instituting a truly universal regime of control over nuclear weapons materials and technology. The March 1995 review conference of the 25-year Nuclear Nonproliferation Treaty (NPT), which took effect in 1970 and must be extended in 1995, imposes a meaningful political deadline for making significant strides toward the fulfillment of this goal. The impending generational shift in American political leadership and the 40th anniversary of the Atomic Energy Act of 1954 also present symbolic and substantive opportunities for rethinking international approaches to controlling the potential military applications of nuclear energy.

The Reagan-Bush administrations and much of the quasi-permanent national security bureaucracy have proven reluctant to address the urgent technical and verification issues involved in monitoring the storage and dismantlement of some 40,000 former Soviet nuclear warheads and the disposition of hundreds of tons of weapons-usable fissile materials. However, now is *the* politically opportune moment to push for extensive nuclear data exchanges and inspections to help stabilize a potentially dangerous period of political transition and denuclearization on the territory of the Commonwealth of Independent States (CIS). Fearful of demands for reciprocal disclosures and inspections, the Reagan-Bush administrations avoided implementation, or even discussion of international inspection measures in the CIS for nuclear warhead elimination.

Some analysts believe these measures could provide the basis for a universal inspection regime under the United Nations Security Council, and for truly radical arms cuts—down to a few hundred in each nuclear weapon state. But the Reagan-Bush administrations sought to hinder progress in this direction, with the apparent intent of preserving U.S. freedom-of-action regarding future use of its own nuclear weapons materials and warhead production facilities.

The recently completed 102nd Congress did not share the Bush Administration's apparent satisfaction with the nuclear nonproliferation status-quo, passing several provisions that move U.S. policy in the direction of a more universal, non-discriminatory regime for exerting tighter control over the acquisition, production, and disposition of nuclear warheads and fissile materials, including:

- an immediate nine month moratorium on nuclear testing followed by a closely supervised phaseout of all nuclear testing by the end of 1996;
- a binding condition to the Senate's START Treaty approval resolution that directs the President to pursue monitoring arrangements with states of the FSU covering nuclear warheads and inventories of fissile materials;
- a recommendation to the President to negotiate a global ban on the production of fissile material for weapons, and creation of a DOE demonstration program for monitoring techniques needed to verify nuclear warhead elimination and a global ban on the production of fissile materials for weapons;

- a declaration that the goal of U.S. policy should be multilateral negotiations to achieve further reductions "in the number of nuclear weapons in all countries," including further reduction of U.S. strategic forces to a level of 1000–2000 warheads.

The historic changes in international superpower relations afford an unprecedented—and very real—opportunity to make major reductions in the burdens and risks imposed by nuclear weaponry on individual nations and on the entire international security system. The United States has halted both the production of nuclear warheads (for the first time since 1945) and the production of nuclear weapons materials, and is now on a trajectory to phase-out nuclear weapons testing by September 30, 1996. Under the START Treaty and various unilateral initiatives, the United States and Russia have agreed to dismantle approximately 80 percent of the estimated 55,000 nuclear warheads remaining in their combined deployed and reserve stockpiles. The United States is slowly abandoning the nuclear-armed standoff of "deterrence" as the organizing principle of its security policy, but the shape of a more cooperative new world order is not yet clear.

The international security system of the Cold War was essentially bi-polar. The boundaries of two rival ideological and economic systems were enforced by massive deployments of conventional forces backed by tens of thousands of "tactical", "theater", and "strategic" nuclear weapons. At the height of the Cold War frenzy, from 1960-62, the United States was producing some 6000 warheads *per year*, a number which now appears grossly excessive, if not completely irrational. Even more odd was that the size and general features of these imposing arsenals, nominally built to "deter" the opposing side, were kept secret both from the people they were "protecting" and from their intended targets. Instead, to protect its far-flung alliances from monolithic "Communism" and "Soviet expansionism," U.S. forces overseas were trained and equipped to pose an explicit "extended deterrent" threat of "first use" of nuclear weapons in a conventional conflict. Former Soviet forces were similarly trained and equipped, but for propaganda purposes the Kremlin authorities paid lip service to a policy of "no first use."

In this Cold War world, characterized by a utilitarian emphasis on the "containment" of Soviet communism above all other foreign policy goals, a subsidiary objective was to "manage," "limit" or "slow-down" nuclear weapons proliferation through a patchwork of partially effective but discriminatory control regimes—the Nonproliferation Treaty; International Atomic Energy Agency (IAEA) safeguards agreements, Nuclear Suppliers Group export restrictions, ad hoc foreign policy controls in the form of aid and trade incentives or embargoes, and unilateral diplomatic pressures. Because the United States and the former USSR were unwilling to reduce their own reliance on nuclear weaponry, no serious attempts were made to control or reduce global inventories of nuclear warheads and weapons-usable fissile materials. On the contrary, under the NPT the price paid for pursuing an escalating U.S.- Soviet nuclear weapons balance was the "legal" proliferation of fissile material production facilities and expertise through nominally "peaceful" nuclear fuel cycle activities. Neither the U.S. nor the former USSR was in a position to promote agreements denying other countries what they were unwilling to deny themselves.

The steps outlined in this paper are based on the assumption that the decaying bipolar balance of nuclear terror should not be replaced by a multipolar "nuclear-armed crowd", but rather by a cooperative security system characterized by a greatly diminished role for nuclear deterrence, including abandonment of the threat of nuclear "first use," and a gradual shift in strategy from deterring nuclear and large-scale conventional attack to discouraging further proliferation. Not all security experts necessarily agree with this denuclearizing vision, particularly those associated with the complex of institutions that design, test, and manufacture nuclear weapons.[1] But this paper assumes that a definitive end to the problem of nuclear weapons proliferation can be brought about by cooperative control measures, including a non-discriminatory global system of nuclear materials accounting and control, verified elimination of nuclear warheads, and universal arms control obligations that apply to nuclear weapon- as well as non-weapon-states, such as a Comprehensive Test Ban and a cutoff in the production of weapons-usable fissile material for both military and civil purposes.

This paper likewise assumes—rather than demonstrates—that such a universal regime of control over the military applications of nuclear energy would comprise an important building block of a new world order—an order based on cooperative international security arrangements in place of "deterrent stability" imposed by offsetting and continually evolving threats of devastating military force, both conventional and nuclear. This new world order will presumably be a far more multipolar world, with established global norms of international conduct and human rights backed-up by international sanctions regimes, international peacekeeping forces, and if necessary, multilaterally-sanctioned use of modern conventional forces.

This paper presents the case for pursuing the following steps toward an effective control regime aimed at ending—as opposed to merely "managing"—nuclear weapons proliferation in its qualitative, quantitative, and geographic aspects:

I.   A.   Negotiate an amendment or protocol to the Nuclear Nonproliferation Treaty (NPT)—or a separate treaty—banning further production, transfer, and acquisition of *weapons-usable* fissile materials, including international safeguards on all fissile material production facilities and all civil stocks of nuclear-weapons usable materials; *or*

    B.   Approach the same goal more gradually by negotiating a multilateral treaty barring further production of fissile materials for weapons purposes, couple it with a voluntary deferral in the separation of plutonium from civil and naval reactor spent fuel, and phase-out the civil use of highly-enriched uranium (HEU).[2]

II.   Verify the nuclear warhead elimination process in weapon states, beginning with comprehensive data exchanges on nuclear weapons stockpiles and fissile material inventories, (as required by the "Biden Condition" to the Senate's ratification of the START I Treaty), and storage of surplus plutonium and highly-enriched uranium removed from weapons under international safeguards.

III.   As deep nuclear and conventional force reductions proceed and international control mechanisms are strengthened, shift the international security role of nuclear weapons from "deterring" nuclear and large-scale conventional attacks to "discouraging" potential proliferants. This can be achieved through secure deep underground storage of residual nuclear weapon component inventories—under international monitoring—that could readily be reassembled in the event a serious nuclear threat to international security emerges that would justify redeployment of a nuclear deterrent force.

IV.   Negotiate a universal ban on nuclear weapons test explosions, i.e. a "Comprehensive Test Ban (CTB)".

V.   In the near-term, improve disclosure of, and export controls on, transfers of nuclear technology and equipment and so-called "dual-use" items, but if a firm ban can be established on weapons-usable fissile materials, shift the current denial-based system of controls on dual-use technology toward verified end use controls on selected critical items only.

VI.   Create an effective regime for conducting international short-notice special inspections to ensure prompt disclosure of all nuclear activities that may violate treaties and safeguards agreements, including the new elements listed above; and organize an effective international regime for implementing sanctions against states found to be in violation.

Ending the Proliferation of Weapons-Usable Fissile Materials

It is the unanimous opinion of the weapons design and arms control communities that the pacing consideration in a country's acquisition of a nuclear weapon is not the capability to design a nuclear device, but the availability of fissile materials which can be turned to weapons purposes. There are three routes to the acquisition of nuclear weapons-usable materials: through the construction of secret facilities dedicated to weapons production, as occurred in the U.S., U.K., China, Israel, and Pakistan; through largely civilian nuclear power programs, as occurred in India, or through a combination of approaches, as occurred, for example, in Iraq and South Africa.

Ending—as opposed to "managing"—nuclear weapons proliferation will likely prove impossible as long as: production of highly enriched uranium (HEU) and chemical separation of plutonium for national security needs remain legitimate activities in some states; and the international control regime permits civil nuclear fuel reprocessing in any state that asserts a peaceful interest in plutonium recycle and future deployment of plutonium breeder reactors for energy production.

With the end of the cold war, and the reductions in the superpower arsenals, the United States and Russia have huge surpluses of weapon-grade plutonium and highly-enriched uranium. Undoubtedly, there is no need for additional weapons plutonium production in other declared weapons states. By renouncing the production, separation, and isotopic enrichment of weapons-usable nuclear materials, declared weapons states can put pressure on undeclared weapons states to do the same.

Plutonium Requirements for a Bomb

Plutonium in U.S. nuclear weapons is weapon-grade (less than 7% Pu-240) in the form of delta-phase metal (density = 15.6 g/cc). The bare critical mass of delta-phase plutonium metal is dependent on the concentrations of the various plutonium isotopes, and varies from about 15 kg for plutonium with 6% Pu-240, to about 22 kg for plutonium with 30% Pu-240, reactor-grade plutonium from high burn-up fuel.

Thus, regardless of the fuel burnup level, the critical mass of plutonium will be between that of Pu-239 and U-235.[3] The Trinity device (and the Nagasaki bomb) used 6.1 kg of weapon-grade plutonium, and modern compact fission warheads require as little as 3–4 kg of weapon-grade plutonium. Consequently, a fission device could be made from as little as 6 to 10 kg of delta-phase plutonium recovered from high burnup fuel. We assume one bomb's worth of reactor-grade plutonium is about 8 kg (although in reality it can be smaller). Plutonium with a high Pu-240 content is less desirable for weapons purposes than weapon-grade plutonium, because for low-technology weapons

TABLE 1a　Rough Design Criteria for a Weapon

Critical mass M_c = amount needed to sustain fission chain reaction.
The assembled weapon system needs to contain about 2 "crits" (two critical masses) or more. For example:

No. of Crits	Explosive Yield (KT)
1.5	0.6
2.0	4.6
2.5	15.0 (Hiroshima)
	20.0 (Nagasaki)
3.0	34.0

The mass required for criticality (M_c) can be greatly reduced by use of a neutron reflector (e.g. beryllium, tungsten, U-238) and compression.
Example (Alpha-phase Pu):
M_c = 10 kg at normal density, unreflected
M_c = 6 kg at normal density, reflected
$M_c = 6/x^2$ kg with x-fold uniform compression
Therefore, if an assembled weapon system requires at least two crits, with uniform 2-fold compression an alpha-phase Pu weapon could be made with 2 x $(6/2^2)$ = 3 kg.

TABLE 1b　Nominal "2-Crit" Requirements for Weapons (kg)*

Fissile material	Bare No reflector	With moderate reflector	Compressed 2-fold
U-235 (90%)	100	50	12.5
Alpha Pu-239	20	12	3.0
Delta Pu-239	32	17	4.25
Delta Pu-239(30% Pu-240) "Reactor-Grade"	44	24	6.0
Delta Pu-238	30	16	4.0
Delta Pu-240	80	42	10.5
U-233	30	17	4.25

*Uncompressed values for plutonium are hypothetical only, as the high spontaneous fission rate of plutonium severely complicates assembly of an explosive "supercritical" mass at normal density.

designs the neutrons generated by the high rate of spontaneous fission of Pu-240 can increase the statistical uncertainty of the yield by "pre-initiating" the chain reaction before the desired compression of the plutonium core has been achieved. Militarily useful weapons, with reliable yields in the kiloton range can be constructed based on low technology designs with reactor-grade plutonium. Using sophisticated designs, well within the capabilities of the U.S. and the Russian weapons programs, reliable light-weight efficient weapons and high yield weapons whose yields have small statistical uncertainties can be constructed with plutonium regardless of the Pu-240 content.[4]

Pure PuO_2 as well as MOX blends with PuO_2 concentrations greater than about 20-30% appear to be directly usable in an illicit nuclear device.[5] However, the material requirements are substantially larger and the explosive yields of such devices would be substantially less than if plutonium metal were used, other design factors being the same.[6]

Despite the fact that all isotopic grades of plutonium in relatively small quantities, irrespective of their designation as civil or military, have an inherent capability to be used in weapons, the current nonproliferation regime allows national separation and acquisition of plutonium under an internationally monitored commitment of peaceful use. The defects of this arrangement are threefold: (1) it places a heavy burden on the IAEA safeguards system to detect promptly relatively small diversions of material from peaceful use; (2) it sustains a worldwide plutonium separation technology base that itself is subject to diversion into clandestine military production programs; and (3) it ignores the longer-term problem of "break-out" from the NPT by a nation that has "legally" acquired a stockpile of separated plutonium under safeguards, but then undergoes political upheaval and emerges as a nation seeking to build a nuclear arsenal. Given these realities, a more effective nonproliferation measure would be a global ban on the chemical separation and acquisition of plutonium.

Option One: Strengthening the NPT. Banning weapons-usable fissile material production and a ban on any acquisition, transfer, or use of such material except for the purposes of irradiation and/or disposal under international inspection.

The most far-reaching and effective measure to end the proliferation of "weapons usable fissile materials" (principally uranium enriched to greater than 20% in the isotope U-235, and plutonium and U-233 produced in reactors and then chemically recovered) would be the adoption of a protocol at the 1995 NPT extension conference barring weapon-state parties from either producing or transferring to any non-weapon state—and non-weapon state parties from either producing or acquiring—fissile materials usable in weapons. In one fell swoop, such a measure, if effectively inspected and enforced, would halt production of weapon-grade plutonium in Russia, commercial separation and stockpiling of "civil" plutonium in Russia, Japan, France, and the United Kingdom, and the current "legal" route to acquisition under safeguards of weapons-usable fissile materials and chemical separation facilities.

By foreclosing further development and forcing the shut-down of the plutonium separation business worldwide, such a measure would also deprive future proliferators of the specialized industrial base from which to *illegally* divert materials, equipment and technology. While the United States has no plans to develop a commercial plutonium industry—and has already ceased military production—the U.S. government has never developed a decisive policy against the development and operation of plutonium fast-breeder reactors, chemical separation plants, and plutonium-fueled thermal reactors for safeguarded commercial uses in other countries. The heavy commitment of some U.S. allies to spent fuel reprocessing and recycle of plutonium, and the lingering hopes of a future revival of the plutonium fast breeder program in the United States and abroad, have effectively barred consideration of such a simple and direct step as outlawing production and acquisition of weapons-usable fissile materials on a global basis.

Option Two: Military Ban/Civil "Deferral". A separate multilateral treaty barring the production of fissile material for weapons, coupled with a voluntary deferral of the commercial separation of plutonium from spent fuel, and phase-out of the civil uses of highly-enriched uranium.

This option differs from Option One above in that it seeks to resolve permanently only the question of fissile material production for weapons purposes, while encouraging an informal "deferral " of civil spent fuel reprocessing and plutonium recycle programs. In exchange for such a deferral, this option would permit IAEA-supervised international transactions in plutonium-bearing Mixed Oxide (MOX) fuel pursuant to a cooperative "once-through" program to 'burn-up"—possibly in European and Japanese thermal reactors that already use MOX fuel—*existing* weapon-grade plutonium made surplus by deep reductions in nuclear weapons stockpiles. Instead of business as usual, which will lead to a doubling of the world inventory of separated plutonium in the next decade, Option Two would attempt to cap and then draw down the world inventories of HEU and separated plutonium.

A cutoff in the production of fissile material for weapons. While the former Soviet Union announced in 1989 that it had ceased production of HEU for weapons, the Russian Ministry of Atomic Energy (MINATOM) continues to produce and separate annually about one metric ton (MT) of weapon-grade plutonium, and to separate annually about one MT of reactor-grade plutonium from civil power and naval reactor spent fuel.[7] The United States, on the other hand, has not produced HEU for weapons since 1964, or plutonium for weapons since 1988, and has announced that it will not produce either material for weapons purposes for the foreseeable future. The United States does not chemically separate plutonium in its civil nuclear power program, and maintains a discriminatory policy of discouraging most, but not all nations from doing so in the interest of limiting the spread of nuclear weapons production capability.

As noted in the discussion of Option One above, a global ban on the production and acquisition of nuclear weapons material, if verified and enforced by an international sanctions regime, would effectively bar further proliferation of nuclear weapons, and would provide the basis for a strengthened international inspection system assuring permanent deep reductions in nuclear weapons stockpiles. On May 29, 1991, President Bush called on the nations of the Middle East to "implement a verifiable ban on the production and acquisition of weapons-usable nuclear material" and "place all nuclear facilities in the region under International Atomic Energy Agency safeguards."[8] This unheralded regional initiative stands in sharp contrast to U.S. policy under the Bush Administration toward a U.S.-Soviet or comprehensive global agreement. Beginning in 1989, the USSR and then Russia sought negotiations with the United States to ban the production of fissile material for weapons. These overtures were rebuffed or ignored by the Executive Branch.

However, in testimony before the Senate Foreign Relations Committee on June 23, 1992, Secretary of State Baker noted that "we haven't produced any [fissile material for weapons] for a long time" and that "right now, we have all we need." Despite the vast surpluses of weapons-usable material generated by deep reductions in nuclear stockpiles, Secretary Baker nevertheless testified, "if we are going to maintain a nuclear deterrent, and have to have some fissile material, then we would have to have *the right* to produce it (emphasis added)"

This position was without merit. Given that the radioactive "half-life" of the existing U.S. weapons material inventory is measured in tens of thousands of years, Secretary Baker's statement implied that the Bush Administration was seeking to reserve a U.S. "right" to revert to a potential nuclear force even larger than average U.S. stockpile of 20,000–30,000 weapons maintained throughout most of the Cold War. The implication was technically unjustified, and politically unsustainable in light of the overriding U.S. objectives of ensuring stable long-term deep reductions in nuclear arsenals and a halt to the proliferation of fissile material production capabilities.

On July 13, 1992, President Bush made it official—after a fashion—by issuing a statement declaring that as a matter of unilateral policy, the United States "shall not produce plutonium or highly-enriched uranium for nuclear explosive purposes." No time period for this commitment was indicated. However, as in the cases of warhead dismantlement and fissile material control, the Bush Administration declined to seek a bilateral or multinational agreement to halt the production of fissile material for weapons in other states.

Status of U.S. and Russian production facilities for weapons-usable fissile material. All 14 U.S. plutonium production reactors at the Hanford Reservation, Washington, and the Savannah River Site (SRS), South Carolina, have now been shut down. Limited chemical separation activities may continue at the SRS site, but only for recovery of highly enriched uranium from research and test reactor fuel, and for stabilization of plutonium residues in preparation for long-term disposal. A single refurbished heavy-water reactor for tritium production at SRS is currently undergoing testing prior to placement in a cold standby status. Construction design activities for a new tritium production reactor at SRS have been deferred for at least a decade.

The former Soviet Union announced in 1989 that it had ceased production of HEU for weapons—exactly when is still not clear—and was phasing out the production of plutonium for weapons by the year 2000. All former Soviet plutonium production reactors and enrichment plants are located in Russia.

Plutonium production for weapons in Russia has taken place at three locations:

- Chelyabinsk-65 (previously Chelyabinsk-40, and for many years known in the West as the ``Kyshtym Complex''), near Kyshtym in Chelyabinsk Oblast;
- the Siberian Atomic Power Station, located at the Siberian Chemical Combine (Tomsk-7) on the Tom River 15 km northwest of Tomsk; and

- the Mining and Chemical Combine (Krasnoyarsk-26) on the Yenisey River, 10 km north of Dodonovo, and 64 km northeast of Krasnoyarsk in Siberia.

Prior to 1987, there were as many as fifteen production reactors at these three sites—seven at Chelyabinsk-65, five at Tomsk-7 and three at Krasnoyarsk-26. At Chelyabinsk-65, five graphite reactors used for plutonium production were shut down between 1987 and December 31, 1990. Two light water reactors (one converted from a heavy water type in the 1980's) continue to produce special isotopes, such as Pu-238 and tritium. At Tomsk-7 three of the five graphite reactors used for weapon-grade plutonium production were also shut down between 1987-1992. At Krasnoyarsk-26 two of the three graphite production reactors were shut down in 1992.

Thus, in December 1992, five production reactors were in operation—two at Tomsk-7 and one at Krasnoyarsk-26 for weapon-grade plutonium, and two LWRs at Chelyabinsk-65 for special isotopes. The three graphite reactors are dual-purpose reactors that also supply electricity and steam heat to Tomsk-7 and Krasnoyarsk-26, the industrial sites and closed cities where they are located. No tritium production takes place at Krasnoyarsk-26. It is assumed that there are tritium separation facilities at Chelyabinsk-65 and Tomsk-7.[9]

MINATOM says that they cannot shut down the last three reactors until replacement power sources are constructed. By increasing the fuel burnup of these reactors, MINATOM could optimize their fuel cycles for electricity and heat production, rather than for weapon-grade plutonium production; and could also shut down the chemical separation facilities and store or bury the spent fuel.[10] To date MINATOM has not implemented either option, nor was it urged to do so by the Bush Administration or the Russian Foreign Ministry.

A halt in the chemical separation of "civil" plutonium from spent reactor fuel. Reprocessing of spent fuel and the recycling of plutonium[11] into fresh fuel for reactors permit non-nuclear weapons states to justify the acquisition and stockpiling of nuclear weapons-usable material—ostensibly for peaceful purposes. At the same time, without violating any international safeguards agreements, these countries could design and fabricate non-nuclear weapon components. By moving to a point of being within hours of having nuclear weapons—perhaps needing only to introduce the fissile material into the weapons—a nascent weapons state would have all of its options open. Under these conditions, international safeguards agreements can serve as a cover by concealing the signs of critical change until it is too late for diplomacy to reverse a decision to "go nuclear."

Likewise, acceptance of the plutonium breeder as an energy option provides the justification for the early development of a reprocessing capability by any country. A non-nuclear weapons country would always have the option to shift its "peaceful" nuclear program to a weapons program. Without national reprocessing facilities and breeder reactors, countries wishing to develop nuclear weapons capacity face very considerable political problems and cost. Obtaining large quantities of weapon-usable plutonium requires that they build one or more specialized production reactors and chemical separation facilities. By establishing their nuclear weapons option through a plutonium-using nuclear electric generation program, they can circumvent these obstacles.

Development efforts worldwide have demonstrated that plutonium fast breeders are uneconomical—unable to compete with thermal reactors operating on a once through uranium cycle—and that breeders will remain uneconomical for the foreseeable future. The putative benefits of the plutonium breeder, associated with its ability to more efficiently utilize uranium resources, are not diminished if commercial breeder development is postponed for decades, and the spent fuel from existing conventional reactors is stored in the interim. In the near term the energy security benefits of the plutonium breeder can be achieved more cheaply and more quickly by stockpiling uranium.[12] Deployment of plutonium fast breeders would entail staggering amounts of nuclear weapons-usable plutonium in the reactors and the supporting fuel cycle. There is no adequate means of safeguarding this material to prevent some of it from being used for nuclear weapons.

The continued development of plutonium breeders in the few remaining countries that have strong breeder research and development programs will legitimize breeder programs and large plutonium stockpiles in non-nuclear weapons states that may use these programs to cover the development of a weapons option. Consequently, the breeder research and development programs should be phased out. To the extent that this is politically impossible, sufficient plutonium has already been separated to meet the needs of R&D programs, so there is no requirement to continue separating plutonium for this purpose.

The use of plutonium in the form of mixed-oxide (MOX) fuel in thermal reactors is also uneconomical, because the costs of using MOX fuel cannot compete with those of enriched fresh uranium fuel for the foreseeable future. Consequently, there is no economic or national security justification for continued commercial reprocessing.

The chemical separation facilities in operation or planned are identified in Table 2a. Facilities that have been terminated or whose operations have been suspended are identified in Table 2b. Operating and planned commercial reprocessing plants are summarized in Table 2c. The status of chemical separation programs in several key countries is discussed below.

United States. The U.S. has four principal chemical separation facilities: the F area and H area chemical separation facilities at the Savannah River Site (SRS), the PUREX plant at the Hanford Reservation, and the Idaho Chemical Processing Plant (ICPP) at the Idaho National Engineering Laboratory (INEL).

At SRS the H canyon is used for chemical separation of highly enriched production reactor fuel; and the F canyon is used for processing natural uranium production reactor targets. H canyon has also been used to process limited quantities of research and test reactor fuel. In addition there are small processing lines at each facility: the HB-Line at the H area which converts liquid Pu-238 and Np-237 to powdered oxide, and the FB-Line (or JB-Line) at the F area that concentrates and purifies Pu-239. Although the H and F canyons are currently shut down, a DOE official stated in August 1992 that reprocessing of spent fuel will continue at SRS for "clean-out and stabilization." There also continues to be limited operations at the HB- and FB-Lines.

The PUREX plant at Hanford was used to chemically separate N-reactor fuel. PUREX was shut down on December 7, 1988, and placed on cold standby. There are no plans to resume operations and an Environmental Impact Statement would have to be prepared if the Department of Energy (DOE) intended to do so.

The ICPP at INEL was used to chemically separate naval reactor spent fuel and limited quantities of research reactor fuel. ICPP was shut down in July 1989. On February 24, 1992, DOE Secretary Watkins announced that ICPP would not be reopened or replaced.

Russia. There are three large chemical separation facilities in Russia: one each at Chelyabinsk-65, Tomsk-7, and Krasnoyarsk-26. The RT-1 chemical separation plant at Chelyabinsk-65 was formerly used to process Chelyabinsk-65 production reactor fuel to recover plutonium for weapons. In 1977 it shifted to processing spent fuel from naval (both submarine and civil icebreaker) reactors (which apparently occurred first), test reactors, and 210 Mw_e and 440 Mw_e light-water moderated and cooled power reactors (VVER-210s and VVER-440s). It is the only operating Russian facility for power and naval reactor fuel reprocessing. The RT-1 reprocessing plant capacity is about 400 metric tons of heavy metal per year (MTHM/y), or 300–900

TABLE 2a   World Reprocessing Capabilities in Operation or Planned

Country	Facility	Location	Purpose	Capacity (MTHM/y)	Startup-Shutdown
China	Pilot Plant at JAEC	Subei	W	70	1968–
	Production plant at				
	Subei	Subel	W	large	
	"Plant 821"	Guangyuan	W	large	?
France	UP1 (metal)	Marcoule	W	400	1958–
	UP3 (oxide)	La Hague	C	800	1990–
	UP2-800	La Hague	C	800	1993/4–
India		Trombay	W,R	70	1964–1974
			R,R	larger	1983–
	PREFRE	Tarapur	R	30–150	1975–
	Phase I	Kalpakkam	R	LS	1985–
	Phase II	Kalpakkam	C	100–200	1993/4–
Israel		Dimona	W	20–40	ca. 1966
Italy		Saluggia	R	10	1983–?
Japan	PNS, Tokai	Tokai-mura	R,C	210	1978–1983/ 1985–
	JNFS, Rokkasho	Rokkasho-mura	C	800	2002–
North Korea	Yongbyon		W	PS	1990 (partial)–
Pakistan	"New Labs"	Rawalpindi	W	100	?
	PINSTECH				
Russia	RT-1	Chelyabinsk-65	C,N	400	1976–
		Tomsk-7	W	6000	ca. 1959–
		Krasnoyarsk-26	W	3000	?
Spain	Juan Vigon Center	Madrid	R	PS	?
U.K.		Dounreay	W	8	1980–
	B205 Metal (Magnox)	Sellafield	C	1500	1964–
	THORP	Sellafield	C	700	1993–
	DNPDE	Thurso	R	<1	1959–
			R	7	1980–
U.S.	200 H-Area (HEU fuel)	SRS	W,R		1954–
	200 F-Area (U targets)	SRS	W	>4000	1954–

Abbreviations:
C = for reprocessing civil (power) reactor fuel
CC = cancelled during constructionl the facility never operated
CIS = construction indefinitely suspended
D = destroyed
JAEC = Jiuguan Atomic Energy Complex
LS = laboratory scale
N = for processing naval reactor fuel
OIS = operation indefnitely suspended
R = for processing research and test reactor fuel
W = for the production of plutonium for weapons

TABLE 2b World Reprocessing Capabilities Terminated or Suspended

Country	Facility	Location	Purpose	Capacity (MTHM/y)	Startup-Shutdown
Argentina	Ezeiza I	Ezeiza	W	LS	1969–1973
	Ezeiza II	Ezeiza	W	5	1989–1990
Belgium	Eurochemic-Mol	Mol	C	100	1966–1974
Brazil	Resende		W	2	OIS
	IPEN	Sao Paulo	W	LS	?
France	UP2 400 (metal)	La Hague	C	400	1966–1987
	UP2 400 (oxide)	La Hague	C	400	1976–1990
Germany	MILLI	Karlsruhe	R	1 kg/d	?
	DWK	Karlsruhe	R	40	1971–
	Wackersdorf	Dragahn	C	350	CIS (1989)
Iraq		Al Tuwaitha	W	LS	1983–1991 (D)
Israel		Nahal Soreq	W	LS	ca. 1960–
Pakistan	New Labs	Rawalpindi	W		?–C/OIS
Russia		Chelyabinsk-65	W	?	1948–?
	RT-1	Chelyabinsk-65	W	?	1958–1976
	RT-2	Krasnoyarsk-26	C	1500	CIS (1989)
South Africa		Pelindaba	W		1987+
Taiwan	Nuc. Energy Res. Inst.		W	LS	?–C/OIS (1988)
U.K.	B204/205 Oxide	Sellafield	C	300	1969–1973
U.S.	Nuclear Fuels Service	West Valley, NY	C,R	300	1966–1972
	Midwest Fuel Recovery Plant	Morris, IL	C	300	CC
	AGNS	Barnwell, SC	C	500	CC
	PUREX	Hanford	W	3000	1956–1989
	REDOX	Hanford	W	?	?–1967
	Bismuth/Phosphate B-Plant	Hanford	W	1000	1944–1968
	Bismuth/Phosphate T-Plant	Hanford	W	1000	1945–1956
	ICPP	INEL	N,R	1030	1953–1989
Yugoslavia	Boris Kidric Inst.			LS	

Abbreviations:
C = for reprocessing civil (power) reactor fuel
CC = cancelled during constructionl the facility never operated
CIS = construction indefinitely suspended
D = destroyed
INEL = Idaho National Engineering Laboratory
LS = laboratory scale
N = for processing naval reactor fuel
OIS = operation indefnitely suspended
R = for processing research and test reactor fuel
W = for the production of plutonium for weapons

fuel assemblies/y, comparable to the UP-400 plant operated by Cogema at La Hague in France.

In 1992, RT-1 reprocessed 120 MTHM, down from 160 MTHM in 1991, due to the falloff in imports of spent fuel from Ukraine and Eastern Europe, which are now illegal under Russian environmental law. Processing mainly low enriched uranium VVER spent fuel, it has been recovering an estimated 1 MT of plutonium annually, sufficient to construct in the range of 100–180 nuclear weapons, depending on the level of weapons technology employed in their design. From 4000–9000 weapons annually could be constructed from the recovered plutonium if RT-1 were operating near design capacity processing breeder reactor fuel!

Following the modification of RT-1 to process civil fuel in 1976, the irradiated fuel elements from the production reactors at Chelyabinsk-65 were shipped by rail to Tomsk-7 for processing. Efforts to build a mixed oxide (MOX) fuel fabricating plant at Chelyabinsk-65 were suspended and the thermal power reactor fuel cycle was never closed. Consequently, the plutonium recovered from naval and power reactors, now about 30 MT, is being stockpiled at Chelyabinsk-65. It is assumed that chemical separation of plutonium from the spent fuel from the two operating production reactors at Tomsk-7, about 0.75 MT/y, continues at that site; and that about half that amount comes from the single operating production reactor at Krasnoyarsk-26.

As a consequence of START, and the Gorbachev and Yeltsin initiatives, the Russians could remove over the next decade on the order or 70-80 MT of weapon-grade plutonium from dismantled weapons. Currently it costs more to use this plutonium as power reactor fuel than it does to mine, enrich, and fabricate uranium into fuel. The plutonium requirements for fast reactor and other R&D needs are small. Consequently, there is currently no foreseeable commercial market for plutonium. It makes no sense for Russia to continue to separate additional plutonium for weapons or other uses given the large surplus of unusable materials already available. As noted above, Russia should shut down all its chemical separation facilities and store or bury, rather than reprocess the spent fuel.

Europe and Japan: The French government-owned Cogema Corp. is now operating two chemical separation plants—UP1 at Marcoule and UP3 at La Hague, and a third plant, the new UP2-800 facility at La Hague, is scheduled to come on line in 1993. These plants have a combined capacity of 2000 MTHM/yr. Through 1990 France had separated 23.6 metric tonnes of plutonium, and is projected to separate an additional 45 tons in the period 1991-2000.

The British government owned British Nuclear Fuels, Limited (BNFL) operates the B205 chemical separation plant at Sellafield along the shores of the Irish sea just west of England's fabled Lake District. B205 has a capacity of 1500 MTHM/y, and will be joined some time in early 1993 by the THORP facility with a capacity of an additional 1200 MTHM/y. Through 1990 the U.K. is reported to have separated 42.5 MT of plutonium, and is projected to separate another 25 MT in the period 1991-2000. The main scheduled mission of THORP over this period, however, will be to separate plutonium from Japanese spent fuel.

Japan's Tokai-mura chemical separation plant has a nominal capacity of 210 MTHM/yr. A full-scale commercial plant of 800 MTHM/y capacity at Rokkasho-mura is planned for startup in the year 2002. In the meantime, Japan plans to expand its plutonium stockpile by separating an estimated an estimated 49 metric tons of plutonium in British and French plants by the year 2000.

Thus by the end of the decade France, the U.K and Japan alone will have separated an additional 120 metric tons, more plutonium than in the U.S. nuclear weapons stockpile. The global inventory of surplus separated civil plutonium (i.e. not fabricated into fuel or in use in reactors) will rise to an estimated 180 metric tonnes, a figure about twice the size of the U.S. weapons plutonium stockpile at its peak.[13] This amount would be in addition to more than 100 MT of plutonium from retired US and former Soviet weapons.

TABLE 2c   World Oxide-Fuel Reprocessing Plants

Plant/Location	Operating Dates	Capacity (MTHM/y)	Output (MTHM/y)	Output (kg.Pu/y)
RT-1, Mayak Chemical Combine Chelyabinsk-65, Russia	1976–	400	120	1080
PNC, Tokai-Mura, Japan	1978–83 1985–	210	90	810
UP3, La Hague, France	1990–	800	800	7200
Subtotal		1410	1010	9090
THORP, Sellafield, UK	1993–	700	600	5400
UP2-800, La Hague, France	1993–	800	800	7200
JNFS, Rokkasho-mura, Japan	2002?–	800	800	7200
TOTAL		3710	3210	28,890

Civil Plutonium Risks. As is becoming clear in Russia, Japan and France, by sanctioning reprocessing the world is confronted with large flows of recovered plutonium and plutonium stockpiles. With a plutonium breeder economy the quantity of plutonium involved would be enormous. The 280 Mw_e Monju fast reactor in Japan requires 1.4 MT of fissile plutonium (Pu_f) for its initial core and 0.5 MT Pu_f annually thereafter. The 350 Mw_e Clinch River Breeder Reactor in the U.S. was to have been loaded with 1.7 MT of plutonium (86% Pu-239), about the same Pu_f inventory as Monju.[14]

The plutonium inventory in a commercial-size breeder is about 5 MT, of which 3.5 MT is fissile[15]—about 600 atomic bombs worth. A Russian BN-800 would require over 4 MT. Although the net amount of plutonium produced in a fast breeder reactor annually is generally less than that produced in a conventional thermal power reactor of the same size,[16] one-third to one-half of the FBR fuel must be removed annually for reprocessing, plutonium recovery, and remanufacture into fresh fuel.[17] Since the fuel will be outside of the reactor for 3.5 to 7 years the plutonium inventory needed to support a single commercial-size plutonium breeder is 11-22 MT, about 1400 to 3700 bombs worth.

If only 10 Gw_e of nuclear capacity were supplied by breeders—hardly enough to justify the R&D effort in any country even if the economics were otherwise favorable—the plutonium inventory in the reactors and their supporting fuel cycle would be on the order of 100-200 MT, or about 12,000-25,000 bombs' worth. By comparison, U.S. nuclear weapons stockpiles in 1987 consisted of 23,400 warheads, and the weapon-grade plutonium inventory, most of which was in weapons, was about 100 MT. The Russian warhead plutonium stockpile consists of an estimated 130 MT of plutonium in a total stockpile which peaked in 1985 at about 45,000 warheads.

About one half of the plutonium created in a breeder reactor is bred in the blanket rods. The burnup of the blanket material is low. Consequently, the resulting plutonium is weapon-grade, with a Pu-240 concentration lower than that used in U.S. and Russian weapons. Thus, any non-weapons country that has large stocks of breeder fuel, has the capacity to produce a ready stock of weapon-grade plutonium. It only has to segregate and reprocess the blanket assemblies separately from the core assemblies.

Inadequate Security of Plutonium. Adequate physical security is essential to prevent the theft of any quantity of material, even as little as one bomb's worth. Highly accurate material accounting and control measures are essential to determine whether a theft has taken place, and to provide timely warning to prevent the material from being used for illicit purposes. It is well established—from experience at existing civil and military chemical separation (reprocessing) plants, naval fuel facilities, and mixed-oxide fuel facilities—that it is extremely difficult (some would argue impossible) to provide in practice a sufficient level of physical security, or material accounting and control, at bulk handling facilities that process large amounts of nuclear weapons-usable material.

Inadequate Physical Security. The difficulty in providing adequate physical security is that theft of materials can involve a collusion of individuals, including the head of the guard force, or even the head of the company. This was alleged to have occurred at the NUMEC facility in Apollo, Pennsylvania in the 1960s. Despite having guards at every bank, employees at the Bank of Credit and Commerce, Inc. (BCCI) allegedly were able to steal millions of dollars from bank customers because the thieves were running the bank—the collusion was at the top. If the threat includes the potential for collusion involving the guard force and company directors, providing adequate physical security in the West would require turning the facility into a heavily armed site occupied by an independent military force. In Russia physical security has relied on heavily guarding not only the facilities, but also the towns where the work force resides. These closed cities are anathema to a democratic society. And of course the principal role of physical security is completely reversed when the collusion involves elements of the government itself. In this case the primary mission of the security apparatus is to hide the program from outside scrutiny. It is now known that at various times in the past, the governments of the United States, Japan (during World War II), Soviet Union, United Kingdom, France, China, Israel, India, South Africa, Sweden, Argentina, Brazil, Taiwan, Pakistan, North Korea, South Korea, and Iraq have had secret nuclear weapons development programs.

Inadequate Material Accounting and Control. Material accounting and control procedures, collectively referred to as safeguards, are meant to provide timely detection of the diversion of significant quantities of weapons-usable material.

The safeguards goals of the International Atomic Energy Agency (IAEA) have been summarized by Marvin Miller.[18] The IAEA's Standing Advisory Group on Safeguards Implementation (SAGSI) in 1977 defined a significant quantity of plutonium as 8 kg. As noted in subsection A above, the use of alpha-phase plutonium, thicker reflectors, and compression by chemical explosives mean that the true significant quantity is considerably less—on the order of 3–4 kilograms. This roughly corresponds to the critical mass of delta phase plutonium metal with a moderate neutron reflector.

To provide assurance that a significant quantity of fissile material has not been diverted, the uncertainty in the inventory accounting must be small compared to the quantity of fissile material considered significant, e.g., compared to 8 kg of plutonium or less. At a bank each deposit and withdrawal has a precise numerical value which, if accurately recorded, permits a precise daily balancing of the books. At a bulk handling facility the books never balance because of inherent limitations in the ability to measure the material quantities entering the plant. To this inherent uncertainty must be added a further allowance for variance in equipment calibration and sampling techniques. In the parlance of nuclear material accounting the inventory difference (ID) is defined as

$$ID = BI + I - R - EI,$$

where BI is the beginning inventory, EI is the ending inventory, and I and R are, respectively, the material added and removed during the inventory period.[19] For the minimum amount of diverted plutonium (assumed here to be 8 kg) to be distinguished from measurement noise with detection and false alarm probabilities of 95% and 5%, respectively, it can be shown that 3.3_{ID} must be less than 8 kg, where ID is the uncertainty in the inventory difference.[20]

At existing reprocessing plants in the West that handle tons of weapons-usable plutonium, ID is dominated by the error in measuring the plutonium input into the plant, which is about one percent of the throughput. The Japanese Tokai Mura plant, one of the smallest plants in the West, has an average output of about 90 Metric Tons of Heavy Metal per year (MTHM/y), and the LWR spent fuel processed has an average total plutonium content of about 0.9 percent. Thus, 3.3 ID for Tokai Mura is about 27 kg of plutonium per annual inventory. Even if inventories were taken every six months, 3.3 ID would be about 14 kg, which is still greater than 8 kg. One simply cannot detect the diversion of several bombs' worth of plutonium annually from Tokai Mura.

We are told that material accounting and control at Russian plants handling nuclear fuel in bulk form is rudimentary at best. The RT-1 chemical separation plant at Chelyabinsk-65 has a capacity of about 400 MTHM/y, and until 1991 had been operating at about 200 MTHM/y. Therefore, the situation at RT-1 would be two to six times worse than at Tokai Mura, even if it were brought up to current western standards.[21] It is difficult to imagine running a bank in which you counted the money only a few times a year, and then only counted the notes larger than 10,000 rubles. Yet the Russian nuclear establishment sanctions the commercial use of nuclear weapons-usable material under safeguards that are no better.

Detection time (the maximum time that should elapse between diversion and its detection) should be the same order of magnitude as the conversion time, defined as the time required to convert different forms of nuclear material into components of nuclear weapons. For metallic plutonium and HEU, conversion time was estimated by SAGSI as 7-10 days; for pure unirradiated compounds of these materials, such as oxides and nitrates, or for mixtures, 1–3 weeks.[22] These times are already much shorter than the period between cleanout inventories at any fuel reprocessing plant operating today. Thus, there can be no assurance that the primary objective of safeguards—the timely detection of significant quantities of plutonium—can be met.

To meet the timely detection criteria reprocessing plants would have to undergo clean-out inventories every few days, or weeks. But this would reduce their annual throughput—and utility—practically to zero. It would also drive up the cost of reprocessing. Plutonium recycle, the use of MOX fuel in LWRs, is already uneconomical due to the high cost of reprocessing. Similarly, the cost of the fast breeder fuel cycle is greater than that of the LWR operating on the once-through cycle, that is, without plutonium recycle.

In the West consideration is being given to Near-Real-Time Accountancy (NRTA) as a means of improving the sensitivity and timeliness of detection.[23] NRTA involves taking inventories at frequent intervals, typically once a week, without shutting down the facility. It and similar concepts are likely to be opposed by operators due to the added costs that would be imposed.

In any case the methods and adequacy of practical NRTA system implementation are open questions.[24] If Russia and Japan continue to develop their fast breeder programs, other countries that want to preserve the weapons option will point to them as the basis for legitimizing their own breeder development efforts. India, as noted previously, recovered the plutonium for its first nuclear device in a reprocessing plant that was ostensibly developed as part of its national breeder program.

General Electric and Argonne National Laboratory have proposed a modular Liquid Metal Reactor (LMR) that they argue is more "proliferation resistant" than other fast reactor designs. With the possible exception of the initial inventory, the fuel in General Electric's proposed PRISM[25] modular Liquid Metal Reactor (LMR) will always contain highly radioactive fission products and actinides. Consequently, illicit diversion from the plant will be more difficult than diversion from the breeder fuel cycle currently employed.

However, the PRISM design places plutonium metal fuel processing and manufacturing facilities at each reactor site.

Also at the site will be a ready supply of about 25 MT of plutonium—about 3000 bombs worth.[26] Finally, a large cadre of nuclear fuel specialists with hands-on experience in plutonium metallurgy will have access to these materials and equipment. No country that wants to preserve a nuclear weapons option could ask for a better cover for its military interest. Early drafts of the Clinton Administration's FY 1994 budget reportedly eliminate DOE's LMR Program, but this may be reversed by DOE advocates of the technology and Congressional supporters of the program. Because it will lose its facility for burning experimental fuel if Congress approves the budget cut, DOE is reportedly planning to fly plutonium fuel rods from Argonne's Integral Fast Reactor (IFR) project to Russia for testing.[27]

Energy Independence and the Breeder. It is useful to ask whether there is another way of achieving a secure nuclear fuel supply without relying on nuclear weapons-usable material. We conservatively assume that a 1000 Mw_e LWR can be built today in the West for about $2000/kw,[28] and that the cost of an LMFBR would be only about 50% greater. We also ignore the fact that the cost of reprocessing and other breeder fuel cycle requirements is currently more than twice the cost of direct disposal of LWR fuel. (It is likely to remain at least twice the cost after the year 2000 assuming current uranium prices.[29]) Today the average price of imported U_3O_8 is about $30/kg.[30] By purchasing an LWR instead of a breeder, the $1,000 million capital cost saving could be used to buy 30,000 MT of U_3O_8 at today's prices, enough uranium to operate the LWR for about 150 years! If more advanced high burnup LWR fuels were used, the LWR could be operated for 300 years. While the economic situation in Russia is quite different, the ratio of the cost of a BN-800 to the cost of a VVER is also at least 1.5, therefore the results will be similar. Moreover, given the enormous surplus of enriched uranium from weapons to be retired, the economics of the breeder should be worse, not better in Russia. Clearly, if energy independence, or wise economic investment were the objective, countries such as Russia and Japan would abandon their breeder programs and invest in technologies that would contribute more to economic efficiency and growth.

Reducing World Inventories of Separated Plutonium Removed from Weapons. As noted in connection with Option Two above, a program for capping and reducing world inventories of plutonium could include a carefully circumscribed Pu/MOX option, with the primary objective of converting Weapon-Grade Plutonium (WGPu) to waste in a once-through MOX cycle in exchange for an indefinite deferral of reprocessing. The basic outline of this option (shown schematically in Figure 1) is as follows:

(a) Japan: Japanese utilities with contracts to reprocess spent fuel at the British Nuclear Fuels Limited (BNFL) THORP plant—Kansai Electric Power Co. and Tokyo Electric Power Co. are the key players—would agree to forego reprocessing of the spent fuel at THORP. The utilities, at least for a limited time period, would have the option of sending their spent fuel to the new THORP plant in the U.K. for interim storage if they have a spent fuel storage problem. The utilities would agree to burn MOX fabricated in Russia from WGPu, and agree not to reprocess the spent MOX fuel. The utilities would agree to support deferral of the construction of the Rokkasho commercial-scale reprocessing plant in Japan and place the Tokai pilot plant on standby. The Japanese utilities would reduce their payments to BNFL under the outstanding reprocessing contracts, and agree to purchase MOX from Russia, possibly from a MINATOM/BNFL joint venture. The utilities would pay for spent fuel storage at THORP if they exercise that option.

(b) United Kingdom: BNFL would agree to defer the opening of the THORP plant, and continue to store Japanese spent fuel for an interim period. BNFL would receive its profit in the form of reduced fees from the Japanese utilities under the existing reprocessing contracts and would be paid for interim spent fuel storage. BNFL would have the option of completing, perhaps with Japanese partners, the MOX fuel fabrication plant at Chelyabinsk-65, and would manage its operations, perhaps jointly with MINATOM.

(c) Russia: MINATOM would complete its MOX fuel facility at Chelyabinsk-65—built and operated with BNFL assistance and operated under IAEA safeguards. (Seimens in Germany has also expressed an interest in completing this facility.) Russia would agree to halt all military and civil reprocessing. Russia would receive hard currency for MOX fuel, and reduce its long-term ruble costs for securing WGPu in storage.

The idea of direct disposal of the WGPu as vitrified waste, either with or without mixing it with fission products, may be an attractive option in the U.S., but is unlikely to be politically saleable in Russia. Quite literally hundreds and perhaps thousands of Russian lives were sacrificed, billions of rubles expended, and the environment severely contaminated to produce and separate the Russian weapons plutonium stockpile, to say nothing of the professional careers and reputations invested in the task. The opposition by MINATOM's current leadership to treating this plutonium as a "waste" to be thrown away

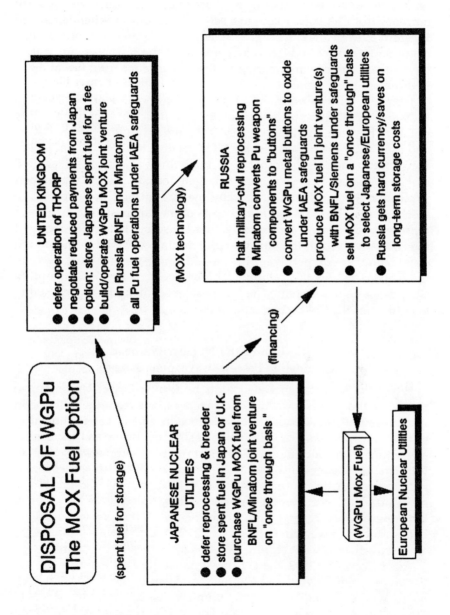

DISPOSAL OF WGPu
The MOX Fuel Option

(spent fuel for storage)

UNITED KINGDOM
- defer operation of THORP
- negotiate reduced payments from Japan
- option: store Japanese spent fuel for a fee
- build/operate WGPu MOX joint venture in Russia (BNFL and Minatom)
- all Pu fuel operations under IAEA safeguards

(MOX technology)

RUSSIA
- halt military-civil reprocessing
- Minatom converts Pu weapon components to "buttons"
- convert WGPu metal buttons to oxide under IAEA safeguards
- produce MOX fuel in joint venture(s) with BNFL/Siemens under safeguards
- sell MOX fuel on a "once through" basis to select Japanese/European utilities
- Russia gets hard currency/saves on long-term storage costs

(financing)

JAPANESE NUCLEAR UTILITIES
- defer reprocessing & breeder
- store spent fuel in Japan or U.K.
- purchase WGPu MOX fuel from BNFL/Minatom joint venture on "once through basis "

(W/GPu Mox Fuel)

European Nuclear Utilities

is likely to remain strong. On the other hand, these officials may be willing to defer reprocessing for some time in exchange for hard currency from MOX fuel sales to a select group of utilities in Japan and Western Europe. BNFL might be willing to defer THORP if they continue to receive reduced payments from the Japanese and if they have the option of participating in the construction and operation of the Russian MOX plant.

Japanese utilities are not in favor of continued reprocessing and MOX use, but feel compelled by government policy to support the MOX option. They can continue their MOX program (with Russian MOX) and can justify the higher cost for MOX relative to conventional fuel as their contribution to world peace. Actually they would pass the added cost on to the Japanese consumer, enlarging the cost base on which their profit margin is calculated, thereby making an additional profit on world peace. The exact terms and costs of the Japanese-British/French reprocessing contracts are a closely guarded secret, but it is known that the costs involved in the Japanese plutonium recycle program are not even remotely competitive with an LEU once-through fuel cycle at today's prices. So the relatively higher cost of the WGPu option should not be a deterrent. The Japanese are looking for a face saving way to defer the Rokkasho plant, and this may be it.

Verification of the Nuclear Warhead Elimination Process in Weapons States

When the Ministry of Defense of the former Soviet Union began removing thousands of tactical nuclear weapons from the Ukraine in December 1991, no U.S. or United Nations inspectors were on hand to verify the process, despite the desire of the new Ukrainian government for international inspection to assure elimination of Russian warheads, and the willingness of at least some senior political authorities in the new Russian government to grant it. The main problem, as it turned out, was not in Moscow or Kiev but in Washington, where erstwhile advocates of "effective verification" had suddenly reversed field, arguing that U.S.-Soviet "unilateral" arms reductions did not require any mutual verification measures.

As of December 1992, the U.S. government had yet to advance a co-herent program for verifying elimination of tens of thousands of former Soviet warheads and tracking the ultimate disposition of hundreds of tons of surplus bomb-grade materials in the Russian nuclear stock-pile.[31] Once invoked as a kind of magic mantra to ward off unwanted arms control agreements, "on-site inspection" is now viewed by some in the national security establishment as a dangerous Trojan horse that will pry open the gates to global nuclear disarmament. But to reject extensive cooperative monitoring measures on nuclear warheads and materials now, at the very moment when the international community is seeking to upgrade similar controls in non-weapon and threshold nuclear states, would do more than perpetuate the "do as I say, not as I do" dichotomy that has plagued U.S. nonproliferation efforts for decades. It could undermine the technical and political basis for achieving even deeper reductions in the future. A failure to properly account for disposition of the vast Cold War excess of nuclear destructive power now being "eliminated" could actually make the proliferation problem worse, by increasing uncertainty about who does or does not have access to nuclear weapons materials and technology. At the very least, this uncertainty creates a lofty floor for nuclear arms reductions below which, it will be argued, "a prudent national security posture" can not go.

At the very moment of maximum political opportunity—and genuine technical need—for extensive nuclear inspections throughout Russia and the other states of the CIS with nuclear weapons on their territory, the Bush Administration ducked the chance to establish verification arrangements that would assure nuclear warhead elimination and monitoring of the nuclear explosive materials removed from dismantled warheads. These monitoring arrangements could lay the groundwork for a universal nuclear inspection regime under the UN Security Council and truly radical arms cuts down to a few hundred weapons in each nuclear weapon state. Instead of trying to move the U.S.-CIS nuclear monitoring regime closer to the current international nuclear inspection regime—now receiving increased understanding and support worldwide as a result of the UN Special Commission inspections in Iraq—the Bush Administration continued to place future U.S. freedom of action with respect to its own nuclear arsenal ahead of the global nonproliferation agenda. A few days after his retirement in August 1992 as Assistant to the Secretary of Defense for Atomic Energy, Dr. Robert Barker testified against mutual verification of nuclear stockpiles as follows:

> A concern about Russian nuclear weapons security should not result in a mandate for Russian inspection of U.S. facilities. An automatic requirement for reciprocity is, frankly, old-think.[32]

However, as matters now stand, an indeterminate number of former Soviet warheads have been returned to storage sites in the Russian heartland east of the Urals, an indeterminate number of these may be dismantled, and an indeterminate amount of nuclear explosive (fissile) material from the weapons will go who knows where. Intact warheads, weapon components, or bulk fissile material could disappear from this process at any time and the international community would be none the wiser.

That frightening uncertainty is the price we are paying today for the Bush Administration's failure to pursue negotiations, first with Gorbachev, and then with Yeltsin, on a fissile material production cutoff and verified storage and destruction of nuclear warheads. Since the spring of 1989, House and Senate peppered the Administration with report requirements, research programs, and "sense of the Congress" resolutions urging preparations for these initiatives, but the Bush national security team sidetracked or ignored all of these efforts.

As evident in Table 3, there is considerable uncertainty surrounding the number and status of former Soviet weapons. According to Minatom Minister Mikhailov, the Soviet nuclear weapons stockpile grew rather steadily until it peaked in 1986 at 45,000 warheads;[33] and then declined by 20 percent to 35,000 warheads as of mid-1992.[34] An official CIA estimate given in May 1992, placed the stockpile of the former Soviet Union at 30,000 nuclear weapons with an uncertainty of plus or minus 5,000.[35] The upper limit of the CIA estimate is consistent with the Mikhailov figures.

According to senior Minatom officials in June 1992, the FSU stockpile was projected to decline to 40–50 percent of its mid-1992 level as a result of arms control initiatives through early 1992.[36] This implies a 17,500 to 21,000 reduction, bringing the stockpile down to 14,000 to 17,500 warheads. The CIA, in contrast, informed Congress in May 1992:

> the Russians have something on the order of 9,000 to 16,000 nuclear weapons slated for dismantling. They have not given us an official figure for how many weapons are slated for dismantling as a result of the Gorbachev-Yeltsin initiative. This is our estimate. We have a highly uncertain estimate of the size of their tactical nuclear weapon inventory. Their initiative included something on the order of 1,200 strategic weapons; 5,000 to 12,000 tactical nuclear weapons, and our estimate of 2,700 weapons remaining from the INF treaty.[37]

The CIA upper limit on the number of warheads slated for dismantlement is 1,500 warheads less than that derived from the Minatom statements.

As a consequence of the Bush/Gorbachev initiative of September/October 1991, and the Strategic Arms Reduction Treaty (START I), the deployed Russian stockpile would be reduced to 10,500–13,000 warheads by the year 2000. On June 17, 1992, Presidents Bush and Yeltsin announced that the U.S. and Russian strategic arsenals would

TABLE 3: U.S. and Former Soviet Nuclear Weapon Stockpiles

	1980	1988 (end)	1992	2002(START II)
No. of US Warheads				
Strategic Offense	10,600	12,750	8,420	3,500
Nonstrategic[a]	13,700	10,650	3,000	1,600
TOTAL	24,300	23,400	11,400	5,100
Est. No. of FSU Warheads				
Strategic Offense	7,500	10,850	9,650	3,000–9,650[b]
Nonstrategic	28,500	31,700	25,350[c]	11,000–16,350
TOTAL	36,000	42,550[d]	35,000	14,000–26,000[e]

[a]Category includes air/missile defense warheads.

[b]Since START II does not require the dismantlement of warheads, the number of strategic warheads that will be retained in the reserve stockpiles of each side is unknown. The low figure assumes the dismantlement of the maximum number of warheads likely to be removed from service under the treaty; the high figure assumes that all such warheads would be stored.

[c]Includes thousands of tactical and air-defense weapons removed from active service but not yet dismantled.

[d]According to remarks by Victor Mikhailov, Russia's Minister for Nuclear Energy, at a Feb. 17, 1993 meeting in Washington D.C. hosted by the Committee on International Security and Arms Control of the National Academy of Sciences, the Soviet nuclear weapons stockpile peaked in 1986 at 45,000 warheads, and then declined by 20% to 35,000 warheads as of mid-1992. This implies a dismantlement rate of about 1670 warheads per year. At this rate, the Russian nuclear stockpile will decline to 21,500 warheads by the year 2000.

[e]This range is bounded by the low end of a June 1992 projection by Minatom officials of the weapons remaining in the Russian nuclear stockpile after implementation of disarmament initiatives, and the low end of a May 1992 CIA estimate of the number of Russian warheads that might be dismantled.

each be reduced by 2003 to 3000–3500 warheads associated with deployed strategic delivery vehicles. This agreement was codified as the second Strategic Arms Reduction Treaty (START II)—signed in Moscow by Yeltsin and Bush on January 4, 1993.

Nuclear Stockpile Data Exchanges and
Cooperative Inspections for Data Confirmation

There is a natural tendency in any government bureaucracy to "complexify" those tasks which are obviously too important to be dismissed out of hand, but are nonetheless perceived as inimical to the interests of the organization. Verifying the elimination of former Soviet nuclear weapons and subsequent disposition of the removed fissile materials are two such tasks. While the prospects for implementation may be shrouded in a bureaucratic fog , the essential purposes to be served by such arrangements cannot be hidden, and are not difficult to describe. Nuclear stockpile data exchanges and cooperative inspections have the potential to:

- reduce the uncertainties in our estimates of nuclear weapons material in Russia and the other new nations formed from the former Soviet Union
- assure the American people and the international community that significant quantities of these materials are not being diverted to unauthorized uses or secretly kept in reserve for future use in nuclear weapons
- provide a firm political basis for agreement on strengthened proliferation controls at the 1995 conference to extend the Nuclear Nonproliferation Treaty (NPT)
- provide a verified basis for confidently reducing stockpiles well below the currently agreed upon levels of 5000–6,000 deployed weapons (tactical and strategic); and
- provide a coherent record of nuclear weapons elimination that could be relied upon by other countries with smaller or undeclared nuclear arsenals, such as China and Pakistan, in reaching a decision to join the nuclear arms reduction process.

On July 2 1992, the Senate Committee on Foreign Relations (SFRC) adopted a condition to the resolution of ratification for the START I Treaty—approved by the full Senate in October—that directs the President to seek an appropriate arrangement, "in connection with any further agreement reducing strategic arms," for monitoring nuclear stockpile weapons and fissile material production facilities, through the use of reciprocal inspections, data exchanges, and other cooperative measures (text of the so-called "Biden Condition" is included in a footnote below.)[38]

Russian officials estimate that as much as 70–80 metric tons of plutonium and 300–500 tons of highly-enriched uranium will be released from weapons before the year 2003, when the Russian arsenal of deployed strategic weapons is to have been reduced to 3500 weapons. As Ambassador Robert Gallucci, the State Department's Senior Coordinator for nuclear nonproliferation assistance to the CIS, recently observed, "if this situation doesn't get fixed, in the long term it will be an area in which we will have real worries about materials disappearing."[39] There is every reason to be concerned about the short-term problem of nuclear material diversion as well. The new administration should therefore place a high priority on the prompt achievement of the monitoring objectives set forth in the Committee's resolution.

Agreement between the United States and the appropriate states of the CIS on the desired verification arrangements would lend momentum and credibility to President Bush's important—but politically sidelined—initiative in the Middle East for a weapons material production ban. The extensive on-site inspection measures needed to verify a production ban would guard against a recurrence anywhere in the Middle East of secret programs to produce weapons usable nuclear materials like that mounted—with foreign assistance—by Iraqi dictator Saddam Hussein.

On February 12, 1992, Russian Foreign Minister Andrei Kozyrev formally proposed a reciprocal exchange of data between all nuclear weapon powers on inventories of nuclear weapons and fissile materials, and on nuclear weapons production, storage, and elimination facilities. The Bush Administration failed to respond positively to this Russian initiative at the time, and ignored the offer for the remainder of its term in office.

The Clinton Administration should seriously examine the following measures for inclusion in supplemental monitoring arrangements that meet the verification objectives of the Senate START condition:

- a data exchange, including the total number of warheads of each type, and the total masses of plutonium and highly-enriched uranium metal within and outside of nuclear weapons;
- an exchange of serial numbers and storage locations of warheads and bombs, which could be updated at six- or twelve-month intervals;
- application by the owning party of tamper-resistant, laser-readable bar-codes and/or "intrinsic fingerprint" tags on all nuclear weapons (or on their containers sealed with tamper-indicating locks), accompanied by immediate provision of these data to the verifying party at the inspection site;
- random on-site inspection of weapon storage sites to verify the disposition of warheads as set forth in the periodic exchanges of data; identification of all nuclear weapons or sealed weapon canisters entering a dismantlement facility or leaving a production facility by matching the serial number to a unique barcode and/or "fingerprint" tag;
- international safeguards over fissile material permanently removed from weapons use, civil stocks, and plants capable of producing such material.

The Clinton Administration and the Congress should also consider exchanging the following or similar categories of data (shown in Table 4), on an annual or semi-annual basis:

TABLE 4: Sample U.S.-C.I.S. Nuclear Stockpile Data Exchange Under Biden Condition to START

A	B	C	D	E
1 DATA CATEGORY	Weapon and Fissile Material Inventories			
2	(Status as of 9/30/91 and each year thereafter)			
3	# of weapons	Pu (kgs)	HEU (>20% U-235)	
4			U-235 (kg)	Total (kg)
5 Warheads/bombs for SNDV's				
6 on strategic ballistic missiles				
7 at bases for operational strategic bombers				
8 in storage				
9 Total - strategic weapons				
10				
11 Nonstrategic Nuclear Weapons				
12 land-based missiles/artillery/mines/air-defense				
13 gravity bombs (Navy and Air Force)				
14 ship-launched weapons/sea mines				
15 Total - nonstrategic weapons				
16				
17 Other stocks available for weapons				
18				
19 Total nuclear weapons stockpile				
20				
21 Non-weapons Stockpile				
22 Transferred from weapons use				
23 Recovered from spent fuel				
24 In fresh enriched uranium (unirradiated)				
25				
26 Total weapons-usable				
27 fissile material inventory				
28				

Notes:

Cell A1: Only data in unshaded boxes would be exchanged, protecting specific weapons design information.

Cell A17: "Other stocks available for weapons" includes stored fissile material components of previously dismantled and any other fissile materials usable in weapons without further chemical separation or isotopic enrichment

(1)   the numbers of CIS/Russian and U.S. nuclear stockpile weapons added, retired, dismantled, and remaining in service (if any) in each of the following categories:

(i)   total stockpiles;
(ii)   strategic ballistic missile warheads;
(iii)   strategic bomber weapons;
(iv)   non-strategic land-based missiles (incl. air defense), artillery, mines;
(v)   gravity bombs;
(vi)   ship-launched weapons/sea mines;

(2)   the total masses of CIS/Russian and U.S. plutonium and highly-enriched uranium in:

F	G	H	I	J	K	L	M
Weapons Committed/Scheduled for Elimination				**Nuclear Weapons Dismantled**			
(cumulative weapons and fissile material since 9/30/91)				(cumulative number of weapons and fissile material)			
# of weapons	Pu (kgs)	HEU (>20% U-235)		# of weapons	Pu (kgs)	HEU (>20% U235)	
		U-235 (kg)	Total (kg)			U-235 (kg)	Total (kg)

Cell A23: "Recovered from spent fuel" category includes fissile material recovered from naval propulsion, research, test, and defense production reactors, and from nuclear power generating stations.

Cell A24: "In fresh enriched uranium" category includes fresh HEU fuel elements for naval propulsion, research, test, isotope production, and prototype power reactirs, HEU fuel fabrication pipeline inventory, and stored inventories of highly enriched product.

(i)   the total nuclear weapons stockpile

(ii)   weapons on or available for strategic nuclear delivery vehicles;

(iii)   all other nuclear stockpile weapons;

(iv)   other stocks outside of but available for weapons

(v)   irrevocably transferred from weapons use to peaceful use;

(vi)   recovered from spent fuel

(vii)   fresh (>20%) enriched uranium (unirradiated)

(viii) the combined total inventory of potentially weapons-usable fissile material.

(3)   the current status, fissile material inventories, and output of all known CIS/Russian and U.S. facilities with the capacity

for producing or processing significant quantities of fissile materials.

In developing the verification arrangements required by the Biden condition, Executive Branch agencies, particularly the DOE and its national laboratories, should seek to engage nuclear weapon experts of the former Soviet Union in the joint development and implementation of:

(1) reliable techniques and procedures for verifying a global ban on the production of fissile materials for weapons purposes;

(2) reliable techniques and procedures for permanently transferring agreed quantities of fissile materials out of the nuclear weapons production cycle, and for safeguarding the secure storage of these materials pending future nonweapon uses or permanent disposal;

(3) techniques to permanently dispose of nuclear weapons components and materials in a verifiable and safe manner so as to prevent recovery for use in weapons;

(4) increased technical assistance to the IAEA to aid in the accomplishment of its global safeguards and inspection responsibilities.

Through four decades of international arms control and disarmament negotiations, the United States government has consistently stressed strict nuclear materials accountability and openness to on-site-inspection as the bedrock of the nuclear nonproliferation regime. The need for mutual openness, accurate and complete baseline data exchanges, and on-site inspection has also been a consistent feature of the U.S. position in bilateral arms control negotiations with Russia and the former Soviet Union. The "Biden Condition" is completely consonant with and supportive of these longstanding pillars of U.S. nuclear policy.

While differences in the technical community persist over the extent of the prospective reduction in the margin of error that might be gained from the measures called for in the Biden Condition, no serious student of the subject disputes that at least some reduction in uncertainty would be forthcoming, and some scholars and intelligence professionals believe it could be significant, particularly if production records were exchanged to substantiate authoritative nuclear stockpile declarations. For example, at present the United States government does not know whether Russia has 750 or 1050 metric tons of highly enriched uranium, and it lacks the technical data to substantiate either number.

We note that officials of the Russian Foreign Ministry itself, nominally charged with the responsibility of controlling Russia's nuclear exports, have stated that they have no knowledge of, and no reliable technical basis for ascertaining, the total amount of fissile material in Russia, which is under the sole control of MINATOM. Thus the reciprocal exchange of nuclear stockpile data called for under the Biden condition could not only reduce the large uncertainty in US estimates, but it could also significantly assist the process of asserting democratic control over the Soviet nuclear industrial complex.

The purpose of data exchanges and on-site inspections is not to render a black or white judgement by categorically excluding all possibilities for cheating, but rather to increase confidence in our own compliance judgements and intelligence assessments. This logic is clearly accepted in other areas of arms control. For example, in the biological weapons area, the disclosure by Yeltsin of the Soviet military's noncompliance with the 1972 Biological Weapons Treaty recently prompted the US and UK to seek increased inspection rights to provide greater assurance of Russian military compliance.

According to the joint U.S.-Russian-UK statement issued on September 14, inspection visits to suspect non-military biological facilities will include "unrestricted access, sampling, interviews with personnel and audio and video taping." The agreement provides for Russian visits to American and British sites on the same basis. According to State Department spokesman Richard Boucher, "the steps in the statement are designed to launch *a process that could, over time, give us confidence* that Russia has terminated the offensive biological warfare program illicitly carried out for years by the Soviet regime."[40]

Another concern raised about the Biden Condition during Senate consideration of the START Treaty was "the legality under current U.S. law of the reciprocal monitoring and inspection regime envisioned in the proposed Condition."[41] In fact, the Secretary of Energy already has the authority under current law to reclassify nuclear information from the "Restricted Data" category, classified under the statutory authority of the Atomic Energy Act, to "Formerly Restricted Data," which is controlled by Executive Order. Thus there is already a clear path in existing law for the President to make whatever changes are necessary in the current information security system to accommodate the types of data exchanges and inspections and exchanges called for under the Biden Condition. But to remove any doubt about the matter, the Congress including a provision in the FY 1993 Defense Authorization Bill that amends the Atomic Energy Act to clearly permit release of Restricted Data regarding the nuclear weapons stockpile if the US and Russia reach agreement on reciprocal release of such data.[42]

There is a disturbing contradiction at the heart of some of the official testimony received by the Senate Armed Services Committee concerning the Biden condition. Officials who only a short time ago were insisting on the need for the most stringent verification measures now suggest that the kind of measures contemplated by the Biden Condition are "not needed" given the friendly, cooperative relationship we supposedly now enjoy with a new "democratic" Russia. This stance not only begs the question of what might happen under a less hospitable Russian government, but it vastly overstates the democratic nature and degree of popular control which characterize the current government, Yeltsin's revolutionary ambitions notwithstanding.

Precisely because events in the CIS could take a turn for the worse, the US government and the international community needs to establish now, while the political opening exists, the baseline data and inspection rights which we can rely on in the future to track changes in the CIS nuclear stockpile regardless of the political tendencies of the governments in power. This principle is well acknowledged as it applies to stocks of enriched uranium in Argentina, South Africa, or Pakistan, or stocks of plutonium held by former enemies-turned-allies such as Germany and Japan. Indeed, it is this basic principle of openness and nuclear accountability that underlies the entire international safeguards system, which virtually all observers agree needs to be supported and strengthened.

Beyond the imperative of nonproliferation, however, there is the additional consideration of holding open the prospect of making even deeper nuclear weapon reductions in the future. These would be on a scale that could induce lesser nuclear weapon powers to accept verified limitations on their arsenals, thereby establishing the basis for a universal system of control over nuclear weapons and fissile materials. In a little-noticed provision of the FY 1993 Defense Authorization Act regarding future US policy on nuclear weapon reductions, the Congress stated:

> It shall be the goal of the United States— . . . (4) to build on the agreement reached in the Joint Understanding of June 16-17, 1992, by entering into multilateral negotiations with the Russian Federation, the United Kingdom, France, and the People's Republic of China, and, at an appropriate point in that process, enter into negotiations with other nuclear armed states in order to reach subsequent stage-by-stage agreements to achieve further reductions in the number of nuclear weapons in all countries.[43]

To sustain this prospect for the future requires a careful accounting now of the disposition of the former Soviet and US nuclear arsenals. Under the SFRC condition, the U.S. position on the scope, frequency, and relative intrusiveness of nuclear stockpile data exchanges and monitoring arrangements is left to the discretion of the Executive Branch. And that is where the real problem lies. The constant refrain that reciprocal nuclear stockpile monitoring measures are too "sensitive" and "complex" to negotiate is less a reflection of diplomatic reality than a sad commentary on the somewhat aimless monitoring debate within our own national security establishment.

After four decades of lecturing the Russians and the world on the importance of openness and reliable verification, it is something of an embarrassment for the United States to be having difficulty with nuclear data exchanges, fissile material accounting, "tagging" of treaty-limited items, and on-site inspections at the very moment in history when such initiatives appear feasible to implement on a global basis.

Creating the Basis for a Steady Reduction in the Politico-Military Role of Nuclear Weapons in the International Security System

As deep nuclear and conventional force reductions proceed and international control mechanisms are built-up, it should become both possible and desirable to shift the international security role of nuclear weapons from "active" day-to-day deterrence of nuclear and large-scale conventional attacks to "passive" discouragement of potential proliferant nations. This shift can be achieved initially through international commitments to "no-first-use" of nuclear weapons, and through the retention of modest internationally-monitored nuclear reserve forces, the size and combat readiness of which are steadily diminished over time. Over the long term, as greater confidence is achieved in a $NEMC^2$ system, this proliferation "discouragement" mission could be performed by secure deep underground storage of residual nuclear warhead component inventories—under international monitoring—that could be reassembled in the event a serious nuclear threat to international security emerged that justified redeployment of a nuclear deterrent force.

Storage of Fissile Material from Weapons (i.e., Plutonium and Highly Enriched Uranium) Under International Safeguards

The major reductions now taking place in nuclear warhead stockpiles have raised anew the issue of whether U.S. and Russian warhead plutonium should be regarded as an energy resource or a waste.

Attitudes toward this question affect the type of storage facilities that may be built, and the methods adopted for ultimate disposition of the material. With respect to plutonium storage, then MAPI First Deputy Minister Victor Mikhailov visited Washington in October 1991, before the breakup of the Soviet Union, and met with U.S. senators to discuss the need for U.S. financial assistance in constructing a large secure facility to store fissile material components from dismantled Soviet weapons. Without such a new storage facility, he maintained, the dismantlement of Soviet warheads would be delayed.

Based in part on the representations made by then Deputy Minister (now Minister) Mikhailov and other former Soviet officials, in November the U.S. Congress passed the *"Soviet Nuclear Threat Reduction Act (SNTRA) "* of 1991,[44] allocating $400 million in Department of Defense funds to assist the states of the former USSR in nuclear and chemical warhead destruction. Congress added another $400 million for FY1993, bringing the total "Nunn-Lugar" program to $800 million.

The main purposes of the Nunn-Lugar bill are to:

- Destroy nuclear and chemical weapons;
- Transport, store, disable and safeguard weapons in connection with their destruction;
- Establish verifiable safeguards against proliferation.

Nunn-Lugar funds provided by Congress may not be spent by the Executive Branch unless the President certifies to Congress that the proposed recipient is "committed to"—

- foregoing any re-use of fissionable and other components of destroyed weapons in new weapons;
- facilitating US verification of weapons destruction;

With respect to the first condition, the State Department certified to Congress in April 1992 that, based on the results of informal discussions with Minatom and military officials, Russia did not intend to reuse fissile material components in weapons:[45]

> Russian willingness to allow U.S. participation in the construction and joint Russian-U.S. or international operation of a storage facility (even to the extent of a dual-key access system) demonstrates their intention not to reuse this fissionable material in weapons.

However, the State Department also noted, "the Russian government has made no official declarations in this regard."

With respect to the second condition, the State Department informed the Congress that none of the Nunn-Lugar projects "identified so far" envisioned U.S. assistance for the actual destruction of warheads. Therefore, the requirement to facilitate U.S. verification of weapons destruction did not apply to the current U.S. assistance program. This apparently remains the case today. In October 1992, the Congress passed the "Former Soviet Union Demilitarization Act of 1992," providing an additional $400 million in funding for Nunn-Lugar activities, including $40 million in FY 1993 for "industrial demilitarization projects" in the former Soviet Union "that would directly contribute to the elimination of military production capability, especially in the area of weapons of mass destruction."

Using the $800 million as leverage, the U.S. government plans to obtain whatever level of safeguards can be negotiated on the Russian fissile material without involving reciprocal controls on the U.S. materials removed from weapons. The Ministry of Atomic Energy (MINATOM) has stated that Russia will permit some degree of U.S. monitoring of the contents of the storage facility. Apparently, the Russians do not have anything approaching the material accounting and control requirements and procedures of the United States or even the International Atomic Energy Agency (IAEA) at Russian facilities where nuclear weapons materials are processed and stored. The U.S. government is reportedly considering providing the Russians with computer systems and software for fissile material control.

According to a September 1992 report of the Senate Armed Services Committee[46], the "Nunn-Lugar program has been a major success in facilitating the disabling, transport, storage and safeguarding of the nuclear weapons of the former Soviet Union." In reality, as of December 1992 not a single former Soviet warhead had been disabled, transported, stored, safeguarded, or destroyed with the assistance of U.S. funds or personnel. In fact, the principle premise of the Nunn-Lugar effort—to assist in the swift disablement, transportation, and destruction of excess former Soviet weapons located outside of Russia—has turned out to be misdirected, as the Russians have maintained that they do not require assistance in this area.

Instead, there has been a proliferation of marginally useful but essentially peripheral "Nunn-Lugar projects"—each of which requires its own implementing agreement above and beyond a broad "framework agreement" with the proposed recipient nation. Most of these projects remain to be implemented and are unlikely to yield the comprehensive stockpile data called for by the Biden Condition. Fourteen months after Congress made available $400 million in

TABLE 5a   "Nunn-Lugar" Assistance Projects in Russia

Projects	Proposed Funding (as of Jan. 30, 1993)	Obligated Funds (Dec. 31, 1992)	Start/End Dates
Russia			
2500 armored blankets for Russian warhead containers	$5,000,000	$2,691,000	July 1992–1995
accident response equipment	15,000,000	8,168,000	Jan.–Dec. 1993
10,000 containers to ship/ store fissile material weapon components	50,000,000	600,000	"early 94"–Dec. 95
assessment of chemical weapons demilitarization	25,000,000	1,553,000	July 1992–1993
115 safety upgrade kits for Russian railcars to transport fissile material components	20,000,000	3,080,000	Dec. 92–April 1994
technical design review of weapon component storage facility	15,000,000	3,363,000	Aug. 92–March 93
storage facility construction	75,000,000	0	late 1993–1997
Science and Technology Centers (Moscow)	25,000,000	150,000	June 93–?
export control training and equipment	2,260,000	0	not yet implemented
Subtotal Russia	$232,260,000	$19,605,000	

Sources: USGAO; U.S. State Department.

emergency disarmament assistance, the Pentagon had actually expended almost none of it, and planned to spend only about two-thirds of the money Congress provided (see Table 5). The bulk of the funds obligated to date are being paid to US contractors to provide in-kind assistance in the form of equipment and training, and a year after its founding, the much ballyhooed Science and Technology Center program, to offset incentives for the migration or sale of nuclear weapons expertise, had yet to make a single grant.

In 1991–92, the Bush Administration and Senators Nunn and Lugar were content to rely on the Russian Nuclear Ministry's desire for U.S. funding of a large facility to store fissile material components removed

TABLE 5b "Nunn-Lugar" Assistance Projects in Other FSU States

Projects	Proposed Funding (as of Jan. 30, 1993)	Obligated Funds (Dec. 31, 1992)	Start/End Dates
Ukraine			
nuclear accident response	$5,000,000	0	agreement pending
Communications link for INF and START Treaty data	2,400,000	0	agreement pending
Export control training and equipment	2,260,000	0	agreement pending
fissile material accounting and control system	7,500,000	0	agreement pending
Science and Technology Center (Kiev)	10,000,000	0	agreement pending
Subtotal Ukraine	$27,160,000	0	agreement pending
Belarus			
nuclear accident response	$5,000,000	0	agreement signed
START/INF data link	2,300,000	0	agreement signed
export control training and equipment	2,260,000	0	agreement signed
Subtotal Belarus	$9,560,000	0	
Kazakhstan			
nuclear accident response	$5,000,000	0	US proposal provided
START/INF data link	2,300,000	0	US proposal provided
export control training and equipment	2,260,000	0	US proposal provided
fissile material accounting and control	5,000,000	0	US proposal provided
ballistic missile dismantling	amount TBD	0	US proposal provided
Subtotal Kazakhstan	$14,560,000		
Program Management/ Assessment	$10,000,000	$778,000	
Total (Russia + Other FSU)	$303,540,000	$20,383,000	

from weapons use as sufficient evidence of a "commitment" not to reuse this material in weapons. From the technical point of view, however, without knowing the total universe of fissile material in and withdrawn from weapons and all the locations where it is being stored, the State Department's certification provides no meaningful assurance against proliferation or possible reuse of the material in weapons.

Dr. Robert Barker, then Assistant to the Secretary of Defense for Atomic Energy, testified to Congress in August 1992 as follows:

> For nuclear material *in excess of Russian nuclear weapon requirements*, we the United States, have already been offered the opportunity to help design a secure storage and accounting system.[47]

Dr. Barker stated that during discussions of potential assistance under the Nunn-Lugar program:

> a representative of the Russian General staff . . . surprised me when he freely agreed, without any discussion whatsoever, that should the United States fund any facility in which fissile material would be stored, the U.S. would, of course, have free access *to that facility* to determine that the facility was used *in the manner in which the funding was intended*.
> . . . With this kind of access to facilities and information, we will have a sound basis for any judgements about the *potential for the loss of Russian nuclear material* into the hands of potential proliferators.
> . . . Further, we should not forget that they will always have the option of adapting the technology we will share with them for storage and accountability of non-weapons material. *They can apply the same techniques themselves* to nuclear weapons storage if they see a need for it (emphasis added).[48]

The underscored portions of Dr. Barker's testimony clearly indicate that current U.S.-Russian denuclearization policy does not contemplate declarations and controls that would apply to all nuclear-weapons usable material, but only to that portion of the total inventory that would be declared in excess of weapon requirements and stored in a facility built with U.S. funds. Weapons usable nuclear material stored at other military sites, and the 30 metric tons of separated plutonium (and an unknown amount of HEU) in the Russian civil nuclear program, would not be covered under such an arrangement.

Even for the material that would be covered, controls would appear to be limited to determining that the storage facility is used in a manner consistent with the purposes of the Nunn-Lugar funding, thereby permitting the U.S. to acquire a basis for making judgements about the "potential" for the loss of Russian nuclear material from this facility. It should be noted that the standard for genuine safeguards is considerably different—namely, to account for the disposition of all nuclear material with sufficient accuracy to detect promptly whether a diversion of material has actually occurred.

The Russians have proven less than eager to implement genuine controls as long as they are not applied in a reciprocal manner, and in the face of the Bush administration's opposition to reciprocal measures, Nunn and Lugar backed away from pursuing the verification aspect of their legislation to obtain executive branch cooperation in implementing what they hoped would be a warhead elimination assistance program. According to the General Accounting Office, the U.S.- Russian framework agreement merely states that the United States "shall have the right to examine the use of any material, training, or other services" that it may provide.[49]

Thus in December, 1992, nuclear energy minister Mikhailov could mount a public defense against Russian nationalist attacks on the "unilateral" monitoring provisions of the Nunn-Lugar program by noting that these provisions provided no real access to, or information on, Russia's nuclear weapons activities:

> The U.S. Congress . . . set us six conditions. Two of them—U.S. monitoring of our scientific research and experimental design work in the defense sphere to ensure that this work does not exceed the bounds of Russia's "defense sufficiency" needs—"sufficiency from the American viewpoint, that is—and monitoring by their specialists of the process of nuclear disarmament in Russia—were totally unacceptable.
>
>   . . . the [American] specialists invited have the status of consultants. All decisions will be made by us and all supplies are strictly monitored by us. The Russian side alone is responsible for all operations involving U.S. equipment. We, in turn, must guarantee the U.S. side that the equipment we receive will be used only for its specific purpose, will not end up in any part of the Third World, and will not be used to produce weapons.[50]
>
>   . . . G. Bush's active personal support helped to decide the question. As a result, it was possible to ensure that the preliminary conditions set by the U.S. Congress were not reflected in the text of the [June 1992 framework] agreement. . . . The [framework and implementing] agreements do not provide for the admission of U.S. specialists to facilities in the Russian nuclear weapons complex in order to participate in any work or operations involving nuclear weapons. The U.S. side will have the usual right in such cases to occasionally verify that [U.S.-provided] equipment is being used for its intended purpose. The verification procedures are subject to additional agreement."[51]

A Ban on All Nuclear Explosions,
i.e., a Comprehensive Nuclear Test Ban (CTB)

The New Test Ban Debate 1985–1992

Nuclear explosions were banned in all environments except underground by the Partial Test Ban Treaty of 1963. The implications of a Comprehensive Test Ban can be examined and debated at several levels. Proponents of a complete test ban have long believed that any military technology benefits that might come from continued testing underground are outweighed by the risks of radioactive contamination and advanced thermonuclear weapons proliferation entailed by further nuclear weapons tests. At the level of international diplomacy, virtually all the signatories to the Nuclear Nonproliferation Treaty (NPT), including nuclear weapon states such as Russia and France, and new nuclear powers such as India and Pakistan, support a Comprehensive Test Ban as one important means of minimizing discrimination between nuclear weapon- and non-weapon-states when the NPT comes up for extension in 1995. A test ban could also help to stabilize the so called "existential" nuclear deterrent balance that now exists in South Asia between India and Pakistan, without either state feeling compelled to develop and deploy a sophisticated nuclear arsenal. Perhaps, above all, a test ban is an important symbolic and political component of a broader nonproliferation strategy which seeks to stigmatize acquisition nuclear weapons and thereby diminish the potential for their threatened or actual use.

When the Cold War ended and the Soviet Union disintegrated, the primary U.S. justification for continuing nuclear weapons testing abruptly shifted from staying ahead in the arms competition to "enhancing nuclear weapons safety." Under this rubric, proponents of nuclear testing proposed to spend billions of dollars over the next decades developing a new generation of nuclear warheads which can endure severe collisions and plane crashes without detonating their *chemical* explosive, thereby scattering toxic plutonium into the environment. Current weapons are already designed to be safe against an accidental *nuclear* explosion under a wide, if not exhaustive, set of possible accident scenarios. In the 45 year history of the nuclear arms race, despite numerous accidents involving nuclear weapons less "safe" than today's designs, no such accidental nuclear explosion has ever occurred.

Opponents of continued nuclear weapons tests argue that there are far more cost-effective ways to reduce the public's exposure risk to cancer-causing agents than spending billions of dollars building so-called "safer" nuclear weapons. If public health is really the new measure of merit by which the need for nuclear explosions will be judged, then the scatter of warhead plutonium by fire or chemical explosion constitutes one of the *least likely* public cancer exposure risks, and the most obvious way to further reduce this risk is not to transport nuclear weapons by air in peacetime. Further reducing the public's environmental and occupational exposure to lead, benzene, and cadmium, for example, would be a far more effective use of a billion taxpayer dollars than further refinements in nuclear weapons technology.

Beginning in 1985 with the ascendancy of President Gorbachev, the former Soviet Union went out of its way to demonstrate a willingness to stop all nuclear weapons testing if the United Sates would agree to do the same. In August 1985, the USSR began a 19-month unilateral testing moratorium, and in June 1986 President Gorbachev agreed to a joint proposal by the Natural Resources Defense Council (NRDC) and the Soviet Academy of Sciences to install seismic stations around the main Soviet test site in Kazakhstan.

The first step in a long-standing campaign in Congress to end nuclear testing was a surprise victory in an August 1986 House vote that was influenced by NRDC's surprise success only weeks before in setting up the first "in-country" seismic stations for monitoring a test ban. The House of Representatives approved an amendment that barred all U.S. nuclear tests with a nuclear energy release exceeding one kiloton (1000 tons) of chemical explosive equivalent provided the USSR showed similar restraint. NRDC's stations boosted confidence in Congress that the USSR would observe a reciprocal test moratorium, and the same restriction passed the House again in 1987 and 1988. But it twice failed passage in the Senate, where similar Hatfield-Kennedy amendments were held to a maximum of 40 votes.

The Reagan Administration declined to join the moratorium or begin CTB negotiations, and the Soviet Union resumed testing in February 1987. Despite the moratorium, the Soviet Union still managed to conduct 61 underground nuclear explosions in the four year period from 1984 through 1987. Over the same period, the United States conducted 62 underground explosions.

As the Reagan era gave way to the Bush Administration, Senators Ted Kennedy and Tom Harkin and Representatives Ed Markey and Martin Sabo arranged for government funding and expansion of NRDC's seismic monitoring network in the former Soviet Union under the auspices of a large university consortium, the Incorporated Research Institutions for Seismology (IRIS). Technical support for the IRIS stations came from the same geophysics research group at Scripps Institute, U.C. San Diego, that had earlier collaborated with NRDC.

From 1987-91, congressional supporters of a test ban also vigorously pursued the other ostensible technical barriers to a test ban, by mandating a DOE study of the test requirements, including any needed safety upgrades, that would permit reliable remanufacture of weapons under a future test ban, and by commissioning an independent evaluation of the weapon reliability and safety issue by Livermore physicist Ray Kidder. Both these studies eventually turned out to play an important role in the deliberations leading to the successful compromise and historic first Senate vote on Aug. 3, 1992 to end nuclear testing. The estimated number of tests needed for certifying various safety upgrades, to warheads regarded as candidates for retention in the future stockpile, is given in Table 6.

Two years after the Soviet Union resumed testing, two of its underground tests leaked radioactive material into the atmosphere. The accident initiated a grassroots environmental movement calling for the closure of the Soviet test site in Kazakhstan. At the beginning of 1990, Moscow announced that testing at Kazakhstan would be phased out over three years and moved to an existing test site on the Arctic Island of Novaya Zemlya. Testing in the Arctic, however, also faced opposition, notably from the newly elected President of the Russian Republic, Boris Yeltsin, whose election platform included opposition to testing on Novaya Zemlya. The last test in Kazakhstan occurred on October 19, 1989, and the last test conducted by the former Soviet Union was on Novaya Zemlya on October 24, 1990.

While the debate over the technical requirements for a comprehensive ban continued in Congress, the Bush Administration never delivered on President Reagan's pledge to Congress to resume test ban negotiations "immediately" following ratification of the Threshold Test Ban Treaty, an agreement dating back to the Nixon Administration that had become a convenient obstacle to progress on a CTB. After years were wasted negotiating cumbersome on-site technical measures—to more exactly determine the size of large nuclear explosions permitted by the Threshold Treaty—this agreement finally received Executive and Senate approval in September 1990.[52]

In August 1991, the Semipalatinsk test site was permanently closed at the direction of the newly independent Kazakh Republic. Following the disintegration of the Soviet Union in December 1991, Russian President Boris Yeltsin continued to seek negotiations on a CTB and pledged that Russia would adhere to the one-year unilateral moratorium on testing initiated by then Soviet President Gorbachev on October 5, 1991. French Prime Minister Pierre Beregovoy announced on April 8, 1992 that France, long considered one of the staunchest opponents of a test ban, would suspend testing for the remainder of the

TABLE 6:   Estimated Numbers of Nuclear Explosive Tests Required to Install Safety Upgrades (and Other Permitted Tests) Under the "Hatfield Exon Mitchell Amendment" (HEMA) of 1992

Warhead/Bomb	Safety Upgrade(s)	# of Explosions Min #	Max #	Source
W76 Trident I/II	Add IHE/FRP[a]		3	DOE, Dec. 1990
W88 Trident II	Add IHE/FRP		2–4	DOE, Dec. 1990
[W76/88 Trident I/II	No change needed	0		DoD, March 1992][b]
[W76/88 Trident I/II	Test W89 replacement	4		R. Kidder, 1992]
W78 MM III	Add IHE/FRP		2	DOE, Dec. 1990
	No change needed	0		DoD, March 1992
[DeMIRV W78 MMIII	Replace with MX/W87	0		R. Kidder, 1992
W80 ALCM/ACM	Add FRP		2	DOE, Dec. 1990
B61 bomb	Add FRP		1	DOE, Dec. 1990
[W80/B61	Do not add FRP's	0		DoD/Air Force,[c] 1991-92
Subtotal— safety upgrade tests		0–4	10–12	
"Reliability" tests (incl. DNA) @ 1 per year		0	3	President must certify
British tests @ 1 per year		0–3	3	President makes determination
Est. Hatfield-Exon-Mitchell tests[d]		0–7	16-18	

[a] IHE = "Insensitive High Explosive;" FRP = "Fire Resistant Pit."

[b] As recently as March 31, 1992, the Asst. to the Secretary of Defense for Atomic Energy testified "that there is not now sufficient evidence to warrant changing either warheads or propellants" in the Trident SLBM force."

[c] The Air Force response to the Drell Panel in August 1991 stated that it would not be cost effective to remanufacture the W80 and B61 weapons with fire resistant pits: "Qualitative Assessment indicates that safety risk associated with incorporating FRP into bombs and cruise missile warheads which already have ENDS and IHE would exceed the safety gain." Air Force Response to the Drell Panel, NWCWSC 1 August 1991, Lt. Col John R. Curry SAF/AQQS.

[d] The number of tests ultimately arrived at in the "Hatfield-Exon Mitchell" legislation was 15, between the upper end of the minimum and the low end of the maximum credible estimates. As the final vote neared, DOE officials testified that 25 tests would be needed to accomplish these tasks, apparently on the basis that additional tests should be included as a buffer, to insure against the failure to accomplish the safety upgrade objectives within the forecast number of tests.

year, and he urged the United States and other nuclear weapon states to follow suit.

On February 27, 1992, President Yeltsin quietly ordered the Russian Ministry of Atomic Energy and the Russian Navy to resume preparations for conducting 2-4 tests at Russia's Arctic site "in case of termination of the existing moratorium."[53] On October 13, 1992, responding to the enactment of a 9-month U.S. test moratorium imposed by the U.S. Congress, Russian Defense Minister Pavel Grachev announced, "If the tests resume, it will not be before mid-1993."

On May 21, 1992 China conducted a nuclear test with an estimated yield of 660 kilotons. The next day the U.S. State Department called on China to restrain its program of underground nuclear testing. However, the Bush Administration continued to adhere to the essentials of the Reagan doctrine on testing, namely, "as long as we rely on nuclear weapons as a deterrent, we must continue testing." In the minds of at least some senior Bush Administration officials, this imperative applied to *foreign* nuclear testing programs as well. Despite the ongoing Russian and French test moratoria, Richard Claytor, the DOE's Assistant Secretary for Defense Programs, told the Senate Armed Services Committee in August 1992:

> With respect to the French, I know in their technical community there is strong support from a safety and reliability standpoint that this is very important, that *any nation that has nuclear weapons feels the necessity to test to assure the safety and reliability of the stockpile.* Sometimes the political considerations have overridden that, but I believe that those nations with whom we deal would want to resume testing. . . .
>
> I do not think it would make any difference if we have a moratorium. I am sure the Chinese would not be affected one way or the other. That is my view. . . .
>
> Our laboratory directors from our weapons laboratories have been in touch with their [Russian] counterparts and have actually visited the former Soviet Union. I am suggesting to you, sir, that the technical community in Russia, from the information fed to me, feel it is very important to continue testing for safety and reliability of their stockpile. That is the only view I have.

The possible implications for nonproliferation and regional security of his "any nation that feels the need to test should test" position seems to have escaped Mr. Claytor, and other senior officials as well. Douglas Graham, the Deputy Assistant Secretary of Defense for Strategic Defense, Space, and Verification Policy, agreed with Claytor's testimony:

In our view, the reasons we test have nothing to do with the fact that the Russians are testing or the French are testing, and in our view the Russians and the French have very compelling reasons to be doing testing of their own. . . . As long as those two countries rely on nuclear weapons, it seems to us that the United States has an interest in their having as safe and secure a stockpile as possible.

Dr. John Birely of Los Alamos National Laboratory, the Acting Assistant to the Secretary of Defense for Atomic Energy, testified that in a recent discussion with "a top-level official of the Russian defense establishment," he and Mr. Graham had asked him why the Russians had formally notified the U.S. in accordance with the TTBT of their intent to resume testing:

And he said, "well, just read your own President's policy." So the top-level policymakers in Russia, in addition to the technical people, are also actively debating the resumption of testing, for the exact technical reasons that we have incorporated in our policy. . . for the foreseeable future..both sides will have a substantial stockpile. As long as we have that stockpile, improving and assuring its safety and reliability is the responsibility of both sides, and *one could make an argument based on those concerns that it would be to our advantage to have them testing.*[54]

The Bush Administration had scheduled 6 nuclear tests during FY 1993. Facing the likelihood of a one-year nuclear test moratorium imposed by Congress if it failed to act on its own, on July 10, 1992 the Bush Administration "modified" U.S. nuclear testing policy by impos-ing new unilateral restraints on the conduct of U.S. tests. "The purpose of all U.S. nuclear tests of our weapons will henceforth be for safety and reliability of our deterrent forces. . . . We do not anticipate, under current foreseen circumstances, more than six tests per year over the next five years, or more than three tests per year in excess of 35 kilotons."[55] This policy resulted in the cancellation of one test for FY 1992—"Greenwater"—the final test planned prior to the congressionally mandated phase-out of the controversial x-ray laser program.

In June 1992 the House of Representatives approved by a vote of 237 to 167 an amendment imposing a one year ban on all nuclear tests unless the President certified that Russia or another nation that was part of the former Soviet Union conducted a nuclear test during that period. On August 3, 1992 the Senate voted 68 to 26 in favor of a more extensive and complex provision, the "Hatfield-Exon-Mitchell" nuclear testing amendment to the Energy and Water Appropriations Bill. With the seemingly mundane pronouncement by President Bush on October 2,

1992, that he had "signed into law H.R. 5373, the Energy and Water Development Appropriations Act, 1993," a long-sought milestone was achieved on the road to a CTB. The President's signature immediately triggered the Hatfield-Exon-Mitchell provision mandating a nine-month moratorium on underground nuclear test explosions, renewed negotiations for a global CTB treaty, and complete phase-out of U.S. nuclear weapons testing by December 31, 1996 if other nations refrain from testing after that date.

Congress and the Nuclear Testing Issue in 1992

In the spring of 1992, first-term Representative Mike Kopetski from Oregon and the "Plutonium Challenge," a coalition of national arms control and environmental organizations, sparked a revival of the test-ban issue in the House, which passed a 12-month test moratorium in June conditioned only on Russia's continuation of the test halt inaugurated by President Gorbachev shortly before the Soviet Union came apart in December 1991. In the Senate meanwhile, a painstaking office-by-office coalition lobbying effort, spearheaded by Plutonium Challenge Legislative Coordinator David Culp, assembled a potential 53-vote majority in support of an identical provision sponsored by Senator Mark Hatfield from Oregon and the Democratic Majority Leader, Senator George Mitchell from Maine.

A narrow majority is usually insufficient to assure a win in the Senate, given the ability of the President to turn at least a few votes, and the inherent power of the Vice-President to break a tie. The path to victory lay in winning over a group of moderate Senators, whose views were represented by Senator Jim Exon, Chairman of the Armed Services Subcommittee on Strategic Forces and Nuclear Deterrence. These "swing" Senators were sympathetic to the political need to end U.S. nuclear explosions as a means of enhancing U.S. credibility on nuclear nonproliferation issues, but they were also persuaded of the need to test a few safety modifications to existing weapons before entering a permanent test ban.

With the Administration promising a veto and neither side sure of victory, negotiations commenced between the Exon and Hatfield camps to find a compromise formula that could command a convincing margin of votes. The resulting provision—the "Hatfield-Mitchell-Exon" Amendment to the Energy and Water Appropriation Bill—represented a compromise, but in many respects it went beyond the House position by specifying a restrictive program and timetable for phasing-out all U.S. underground nuclear explosions by the fall of 1996.

Between July 1, 1993, and October 1, 1996, the Hatfield amendment provides for a possible limited resumption of testing, with a quota of 15 explosions over the 39 month period. In general, only tests required for installation of modern safety features in warheads to be retained in the arsenal may be conducted, and the justification for each such test proposed to be carried out in a given fiscal year must be provided in a comprehensive report by March 1 of the preceding year. Of the maximum five tests permitted for safety in each of these three "report periods," one may be replaced by a joint test of a United Kingdom nuclear weapon, and one may be conducted—subject to Congressional disapproval of a Presidential certification of need—using a weapon that has not been modified for safety purposes, but rather is proposed for detonation to ascertain its "reliability."

When it became clear that the Hatfield-Mitchell-Exon compromise had the votes, the leading opponent of the amendment, Energy and Water Subcommittee Chairman Bennett Johnston at first sought to accept the amendment without a record vote, thereby diminishing its importance with the intent of undoing it in conference committee. When Hatfield insisted on a recorded vote, Johnston urged "all Senators to vote yes on this," a tactic sometimes employed in the Senate to deprive a vote of its political meaning. The Armed Services Committee Chairman Sam Nunn, announced that he was voting for the amendment but would seek to modify it later to permit additional testing when his own committee's Defense Authorization Bill reached the floor after the August recess. The Senate adopted the Hatfield-Mitchell-Exon amendment on August 3, 68-26.

The promised attempt to weaken the Hatfield-Mitchell-Exon provision materialized after the recess on September 18. Senator Cohen of Maine offered an amendment to extend the cutoff date for testing to September 30, 1998, and to create loopholes for nuclear "effects" testing of non-nuclear military systems, and for resumption of testing after 1998 if the President certified to Congress that he was "actively engaged in negotiations" for a test ban. While backing Cohen, Senator Nunn kept an unexpectedly low profile in the debate, declaring at one point that "I did not draw up this amendment" and that the gap between his views and the original amendment had been narrowed "a lot" by a change making a nuclear test after 1996 by any nation—not just Russia—sufficient cause to terminate the restriction. Hatfield and Exon offered their slightly modified Energy and Water bill provision as a replacement to Cohen's amendment and prevailed, 55–40.[56]

Test-ban provisions had now been added to a total of four House and Senate bills, and the remaining question to be resolved was the most effective strategy to prevent the promised veto by the President. A great political struggle ensued to keep the Senate-passed provision on the Energy and Water Bill, because this bill contained funding for a great variety of federal projects, including $500 million of an eventual $8 billion for the Super Conducting Supercollider atom-smasher in Texas, a must win State for the President in the November election.

Test ban advocates in Congress held their ground against Appropriations chairmen Johnston and Bevill, who initially sought to drop the provision from the conference report, and resisted political pressures from members anxious to protect projects in their districts and adjourn quickly without risking a veto of the Energy and Water Bill. With support from Majority Leaders Mitchell and Gephardt, Armed Services Committee Chairman Les Aspin, and other key test ban leaders in the House, the House finally adopted the Hatfield-Exon-Mitchell provision on September 24 and sent the completed bill to the White House.

While he signed the bill into law on October 2, President Bush nonetheless characterized the test ban provision as "highly objectionable," and he pledged to "work for new legislation to permit the conduct of a modest number of necessary underground nuclear tests." In transmitting a classified report on nuclear testing to Congress on January 19, President Bush noted in an accompanying unclassified letter to the departing Chairman of the House Armed Services Committee, defense-secretary designate Les Aspin, that

> the framework of the law is far too restrictive to provide a basis for a proper test program that ensures the safety and reliability of U.S. deterrent forces. The enclosed report, therefore, does not propose a specific test plan to the Congress."[57]

In fact, late in 1992 the departing Bush Administration had formally notified the Russian government of a scheduled resumption of U.S. underground testing. According to Russian sources, on March 4, a Russian Defense Ministry spokesman announced that the U.S. Department of Energy, in accordance with the verification protocol of the Threshold Test Ban Treaty requiring four months notice of preparations for a test, had officially informed the Russian government that "on July 7, 1993, the DOE will be lowering a nuclear device into a shaft at the Nevada Test Site." According to Victor Ivanov of the Russian Ministry of Atomic Energy, the notification specified that the test, codenamed "Icecap," was scheduled for July 28 and that a delegation of U.S. testing experts would arrive in Moscow on March 15 to discuss a schedule of tests.[58]

The incoming Clinton administration promptly notified Congress that the Bush testing report was null and void, and notified the

Russian government that the U.S. test planned for July 1993 had been, not "cancelled," but rather "postponed."

Phasing-Out Nuclear Tests—1993-95

Overall Approach. Rather than seeking a dramatic new departure on the nuclear testing issue—such as indefinite extension of the current moratorium into a *de facto* CTB—the Clinton-Gore Administration began by building on the bipartisan Congressional compromise established by the "Hatfield-Exon-Mitchell" amendment to the FY 93 Energy and Water Appropriations Bill. In a "Roundtable Discussion" with employees of Sandia National Laboratory on September 18, 1992, Governor Bill Clinton was asked whether he favored a CTB:

> Yes, I'm in favor of the one that I think Congress is developing that I believe this [Bush] administration will finally sign off on, which would permit some testing for a few years, working toward and absolute ban, providing testing for safety in the near term. I know there is a big dispute about this. But let me say that France has stopped testing; Russia has stopped testing. And I perceive the biggest threat in the future to be...the proliferation of nuclear technology, as well as other weapons of mass destruction, to other countries. And I think to contain that, we ought to get out there and join the parade on working toward a comprehensive test ban, and then focus our energies on this proliferation issue."[59]

While setting a near-term deadline for ending testing worldwide, this approach sought to defuse conservative domestic opposition to a test ban by allowing the President the option of a carefully circumscribed resumption of testing for the purpose of incorporating additional weapon safety features that were deemed cost-effective after review by the President and relevant Congressional committees. The key provisions of the legislation are as follows:

- Minimum 9-month moratorium expiring July 1, 1993, or 90 days of continuous session after Congress has received the first of three Presidential annual reports on testing.
- First annual report, due March 1 (but likely to be delivered later than July 1993), must outline a plan for resuming negotiations and achieving a multilateral CTB by September 30, 1996, and describe the specific safety or other objectives of each test proposed to be conducted under the annual quota established by the amendment.
- Up to five tests may be conducted in each of three "report periods" (4th quarter FY93-94, FY95, FY96) for the primary purpose of adding one or more specified safety features—"insensitive

high-explosive (IHE)," "fire-resistant pits (FRP's)," and
"enhanced nuclear detonation safety (ENDS)"—to existing
weapon designs that will be retained in the stockpile.

- *Exceptions*: Of the maximum 15 tests conditionally permitted
  by the amendment, 3 need not involve certification of added
  safety features, but may be conducted to confirm the reliability
  of unmodified weapons, and three may be conducted jointly
  with the UK; no tests may be conducted after September 30,
  1996, "unless a foreign state conducts a nuclear test after this
  date."

Opponents of resuming testing for improved safety note that: (1) all
weapons planned for retention in the stockpile already have ENDS,
and all air-delivered weapons (i.e. those with the highest accident
risk) already have IHE and will not be deployed on aircraft in
peacetime; (2) the Department of Defense, the Air Force, and the
Navy have all maintained that the weapons they plan to retain in
the stockpile are adequately safe, and that additional safety features
for air-delivered weapons (FRPs) or sub-launched weapons
(IHE/FRPs) are not required; and (3) replacement of the current
stockpile with entirely new warhead designs that ensure an even
higher level of safety, by physically separating the plutonium from
the high explosive, cannot be accomplished within the 15 test quota
and could delay a test ban by a decade or more.

The congressional cutoff date for testing (September 30, 1996)
extends 18 months beyond the anticipated March 1995 opening of the
critical conference to extend the NPT. Test ban proponents and some
supporters of the NPT therefore argue that strict adherence by the
Administration to the congressional timetable could deprive the
United States of the moral and political leverage needed to gain
indefinite extension or strengthening of the NPT.

The apparent conflict between safety and nonproliferation
objectives could be resolved by one or more of the following steps:

(a) an early joint understanding with the other nuclear weapon
     powers on a deadline for ending all tests before resuming US
     testing;
(b) curtailment and/or acceleration of the permitted program of up
     to 15 tests to afford termination before the 1995 NPT conference;
(c) completion of a draft treaty before the opening date of the NPT
     extension conference, but delay of the treaty's effective date by
     12-18 months (such a delay may be implicit in any case because
     multilateral treaties usually do not enter into force until some

significant number of parties (40-65) "collectively" ratify the agreement)

Negotiating Strategy. Simple resumption of the trilateral talks with Russia and the U.K. will no longer suffice, as the test ban is now firmly entrenched as a multilateral issue with strong political implications for nonproliferation diplomacy. The immediate objective should be to convene meetings with the five avowed nuclear weapon powers (i.e including France and China), with the intent of reaching joint understandings on:

- a target date on or before September 30, 1996, for phasing out all nuclear weapons test explosions;
- restraint in any interim testing that may be conducted;[60]
- the forum(s) and timetable for completing a draft CTB Treaty and any accompanying verification protocols.
- an agreed approach to defining what constitutes a "nuclear weapons test explosion" to be banned under the treaty (e.g. limit(s) on the permitted amount of explosive fission/fusion energy release, or on above-ground containment structures and shielding for permitted nuclear "experiments)."
- the seismic source detection/location/identification performance objectives for open seismic monitoring networks in their respective countries;

If the CTB is to have the desired restraining political effect on proliferation, it will be necessary to fashion a process which involves important nuclear threshold nations and non-weapon states with an existing stake in the issue (e.g. India, Sweden, Indonesia, Mexico, Argentina, Kazakhstan, Ukraine, etc.). While much can be accomplished by the nuclear weapon powers operating as a subcommittee, they should be seen as being responsible to some larger multilateral body, such as the PTBT Amendment Conference, or the Conference on Disarmament in Geneva, rather than simply presenting a take-it-or-leave it treaty to the rest of the world.

One efficient but inclusive way of proceeding would be for the five nuclear weapon powers to reach early agreement among themselves on the difficult issues especially relevant to them as outlined above. A partly completed joint draft treaty text could then be presented to the Partial Test Ban Amendment Conference.[61] At the same time, the CD in Geneva and its Group of Scientific Experts could complete a draft Protocol on:

- expanding and sharing data between various existing national and international seismic networks that could be used to verify a universal test ban;
- conducting inspections to resolve the identification of ambiguous facilities, activities, or events, and;
- enforcing sanctions against violators.

The CD would submit this monitoring protocol to the PTBT Amendment Conference, which would combine it with draft treaty elements agreed upon by the nuclear weapons powers, consider any further amendments, and approve the final combined result by majority vote rather than the consensus required at the CD. The Amendment would become technically become binding on all 117 parties to the original treaty after only 59 had ratified it. China and France would accede to a CTBT by ratifying the PTBT as amended. To assure their participation as equal partners in the Amendment Conference negotiations, China and France could each promptly sign and ratify the Limited Test Ban Treaty with a reservation stating that an amendment to the treaty banning all tests shall not be considered binding upon them unless it meets with their approval.

Two Important Guidelines for Success: To avoid being bogged-down in politically enervating technical debates within the national security establishment over the *definition of a nuclear explosion* and the *performance objectives of a seismic monitoring system*, the Clinton-Gore administration needs to resolve these issues early. It could prove difficult, if not impossible, to conduct successful CTBT negotiations if these two issues are not firmly resolved internally at the outset.

For example, assigning an as yet nonexistent "international seismic monitoring system" the task of monitoring the entire globe for the occurrence of 1 kiloton "fully decoupled nuclear explosions" raises the verification cross-bar so high that the Clinton-Gore CTB negotiating team will never be able to surmount it. And yet this is precisely the kind of objective that is now being talked about in the monitoring R&D community, which envisions the prospect of ever larger contracts for the development of ever more complex seismic analysis systems for automated processing of ever larger numbers of small seismic events.

The way around this problem is an early national security decision directive that authoritatively establishes reasonable parameters for the CTB "verification problem."[62]

Reforming Export Controls

Improved International Controls on Exports of
Nuclear-related and Dual Use Technology

The major vehicle in 1991–92 for improving export controls was the Export Administration Act (EAA) reauthorization. Title III of the House (but not Senate) passed version of this bill contained an amended version of H.R. 2755, the "Nuclear Proliferation Prevention Act of 1991" introduced June 25 by Representatives Edward Markey, Gerald Solomon, Howard Wolpe, and Pete Stark. In its original form Title III would have essentially created the same statutory tests for nuclear "dual-use" items, nuclear technology transfers, and nuclear components that now must be met for nuclear fuel and reactor exports—namely, that to receive such goods, a country must have in force full-scope international safeguards on all its nuclear facilities, and a nuclear cooperation agreement with the United States. The bill also sought the phase-out of U.S. HEU exports by January 1, 1996, trade sanctions against foreign individuals, companies, or countries which violate nonproliferation controls, and improvements in IAEA safeguards.

Despite the recent experience of just such "dual-use exports" (e.g. super-accurate computer controlled milling machines, high speed "streak" cameras, flash X-ray machines) flowing to Iraq's secret nuclear weapons program, the Bush Administration threatened to veto the EAA if it contained Title III, creating ambivalence among some key Democrats whose industrial constituents were pressing for the liberalized export authority contained in other portions of the bill. Of course, this was also a reason to send the bill as is to the President's desk, and confront him with the choice of vetoing a popular export expansion/non-proliferation bill in an election year. In the end, the final obstacle proved to be not the Administration—which ultimately signed-off on a much revised compromise version of the bill—but House International Trade Subcommittee Chairman Sam Gejdenson, whose moves on the bill were frequently reviewed by the Israeli Embassy and the American Israel Public Affairs Committee. Apparently the Israeli government and some of its supporters feared that the Bush Administration would seek to use tightened export control requirements as a lever to pressure Israel in the Mideast peace talks.

Meanwhile, a bill introduced by Senator Glenn, to give the President expanded authority to impose procurement and aid sanctions on countries and companies that violate nonproliferation norms, passed the Senate but not the House. A complex negotiation ensued in August-September 1992 to combine the two bills in a manner that would satisfy the objectives of the House and Senate principals without prompting a presidential veto.

Despite commitments made to Markey and Wolpe to support passage of Title III, Gejdenson managed first to delay and then to sabotage final Congressional approval of the House passed provisions. In the final stages, a "Markey-Glenn" compromise package was worked out that merged Glenn's nuclear sanctions bill with revised elements of the House-passed Title III. The State Department signed off on this draft, but Gejdenson skewered it by insisting on a blanket set of (thinly disguised) export control exemptions for Israel that neither Senator Glenn nor the Administration could accept.

To salvage what they could from this imbroglio, the principle organizations backing the Markey-Wolpe bill urged Markey to withdraw the bulk of Title III from the conference report, thereby allowing passage of the EAA with the weakened Glenn sanctions provisions. The only part of Title III to survive this process was a congressional reporting requirement for nuclear-related and dual-use export approvals. But in the waning hours of the 102nd Congress, the EAA itself foundered in the House, not as a consequence of the attached Glenn provisions, but due to a series of time consuming procedural moves from Republican Armed Services Committee opponents of the Title I export liberalization provisions. In the final crush to complete other legislation, the Democratic leadership instructed Gejdenson to yield the floor. The combined result of the Administration's prolonged opposition to the bill and Gejdenson's solicitude for Israel's perceived security interests is that two years of hard work on nonproliferation in both House and Senate went down the drain. It was a tough defeat for everybody involved, and may dampen future legislative efforts to tighten-up U.S. nuclear export controls.

Export License "Sunshine" Amendment

Attempts to compel disclosure of sensitive proposed military export transactions invariably arouse stiff opposition from industry and the export control bureaucracy, which for different reasons strongly prefer that such matters be handled in secret. Industry claims to be worried about disclosure of so-called "proprietary" business information to competitors, and State Department bureaucrats fret that such disclosure would hamstring the President's ability to engage in "quiet diplomacy" to achieve U.S. nonproliferation objectives. The answers to these objections are straightforward: some weapons-related export transactions pose sufficient dangers that they no longer merit the cloak of commercial secrecy; and "quiet diplomacy" is often a synonym for "ineffective diplomacy" or tacit tolerance of dangerous nuclear export activity.

Legislation is needed that would permit public access to export license application information concerning licenses that meet two statutory standards:

- First, the license information must concern the export of equipment or technology that would assist a foreign country in acquiring nuclear-related or dual-use items, chemical or biological agents, or advanced conventional weapons;
- Second, the license information must be for export to a country that has used or made preparations to use chemical or biological weapons, repeatedly supported international terrorism, engaged in a pattern of gross violation of human rights, failed to implement an effective export control system, declined to accept full-scope IAEA safeguards on its nuclear activities, or been placed under a U.S. or UN trade embargo that remains in effect.

A companion provision would require the President to report to Congress twice a year on diversions of controlled goods or technology to unauthorized uses or consignees in violation of the conditions of US export licenses.

Such a provision could be the entering wedge of what is undoubtedly a longer term effort to extend to the process of weapons-related export licensing the same provisions for public notice, participation, comment, and litigation that now apply only to proposed exports of nuclear reactors and fissile material. Success in this effort would represent a quantum leap forward in the "democratization" of foreign policy.

An Alternative Approach: Less Regulation of Technology Transfer in Exchange for Verifiable End-Use Commitments and Full Disclosure of Military Programs and Facilities

In lieu of an ever multiplying array of controls based on preserving the option to block "dual-use" technology transfers, some observers favor a new approach that places increased emphasis on the transparency of the activities of both buyers and suppliers. They suggest creation of an "international registry" to record the manufacturer, the user, and the end use of all weapons products, major components, and sensitive technologies. "Encoded labels" could be attached to all these items containing all the information that had been sent to the registry. Any such registered transactions would naturally have to be in compliance with relevant negotiated force level ceilings and categorical prohibitions on certain types of weaponry.

If full disclosure were the norm, then unregistered products or products without labels would be illegal. Individuals involved with such products would be subject to criminal proceedings, and states in violation would be subject to international sanctions. Monitoring of the registry and selected inspection of products would make it much more difficult to conceal clandestine national weapons programs or international transfers. It would also provide the basis for bringing sanctions to bear. Access to trade credits and other sources of international capital could be made contingent, for example, on participation in the registry and compliance with its rules.[63]

In the long run, however, as the number of high technology products with a potential military use proliferate in the world marketplace, attempts to control nuclear proliferation through selective denials of "dual-use" items to certain countries becomes an unwieldy and virtually hopeless task. Such controls also run counter to prevailing free market doctrines and trade liberalization efforts. In the long run, a more selective, efficient, and effective approach is to ban production, acquisition, and transfer of the unique, irreplaceable weapon-usable fissile materials.

An Effective Regime for International Nuclear Inspection of States, and for Applying Sanctions Against States Found to be in Violation of International Treaties and Agreements

The discovery of a substantial clandestine nuclear weapons development program in Iraq, the full scope of which neither national intelligence services nor the IAEA accurately comprehended, has exposed glaring deficiencies in the current nonproliferation regime comprised of the NPT, the IAEA, and the Nuclear Suppliers Group. The ongoing inspections of Iraq, conducted under UN Security Council auspices, have highlighted the need for a permanent international inspection authority with considerably more clout than the IAEA's current international safeguards system. This permanent inspection should apply to all states, including those not currently signatories to the NPT; and the inspections must be backed by tough sanctions.

There are 144 signatories to the NPT. Although France and China have recently agreed to sign the NPT, approximately 36 other states are still not signatories, including Algeria, Argentina, Brazil, India, Israel, North and South Korea, Pakistan, South Africa and the newly formed states of the former Soviet Union. Several of these states have undeclared nuclear weapons programs and others currently represent, or have represented in the recent past, serious proliferation threats. The number of non-IAEA states is even larger, about 66 in all.

Under the "new world order" it should no longer be acceptable for states to avoid the norms of behavior required of NPT members by refusing to join. The current members of the NPT, therefore, should treat all non-member states as if they were members of the NPT, and require full scope safeguards on all nuclear source or special nuclear material, as a prerequisite for any commerce in nuclear and dual-use items covered by Zangger Trigger list and the Nuclear Suppliers' Group's new Export Regime for Nuclear-related Dual-Use Items. All members of NPT should endorse the Nuclear Suppliers' Group (formerly the London Club) uniform code for nuclear exports which goes beyond NPT obligations (covered by the Zangger Trigger List) to include a common policy to exercise restraint in the transfer of sensitive nuclear technology. These new obligations could be incorporated into the NPT by amendment.

The IAEA has the authority, which it has never used, to undertake special inspections to ensure that nuclear materials subject to IAEA safeguards are being used for peaceful purposes. One proposal for beefing up the IAEA is to establish a new office of inspection that would report directly to the Director-General of the IAEA. With a staff whose sole mission would be to carry out special inspections, it is argued that Director-General on his own initiative, or at the request of the Security Council, would initiate special inspection as appropriate.

There are, however, several drawbacks to giving IAEA the primary authority for special inspections. First, the IAEA has no intelligence gathering capability. The United States, Russia, and other countries with significant intelligence capabilities, will be reluctant to share their intelligence data with the IAEA staff. Similarly, it would be awkward to develop within the IAEA in-house expertise and documentation on nuclear weapon design and production activities given that the IAEA staff is drawn from non-weapon countries. Also, the IAEA has no enforcement mechanism. The Director General, or the Board of Governors, of the IAEA would have to request assistance from the UN Security Council. Approval by the Board of Governors could introduce lengthy delays, and in any case the very existence of the Board of Governors with its large membership would likely constrain the actions of the Director General. Finally, the IAEA is already strapped for funds and cannot adequately perform its current inspection requirements.

A preferred alternative would be to have the permanent office for special nuclear inspections report directly to the UN Security Council rather than the Director General of the IAEA. The five permanent members of the Security Council are all nuclear weapons states. These countries have perhaps the greatest interest in insuring that other countries do not join the nuclear club. Countries with the largest intelligence capabilities and greatest nuclear weapons expertise are represented on the Security Council. Most importantly, the UN Security Council would be more inclined to back up its own inspectors with timely sanctions if necessary.

Conclusions and Recommendations

Ending the Production, Chemical Separation, Enrichment and Acquisition of Weapons-Usable Fissile Materials

1. *Overall Policy Objective*: Make the capping and reduction of global HEU and separated plutonium inventories (both military and civil) a major objective of U.S. foreign, energy, and security policies.
2. *Policy Option*: As a first step, negotiate a verified agreement with Russia and other nuclear weapon states banning production of either (a) fissile materials for weapons, or (b) fissile materials usable in weapons, the latter being the more restrictive.
3. *Policy Option*: Seek agreement at the 1995 NPT Extension Conference on a protocol to the treaty banning the production, acquisition or transfer by any treaty party of weapons-usable fissile materials from or to any other state.
4. *Policy Recommendation*: Strongly encourage near-term phase-out in all countries of plutonium separation from commercial and naval spent fuel.
5. *Policy Option*: If Russia/UK/Japan agree to cease plutonium separation, structure three-way deal for converting Russian warhead plutonium into mixed-oxide (MOX) fuel for "once-through" use in approved commercial nuclear reactors, with subsequent geologic disposal of the spent fuel.
6. *Existing Policy, But Not Yet Implemented*: Dilute HEU into low-enriched uranium for use in commercial reactor fuel with subsequent direct geologic disposal of the spent fuel.
7. *Existing Policy, But Not Yet Implemented*: Support shut-down or conversion to alternative reduced-enrichment fuel of all research and test reactors currently supplied with U.S. produced HEU fuel, fulfill existing spent fuel "take-back" commitments, and set a final cutoff date for US HEU exports.

Verification of the Nuclear Warhead Elimination Process in Nuclear-Weapon States

1. *Overall Policy Objective*: Create a verifiable basis for a universal regime to cap, monitor, and reduce nuclear war-

head stockpiles and inventories of weapons-usable fissile materials.

2. *Policy Recommendation*: Pursue negotiations in good faith with Russia to obtain the reciprocal warhead stockpile and fissile material monitoring arrangements required by the "Biden Condition" to START, beginning with a comprehensive nuclear stockpile data exchange and inspections to help confirm the validity of the data.

3. *Policy Recommendation*: Apply IAEA safeguards and nuclear material accounting standards to all inventories of fissile material in weapons states that are outside of or removed from weapons.

4. *Implementing Action*: Within the U.S. Department of Energy, create a new Assistant Secretary for Nonproliferation, Arms Control, and Intelligence, with a purview that consolidates and effectively integrates DOE's current functions in intelligence, arms control policy, nonproliferation policy, verification technology development, and export control.

A Universal Ban on Nuclear Weapons Test Explosions (a "Comprehensive Test Ban")

1. *Overall Policy Objective*: Conclude a draft Comprehensive Test Ban Treaty by 1995, and seek multilateral "collective ratification" and entry into force of the agreement not later than October 1, 1996, the Congressional target date for phasing-out U.S. underground nuclear explosions.

2. *Policy Recommendation*: Use existing bipartisan congressional compromise in the FY 93 Energy and Water Bill (the *"Hatfield-Exon-Mitchell"* amendment) as the basis for administration policy, recognizing that the amendment specifies the *maximum* —not the minimum—number of tests that *may* be conducted to incorporate safety upgrades *if* these improvements are found to be warranted by *both* the new Administration and the Congress.

3. *Policy Recommendation*: Show respect for the views and previous efforts of other nations by making use of existing multilateral forums—the *Partial Test Ban Treaty Amendment Conference* and the *Conference on Disarmament* in Geneva—to conclude the final CTB Treaty and accompanying Verification Protocol.

4. *Recommended Implementing Action*: Convene early meeting(s) of the five declared nuclear weapon powers to reach agreement on:
   a. a target date in the 1995-96 period for phasing-out all nuclear weapons test explosions;

    b. restraint in any interim testing that may be conducted;

    c. the forum(s) and timetable for completing a draft CTB Treaty (or Partial Test Ban Treaty Amendment) and an accompanying verification protocol;

    d. definition of a "nuclear weapons test explosion", and;

    e. the performance objectives of global and regional in-country seismic monitoring capabilities.

5. *Recommended Implementing Action*: By means of a national security decision directive, establish early and firm White House control over two key "land mine" issues which, if not handled properly, have the potential to undermine the Administration's ability to deliver a test ban—definition of a "nuclear weapons test explosion" and the performance objectives of U.S. global seismic monitoring capability.

Export Controls

1. *Overall Policy Objective*: Achieve stronger domestic and international controls over both direct and indirect transfers of sensitive goods and technology to countries that fail to meet strict nonproliferation standards.

2. *Policy Recommendation*: Increase the role of the media and nongovernment organizations in reviewing the wisdom of proposed nuclear- and other weapons-related exports.

3. *Implementing Action*: Require Federal Register notice and disclosure at least 30 days prior to approval of export license information concerning proposed transfers of controlled nuclear-related and "dual-use" items (and other advanced weapon technologies) to countries that fail to meet strict nonproliferation standards.

4. *Policy Option*: Seek legislation plugging loopholes in US statutory criteria governing eligibility for exports of sensitive nuclear technology and nuclear "dual-use" items.

5. *Policy Option*: Provide increased leverage for the President to deter and punish violations of export control norms by passing legislation increasing Executive authority to impose procurement and trade sanctions against individuals, companies, and foreign governments.

6. *Policy Option*: With a strong fissile material control regime in place, shift burden of controlling dual-use items from unilateral/multilateral denial via export controls to a more open, cooperative regime based on full disclosure of military programs, tamper-proof identification and tracking of sensitive equipment and on-site inspection of end-user applications.

New Regimes for Special Inspections and Sanctions Against Violators

1. *Overall Policy Objective:* Establishment of a permanent international inspection authority for control of mass destruction weapons backed by a tough UN sanctions regime.
2. *Policy Recommendation:* As a matter of US policy, treat all states as if they were parties to the NPT, thereby requiring full-scope safeguards on all nuclear source or special nuclear material as a prerequisite for commerce in nuclear and dual-use items.
3. *Policy Option:* Seek amendment of the NPT to require that all member states treat non-member states as if they were members of the NPT bound by identical standards for nuclear trade, and upgrade these standards to include a uniform code for transfer of sensitive nuclear technology and dual-use items.
4. *Policy Option:* Seek establishment of, and extend financial and technical support for, a new Office of Special Inspections at the IAEA reporting directly to the Director-General.
5. *Policy Option:* Seek establishment of Permanent Office of Nuclear Inspections under the authority of the UN Security Council.
6. *Policy Recommendation:* As new arms control and disarmament treaties and agreements are negotiated, seek incorporation of provisions specifying international mechanisms for the imposition of sanctions against violators.

Notes

1. For example, Thomas W. Dowler and Joseph S. Howard II of the Los Alamos National Laboratory argue in a recent briefing paper that the United States should continue to deploy "low-yield nuclear forces" to "help deter future third-world nuclear states from employing their own nuclear weapons." They recommend that "any long-term stockpile should include several hundred low-yield nuclear systems," including new types of "stand-off tinynukes for battlefield deterrence" (yield: 1000 tons); "theater-ballistic missile defense mininukes" (100 tons); and "accurate micronuke EPWs [earth-penetrating weapons]" (10 tons). Source: "Potential Uses for Low-Yield Nuclear Weapons in the New World Order, (Roles and Missions)," undated briefing documents, Los Alamos National Laboratory, circa Spring, 1992.

2. In both of the above cases, U.S. use of HEU to fuel naval reactors could continue as long as the HEU came from existing surplus weapons stocks and not from new production.

3. J. Carson Mark, *Reactor-Grade Plutonium's Explosive Properties*, Nuclear Control Institute, August 1990. The bare critical masses of the fissile isotopes Pu-239 and Pu-241 are both about 15 kg. For the more brittle alpha-phase Pu-239, the bare critical mass is about 10 kg. The other isotopes of plutonium, Pu-238, Pu-

240, and Pu-242, are fissionable by fast neutrons and as delta-phase metal have critical masses of about 15, 40 and 177 kg, respectively.

4. For further discussion see, J. Carson Mark, *Reactor-Grade Plutonium's Explosive Properties*, Nuclear Control Institute, August 1990; Thomas B. Cochran, et al., *Nuclear Weapons Databook, Volume I, U.S. Forces and Capabilities*, (Boston: Ballinger Publishing Company, 1984), p. 24, footnote 17.

5. U.S. Nuclear Regulatory Commission, *Safeguarding a Domestic Mixed Oxide Industry Against a Hypothetical Subnational Threat*, NUREG-0414, May 1978, p. 6-9.

6. The bare critical mass for reactor-grade plutonium oxide (PuO2) varies from 30 to 70 kg. Bare critical masses for MOX at 30 and 10 percent PuO2 concentrations vary between 250 and 600 kg and 3,000 to 10,000 kg, respectively; ibid.

7. Notes of seminar paper presentation by E. G. Dzekun, "Experience with the Management of Fissile Materials at Mayak," International Workshop on the Future of Reprocessing and Arrangements for the Storage and Disposition of Already-Separated Plutonium, Moscow, December 14-16, 1992.

8. *White House Fact Sheet on the Middle East Arms Control Initiative*, May 29, 1991.

9. For a complete description of former Soviet nuclear weapons production facilities, see T.B. Cochran and R.S. Norris, "Former Soviet Nuclear Weapon Production Facilities" NWD 92-4, Natural Resources Defense Council, June 1992.

10. Minatom officials argue that the aluminum-clad fuel of its dual-purpose reactors can not be stored safely for long periods, thereby compelling reprocessing. The obvious alternative would be to use a more stable zircalloy clad-fuel that could be placed in a permanent underground repository.

11. Or any other weapon material, such as highly enriched uranium or U-233.

12. See, for example, P. Leventhal and Steven Dolley, "A Japanese Strategic Uranium Reserve: A Safe and Economic Alternative to Plutonium," Nuclear Control Institute, Washington D.C., April 12, 1993.

13. Capacity data and production estimates are from F. Berkhout, et al., "Disposition of Separated Plutonium," Center for Energy and Environmental Studies, Princeton University, July 8, 1992, Appendix A.

14. U.S. Nuclear Regulatory Commission, *Safety Evaluation Report Related to the Construction of the Clinch River Breeder Reactor*, NUREG-0968, Vol. 1, Main Report, March 1983, p.4-122.

15. The initial core of the Superphenix contained 5.2 MT of plutonium; Nuclear Engineering International, *World Nuclear Industry Handbook*, 1991, p. 126. European commercial FBR designs contain 3.4-4.1 MT of fissile plutonium; *Nucleonics Week*, April 28, 1988, p. 6.

16. The net excess fissile plutonium for a European design commercial FBR with a breeding ratio of 1.17 is 10 kg, while the excess is 194-220 for a design with a breeding ratio of 1.26; *Nucleonics Week*, April 28,1988, p. 6.

17. Superphenix requires 1.1 MT of plutonium fuel annually; 0.9 MT of plutonium for the Japanese advanced reactor program; Frans Berkhout and William Walker, *Thorp and the Economics of Reprocessing*, Science Policy Research Unit, University of Sussex, November 1990.

18. Marvin Miller, "Are IAEA Safeguards at Bulk-Handling Facilities Effective?," Nuclear Control Institute, Washington, D.C., August 1990.

19. In the literature "inventory difference" (ID) is sometimes called "material unaccounted for" (MUF).

20. Marvin Miller, op. cit.

21. According to Evgeni Dzekun, chief engineer of the Mayak civil reprocessing plant at Chelyabinsk-65, a plutonium input-output balance for the plant is calculated every 3-4 months when the plant is cleaned out between reprocessing campaigns. About one percent of the plutonium is lost to waste streams, and a lesser amount to plateout in the plant's plumbing. The ID is typically 15 kilograms of Pu per campaign, amounting to a total ID of about 3% percent of throughput. In other words, the ID is almost twice the IAEA's significant quantity for plutonium. According to Dzekun, if the ID in a given campaign is larger than can be explained by measurement errors, a "special investigation" is carried out, but what this consists of is not known. To assure detection of an 8 kg. diversion at this plant with 95% confidence and a 5% false alarm rate, 3.3 x ID must be less than 8 kg., so this plant apparently falls short of the minimum IAEA standard by a factor of six. If 4 kilograms is regarded as the amount needed for a weapon, then the "safeguards" at Mayak need to be improved by a factor of twelve in order to provide confident detection of diverted material. See "Report on an International Workshop on the Future of Reprocessing, and Arrangements for the Storage and Disposition of Already-Separated Plutonium (Moscow, 14-16 December 1992) by F.v.Hippel, Princeton University, and T.B. Cochran, C.E. Paine, Natural Resources Defense Council, 10 January, 1993, p. 5.

22. Marvin Miller, op. cit.

23. Ibid.

24. For a more detailed treatment of the deficiencies of international safeguards, see William Walker and Frans Berkhout, "International Safeguards and the New British and French Reprocessing Plants," Science Policy Research Unit, University of Sussex, DRAFT, 1991.

25. PRISM is an acronym for the "Power Reactor Innovative Small Module" concept, which utilizes nine reactor modules arranged in three identical 415 Mwe power blocks for an overall net rating of 1245 Mwe (3825 Mwt). GE is working with an industrial team consisting of Bechtel Power Corp., Borg Warner, Foster Wheeler, and United Engineers and Constructors on the PRISM design. Supporting R&D is being performed by Argonne National Laboratory, the Energy Technology Engineering Center, Hanford Engineering Development Laboratory, and Oak Ridge National Laboratory. For an independent evaluation of PRISM, see MHB Technical Associates, Advanced Reactor Study, prepared for the Union of Concerned Scientists, July 1990, p. 2-37.

26. Assumes one reactor core and two reloads for each of nine 155 Mwe modules. A fresh fuel load for one module will contain about 1722 kg of plutonium (23% Pu-240). At each refueling (every 18 months), approximately 536 kg of plutonium will be discharged from, and 508 kg of plutonium loaded into, the reactor. Data supplied to T.B. Cochran by P.M. Magee, General Electric Company, September 13, 1991.

27. *Science News*, April 17, 1993.

28. Charles Komanoff, *Variations in Nuclear and Coal Plant Capital Costs,* Komanoff Energy Associates, November 13, 1989. According to Komanoff for a sample of 30 U.S. nuclear plants completed during the period 1983-1991, the average cost of construction without interest was $2300/kw. One utility, Duke Power Co., was able to construct two plants for $1300/kw (1987 dollars). In 1991 dollars the costs would be about $2800/kw (30 plant avg.) and $1600/kw (Duke Power Co.) Adding 15% for real interest during construction would bring the costs to $3300/kw (avg.) and $1800/kw (Duke Power Co.).

29. According to Frans Berkhout and William Walker, *Are Current Back-End Policies Sustainable*, Science Policy Research Policy Unit, University of Sussex, April 1991: The total undiscounted cost for the direct disposal of LWR fuel is around $900/kg of heavy metal (kgHM). Fuel reprocessing services at La Hague and Sellafield during the 1990s will cost between $1400-$1800/kgHM, not counting the cost of long term high level waste (HLW) storage, transportation and disposal. Even with the reduced prices now being offered for reprocessing in the post-2000 period—$900/kgHM—reprocessing seems to double the cost of dealing with spent fuel, assuming that vitrified HLW cost about as much to bury as spent fuel. Even if the plutonium is treated a free good, MOX fuel is more costly than low enriched uranium fuel given the higher cost of fabrication of MOX fuel.

30. The average price of uranium imported into the United Stated in 1990 was 12.56 per pound, a decrease of 25 percent from the 1989 price; U.S. Department of Energy, Energy Information Administration, *EIA Reports*, EIA-91-12, June 24, 1991.

31. This still remained the case as of May 30, 1992, when this chapter was submitted for publication.

32. Testimony of Dr. Robert Barker before the Senate Armed Services Committee, August 4, 1992 (committee transcript), subsequently printed as "Military Implications of START I and START II," SASC Hearings, 102nd Cong., 2nd Sess., USGPO, 1992, p.173.

33. Viktor Mikhailov, remarks at a meeting in Washington, D.C. hosted by the Committee on International Security and Arms Control of the National Academy of Sciences, February 17, 1993.

34. Viktor Mikhailov and Evgeniy Mikerin, in remarks at the International Symposium on Conversion of Nuclear Warheads for Peaceful Purposes, Rome, Italy, June 15-17, 1992, stated that the stockpiled had declined by 20 percent since it peaked in 1986. In an interview with Yevgeniy Panov, *Moscow Rossiyskaya Gazeta*, in Russian, December 11, 1992, p. 7 (Translated in *Foreign Broadcast Information Service*, FBIS-SOV-92-239, December 11, 1992, p.3), Viktor Mikhailov is quoted as having said, ``...if destruction of nuclear weapons in our country is halted as a result of financial and technical difficulties, by the year 2000 the Americans will be scrapping their own weapons but we will be unable to. They will have 10,000 charges left, we will have 35,000.''

35. Lawrence K. Gershwin, National Intelligence Officer for Strategic Programs, Central Intelligence Agency, Hearings before the House Committee on Appropriations, DOD Appropriations for 1993, Part 5, May 6, 1992, p. 499.

36. Viktor Mikhailov and Evgeniy Mikerin, Rome, June 15-17, 1992.

37. Lawrence K. Gershwin, Hearings before the House Committee on Appropriations, DOD Appropriations for 1993, Part 5, May 6, 1992, p. 499.

38. Condition Eight to the Resolution of Ratification for START Adopted by the Senate Committee on Foreign Relations, July 2, 1992: "(8) Nuclear Weapon Stockpile Arrangement.—In as much as the prospect of a loss of control of nuclear weapons or fissile material in the former Soviet Union could pose a serious threat to the United States and to international peace and security, in connection with any further agreement reducing strategic offensive arms , the President shall seek an appropriate arrangement, including the use of reciprocal inspections, data exchanges, and other cooperative measures, to monitor—

(A) the numbers of nuclear stockpile weapons on the territory of the parties to this Treaty; and,

(B) the location and inventory of facilities on the territory of the parties to this treaty capable of producing or processing significant quantities of fissile materials."

See "The Start Treaty," Report of the Committee on Foreign Relations, U.S. Senate, USGPO: 1992, p. 101.

39. Quoted in William Broad, "Nuclear Accords Bring New Fears on Arms Disposal," New York Times, July 6, 1992, p. A1.

40. William J. Broad, "Russia Has Far More A-Fuel Than U.S. Thinks, Study Says," New York Times, September 11, 1992, p. A8.

401 (emphasis added) Michael R. Gordon, "Russia and West Reach Accord on Monitoring Germ-Weapon Ban," *New York Times*, September 15, 1992, p. A6.

42. SASC "Report on the START Treaty," op. cit.

43. DoD Conference Report 102-966, Oct.1,1992, p. 338. Sec. 3152 of this Act amends Section 142 of the Atomic Energy Act of 1954 (42 U.S.C. 2162).

44. Sec. 1321. Nuclear Weapons Reduction, DoD Conference Report 102-966, October 1,1992, page 244.

45. *Congressional Record*, November 27, 1991, S18798.

46. Lawrence S. Eagleburger, Deputy Secretary of State, "Certification Pursuant to the Soviet Nuclear Risk Reduction Legislation," Department of State, April 8, 1992, p. 5.

47. "Report of the Armed Services Committee on the START I Treaty and the Prospective START II Treaty," September 18, 1992, included as Appendix D in "The START Treaty," Report of the Committee on Foreign Relations, United States Senate, USGPO: 1992, p. 206.

48. However, as of March 9, 1993, Russia and the U.S. had yet to conclude an implementing agreement on assistance for nuclear material control and accounting, and none of the $10,000,000 set aside for this effort had been spent.

49. Testimony of Dr. Robert Barker before the Senate Armed Services Committee, August 4, 1992, as recorded in unedited committee transcript.

50. Statement of Joseph E. Kelley, Director in Charge, International Affairs Issues, National Security and International Affairs Division, USGAO, March 9, 1993, footnote, p. 8.

51. "Atomic Energy Minister Defends Treaty," *Rossiyskaya Gazeta*, 11 Dec. 92, p. 7, translation printed in FBIS-SOV-92-239, 11 December 1992.

52. "How We Will Destroy Nuclear Weapons: Concerning the Agreement on Cooperation Between Russia and the United States," by Foreign Minister Andrei Kozyrev and Atomic Energy Minister Victor Mikhailov, *Krasnaya Zveda*, 10 Dec. 92, p. 3, translation printed in FBIS-SOV-92-239 11 December 1992.

53. For a detailed discussion of the technical issues and political lessons of the TTBT verification debate, see G. van der Vink and C.E. Paine, "The Politics of Verification: Limiting the Testing of Nuclear Weapons," *Science and Global Security*, Vol. III, No. 3/4, Gordon and Breach Science Publishers, New York, 1992.

54. The English text of Yeltsin's decree is reproduced in "Report of the Fourth International Workshop on Nuclear Warhead Elimination and Nonproliferation, FAS/NRDC Washington, D.C., Feb.26-27, 1992, Appendix G-20).

55. (emphasis added) "Military Implications of START I and START II," SASC Hearings, 102nd Cong., 2nd Session, USGPO:1992, p. 213-215.

56. (Letter from National Security Advisor Brent Scowcroft, Secretary of Defense Richard B. Cheney and Secretary of Energy James D. Watkins to Senator J. Bennett Johnson, July 10, 1992).

57. For the transcript of this second test ban debate, see Cong. Record-Senate, Sept. 18, 1992, S13949-68.

58. Letter from George Bush to Les Aspin, (HASC Control No. 93-14) January 19, 1993.

59. Physicians for Social Responsibility, Washington D.C., Faxmemo to R. Degrasse, DOE from D. Kimball, Associate Director for Policy, re: "communication from Russia concerning U.S. preparations for resuming nuclear weapons tests," March 10, 1993.

60. On July 3, 1993, President Clinton extended the U.S. moratorium on nuclear testing "at least through September of next year, as long as no other nation tests." Radio Address by the President, text released by White House Press office, July 2, 1993.

61. Clinton-Gore Campaign media release, "Remarks by Governor Bill Clinton: A Roundtable Discussion with Employees of Sandia National Laboratories, Albuquerque, N.M., September 18, 1982, p. 9.

62. Unless they ratified the PTBT Treaty beforehand, France and China would technically be "observers" at the PTBT Amendment Conference. Despite this fact, they are likely to demand the same privilege of concurrence over the final draft treaty text that now belongs solely to the original parties, U.S., USSR/Russia, and the U.K.

63. For example, such a directive might stipulate the following: "The detection of illegal explosions conducted in secret underground test cavities designed to muffle the explosion's seismic signal is one aspect of a broader intelligence mission to obtain early warning of clandestine nuclear weapon development that relies upon a wide range of nonseismic means of intelligence. Seismic monitoring capability optimized for detection of decoupled nuclear explosions shall be deployed only in particular countries, or regions of countries, where combined intelligence suggests that a plausible threat of decoupled nuclear test activity exists.")

64. A.B. Carter, W.J. Perry, and John D. Steinbruner, "A New Concept of Cooperative Security," The Brookings Institution, Washington, D.C., 1992, p. 40.

2

Public Access to Nuclear Energy and Weapons Information

Allan Robert Adler

Through nearly a half century of controversial development, the operations of the nuclear weapons complex and, to a lesser extent, the commercial nuclear power industry have been shielded from public scrutiny by a web of federal statutory restrictions on the public disclosure of nuclear-related information.

The reasons for imposing a regime of presumptive secrecy on most information related to nuclear weapons, materials and power production were considered to be self-evident during the Cold War period, when the restrictive laws were put into place. From the late 1940s through the late 1980s, depriving the Soviet Union and its Warsaw Pact allies of competitive nuclear capabilities was a prime national security objective. Broad federal controls over "Restricted Data" and classified nuclear-related information were viewed as necessary means to achieve it. Toward the end of this period, the same urgency regarding threats of international terrorism led to enactment of further restrictions on unclassified information concerning the "security" of nuclear materials and facilities.

Ironically, the deliberate evolution of U.S. law and policy to ensure civilian control over nuclear weapons production and to nurture the growth and success of the commercial nuclear power industry did little to pierce the veil of nuclear secrecy. Apart from the continuing potency of security and nonproliferation concerns, political controversies regarding health, safety and environmental issues associated with the operation of weapons plants and power facilities generated an adversarial environment in which the nuclear weapons complex and the nuclear power industry acted with proprietary zeal to prevent their critics in and out of government from obtaining access to nuclear-related information. In this highly-charged atmosphere, the objectives and consequences of redundant bases for nuclear secrecy became matters of intense public dispute.

Today, the web of federal nuclear information controls is still in place, but the world which justified its creation has radically changed. In the aftermath of events such as Three Mile Island, Chernobyl, the Persian Gulf War, and the extraordinary dismantling of the Soviet Union and its Eastern European bloc, it is a world in which the risks and rewards, and the problems and promises associated with nuclear fission and fusion capabilities must all be reconsidered and reassessed. The American people and their Government must reexamine many of the operative assumptions that have shaped U.S. nuclear weapons and energy development policies over the past decades. To maximize their opportunities for a future based on informed choices, they should begin by reexamining and reforming the federal nuclear secrecy laws.

Discussion

The Current Regime of Nuclear Secrecy

Restricted Data: Information "Born Classified." The most comprehensive federal statutory controls over nuclear-related information are the "Restricted Data" provisions of the Atomic Energy Act of 1954, as amended ("the AEA").[1] As a legal scholar has succinctly stated, "[n]o law passed before or since gives government such sweeping authority to keep information secret."[2]

What Is Restricted Data?

The definition of Restricted Data has remained essentially unchanged since the time of its original enactment in 1946, when there was relatively little public information or knowledge about atomic energy and the United States was the only nation that had detonated an atomic bomb. It has not been amended to reflect any scientific and technological advances, or the vast amounts of material on atomic energy that have been published over the past four decades in the U.S. and abroad.

Broadly defined to include "all data concerning (1) design, manufacture or utilization of atomic weapons; (2) the production of special nuclear material; or (3) the use of special nuclear material in the production of energy . . .",[3] the expansive reach of the Restricted Data category is rendered even more elastic by the Act's broad definition of "design" as including "research and development data" pertinent to the information contained in any "specifications, plans, drawings, blueprints, and other items of like nature."[4]

As a matter of policy, the AEA states that "dissemination of scientific and technical information relating to atomic energy should be permitted and encouraged so as to provide that free interchange of ideas and criticism which is essential to scientific and industrial progress and public understanding and to enlarge the fund of technical information."[5] However, the AEA's definition of "research and development" puts "theoretical analysis, exploration, or experimentation" and "the extension of investigative findings and theories of a scientific or technical nature into practical application for experimental and demonstration purposes, including the experimental production and testing of models, devices, equipment, materials, and processes," into the realm of Restricted Data.[6] No statutory exclusion is provided for basic scientific and technical information and, under these terms, it is clear that even elementary discussions or demonstrations in an academic or industrial setting could involve the communication of Restricted Data.

Apart from its sheer breadth, the most extraordinary thing about information within the category of Restricted Data is that it is considered to be "born classified."

What Does It Mean for Information to Be "Born Classified"?
The term "born classified" does not appear anywhere in the AEA, but it is a "working assumption" of the Government regarding the manner in which Restricted Data controls operate.[7]

Information is considered to be Restricted Data simply by virtue of falling within the terms of the statutory definition. If information constitutes Restricted Data, it is "born classified" in the sense that it is considered a Government-protected secret immediately upon coming into existence, without any affirmative act on the Government's part[8] and, most significantly, without any regard to its source.[9]

In *The Progressive* case in 1979,[10] the Government tested and prevailed on its assertion that the "all data" language in the statutory definition means that the "born classified" concept and Restricted Data controls are applicable to information created by private individuals who are neither employed nor funded by the Government and did not have prior access to classified government information. Relying on provisions in the AEA that authorize the Government to enjoin publication of Restricted Data,[11] a federal district judge rejected First Amendment objections and granted the government's request to enjoin the publication of a magazine article describing the theory and design of a hydrogen bomb, notwithstanding the author's uncontroverted contention that the article was produced based on public domain materials and without access to classified information.[12]

Although *The Progressive* case was subsequently mooted by newspaper publications of similarly descriptive materials produced by other private individuals, the Government's interpretation of its Restricted Data control authority received judicial approval which has not been contradicted by any subsequent court decision.

The broad reach of the Restricted Data category is matched by the broad range of authority that the Government may rely upon to control access to, or communication or receipt of, Restricted Data:

Security Clearance Required for Access to Restricted Data

Both the Department of Energy (DOE) and the Nuclear Regulatory Commission (NRC), successors to the original statutory jurisdiction of the Atomic Energy Commission, have the duty and authority to safeguard Restricted Data.[13] Pursuant to specific provisions in the AEA, they have issued rules to control dissemination of Restricted Data and to condition access to Restricted Data upon obtaining the proper security clearance.[14] As a result, the Federal Government must maintain a massive and costly "personnel security" bureaucracy to control access to Restricted Data by the Government's employees, the employees of Government contractors and licensees, and others seeking access to Government-controlled Restricted Data.[15]

Unauthorized Communication or Receipt of Restricted Data

Consistent with the espionage laws, the AEA provides criminal penalties for unauthorized communication or receipt of Restricted Data "with intent to injure the United States or . . . to secure an advantage to any foreign nation . . ." [16] The AEA also prescribes criminal penalties for anyone who "communicates, transmits, or discloses" such materials, or attempts or conspires to do so, "with reason to believe such data will be utilized to injure the United States or to secure an advantage to any foreign nation . . ."[17] This standard was applied to the publication at issue in *The Progressive* case and appears to permit criminal prosecution for negligent or reckless disclosure of Restricted Data.[18] In addition, the AEA bars disclosure of Restricted Data by former Government employees, or former employees of Government contractors and licensees, who know or have reason to know that (1) the material communicated is Restricted Data, and (2) the recipient is not authorized to receive Restricted Data under the Act or implementing agency rules.[19]

Restricted Data Exempt from FOIA Disclosure

According to the legislative history of the federal Freedom of Information Act at the time of its enactment in 1966 and its amendment in 1974, Restricted Data in the possession of an agency of the Federal Government is exempt from the mandatory disclosure requirements of the federal Freedom of Information Act, pursuant to that statute's exemption for matters that are "specifically exempted from disclosure by statute . . ."[20]

In 1976, Congress amended this FOIA exemption to limit the kinds of statutes that agencies can rely on as nondisclosure authorities.[21] Although neither the legislative history of this amendment nor any subsequent court decision discusses whether the Restricted Data provision continues to qualify as nondisclosure authority under the amended exemption standards, the Government has repeatedly asserted that it does and the courts are likely to agree.[22]

Periodic Declassification of Restricted Data

The AEA requires the Department of Energy and the NRC to determine "from time to time" what Restricted Data can be published without "undue risk to the common defense and security," and to "declassify" and remove such material from the Restricted Data category.[23] The agencies are also required to maintain a "continuous review" of Restricted Data and any "Classification Guides" used to inform persons "in the atomic energy program" which information may be "declassified" and removed from the Restricted Data category.[24]

The Defense Department has the right to participate jointly in declassification decisions regarding Restricted Data relating primarily to "the military utilization of atomic weapons," and any disagreement regarding a declassification decision must be resolved by the President.[25] Agreement to remove this kind of material from the Restricted Data category does not, however, mean that it will become available to the public. Such information is removed from the Restricted Data category and treated as Formerly Restricted Data only if the information "can be adequately safeguarded as defense information . . ."[26] Similar "declassification" and removal requirements apply to information concerning the atomic energy programs of other nations.[27]

In practice, these provisions have not worked—and cannot reasonably be expected to work—to ensure that the nature and volume of information controlled as Restricted Data are limited by current assessments of what information has entered the public domain and thus should no longer be subject to Government control.

One reason is that the Government continues to assert that information subject to national security controls does not enter the public domain except by the affirmative official actions of persons authorized to publicly disclose it; without specific official acknowledgment, unauthorized disclosure via "leaks" or mistake, or evidence that the information is widely publicly known, will not eliminate the Government's authority to maintain its access and dissemination controls.[28] This doctrine has particular effect with respect to Restricted Data, since all such information is "born classified" and requires an affirmative action by the Government to "declassify" and remove it from that category.

In addition, the sheer mass of material that would have to be reviewed, combined with the bureaucratic inclination to err on the side of security secrecy, will defeat or discourage most systematic efforts to keep controls current in terms of the nonsensitivity or public domain availability of such information.[29]

International Communication of Restricted Data

Although the President is expressly permitted to authorize disclosure of Restricted Data to "another nation" pursuant to a cooperation agreement, the Act prohibits the DOE and NRC from any cooperation that involves communication of Restricted Data relating to the design or fabrication of atomic weapons.[30]

The President may, however, authorize the Defense Department to communicate such Restricted Data to another nation or a regional defense organization, as necessary to develop compatible delivery systems for atomic weapons and to train personnel and evaluate the capabilities of potential enemies regarding atomic weapons and other military applications of atomic energy, when such cooperation will promote and will not constitute an unreasonable risk to the common defense and security.[31]

In addition, under the same standard, the President may authorize DOE, with the assistance of the Defense Department, to (1) exchange Restricted Data concerning atomic weapons, when necessary to improve the atomic weapon design, development, or fabrication capability of a foreign nation that has made substantial progress in the development of atomic weapons, and (2) communicate or exchange with that nation Restricted Data concerning research, development, or design, of military reactors.[32]

But such communications and exchanges of Restricted Data are subject to the requirement that they be made under a cooperation agreement which contains a "guaranty" by the recipient nation that any Restricted Data transferred pursuant to the agreement "will not be transferred to unauthorized persons or beyond the jurisdiction or control of the cooperating party without the consent of the United States." [33] In effect, this means that Restricted Data may be communicated to foreign nations for purposes of international nuclear cooperation, but the possession of such information by such foreign nations does not in any way change the controlled status of the information for purposes of public access or disclosure in the United States.

Does such sweeping control authority remain justified today? It is time for Congress to review the concept of Restricted Data.

Invention Secrecy: Ideas "Born Classified." The Government's ability to reach out and control privately-developed nuclear-related information and technology is aided and abetted by the Invention Secrecy Act ("the ISA") and related provisions in the AEA itself.[34]

The ISA, as enacted in 1951, authorizes Government "defense agencies"—including the Department of Energy—to review patent applications to determine whether disclosure of an invention in which the Government has no property interest "would be detrimental to the national security." An affirmative determination will result in an order requiring a patent grant to be withheld and the invention to be kept secret "for such period as the national interest requires." Initially limited to a period of one year, such orders may be renewed indefinitely for additional one-year periods if the agency that caused the order to be issued makes an affirmative determination that "the national interest continues so to require."[35]

Although the inventor may seek "just compensation" for "the damage caused by the order of secrecy and/or for the use of the invention by the Government,"[36] it is a crime for the inventor or any other person who knows of the order to (1) willfully publish or disclose the invention or "material information" related to it, or (2) file or authorize the filing of a patent application, or design or model registration, for the invention in any foreign country.[37] In addition, such unauthorized disclosure may lead to "abandonment" of the invention, which constitutes a forfeiture by the inventor or his successors of all claims against the U.S. based upon the invention.[38]

Relationship Between the ISA and the AEA

The relationship between the ISA and the AEA raises some interesting questions. Under the latter,[39] patents may not be granted for "any invention or discovery which is useful solely in the utilization of special nuclear material or atomic energy in atomic weapons." A "just compensation" provision, similar to that in the ISA, applies to the extent that such an invention or discovery is so used by the Government.

In addition, the AEA requires any person who makes any invention or discovery "useful in the production or utilization of special nuclear material or atomic energy" to file a complete description of it with the Department of Energy, unless it has been described in a patent application filed with the Commissioner of Patents.[40] In the latter case, it is evidently expected that the DOE would be notified of the application by the Commissioner and thus have an opportunity to request a secrecy order under the ISA.

It is clear that both the ISA and the AEA authorize the imposition of invention secrecy and patent bans on the basis of Restricted Data. But it is also worth noting that the ISA expressly authorizes invention secrecy under a "harm" test which is much more vague and subjective than the minimum standard for classifying "national security information" pursuant to the current Executive Order.[41]

In effect, the ISA provides even broader authority for DOE to impose invention restrictions than does the AEA. Where the AEA expressly bars patents only for an invention or discovery which is "useful solely" in the utilization of special nuclear material or atomic energy in an atomic weapon,[42] the ISA appears to permit the Commissioner of Patents, acting on an ISA determination by the head of DOE, to impose secrecy on a broader range of inventions and discoveries, such as ones that are merely "useful in the production or utilization of special nuclear material or atomic energy."

Yet, even where the AEA would not authorize a patent ban, its interrelationship with the ISA presents an inventor in the nuclear field with a "Hobson's choice" of restrictions: If an application for a patent is filed, the ISA test for a secrecy order will be met if the DOE, upon referral from the Patent Office, finds that the application contains Restricted Data; if a patent application is not filed, the inventor will still be required to file a report on the invention with DOE, which may not be able to impose a patent ban but may nonetheless inform the inventor that the invention involves Restricted Data which cannot be publicly disclosed.

Twelve years ago, the House Government Operations Committee reviewed the history and operation of the ISA in its application to Restricted Data, public cryptography and other areas in which the government asserts authority to control privately-generated information. It found, among other things, that while invention secrecy was clearly conceived and legitimized in wartime, "Congress never set down a rationale" for authorizing invention secrecy on a statutory basis "now assumed to be permanent in time of peace." [43] This finding still looms large in light of the Committee's general characterization of ISA actions:

> The invention secrecy enterprise tends itself, like an automated lighthouse. The basis for issuance of a secrecy order is the opinion of an agency head that disclosure 'would be detrimental to the national security.' . . . How an agency head forms such an opinion is not subject to higher review or Patent Office challenge. His opinion is final until he changes it, yet in the defense agencies his authority to form such an opinion has been delegated and redelegated into the ranks.
>
> There is no mention of invention secrecy in the mandatory annual report of the Commissioner of Patents and Trademarks to Congress . . . Invention secrecy transactions are shielded by Patent Office confidentiality, classified agency documents and, in some cases gaps in public files.
>
> No secrecy order ever underwent judicial review for appropriateness. There has been no First Amendment judicial test of the Invention Secrecy Act, and the statutory right of an inventor to just compensation for secrecy order damages appears more illusory than real.[44]

It appears that this picture of invention secrecy may still be accurate, despite the Committee's detailed recommendations for desired changes. It is time for Congress to take another look at the rationale for and operation of invention secrecy, both under the AEA and the ISA.

National Security Classification: Executive Order 12356. Apart from the protections afforded by the Restricted Data provisions of the Atomic Energy Act, a great deal of nuclear-related information in the possession of the Government and its contractors or licensees is "classified" and controlled by the Government as "national security information."

Unlike the "born classified" status of Restricted Data, all materials that are classified as "national security information" obtain this controlled status only by an affirmative determination and designation by properly authorized federal officials acting pursuant to the standards and procedures of an Executive Order.

Executive Order 12356, issued by President Reagan in 1982, currently governs classification actions.[45] It requires that any information which falls within one of its list of "classification categories" must be classified if the unauthorized disclosure of such information, by itself or in the context of other information, "reasonably could be expected to cause damage to the national security.[46] This threshold standard requires safeguarding of the material as "Confidential" national security information; a higher "Secret" level of protection is provided if unauthorized disclosure of the information reasonably could be expected to cause "serious damage" to the national security, and the highest level of "Top Secret" protection applies if unauthorized disclosure reasonably could be expected to cause "exceptionally grave" damage to the national security.[47] "National security" under the Order means the national defense or foreign relations of the United States.[48]

Even while the Reagan Executive Order was still in draft form, it was widely criticized in Congress and in the press as a backward step which reversed a thirty-year trend of successive presidential efforts to reduce the amount of classified information.[49] After hearings and an extensive review of the ways in which the Executive Order departed from the Carter Executive Order that it superseded, the House Government Operations Committee sharply questioned the asserted reasons for the Order's classification policy changes and reached the following conclusions, among others, regarding them:

> There is little reason to think that Executive Order 12356 will reduce the unnecessary classification of government information. All of the major changes made by the new order loosen the restrictions on classification. These changes will have the effect of—
> Increasing the amount of information subject to classification by the addition of broad, new classification categories;
> Weakening the minimum standard for determining whether information qualifies for classification by dropping the requirement that damage to the national security be "identifiable";
> Dropping the balancing test that required classifiers to consider the public interest in disclosure against the need to protect information;
> Removing limitations on abuse of classification authority that appeared in the previous order; and
> Permitting the reclassification of information that was declassified and publicly released.[50]

Although it is difficult to assess whether Executive Order 12356 has exacerbated the problem of overclassification in the nuclear field, these changes, along with several others criticized by the House committee, appear to be designed to encourage more classification rather than less. Consider the following:

Broad New Classification Categories

While retaining broad Carter Order "classification categories" that could easily be read to cover nuclear-related information, the Reagan Order introduced a new category for "the vulnerabilities or capabilities of systems, installations, projects, or plans relating to the national security."[51]

The Reagan Administration told the House committee that the new category was intended to embrace information relating to the protection of the President, the protection of U.S. embassies, and civil preparedness. If that was its purpose, it is not at all clear why the category is so broad. Moreover, given the Administration's push for enactment of DOE "UCNI" controls during the previous year, a more likely explanation would be that the "vulnerabilities" focus was intended to maximize the Administration's secrecy authority at a time when it was striving to bolster the budget and security of the DOE nuclear weapons complex.[52] But, even if that was the case, it is clear that the existing classification categories were broad enough to serve this purpose, and the addition of the new category would merely encourage broader application of classification stamps to matters that may not warrant such restriction.

Elimination of Restrictions on Classification

The Reagan Order eliminated provisions in the Carter Order that prohibited classifying (1) references to classified documents that do not disclose classified information,[53] and (2) information generated by private research and development which does not incorporate or reveal classified information, and in which the Government has no proprietary interest.[54] In addition, an early draft of the Reagan Order had proposed to drop a prohibition in the Carter Order barring classification of "basic scientific research information not clearly related to the national security."[55]

These prohibitions, as the House committee noted, "allayed fears about the scope of the government's classification authority for private technology and basic scientific research." Although the restriction against classifying basic research was finally restored to the Reagan Order, the elimination of the other prohibitions may have had the effect over the past decade of suppressing private activity and public awareness of classified Government materials concerning nuclear and other technology-related information.

Reclassification Authority

In a similar but more striking vein, the Reagan Order dropped the Carter Order's prohibition against restoring classified status to documents "already declassified and released to the public."[56] In a complete about-face, the Reagan Order provides that previously declassified information may be reclassified if (1) the information requires protection in the interest of national security, and (2) "the information may reasonably be recovered."[57]

This reclassification authority, which is not limited to cases of declassification error, is an extremely disturbing extension of the Government's insistence that it can return squeezed toothpaste to the tube. Government attempts to "un-disclose" what has already been disclosed are particularly unwelcome with respect to nuclear-related information and other areas where official disclosures are seldom forthcoming. They could raise serious liability issues if coercive methods, such as lawsuits, prosecution, and invasive types of investigative or intelligence techniques are considered by the Government to be appropriate means for ensuring that previously-released information will "reasonably be recovered."

Declassification

The Reagan Order eliminated requirements of the Carter Order providing that: (1) each classified document include a date or event for declassification or review;[58] (2) any document classified for more than six years contain additional information, including the name of the classifier and the reasons why classification is still necessary;[59] (3) declassification be "given emphasis comparable" to that accorded to classification;[60] (4) most classified documents undergo systematic review for declassification as they become 20 years old;[61] and (5) "mandatory declassification review" occur at the request of any person, based upon a reasonable description of the information at issue.[62]

Instead, the Reagan Order (1) omits all references to specific periods of time for declassification; (2) permits, rather than requires, documents to be marked with a declassification date or event; (3) deleted the "comparable emphasis" language regarding declassification policy; and, (4) made mandatory declassification unavailable to foreign nationals and to persons who cannot identify specific documents for review.[63]

It is difficult to demonstrate in a quantifiable manner how these policy changes, together with the elimination of the Carter "balancing test" that required declassification if the public interest in disclosure of classified information outweighed the need for its continued protection,[64] have resulted in unnecessary continued classification. However, for nuclear matters and other areas that have experienced pervasive Government control over information in the past, it is clear that they did not signal a determination to address documented problems of overclassification. Instead, the Reagan Order sent the bureaucracy a message that an obsessive emphasis on security would remain "business as usual."

Special Access Programs

Although the Reagan Order retained language identical to the Carter Order on the authority of agency heads to create "special access programs" ("SAPs") to control access, distribution and protection of "particularly sensitive" classified information,[65] it jettisoned key provisions in the Carter Order which were clearly designed to eliminate existing SAPS and prevent the creation of new ones if their continuation or establishment were unwarranted.

These discarded provisions conditioned creation of SAPs on a "specific showing" that "(a) normal management and safeguarding procedures are not sufficient to limit need-to-know or access; (b) the number of persons who will need access will be reasonably small and commensurate with the objective of providing extra protection for the information involved; and (c) the special access controls balance the need to protect the information against the full spectrum of needs to use the information."[66] Moreover, they required that all SAPs be reviewed regularly and, except for those required by treaty or international agreement, automatically terminated every five years unless formally renewed.[67] Finally, the Carter Order told agency heads that, within six months of its issuance, all existing SAPs should be reviewed and continued only in accordance with the Order's "specific showing" requirements; this precedent, too, was rejected by the Reagan Order.[68]

SAPs or "black programs," as they are popularly known, have considerably aggravated the problem of overclassification in recent years. Although it is again difficult to attempt to quantify the impact that changes in the Reagan Order have had on classification actions during the decade since it was issued, it seems clear that they encouraged the proliferation of unnecessary and unaccountable SAPs in the Defense Department. This is evident from the fact that, after enacting a formalized reporting requirement and oversight process for such programs as part of the FY 1988 and 1989 defense authorization legislation,[69] Congress has sharply criticized SAPs as contributing to waste, fraud and poor management in a number of significant weapons development projects.[70]

Application of FOIA, Criminal Laws,
and Clearance Requirements

Unjustified classification of nuclear-related information as "national security information" is extremely troublesome because, as a practical matter, classification actions prevent information controlled by the Government from becoming part of the public record and dis-course regarding official actions and policies on the subjects involved.

Government records constituting matters which are "in fact" properly classified as "national security information" pursuant to an Executive Order are exempt from the disclosure mandate of the FOIA pursuant to that statute's Exemption One.[71]

Moreover, unauthorized communication, receipt or retention of classified national security information—even in circumstances alleged to constitute "whistleblowing" or a "leak" to the news media—may subject an individual to criminal prosecution under the federal espionage and/or theft-of-government property statutes.[72]

Only Government employees and contractor employees who have undergone required personnel security investigations and received appropriate clearances may be given access to properly classified national security information. Such individuals must sign "secrecy agreements" pledging nondisclosure of such information.[73]

Although difficult to quantify, the continuing problem of overclassification has been decried not only by those who see it as an obstacle to informing the American people about the actions of their Government but by those within the Government who fear that it places the ability to protect legitimate national security secrets at risk.[74] The Department of Energy has evidently made its own substantial contributions to the problem.[75]

The changeover of Administrations presents an opportune time to propose a new Executive Order to supersede the Reagan Order as it superseded the Carter Order. But it should also be emphasized that classification policy is not exclusively the domain of the Executive Branch. Because habitual overclassification of Government information is an Executive Branch problem which has so far proved resistant to internal ministrations, it is time for Congress to review the current national security classification program and get directly involved in crafting solutions.

Unclassified Controlled Nuclear Information (UCNI). Even a cursory review of the other legal authorities for Government control over nuclear-related information would lead one to question why, in 1981, the Reagan Administration sought and obtained separate statutory authority to restrict the dissemination of something called "unclassified controlled nuclear information."

At one level, the reasons may have had more to do with the bureaucratic rivalry between the DOE and NRC than any unaddressed information control requirements. The push for enactment of the UCNI statute was something of a sop to the "me-too" demands of the DOE less than one year after Congress enacted a special statute giving the

NRC authority to prohibit the unauthorized disclosure of "safeguards information."[76]

The "safeguards information" statute authorizes the NRC to prohibit the unauthorized disclosure of information "which specifically identifies a licensee's or applicant's detailed" (1) control and accounting procedures or security measures for the physical protection of special nuclear material; (2) security measures for the physical protection of source material or by-product material; and (3) security measures for the physical protection of certain plant equipment "vital to the safety of production or utilization facilities" involving such materials, if the NRC determines that such disclosure "could reasonably be expected to have a significant adverse effect on the health and safety of the public or the common defense and security by significantly increasing the likelihood of theft, diversion, or sabotage" of such material or facilities.[77]

It also explicitly qualifies as a withholding statute for purposes of the (b)(3) exemption of the FOIA, so that the NRC may assert its authority to deny public access to such information in response to FOIA requests for agency records.[78] Any persons who violate any regulation adopted pursuant to the statute, whether or not they are licensees, are subject to the civil monetary penalties provided under the AEA for violations of licensing requirements.[79]

The NRC had expressed uncertainty about its authority to deny public access to specific information regarding security measures taken by its licensees and applicants during the period when events at Three Mile Island had reinvigorated public protest activity over nuclear plant safety and concerns about domestic nuclear terrorism were running high. Because most security materials are generated by the licensees and applicants themselves, as private individuals in the context of commercial nuclear operations, reasonable doubts were expressed about the propriety of allowing the Government to classify such materials as "national security information" under the relevant Executive Order. At the same time, it was not clear whether much of this information could accurately be characterized as Restricted Data under the AEA.

For these reasons, Congress agreed that a narrowly-crafted statute providing the NRC with explicit protective authority was in order. Care was taken to limit the NRC's authority to control only information which "specifically identifies a licensee's or applicant's detailed" security measures; in addition, it was limited with respect to special nuclear material and source or by-product material to apply only to such materials "in quantities determined by the Commission to be significant to the public health and safety or the common defense and security."[80]

The NRC was also directed to apply "the minimum restrictions needed" to meet the public and security protection objectives of the legislation,[81] and was explicitly barred from prohibiting public disclosure of information "pertaining to the routes and quantities of shipments of source material, by-product material, high-level nuclear waste, or irradiated nuclear reactor fuel."[82] This exclusion was a substantial victory for State and municipal officials and local activists who feared that a secrecy blanket over such information would prevent them from ensuring compliance with safety requirements and planning for emergency contingencies in connection with transport of these nuclear materials through highly-populated areas.

For the Department of Energy, however, arguments in favor of similar authority were not terribly convincing.

For one thing, the nuclear materials and facilities within the jurisdiction of the DOE that require physical and other security measures are all part of the weapons program, allowing information concerning security measures to be controlled both as Restricted Data and as classified "national security information" under any of several "Classification Categories," including "United States Government programs for safeguarding nuclear materials or facilities."[83] For another, it is clear that such information is not privately-developed in a commercial context, but is instead generated by Government and Government contractor employees in work that is funded by specific federal appropriations.

Despite these facts, the DOE secured enactment of its UCNI statute as part of the Reagan Administration's early priority effort to ramp up a nuclear weapons production program that had been scaled down in previous years.[84] Although the rulemaking to implement the statute dragged on for two years amidst controversy and criticism of the UCNI concept from Members of Congress, universities, libraries, State officials, labor unions, and a variety of other commenters,[85] passage of the UCNI statute itself, as part of a $6 billion nuclear weapons manufacturing authorization bill, drew little opposition or attention in Congress.

The UCNI statute resembles the NRC "safeguards information" statute in enough ways to support the DOE's position that it was merely seeking the same kind of authority to apply to its "atomic energy defense programs." It contains, for example, the same FOIA (b)(3) exemption reference and uses the same "significant adverse effect" harm standard. It also contains the same "minimization" requirement and the same civil penalty provisions. However, the UCNI statute differs from its ostensible model in ways that provide the DOE with broader and more potent authority than that which is exercised by the NRC.

First, the UCNI control authority applies to unauthorized "dissemination" rather than unauthorized "disclosure" of covered information. The "safeguards information" statute permits the NRC and its licensees and applicants to refuse requests for access to such information, but does not purport to control "dissemination" of the information after it is already publicly available. However, the UCNI statute, in using the broader "dissemination" language, appears intended as authority to deny access requests *and* control further distribution of UCNI in much the same way as controls on Restricted Data and classified national security information operate.

In issuing its implementing regulation, the DOE asserted that only "government information" comes within the reach of UCNI controls and that "privately-generated information" which people acquire by their own or another person's observation (e.g., sightings of "white trains" transporting nuclear weapons or their components) is not "government information" as defined in the regulation.[86] However, the regulation's definition is, at best, a tautology which does not clarify this issue; it states only that information which is "controlled by the United States Government" constitutes "government information."[87]

On the other hand, the definition of "unauthorized dissemination" refers to "the intentional or negligent *transfer*, in any manner, by a person, of *information contained in* a document or material determined . . . to contain UCNI and [so] marked . . . to any person other than" a person authorized to have access to UCNI.[88] The accompanying DOE text confirms that UCNI controls apply to *information*, not the "document or material" in which it appears.[89]

Second, where the NRC statute requires regulations or orders "as necessary" to prohibit unauthorized disclosure of information "which specifically identifies a licensee's or applicant's detailed" security measures, the UCNI statute more broadly orders the Secretary of Energy to issue regulations or orders "as *may be* necessary" to prohibit unauthorized disclosure of "unclassified information pertaining to" three broad subject categories: (1) the design of production or utilization facilities; (2) security measures for the physical protection such facilities, nuclear material contained in such facilities, or nuclear material in transit; and, (3) the design, manufacture, or utilization of any atomic weapon or component if such matter was contained in information declassified or removed from the Restricted Data category.[90] In assessing the breadth of these categories, it must be noted that the latter provision permits the DOE, in effect, to reassert

control over information which, according to the test for
"declassifying" Restricted Data, "can be published without undue risk
to the common defense and security."[91]

Third, in addition to the civil penalty provision included in the
NRC statute, the UCNI statute contains much higher civil penalties
of up to $100,000 per violation, as well as criminal penalties for
willful violation, attempted violation, or conspiracy to violate the
DOE regulations.[92]

These distinctions between the NRC "safeguards information"
statute and the DOE UCNI statute evidence more than an intent to
ensure equilibrium of authority between the two agencies, and it likely
was no mere coincidence or turn of opportunity that led to enactment of
the UCNI statute as part of the funding bill that was designed to
revitalize the nuclear weapons complex. Rather, it appears to have
been part of the Reagan Administration's plan that the controversial
nuclear weapons buildup take place with as much shielding from
public scrutiny as possible.

For this purpose, the UCNI authority provided more than a redundant assurance of the broadest possible control over atomic energy defense information. Its distinct advantage over national security classification and Restricted Data authority is in its ability to selectively
control access and disclosure without the cost, administrative burden
and practical inefficiency of the personnel security clearance requirements imposed by the latter two control regimes.[93] Although there are
some administrative controls regarding who may have "routine" or
"special" access to UCNI, the DOE regulations do not require the extensive measures, such as background investigations, that are a part of
the other personnel clearance programs.[94]

. Without any dispositive legislative history on the subject, it would
be unfair to reject the possibility that, in 1981, the newly-installed
Reagan Administration and the Congress believed in good-faith that
additional nuclear secrecy power was required to address "the
possibility of terrorist or other criminal acts directed against a
government nuclear defense facility . . . based, in part, on the increased
incidence of acts of terrorist-inspired violence, the increased
sophistication of these acts, and the increased availability of the
technological resources, including information in the public domain,
necessary to commit these acts."[95] But, whatever the motive for its
enactment, the UCNI statute epitomizes the redundant, overreaching
nature of Government nuclear secrecy controls.

*More than a decade later, it is time for Congress to reexamine the
rationale for UCNI controls and to determine whether they are*

necessary and appropriate to serve legitimate current safeguarding interests.

Confidentiality of Export License Information. An indirect, more tangential control over nuclear-related information exists in a provision of the Export Administration Act ("EAA") which blocks public access to export licensing information.

The EAA provides that information obtained by the Department of Commerce for the purpose of considering, or concerning, any export license application "shall be withheld from public disclosure unless the release of such information is determined by the Secretary to be in the national interest."[96]

This provision has been judicially confirmed to be a valid nondisclosure statute which, under the authority of the (b)(3) exemption of the Freedom of Information Act, permits the Commerce Department to deny requests for public access to the identities of successful and unsuccessful license applicants, as well as to all information contained in licenses and applications.[97]

The rationale for this secrecy is *not* anchored in security considerations since, as one court concluded, "Congress intended to protect exporters from the disclosure of information that a competitor would use to the exporters' disadvantage."[98] In fact, in this instance, the secrecy authority works *against* important national security considerations.

Federal law places numerous restrictions on the export of certain materials and data in support of nonproliferation goals regarding nuclear weapons, as well as chemical and biological weapons and missile technology. However, inadequate enforcement of these restrictions has been a matter of increasing concern.

Evidence of control problems has appeared in Congressional hearings and press accounts, primarily in discussions concerning certain weapons capabilities of Iraq and in the ongoing battle between the Defense and Commerce Departments for dominance in the enforcement and review process. Of critical concern, however, is the extremely limited ability of nongovernmental parties to obtain information which would permit an independent assessment of the problem, as well as a public role in enforcement efforts.

Not surprisingly, the Federal Government's enforcement efforts are mostly cloaked in a combination of "national security" secrecy and law enforcement "confidentiality." But the most crippling obstacle to public accountability in the area of export control enforcement is the EAA restriction on access to export license information which rests on the asserted need to protect *competitive* interests among exporters.

It is not at all clear why competitive commercial interests must be indulged with such blanket protection, especially in a context in which undue secrecy may contribute to proliferation of nuclear and other weapons of mass destruction. It is particularly puzzling when contrasted with the example of how proliferation and proprietary interests are balanced in connection with the NRC license application process for exporting nuclear equipment and material, as required by the Nuclear Non-Proliferation Act of 1978 and implemented by the NRC.[99]

Under the NRC regulations, the agency is required to give public notice of the receipt of each license application for the export of nuclear equipment and material by placing a copy in the Public Document Room and, in cases involving a production or utilization facility or certain quantities of specified nuclear materials, heavy water, or nuclear grade graphite, publishing a notice in the Federal Register. In addition, the NRC makes "periodic lists" of applications available on request.[100]

The NRC also makes all licenses and documents pertaining to each license available in the Public Document Room, subject to exemptions under the FOIA.[101] Proprietary information in such materials may be exempt from disclosure subject to the (b)(4) exemption of the FOIA.[102]

Beyond notice and access to relevant information, the public is also entitled to participate in hearings regarding such export license applications.[103]

In a recent report on the export licensing system, the House Government Operations Committee concluded that the EAA provision "infringes upon the public's legitimate right to know" both the results of licensing cases and, generally, the types and value of products the U.S. Government permits to be exported.[104]

The Committee's report also concluded:

> Preventing companies from being embarrassed over selling certain items to proliferator nations clearly is not sufficient reason to hide export licensing information from the public eye. . . . The Nuclear Regulatory Commission licenses U.S. nuclear exports in a public process without damaging the ability of U.S. firms to compete internationally. In a similar manner, export licensing review decisions should be made part of the public record. The policy of treating license review as a secret activity, shielded from public and open congressional scrutiny, works against the objectives export controls are trying to accomplish.[105]

During the past two years, Congressional efforts to trace the flow of militarily-useful technology to Iraq produced evidence of secret State

Department intervention that overcame other official concerns and objections to Commerce Department approval of many questionable export license applications. They also discovered that improper alterations had been made to permanent records of these approvals by the Commerce Department officials responsible for maintaining the integrity of the export control system.[106] Both of these activities are disturbing examples of how export controls can be undermined, rather than strengthened, by excluding license application information and review from public scrutiny.

As Congress looks for ways to avoid the kind of export license application review process that benefited Saddam Hussein, it should consider how nonproliferation goals of the export control system can be better served by permitting some much needed "sunshine" to pierce the veil of secrecy surrounding export license information.

The Need for Reform

A clear and convincing case can be made for eliminating much of the secrecy which applies to information about nuclear weapons and nuclear power. Although concerns about the Soviet bloc and international terrorism may have obscured the case in past decades, recent events have diminished these threats and highlighted the need for broader public access to nuclear-related information. The need to maintain the current regime of layered, redundant nuclear secrecy is highly questionable and the drawbacks of this regime now clearly outweigh its benefits. Just as Cold War nuclear politics has become a thing of the past, a sober examination of U.S. nuclear options and opportunities should relegate Cold War nuclear secrecy to the same status as historic artifact.

Simply put, the American people need broader public access to information concerning nuclear weapons and nuclear power in order for our nation to fully understand its nuclear past, adapt to major changes in its nuclear present, and make wise, informed choices for our nuclear future.

We need a complete and accurate history of the nuclear age up to this point so that we can understand our success in releasing the power of the atom and our failure in being unable to prevent that power from threatening the health, safety, security and legacy of mankind. We need to understand our past mistakes in order to remedy their consequences in the present and avoid repeating them in the future.

Looking back, we need to know as much as we can about the validity of past debates over nuclear policies and actions, so that looking ahead, our present debates do not recite old dogma without subjecting it to reexamination in the light of facts, understanding and capabilities that were unavailable to earlier participants.

Information brings knowledge and knowledge brings power to the task of coping with a rapidly changing world and a host of evolving nuclear issues. Without it, our political processes and technical skills cannot confront the challenges they face to secure peace and prosperity in a world full of unsecured nuclear weapons and waste.

Ultimately, what is at stake is human growth and survival, in this nation and throughout the world. Our capability to learn meaningfully from the past, act sensibly in the present, and plan soundly for the future, greatly depends upon our confidence in the correctness of what we think we know. The current regime of nuclear secrecy deprives us of that confidence by blocking our acquisition of a substantial amount of the information which is required to confirm the correctness of what we think we know about nuclear weapons and nuclear power.

The following examples should illustrate the point:

With respect to problems of nuclear proliferation, we know that the end of the Cold War and the collapse of the Soviet Union and its Communist regime offer unprecedented opportunities to create a universal consensus and mechanism for controlling nuclear weapons materials and technologies. Yet our ability to grasp the opportunity is undermined by a lack of public information regarding nuclear weapons stockpiles. Debates over the START treaties and the value of verification agreements to ensure compliance with storage and dismantlement requirements continue to circle around the issue without coming to grips with the importance of addressing it. If we cannot unilaterally acknowledge and act upon the need to remove restrictions on this kind of information, what will become of those "unprecedented opportunities" we are now so confident about?

With respect to health, safety and environmental concerns, we have long known that the aging nuclear weapons complex has had its share of contamination incidents and now presents an urgent need for a plan that will facilitate both cleanup and conversion at a number of key facilities. Yet we probably only know the "tip of the iceberg" because so much information regarding the extent of the health, safety and environmental problems caused by activities at the weapons facilities is still locked away from public scrutiny.

With respect to the economic and energy supply implications of commercial nuclear power production, we know the importance of weaning our society and its economy from its dependence upon fossil fuels in general and foreign oil in particular. Yet the promise of nuclear power in helping to eliminate this dependency has turned into a nightmare of litigation, lost investments, and political recriminations as contending parties remain locked into hardened positions of opposition on a variety of key issues that are critical to plotting the future of the nuclear power industry. Without open general access to the Government's huge store of information on four decades of nuclear power research, development and production, how will these combatants ever be persuaded to reexamine their own contentions and reconsider those of their foes, in the hope of breaking the gridlock and moving ahead to new perspectives on what can or cannot be achieved?

Despite the obvious need for greater public access to nuclear-related information, the Department of Energy remains a bastion of nuclear secrecy. A June 1989 promise by the Secretary of Energy to "create a new culture of accountability" has apparently not led to significant changes in the agency's policies regarding protection of even decades-old records of historical interest.

Pressure to keep up with Japan, Germany, Spain and Italy regarding research into nuclear generation of electrical power has resulted in two recent "rounds" of declassification of materials concerning indirect-drive fusion;[107] however, these actions are more noteworthy for their singularity than for any hope that they may signal a discarding of past nuclear secrecy policies.

Since March 1992, a group of historians, political scientists, and nuclear scientists—many of whom performed significant work for the Government's atomic energy defense programs—have been urging the Department to develop a systematic declassification program for archival documents and to remedy its failure to comply with federal requirements regarding the transfer of historical records to the National Archives.[108] The group has complained that "privileged access" to classified materials has been given to the Department employees and consultants who have been working on the Department's official history of atomic energy in the U.S., "yet independent scholars and journalists outside the Department are deprived of any opportunity to conduct proper evaluations of these official histories, let alone to make authoritative studies covering the same period, because many of the volumes' references remain classified or are simply inaccessible."

Although the group's efforts have achieved some success in stirring administrative action within the agency, the Department has resisted implementing systematic declassification and has dragged its feet regarding the group's request for expedited efforts to transfer records over thirty years' old to the National Archives. Indeed, although the Archivist had specifically requested DOE to transfer records from the

Atomic Energy Commission's Secretariat to the National Archives nearly three years ago, the Department has informed the group that it is only now arranging to transfer the 1947–1951 Secretariat files and has yet to arrange for the transfer of the 1951–1958 Secretariat files.

In its most recent session, Congress authorized spending over $800 million to assist the republics of the former Soviet Union in dismantling their nuclear weapons and converting their military science apparatus to civilian applications; in addition, it has made it possible for some 750 nuclear scientists from the former Soviet Union to come to work in the U.S., with their families, over the next four years.[109] During the same period, the U.S. Senate ratified the Strategic Arms Reduction Treaty (START I) and directed the President to negotiate "appropriate arrangements" for monitoring nuclear stockpiles and production plants. Against this background of expedited post-Cold War activity, it is amazing to contemplate how long it may be before the Department of Energy determines that it is appropriate for the American political, social and scientific communities to have free access to Government information vital to understanding and acting upon a broad range of U.S. public health, safety, environmental, energy, and security interests.

The Cold War presumption in favor of nuclear secrecy is wholly inappropriate and unacceptable for the world and time in which we now live. The key burden of persuasion should no longer be on those seeking disclosure of nuclear-related information, but on those who would suppress it. In this regard, the laws concerning the Federal Government's authority to control nuclear-related information are badly in need of review and reform.

Recommendations

A. Review and Revise Standards and Procedures for Safeguarding National Security Information Through Classification

1. President Clinton should issue an Executive Order which will supersede Executive Order 12356 and revise the standards and procedures for safeguarding "national security information." The new Executive Order should be drafted in a process of consultation with appropriate Congressional committees. Before it is signed by the President, the proposed text should be released in draft form and reviewed in Congressional hearings by designated Administration officials and other interested parties.

2. The new Executive Order should be deemed the only legal basis for restricting access to or disclosure of information on "national security" grounds. Executive Order 12065 should be used as a model for the new Executive Order which, at minimum, should restore the policy requirements and prohibitions that were dropped by President Reagan when Executive Order 12065 was rescinded. These include:

   - the test of "identifiable" damage to national security;
   - the "balancing test" requiring declassification based on overriding public interest in disclosure;
   - the resolution of doubts in favor of disclosure;
   - the discretion not to classify materials that may meet the legal requirements for classification;
   - the prohibitions against classifying privately-developed information and "reclassifying" information that has been previously declassified and disclosed;
   - the review and justification requirements for Special Access Programs; and,
   - the declassification policy requirements, such as the anticipated date or event triggering declassification or review and the 20-year "systematic review" requirement.

3. As additions or alternatives to these changes in current classification policy, the new Executive Order should:

   - eliminate the "Confidential" level of classification, and create a presumption that information currently classified at that level can be declassified unless an upgrading to the "Secret" level is shown to be clearly warranted;
   - eliminate "Special Access Programs" altogether;
   - clarify, narrow and reduce the number and redundancy of "classification categories" by protecting only the specific details of (a) advanced weapons systems design and operational characteristics; (b) plans for military operations; (c) predecisional diplomatic negotiations; and (d) sources and methods actually used for obtaining foreign intelligence information;
   - clarify that the "balancing test" is to be applied with substantial weight on the "public interest" side and no presumption in favor of continued classification whenever disclosure of the information at issue reasonably could be expected to advance identifiable public health, safety and environmental interests, or the national interest in nonproliferation of weapons of mass destruction; and,
   - establish an annual funding authorization requirement for

the Information Security Oversight Office and make appointment of the Director of ISOO subject to Senate confirmation.

B. *Consolidate and Revise Current Statutory Authorities for Nuclear Secrecy Through Enactment of a "Nuclear Information Policy Act"*

1. Through General Accounting Office reports and legislative oversight hearings, Congress should examine current Department of Energy programs for the protection of Restricted Data, UCNI, and "national security information" classified pursuant to an Executive Order. As part of this examination, Congress should review all DOE "Classification Guides" and declassification programs to determine whether and, if so, what information currently being protected in these categories no longer warrants protection from unauthorized disclosure due to its availability in the public domain or to some other superseding event or development.

2. Congress should consolidate all current statutory nuclear secrecy authorities in a new "Nuclear Information Policy Act" which would specify all public access rights and affirmative Government disclosure obligations, as well as any restrictions which continue to be warranted, regarding nuclear-related information that is not classified pursuant to an Executive Order as "national security information." Among other things, the new Act should:

   • eliminate Restricted Data as a control category, and explicitly reject both the "born classified" concept and prior restraint of publication by judicial injunction;

   • establish a presumptive right of public access to any unclassified nuclear-related information that is directly related to identifiable local or national public health, safety or environmental interests;

   • repeal the UCNI statute as unnecessary and redundant, or, at minimum, incorporate it with revisions that limit its scope to the unauthorized disclosure of specific and detailed security measures at particular facilities; and,

   • impose fines and/or administrative sanctions to punish violations of specific statutory restrictions, permit criminal penalties only for espionage-type violations with respect to classified information (i.e., committed with intent to harm the United States), and, in all cases, provide an affirmative defense against liability for disclosures constituting "whistleblowing."

3. As part of such legislation, Congress should enact a title providing for the timely preparation and publication of a "Nuclear Affairs of the United States" historical series, based on the model of provisions in the Foreign Relations Authorization Act for FY 1992 and 1993 (P.L.102-138, Section 198) regarding the "Foreign Relations of the United States" historical series. Such legislation would establish specific requirements for the declassification of records of permanent historical value; set publication deadlines; establish editing integrity principles; and, provide for permanent establishment of an Advisory Committee of non-Government experts to review records and procedures and make recommendations to the Agency Historian at both the Department of Energy and the NRC.

4. As part of such legislation, Congress should enact a title modelled on the JFK Assassination Records Collection Act of 1992, (P.L 102-526) to provide for the expeditious review of currently-restricted Government records concerning a single identified topic in which there is an overriding public interest. It would provide for review of relevant agency records by an appointed panel of independent individuals with necessary subject-matter expertise and authority to provide for the release of such materials at the earliest time possible. Information within the scope of the proposed "Nuclear Weapons Stockpiles Information Act" (H.R.3961), for example, might qualify for such review in connection with public debate over the START II Treaty.

C. *Amend or Repeal Statutory "Invention Secrecy" Authorities*

1. Congress should review the operation of invention secrecy under both the ISA and AEA since the House Government Operations Committee's 1980 report.

2. At minimum, Congress should see whether the Committee's recommendations were implemented, as appropriate; however, unless a strong case can be made for a peace-time invention secrecy regime, with respect to nuclear energy or any other subject area, the existing statutory authorities for such secrecy should be repealed.[110]

D. *Amend the Export Administration Act to Provide for Public Access to Non-Proprietary "Export License Application Information"*

1. Congress should amend Section 12(c) of the EAA to require

public access to export license application information
consistent with (a) the NRC regulations concerning export
license applications for nuclear materials and facilities and
(b) the recommendations of the House Government Operations
Committee.[111]

2. If application of these requirements to *all* export license
application information would prove unjustifiably burdensome, they could be limited to apply only to license applications that raise proliferation concerns with respect to nuclear
weapons.

Such legislation would permit public access *only* to export license
application information concerning licenses that meet 2 statutory
standards:

First, the license is for the export of goods or technology which
would assist a foreign country to develop, produce, deliver, stockpile,
transfer, or use nuclear-related dual use items which are not subject to
controls under the Atomic Energy Act.

Second, the license is for export to a "suspect" country; i.e., a country
that has (1) repeatedly supported international terrorism; (2) failed
to implement an effective export control system; (3) failed to address
diversion of controlled goods or technologies to unauthorized uses or
consignees; (4) refused or failed to accept full-scope nuclear safeguards;
or (5) been placed under a U.S. or United Nations trade embargo which
is currently in effect.

The legislation would also provide for the protection of proprietary
information which qualifies for exemption from disclosure under the
provisions of the Freedom of Information Act, 5 U.S.C. Section
552(b)(4).[112]

Notes

1. 42 U.S.C. Sections 2011-2296 (1991).

2. Cheh, Mary. *The Progressive Case and the Atomic Energy Act: Waking to the
Dangers of Government Information Controls*, 48 Geo. Wash. L. Rev. 163 (1980).

3. 42 U.S.C. Section 2014(y).

4. *Id*. at 2014(i).

5. *Id*. at 2161(b).

6. *Id*. at 2014(x).

7. Hewlett, Richard G. *The "Born-Classified Concept in the U.S. Atomic
Energy Commission*: U.S. Department of Energy, Washington, D.C. (1980),
reprinted in *The Government's Classification of Private Ideas*: House Committee
on Government Operations, H.Rpt.No.96-1540, 96th Cong., 2d Sess. 173, 176
(1980) (hereafter "Private Ideas").

8. This sets Restricted Data apart from "classified" national security information which, as discussed later in this paper, requires a "classification" action on the part of the Government, pursuant to the standards and procedures set out in an Executive Order, before access and dissemination restrictions will apply.

9. *See generally* Cheh, *supra* note 2, at 180-193 ("[I]f Congress intended to control privately developed atomic energy information, it did so in a highly ambiguous, equivocal, and uncertain way.")

10. *United States v. The Progressive, Inc.*, 467 F.Supp. 990 (W.D.Wis.), motion for reconsideration denied, 486 F.Supp. 5 (W.D.Wis.), expedited appeal denied sub. nom. *Morland v. Sprecher*, 443 U.S. 709 (1979), appeal dismissed without opinion, 610 F.2d 819 (7th Cir.1979).

11. 42 U.S.C. Sections 2274(b) and 2280.

12. 467 F.Supp. at 995 (Court held that the statutory provisions as applied were neither vague nor overbroad).

13. The Atomic Energy Commission, established in 1946 under the AEA, was abolished in 1974, when its regulatory functions regarding the nuclear power industry were vested in the Nuclear Regulatory Commission (NRC), 42 U.S.C. Section 5841(a), and its research and development programs were placed under the direction of the Energy Research and Development Administration (ERDA), *id.* at Section 5842. ERDA was abolished in 1977, when its functions (along with those of the Federal Power Commission and the Federal Energy Administration) were vested in the newly-established Department of Energy and its Cabinet-level Secretary. *Id.* at Section 7131. *See generally* Department of Energy Organization Act, P.L.95-91, 91 Stat. 582, 42 U.S.C. Sections 7301-7352.

14. *See* 42 U.S.C. Section 2163 (permitting the Department of Energy and the NRC to authorize access to Restricted Data by government employees, contractor employees, and other private persons upon a determination, in accordance with established personnel security procedures and standards, that permitting such access "will not endanger the common defense and security"); 10 CFR Part 1016 (DOE "Safeguarding of Restricted Data"); 10 CFR Part 725 (DOE "Permits for Access to Restricted Data"); 10 CFR Part 10 (NRC "Criteria and Procedures for Determining Eligibility for Access to Restricted Data or National Security Information or An Employment Clearance"); 10 CFR Part 95 (NRC "Security Facility Approval and Safeguarding of National Security Information and Restricted Data").

15. For example, two years ago, it was reported that annual direct costs to the DOE for administering industrial security programs were at least $85 million. *See* "The National Industrial Security Program: A Report to the President by the Secretary of Defense," November 1990, p.19. Even with substantial funding, these personnel security programs have fallen short of their objectives. *See, e.g.,* "Nuclear Security: Safeguards and Security Weaknesses at DOE's Weapons Facilities," General Accounting Office, RCED-92-39, December 13, 1991; "Nuclear Security: Accountability for Livermore's Secret Classified Documents is Inadequate," General Accounting Office, RCED-91-65, February 8, 1991; "Weaknesses in NRC's Security Clearance Program," General Accounting Office, T-RCED-89-14, March 15, 1989.

16. *See* 42 U.S.C. Section 2274(a) ("Communication of Restricted Data") and 42 U.S.C. Section 2275 ("Receipt of Restricted Data").

17. 42 U.S.C. Section 2274(b).

18. *See* Cheh, *supra* note 2, at 174 ("Under this standard of culpability, prohibited communication could include activities such as public discussion about the efficacy of the government's atomic weapons program, publication of scientific discoveries in the atomic energy field, behavioral or other studies done on victims of atomic bombing or testing, or simply publication of any atomic energy material prior to ascertaining whether it included Restricted Data not yet officially declassified.")

19. 42 U.S.C. Section 2277.

20. 5 U.S.C. Section 552(b)(3).

21. In place of the original (b)(3) language, which simply referred to "matters that are specifically exempted from disclosure by statute," the current exemption refers to matters that are "specifically exempted from disclosure by statute, [other than the Privacy Act] provided that such statute (A) requires that the matters be withheld from the public in such a manner as to leave no discretion on the issue, or (B) establishes particular criteria for withholding or refers to particular types of matters to be withheld."

22. *See, e.g., Weinberger v. Catholic Action of Hawaii,* 454 U.S. 139, 144 (1981) and *Hudson River Sloop Clearwater v. Department of the Navy,* 891 F.2d 414, 421 (2d Cir. 1989) (Exemption Three claims not decided because disputed information was classified "national security information" withholdable under FOIA's Exemption One).

23. 42 U.S.C. Section 2162(a). The DOE safeguards Restricted Data, as well as Formerly Restricted Data (discussed *infra*), at "Top Secret," "Secret," and "Confidential" levels, similar to the way in which national security information is classified pursuant to an appropriate Executive Order. However, as provided in the current Executive Order (discussed *infra*), Restricted Data and Formerly Restricted Data are handled, protected, classified, downgraded, and declassified exclusively in conformance with the AEA and pertinent regulations issued pursuant to its authority. *See* Section 6.2(a) of Executive Order 12356.

24. *Id.* at Section 2162(b).

25. *Id.* at Section 2162(c).

26. *Id.* at Section 2162(d). Formerly Restricted Data remains subject to strict safeguarding standards requiring a "Q" access authorization or clearance in order for an individual to obtain access on a "need to know" basis. *See* 10 CFR Section 1016.3(a)(1).

27. *Id.* at Section 2162(e).

28. *See, e.g., Alfred A. Knopf, Inc. v. Colby,* 509 F.2d 1362 (4th Cir. 1975), *cert. denied,* 421 U.S. 992 (1975); *Hudson River Sloop Clearwater v. Department of the Navy,* 891 F.2d 414, 421-22 (2d Cir. 1989); *Abbotts v. Nuclear Regulatory Commission,* 766 F.2d 604, 607-08 (D.C.Cir. 1985). Courts have even been held that the unofficial publication or inadvertent or unauthorized disclosure does not require the Government to conduct a declassification review of the classified information. *Simmons v. Department of Justice,* 796 F.2d 709, 712 n.2 (4th Cir.

1986). *See also Davis v. Department of Justice,* 968 F.2d 1276, 1280 (D.C.Cir. 1992) (FOIA plaintiff who asserts claim of prior disclosure must bear initial burden of "pointing to specific information in the public domain identical to that being withheld").

29. *See* Cheh, *supra* note 2 at 172 n.59 discussing DOE efforts to declassify atomic energy materials in the 1970s.

30. 42 U.S.C. Section 2164(a).

31. *Id.* at Section 2164(b).

32. *Id.* at Section 2164(c).

33. *Id.* at Section 2153(a)(5).

34. *See* 35 U.S.C. Sections 181-188 and 42 U.S.C. Section 2181.

35. *Id.* at Section 181. Of course, the ISA authorizes secrecy orders with respect to inventions in which the Government *does* have a property interest.

36. *Id.* at Section 183.

37. *Id.* at Section 186.

38. *Id.* at Section 182.

39. 42 U.S.C. Section 2181.

40. *Id.* at Section 2181(c).

41. *See* discussion of Executive Order 12356, *infra*.

42. *See In Re Brueckner,* 623 F.2d 184 (C.C.P A. 1980) (holding that the patent ban under Section 2181 is inapplicable to an invention which has a "nonweapon utility").

43. *Private Ideas,* note 7 *supra* at p.1-3.

44. *Id.* at p.2.

45. Executive Order 12356, "National Security Information," 47 Fed. Reg. 14874 (daily ed. April 2, 1982).

46. *Id.* at Section 1.3(a)&(b).

47. *Id.* at Section 1.1(a).

48. *Id.* at Section 6.1(e).

49. *Executive Order on Security Classification: Hearings Before a Subcommittee of the House Committee on Government Operations,* 97th Cong., 2d Sess. (1982).

50. Executive Order 12065, "Security Classification," 43 Fed. Reg. 28949 (daily ed. July 2, 1978); House Committee on Government Operations, *Security Classification Policy and Executive Order 12356,* H.Rpt.No. 97-731, 97th Cong., 2d Sess. 47 (1982).

51. These categories, identical in both Orders, are: (1) "military plans, weapons or operations"; (2) "foreign relations or foreign activities of the United States"; (3) "scientific, technological, or economic matters relating to the national security"; and, (4) "United States Government programs for safeguarding nuclear materials or facilities." The new "vulnerabilities" category is in E.O.12356 at Section 1.3(2).

52. See discussion of "UCNI" (Unclassified Controlled Nuclear Information), *infra*.

53. E.O.12065 at Section 1-604.

54. *Id.* at Section 1-603.

55. *Id.* at Section 1-602.

56. *Id.* at Section 1-607.

57. E.0.12356 at Section 1.6(h).

58. E.0.12065 at Section 1-401.

59. *Id.* at Section 1-502.

60. *Id.* at Section 3-301.

61. *Id.* at Section 3-401.

62. *Id.* at Section 3-501.

63. E.0.12356 at Section 3.4(a).

64. E.0. 12065 at Section 3-303.

65. Compare E.0.12065 at 4-201 with E.0.12356 at Section 4.2.

66. E.0.12065 at Section 4-202.

67. *Id.* at Section 4-203.

68. *Id.* at Section 4-204.

69. P.L.100-180, Title XI, Part D, Section 1133, codified at 10 U.S.C. Section 119.

70. For example, in a 1990 report, House Armed Services Committee staff concluded that fewer than 10% of all SAPs are subject to meaningful Congressional oversight. *See* "The Navy's A-12 Aircraft Program," House Committee on Armed Services, H.Rpt.101-84, 101st Cong., 2d Sess. 67 (1990). More recently, in a report on FY 1992 and 1993 national defense authorization legislation, the Senate Armed Services Committee concluded that the "vast expansion" in the number of SAPs has led to "serious negative consequences," such as failures of internal management and evasion of Congressional oversight. *See* S.Rpt.No. 102-113, p.269-270.

71. 5 U.S.C. Section 552(b)(1).

72. 18 U.S.C. Section 793; 18 U.S.C. Section 641; *see, e.g., U.S. v. Morison,* 844 F.2d 1057 (4th Cir.), *cert. denied,* 488 U.S. 908 (1988).

73. E.O.12356 at Section 4.1(a); *see also* Department of Defense Directive 5220.6, "Defense Industrial Personnel Security Clearance Program," 57 Fed.Reg. 5383 (daily ed. February 14, 1992).

74. *See, e.g.,* House Permanent Select Committee on Intelligence, "U.S. Counterintelligence and Security Concerns: A Status Report -Personnel and Information Security," H.Rpt.No. 100-1094, 100th Cong., 2d Sess. 16-17 (1988); Senate Select Committee on Intelligence, "Meeting the Espionage Challenge: A Review of U.S. Counterintelligence and Security Programs," S.Rpt.No. 99-522, 99th Cong., 2d Sess. 74-80 (1986).

75. *See, e.g.,* "Nuclear Security: DOE Original Classification Authority Has Been Improperly Delegated," General Accounting Office, RCED-91-183, July 5, 1991 (concerns DOE authorization of contractors to make original classification decisions about national security information).

76. 42 U.S.C. Section 2167.

77. *Id.* at Section 2167(a).

78. *Id.* at Section 2167(a)(1).

79. *Id.* at Section 2167(c). *See also* 42 U.S.C. Section 2282.

80. *Id.* at Section 2167(a)(1)&(2).

81. *Id.* at Section 2167(a)(A).

82. *Id.* at Section 2167(a).

83. *See* note 51, *supra*.

84. Department of Energy National Security and Military Applications of Nuclear Energy Authorization Act of 1982, P.L.97-90, Title II, Section 210, *codified* at 42 U.S.C. Section 2168.

85. After the DOE notice of proposed rulemaking drew 124 written comments and 52 witnesses at three hearings, publication of a revised notice attracted 137 written submissions and 6 witnesses at a fourth hearing. *See* 50 Fed.Reg. 15817 (daily ed. April 22, 1985), *codified* at 10 CFR Part 1017.

86. *Id.* at 15820.

87. 10 CFR Section 1017.3(j).

88. *Id.* at 1017.3(t).

89. DOE Order 5650.3, "Identification of UCNI," February 29, 1988, as amended, at Section 10.i, states that any document or material that has been "widely and irretrievably disseminated in the public domain," as determined by a DOE reviewing official, is exempt from control as UCNI "regardless of its content" where the dissemination was not "under the control of the Government." However, the Order also states that "public dissemination of a document or material containing UCNI does not preclude control of the same UCNI in another document or material."

90. 42 U.S.C. Section 2168 (a)(1). DOE Order 5650.3, *supra*, at Section 8, requires the Director of Classification and Technology Policy to develop and issue "general guidelines" which identify what information is UCNI; it permits, but does not require, the Director and other Government organizations to develop and issue "topical guidelines" which identify what information is UCNI in a specific technical or program area. The Order also permits field and contractor organizations to develop "internal guidelines," based on the applicable general and topical guidelines, to identify what information of interest to the issuing organization is UCNI. None of the guidelines are made publicly available by DOE.

91. DOE Order 5650.3, *supra*, at Section 7.g(5), states that information which has just been declassified from the Restricted Data category "cannot go directly from being Restricted Data to being UCNI." It also states, however, that such information may be controlled as UCNI "in the event that the circumstances surrounding the original declassification have changed."

92. 42 U.S.C. Section 2168(b)&(c).

93. The applicable DOE Order, *id.* at Section 7.g(4), states that UCNI controls should not be used in place of classification under the AEA or an Executive Order "if classification is appropriate." However, there are no penalties provided for such use and, given the broad range of information which may constitute Restricted Data or classified national security information, a substantial overlap between the three control regimes appears unavoidable.

94. *See* 10 CFR Section 1017.16.

95. 50 Fed.Reg. at 15818.

96. Section 12(c)(1) of the EAA, 50 U.S.C. App.Section 2411(c)(1).

97. *See Lessner v. U.S. Department of Commerce*, 827 F.2d 1333 (9th Cir. 1987)

(denying an FOIA request for a list of "United States companies, corporations and individuals holding export licenses to the Soviet Union").

98. *Id*. at 1339.

99. 42 U.S.C. Section 2155, added by the Nuclear Nonproliferation Act of 1978, P.L. 96-280, Section 304(a).

100. 10 CFR Section 110.70.

101. *Id*. at Section 110.72.

102. *Id*. at Section 110.73.

103. *Id*. at Sections 110.80 - 110.91.

104. House Committee on Government Operations, *Strengthening the Export Licensing System*, H.Rpt.No. 102-137, 102d Cong., 1st Sess. 41 (1991).

105. *Id*. at 41 and 53.

106. *See* Hearings Before the House Judiciary Committee, 102nd Cong., 2d Sess. (June 23, 1992) (not yet published); Report on Iraqi Export License Information, Bureau of Export Administration, U.S. Department of Commerce, STD-206-1-0004 (June 4, 1992).

107. *See* "U.S. Is Starting to Declassify H-Bomb Fusion Technology," *The New York times*, September 28, 1992, A1.

108. *See* "Scholars Protest Agency's Handling of Historical and Scientific Papers," *Chronicle of Higher Education*, March 11, 1992, A6.

109. The Freedom for Russia and Emerging Eurasian Democracies and Open Markets Support Act of 1992 (Freedom Support Act), P.L.102-511, and The Soviet Scientists Immigration Act of 1992, P.L.102-509.

110. *See The Government's Classification of Private Ideas*: House Committee on Government Operations, H.Rpt.No. 96-1540, 96th Cong., 2d Sess. 29-33 (1980).

111. *See* House Committee on Government Operations, *Strengthening the Export Licensing System*, H.Rpt.No. 102-137, 102d Cong., 1st Sess. 53 (1991) (urging Congress to require that (1) summaries of completed licensing cases, together with accompanying rationales, be disclosed on a quarterly basis; (2) lists, notes and licensing decisions for all completed transactions be made available upon request; and (3) the names of the exporters should be protected from disclosure as confidential proprietary data.)

112. The legislation could more broadly address proliferation concerns for all weapons of mass destruction, including chemical and biological weapons and advanced conventional weapons and weapons delivery systems, with additional "suspect" nation qualifications (e.g., human rights violations).

3

Managing Change in the U.S. Nuclear Weapons Complex

Kevin T. Knobloch

The Department of Energy's (DOE) problem-plagued nuclear weapons research, development, testing and production complex is managed primarily by the Office of Defense Programs (DP). Because the complex has a legacy of extensive environmental contamination and radioactive waste generation, DOE's Office of Environmental Restoration and Waste Management (EM) and Office of Environment, Safety and Health (ES&H) are also integral players in management of the complex.

The new leadership of President Bill Clinton and Secretary of Energy Hazel O'Leary represents an opportunity for DP and the environmental offices to close a troubled era, shed outdated programs and facilities, and reorient remaining resources around missions that are germane to promoting national and international security in the post-Cold war era.

Problems That Must be Addressed

Costly and Outdated Mission

DOE historically defined the mission of its nuclear weapons program as the research, development, testing and production of nuclear warheads and bombs of the type and quantity "ordered" by its primary "customer," the Department of Defense. If one considers only the "benefits" and not "costs," it can be argued that DOE performed this mission effectively.

In 1967 the United States nuclear stockpile reached an estimated peak of 32,000 weapons, declining slowly to 25,000 weapons by the end of the 1970's.[1] When President Reagan ordered a new generation of modern warheads in the 1980's, the aging, 30-year-old weapons complex rose to the challenge, recycling fissile material from older retired weapons into new weapons and producing additional plutonium to support the Reagan Administration's planned increase in the stockpile of some 15 percent. In total, counting retired warheads, by 1990 DOE and its predecessor organizations had produced some 60,000 nuclear weapons.

The cost of such absolute emphasis on production, however, was to be devastating to the communities neighboring the bomb factories, to the American taxpayer, and to the nation. Today, many of the 15 major production facilities are shut down or inoperative, and collectively bear an environmental cleanup bill estimated by DOE at more than $200 billion. The complex in its present condition can manufacture significant quantities of new warheads only if it recycles the plutonium components intact, without subjecting them to formerly routine chemical processing, casting, and machining operations.

Changes in the international security environment have greatly diminished the need for DOE's traditional mission approach. In unprecedented rapid succession, several major arms control agreements with the former Soviet republics and unilateral arms reductions by both sides will result in sharply reducing the U.S. nuclear arsenal to approximately 5100 warheads in the active nuclear weapons stockpile, of which about 3500 could be delivered promptly by long-range missiles and bombers.

Still Excessive Focus On Weapons Development and Production

Under former President Bush's direction and outgoing DOE Secretary James Watkins' management, DOE responded to these astonishing changes by reducing or canceling a number of programs and shifting a portion of the savings to environmental restoration and waste management programs. Nonetheless, DOE requested and Congress approved nearly in its entirety, some $7.5 billion for its nuclear weapons program in FY 1993 (this number *excludes* environmental cleanup and waste management, which are funded elsewhere within DOE). Even though all new-generation warheads have been canceled, DOE budgeted $4.8 billion for weapons development, testing and production in this fiscal year. DOE has extensive stockpiles of plutonium and highly enriched uranium and DOE's own estimates fail to support a need for new tritium sources until at least 2012—and well beyond that date in the event of further reductions—but the FY 1993 budget request for nuclear materials production was $1.8 billion.[2]

DOE Lacks Vital In-House Expertise

DOE has among its contractors the best nuclear weapons scientists and designers in the world, but there are no new nuclear weapons on order from the Department of Defense, nor are such orders likely to be forthcoming in the future. As that program wanes, the environmental cleanup and waste management budget burgeons. At $5.3 billion in FY 1993 it is larger than the Environmental Protection Agency-managed Superfund toxic waste cleanup program. A Union of Concerned Scientists (UCS) study determined, "(T)he small community of qualified environmental health professionals (at DOE) is woefully inadequate to the task" of cleanup. "Poorly done quantitative risk assessments (QRAs) conducted by under-qualified personnel could be worse than useless, leading to poor decisions and waste of valuable time and resources."[3]

Employees Plagued By Low-Morale, Lack of Professionalism

President Ronald Reagan repeatedly declared his desire to abolish DOE and often denigrated, at least implicitly, federal public service. Not surprisingly, a number of DOE's best employees departed during those eight years. An important characteristic of government employment—pride in service—had been dampened.

DOE has pressured or persecuted "whistleblowers" and other employees who have tried to perform their job professionally and with integrity. An April 1992 investigation by the House Energy and Commerce Committee accused DOE of "bureaucratic execution" of staff professionals who two years ago tried to warn the nation about Iraq's nuclear weapons program.[4] DOE's inspector general, John C. Layton, discovered in the summer of 1991 that security personnel at the weapons plants used illegal surveillance equipment to spy on workers who complained about safety violations.[5]

The price of this disdain for public service is high. The DOE-appointed Advisory Committee on Nuclear Facility Safety concluded in its final November 1991 report that the Office of Defense Programs is "in some respects demoralized and weakened in talent . . . a distressing level of confused and unfocused thinking still exists and the inter-relation among headquarters, field offices and the contractors continues to be characterized by change, overlap and unclear guidance."[6]

DOE Fails to Effectively Manage Outside Contractors

All of the nuclear weapon production facilities are owned by the government but operated by private contractors. A UCS report noted, "(O)ne of the most consistent and worrisome criticisms of DOE has been its unwillingness or inability to discipline and control its contractors . . . both the numbers of DOE oversight personnel and their professional competence are seriously inadequate."[7]

Regrettably, the illustrations of this breakdown are plentiful:

- In a legal settlement announced in March 1992, Rockwell International Corp., the former Rocky Flats contractor, pleaded guilty to 10 environmental crimes and agreed to pay an $18.5 million fine. The U.S. Justice Department conceded that DOE's managers shared in the responsibility for the wrongdoing.[8]
- A May 1991 report by DOE's inspector general detailed illegal transfers of tens of millions of dollars in and out of a construction account to hide huge cost overruns at the Savannah River plant; Secretary Watkins said such practices were widespread in the industry.[9]
- A White House audit released in April 1992 concluded that DOE's reliance on private contractors to clean up the weapons plants has resulted in project estimates being inflated by hundreds of millions of dollars per year.[10]

Over the years, DOE has acted more as an "enabler" towards the contractors' negligence than as a tough overseer—too frequently handing out merit awards to contractors who, it would be later learned, were meeting demanding production orders by endangering the public and fouling the environment.

Immunity From Environmental, Health and Safety Laws

Much of DOE's troubles can be traced to its historic lack of accountability to federal, state and local environmental laws which govern private industry. Accorded the freedom from worrying about the environmental costs of its production activities, by claiming "sovereign immunity," DOE (and other federal agencies) behaved as though those costs were nonexistent. For example, when EPA fined DOE $372,000 in association with the release of some 393,000 pounds of uranium into the environment around the Fernald Plant in Ohio, over the past 30 years, DOE asserted that EPA lacked jurisdiction and refused to pay the penalty. Outgoing Secretary Watkins accepted greater accountability by negotiating several ad hoc agreements among EPA and individual states, committing DOE to comply with all relevant laws. Congress finally acted to correct this double-standard when it passed the Federal Facilities Compliance Act in September 1992, making it unequivocal that DOE facilities must comply with the Resource Conservation and Recovery Act (PL 94-580). President Bush signed it into law on October 6, 1992.[11] The effectiveness of this crucial law is as yet untested.

Weak Base of Scientific Knowledge of Pathways and Effects

DOE has been struggling with its growing environmental cleanup program. One reason it has demonstrated such meager success despite huge infusions of federal dollars is the acute scarcity of scientific knowledge about the key pollutants' environmental pathways or toxic effects in humans. Poor record-keeping—both out of ignorance and recklessness—of releases, spills, dumping and burials of pollutants have given contemporary cleanup managers painfully minimal data on amounts, types and locations of pollutants. Data on past radioactive exposures of populations neighboring the plants is similarly slim to nonexistent.

Also, technologies for stabilizing and safely destroying or storing certain contaminants over the long-term remain to be developed.

Obstacles to Change

The prospects for extensive and lasting change at DOE are poor unless the new leadership gains a keen understanding of three formidable obstacles, and pays dogged attention to removing or minimizing them.

DOE's Professional Culture

Secretary Watkins frequently articulated the need to change DOE's longstanding culture, which placed weapons production above all else, including the public's health and safety. He too occasionally succumbed to this culture's imperatives—such as spending billions of dollars for repairs of the 37-year-old "K" tritium production reactor at Savannah River in South Carolina. He aggressively pressed ahead with restarting the reactor even after it was clear that new tritium would not be needed for at least two decades. Generally, though, his leadership was strong on the need for cultural change. He started what is certain to be a long, frequently painful process.

One of the culture's central characteristics that must be challenged is excessive secrecy. For decades, DOE conducted its nuclear weapons design and production activity in almost total secrecy. Stringent controls remain necessary to prevent disclosure of weapon design and production secrets. But the secrecy which enveloped all aspects of DOE's operations, including the public health and safety impact and financial management of its operations, is less appropriate and less wise. By restricting the flow of vital information to decision makers, excessive secrecy frequently produces bad decisions.

In the fever of the Cold War, DOE exploited this pervasive secrecy to shroud the release of untold tons of radioactive material into the air, land and water. Despite Admiral Watkins' efforts to let a bit of sunshine in, the temptation to retreat behind a "classified" shield persists. As recently as October 1991, DOE reportedly pressured its National Laboratory scientists to avoid multinational seminars on environmental contamination and arms control for fear they would encounter "nongovernmental contacts."[12]

No Public Trust; Perception of Inept Agency

DOE's credibility with the public, Congress and the media is debilitatingly low. For every modest step toward improving its rapport with the public, it seems to take two giant steps backward. When it began to restart the aging K Reactor at Savannah River, in the face of local opposition, radioactive tritium accidentally leaked into the river. In October 1992, the media revealed an internal DOE memo that showed substantial amounts of plutonium were still stored in unstable condition at the Rocky Flats plant in Colorado, nearly three years after the plant was shut down for safety problems.[13] This obstacle will be of special concern as DOE attempts to untangle its stalled efforts to find a long-term repository for radioactive wastes generated by bomb-making activity over the last five decades.

Jobs: 100,000 Employees and Their Dependents

DOE and its management and operations (M&O) contractors employ some 100,000 people at the weapons plants. The future of these jobs is an equity issue and a political issue that undoubtedly will slow the phasing out of weapons activities and implementation of the new mission.

Action Steps

This daunting list of problems and obstacles requires an equally daunting list of remedies. Below, I describe a series of recommended action steps.

Develop a Strategic Plan

This first step, undertaking a strategic planning effort, would produce the framework for assessing and implementing all of the steps which follow. The plan should look at least 10 to 15 years into the future but have the clearest focus on what goals must be accomplished in the next five years. It is essential that staff professionals be involved, especially those currently on staff who are expected to stay aboard, so that they will have an investment in the success of the goals and implementation steps that emerge from the plan.

The strategic planning process is also a crucial opportunity to begin rebuilding public trust and support. DOE personnel in the past referred to the Defense Department, to whom it delivered the weapons it built, as the "customer." This narrow perspective of DOE's constituency was a key weakness that bears some of the responsibility for the ultimate collapse of the complex. If Peter Drucker's observation is accurate that "a customer is a person who can say no"[14]—or at least thwart successful fulfillment of a mission—then the President, Congress, American taxpayers, communities and states which host DOE facilities, Pentagon, labor unions and other employee representatives, and arms control, environment and health advocacy (non-profit) organizations should all be counted among DOE's "customers." The process in which a new strategic plan is articulated and adopted should include each of these constituencies (within reasonable logistical constraints and practical considerations). This investment of time and energy will build support for the difficult decisions which lay ahead.

Draft a New Mission Statement

In a rapidly changing international climate our nation's security needs—in the broadest definition—are great and public funds are scarce. The DP, EM and ES&H Offices are confronted with an array of opportunities to decisively lead the way. Secretary O'Leary immediately recognized those opportunities. At her confirmation hearing on January 19, 1993 before the Senate Energy and Natural Resources Committee, Secretary O'Leary testified in support of shifting resources from weapons production to "other critical missions," including "cleaning up contaminated waste sites to protect the health, safety, and livelihoods of our citizens living in proximity to Federal facilities, beginning to safely reduce our weapons stockpile to comply with international arms reduction agreements, while using the talent of our nation's laboratories to support civilian research and development efforts to encourage innovation and commercialization of products to create economic growth."[15] DOE can also make a vital contribution toward ending the threat of the spread of nuclear weapons and other weapons of mass destruction.

A new mission statement should be drafted which focuses the purposes of DOE's defense and environmental programs in an unequivocal and succinct fashion. In the spirit of Secretary O'Leary's comments, the mission statement would significantly *lessen* the focus on weapons research, development and production while *increasing* the importance of work in these areas:

- Warhead dismantlement and destruction;
- Arms control/nonproliferation verification, both nuclear and conventional;
- Long term storage or disposal of radioactive materials;
- Environmental cleanup and restoration;
- Environmental cleanup technologies;
- Defense technology transfer to civil industrial, medical, and scientific applications.

In the latter four areas, DOE should look for opportunities to enhance U.S. economic competitiveness in international trade.

The mission statement should address the need for sustaining a core capacity to assemble nuclear weapons to counter nuclear threats that might emerge in the future (see further discussion below).

Upgrade Staffing and Address Contractor Issues

The earlier discussion of problem areas identified several acute staffing needs. A premium should be placed on identifying and retaining, wherever possible, exceptional career incumbents. An intensive recruiting effort is needed to attract talented managers and improve the technical depth and versatility of the environmental and health science staff. Adequate resources must be provided to the central personnel operation, the Office of Administration and Human Resource Management, to fulfill these mandates. Emphasis should be placed on reducing reliance on contractors throughout DOE and strengthening management/oversight of those contractors with whom DOE would continue to work.

All staffing decisions should reflect these objectives. As part of the effort to regain public trust, the Office of Congressional and Intergovernmental Affairs and the Office of Public Affairs could be staffed with new personnel who have governmental or community experience at the state and local level. The new mission and goals identified in the strategic plan should be incorporated into the job description, job announcements and personnel evaluations.

Civil service rules and funding limitations will limit DOE's latitude in pursuing these actions. Thus, it is essential to seize opportunities for promoting the best staff from within, and for filling slots vacated through attrition with needed additions.

Alter Budget Priorities

President Clinton must write and submit to Congress a new DOE budget for FY 1994 within the first few months after taking office. This offers a superb opportunity to send an unequivocal message about changed priorities.

This first budget should: 1) begin to phase out weapons development at Lawrence Livermore National Laboratory and consolidate this work at Los Alamos; 2) reduce the underground nuclear testing budget to reflect the Congressionally-imposed test moratorium; 3) significantly reduce the nuclear weapons production and nuclear materials production budgets (in part by canceling restart of the K reactor at Savannah River and placing it in a "dry lay-up" condition pending a decision on decommissioning); 4) cancel the new production reactor program (shifting tritium production research to the linear accelerator technology and other options instead).[16]

New priorities named in the mission statement should be awarded funding increases as appropriate—although some already well-funded programs, such as environmental restoration, may need organizational reform far more than more dollars.

Downsize Production Program, Preserve Minimal Capacity

As noted, DOE is not likely to return to the business of building nuclear weapons anytime soon, but the future is almost by definition uncertain. DOE should maintain a dramatically downsized but high-caliber core staff and facilities that can be activated as needed to remanufacture fully proven useful warhead designs when the current weapons reach the end of their stockpile life, usually about 20-25 years.

Stockpile support activities could be consolidated at Los Alamos and Sandia laboratories in New Mexico. Nuclear materials processing, nuclear component storage and fabrication, non-nuclear parts manufacturing, and warhead assembly could be combined at no more than a few locations within the complex. In the near term, all non-nuclear component operations can be consolidated at the Kansas City Plant, resulting in the closure of the Pinellas, Florida, and Mound, Ohio facilities.

With no ongoing or projected need for nuclear materials processing for the weapons program, the Idaho National Engineering Laboratory has no DOE Defense Program mission and its operations should be phased out and the site transferred to the EM program. Plutonium and tritium processing can be consolidated at the Savannah River Site in South Carolina, resulting in the termination of plutonium processing operations at the Rocky Flats Plant and tritium/plutonium-238 operations at the Mound facility. Uranium components could continue to be shipped to the Y-12 plant in Oak Ridge, Tennessee, for storage and eventual processing into submarine and civil reactor fuel. Thus within five years the active weapons complex could consist of just five sites, down from 15 in 1988: Los Alamos and Sandia Laboratories, Savannah River, Oak Ridge, and Pantex.

In the longer term, all plutonium and tritium operations for a stockpile of a few hundred to 1000 weapons could be consolidated with warhead assembly/disassembly operations at the Pantex Plant near Amarillo, at the new Combined Device Assembly Facility at the Nevada test site (a large highly secure plutonium storage/nuclear device assembly building that is largely empty at the present time), or at the Los Alamos National Laboratory, which already has sizable pilot weapons production capabilities and could be the most appropriate site for an eventual tritium production accelerator.

Numerous studies have been completed by DOE and independent groups on various consolidation approaches. A new, clean assessment is probably needed, given the impact of changing security needs on DOE's mission, but much of the analysis already undertaken should help shorten the process for making decisions on consolidation.

Target Environmental Cleanup Programs for Management Reform

"The key question is no longer whether increased cleanup funding is needed at DOE's defense facilities, but whether we are getting our money's worth for the dollars we are spending," a recent Friends of the Earth report stated.[17] Leo Duffy, outgoing EM Assistant Secretary, recently expressed frustration about DOE and its contractors' "lack of sensitivity in spending the taxpayers' money."[18] Without clear progress in the enormous cleanup effort, Congress might well slash the funding. Because of the size of the budget and its importance to DOE's new mission, this program should be selected as the target of high-profile management reform.

Secretary Watkins and Assistant Secretary Duffy began the reform process. EM developed a Progress Tracking System (PTS) to track program activities, accomplishments and resources and, in so doing, boost communication, reporting and response to information requests across operational jurisdictions. DOE also launched an "in-depth" study and evaluation of overhead allocations at each DOE Field Office, recently completing one of the first, at Hanford, Washington.[19]

An Interagency Review Group (IAG) concluded a three-month study of the EM program in 1992 with recommendations for improving cost control, cost estimation and allocation of overhead costs, as well as increases in personnel, especially at DOE Field Offices.[20] Additional reform steps might include:

- *Redesign the Management and Operations (M&O) Contracting Approach*: Under the current M&O system, DOE's cleanup contractors have little financial incentive to move expeditiously toward project completion. (This dilemma is not unique to DOE, but seemingly endemic in any large, well-endowed government program.) Such incentives might take the form of bonuses for fulfilling a contract on time and penalties for failing to do so; assembling in-house "contractor" teams which could compete with private contractors by bidding for projects, and consequently comparing results; tying potential for future contracts with past performance on effectiveness, timeliness and cost.
- *Give EM Greater Cross-Jurisdictional Authority*: DOE recognized the bureaucratic obstacles to an effective EM program when it instituted the PTS program. The "Operations Offices" in the field—at Albuquerque, Nevada, Rocky Flats and elsewhere— have site-specific and mission-specific interests which are not always harmonious with EM's goals. Yet EM projects must report through the Operations Office to Washington. As one illustration, vitrification facilities—in which radioactive materials is solidified into a durable, solid glass product—are being designed for a number of DOE sites. As lead personnel for each project struggle with the associated technological difficulties (as documented by a General Accounting Office report on the Hanford vitrification project due out in March 1993[21]), they ought to have easy and direct access to staff at other, similar projects. System-wide approaches are especially needed for the low-level and transuranic waste programs.
- *Institute Direct Reporting to EM*: Those sites whose only remaining mission is to be cleaned up, such as Hanford or the Fernald plant in Ohio, should be able to bypass the Operations Office and report directly to EM administrators. Those sites with a continued split mission—environmental cleanup and weapons/ materials research, development, testing and production—should have separate contractors fulfilling each of the two major missions, again with the cleanup contractor reporting directly to EM.

Focus the Technology Development R&D Program

Congress has begun to respond to the need for greater and more effective environmental cleanup options by expanding the budget of DOE's Technology Development Program. The General Accounting Office in February 1992 found significant management problems with the program, however.[22] This program should be refocused on the most promising technologies to clean up the most threatening contaminated sites. The benefits of success could be substantial. Herein is a vital key to cutting cleanup costs, safer long-term handling of wastes and the development of technologies to help boost U.S. exports in international commerce.

Working with other federal and state agencies and leading research universities, DOE should also launch an effort to coordinate and expand knowledge about the toxicity and pathways of contaminants in the environment.

Continue Vigorous Oversight

Inadequate oversight is largely now a former problem. In the wake of revelations about the weapons complex's disastrous environmental legacy, Congress in 1989 established an independent Defense Nuclear Facilities Safety Board to oversee DOE and its contractors. In addition, Congress and the states are far more actively overseeing DOE's facilities than ever before.

A second, "in-house" Advisory Committee on Nuclear Facility Safety had been created by former DOE Secretary Herrington earlier, and did much good work under leadership of its chair, John Ahearne. It was disbanded in 1992. Secretary Watkins, for his part, created the Environmental Restoration and Waste Management Advisory Committee (EMAC) to assist the Assistant Secretary for EM on "both the substance and the process" of the Programmatic Environmental Impact Statement (PEIS) and other EM projects. The 23-member panel includes representatives of environmental advocacy organizations, labor unions and state and local governments.[23]

The oversight institutions are in place and already have valuable operating experience. The challenge is for the oversight to remain vigorous in a constructive, solution-oriented fashion, and for DOE to build the internal capacity to act on the most promising recommendations.

Fully Comply With New Federal Facilities Compliance Law

The Federal Facilities Compliance Act signed into law in October 1992 should sharpen the enforceability of pronouncements from the department's leadership that traditional ways of operating must change. The burden is on DOE to show it is complying with both the letter and spirit of the new law. Thus, by placing priority on bringing its facilities into compliance with federal, state and local requirements, DOE can transform a dictate into an opportunity to begin building public trust. Essential to this transformation is sufficient funding of the "Corrective Activities" account, which represented only one percent of EM's FY 1993 budget request.

Congressional conferees responded to DOE concerns by writing into the compliance law a three-year grace period for federal facilities with mixed hazardous and nuclear waste, to give the department additional time to develop safe disposal technologies. While no single legislative deadline will ensure scientific or engineering advances, this window should be used as a strong incentive for focusing the Technology Development Program.[24]

Design a "Model" Economic Conversion Program at Affected Sites

DOE should ease the pain—both personal and political—of closing many of its defunct facilities by designing a comprehensive program to retrain employees and, wherever there is no longer a clear federal need and contamination can be sufficiently removed, to transfer land and facilities to state and local governments for economic projects. Some DOE- and contractor-employed workers already have the expertise and training appropriate to environmental restoration work; others have basic skills that could be developed. The FY 1993 defense authorization bill requires the Secretary to minimize the economic impacts of plant shutdowns and to provide training and preferential hiring to displaced workers for environmental restoration, but, significantly, no staff or funds have been allocated to carry out these tasks. Savings from the weapons production budget could finance the estimated $75 million cost in FY 1993.

Ensuring Lasting Change

As each action step is implemented, management should concurrently attempt to build the esprit de corps, loyalty to mission and dedication to public service that will be needed to succeed.

Restore Spirit of Public Service to a Dispirited Department

Steven Kelman argues, "(W)here public purpose draws people into government in the first place, it should be nurtured and consciously be made part of a strategy for public management."[25] The strategy at DOE should feature such an appeal to higher purpose.

Even under progressive management, DOE is destined to suffer more than its share of negative news in the years ahead, given the figurative and literal timebombs scattered about the vast complex (serious contamination still to be discovered, decommissioning and decontaminating "hot" plants on a scale never before attempted, and so on). It is essential for reinvigorating employee morale, as well as for making the case to the public that change and progress are occurring, that DOE management as frequently as possible recognize and, when appropriate, publicize the success stories—no matter how small. Also, the unwritten code of persecuting whistleblowers should be vociferously prohibited. This would make it easier and safer for employees to communicate ideas, concerns and information, and through these "listening posts", provide management with "early warning" and "feedback" systems.[26]

Improve Problem-Solving Capacity and Professionalism

The complexity and scope of the problems besetting DOE's Defense and Environmental and Waste Management Programs are such that healthy measures of innovation and flexibility might improve the department's ability to correct its inadequacies and adapt to an abruptly changing environment. This is not so simple as ordering forth creativity, as DOE operates under often strict directives from the President, the Nuclear Weapons Council, Congress and the EPA. But once the program's new goals are clearly defined, the Secretary of Energy should permit her managers and employees as much freedom of initiative in deciding how to achieve them as external limitations permit.

- *Action Teams*: One such innovation would be to make greater utilization of team approaches to difficult problems. Secretary Watkins' "Tiger Teams" were quite effective in sweeping through weapons plants to identify violations and problems, and then repeating the inspection some months later to ensure compliance with its directives. DOE should employ the same zealous spirit of the Tiger Teams to form "Action Teams" which move beyond inspection and enforcement to *problem-solving*. As noted, DOE is currently divided up bureaucratically in a fashion which places responsibility for weapons production, environmental restoration and waste management, and health and safety in three separate offices, each headed up by an assistant secretary, and a tier of Operations Offices further complicate the life of problem-solvers. The Action Teams should be formed across these jurisdictional lines, to include senior administrators, project managers, scientists, environmental specialists, engineers and health specialists. The EMAC, with its diverse geographic mix and technical expertise, could be employed as a resource to the Action Teams. Just as the Interagency Review Group assembled by Secretary Watkins rose above territorial and institutional interests to make recommendations for specific action steps, Action Teams could elevate the art of problem-solving at DOE. They would be charged with flushing out the systemic reasons for persistent, seemingly intractable problems (e.g. why large amounts of plutonium are still stored in unstable condition at Rocky Flats three years after they were cited by Tiger Teams?) and designing and implementing the necessary corrective actions.

- *Performance Indicators:* Concrete performance indicators can be developed to help measure how employees are carrying out the new mission and goals; the indicators should recognize and reward innovation that achieves substantive results (rather than simple adherence to a set of rules and directives).

Meet Resistance Head-On

Some and possibly many career incumbents will greet the dramatic changes recommended here with fear (of the unknown and the new) and resistance. The approaches for transforming opposition to the new agenda into support are many: communication, education, confrontation, negotiation, collaboration. The key, though, is not to ignore or forsake these employees. The Secretary and senior management should appeal to shared values (greater national security, stronger economic health, renewing spirit of public service); demonstrate that changes are being managed in an integrated fashion rather than piecemeal; assure job security during transitions whenever possible; and look for opportunities to create visible symbols that reinforce the feeling the department is moving into a new, brighter era.

Notes

1. Cochran, Arkin, and Hoenig, 1985, Nuclear Weapons Databook, Vol. I, Natural Resources Defense Council, Washington, D.C. p. 14.

2. DOE FY 1993 Congressional Budget Request, Vol. 1, Atomic Energy Defense Activities, p. 5.

3. Krass, Allan, May 1991, *The Future of the U.S. Nuclear Weapons Complex*, Washington, D.C.: Union of Concerned Scientists, p.17.

4. April 25, 1992, "U.S. Accused of Punishing Monitors on Iraq," *The New York Times*, p. 4.

5. Schneider, Keith, August 1, 1991, "Inquiry Finds Illegal Surveillance of Workers in Nuclear Plants," *The New York Times*, p. 18.

6. Lippman, Thomas W., November 16, 1991, "Experts Fault Energy Dept. on Safety at Nuclear Plants," *The Washington Post*, p. 2.

7. Krass, Allan, May 1991, *The Future of the U.S. Nuclear Weapons Complex*, Union of Concerned Scientists, p. 11.

8. Schneider, Keith, March 27, 1992, "U.S. Shares Blame in Abuses at A-Plant," *The New York Times*, p. 12.

9. Schneider, Keith, May 24, 1991, "New Irregularities Found at A-Weapons Plant," *The New York Times*, p. 13.

10. Schneider, Keith, April 30, 1992, "Estimates of Weapons Cleanup Inflated," *The New York Times*, p. 14.

11. Davis, Phillip A., September 26, 1992, "Chambers Vote to Clamp Down on Federal Polluters," *The Congressional Quarterly*, Washington, D.C.: Congressional Quarterly Inc., p. 2930.

12. Schmitt, Eric, October 20, 1991, "Arms Scientists Report Pressure to Skip Conference," *The New York Times*, p. 15.

13. Lippman, Thomas W., October 8, 1992, "Memo Says Plutonium is Not in Safe Storage," *The Washington Post*, p. 3.

14. Drucker, Peter F., *Managing Non-Profit Organizations: Practices and Principles*, p. 55.

15. U.S. Department of Energy, February 1993, "DOE This Month," Washington, D.C.: DOE Public Affairs, p. 2.

16. The recommendations in this paragraph closely parallel those made in: "Reducing the Department of Energy's FY 1993 and FY 1994 Nuclear Weapons Budget," Tom Zamora-Collina and Peter Gray, Friends of the Earth, December 17, 1992.

17. De Gennaro, Ralph, and Kripke, Gawain, January 1993, *Earth Budget: Making Our Tax Dollars Work For the Environment*, Friends of the Earth, p. 127.

18. Ibid, p. 128.

19. Department of Energy Office of Environmental Restoration and Waste Management, Spring 1992, "Interagency Review Group Confirms Validity of Fiscal Year 1993 Budget Request," *EM Progress*, Washington, D.C., p. 6.

20. Ibid.

21. This GAO report was commissioned by the Subcommittee on the Environment of the House Committee on Governmental Relations.

22. Ibid, p. 127.

23. "Energy Department Names Members of New Advisory Group," *DOE News*, July 2, 1992, Washington, D.C.

24. Phillip A. Davis, September 26, 1992, "Chambers Vote to Clamp Down on Federal Polluters," *The Congressional Quarterly*, Washington, D.C.: Congressional Quarterly Inc., p. 2930.

25. Kelman, Steven, Summer 1990, "The Renewal of the Public Sector," *The American Prospect*, p. 53.

26. The terms "listening posts," "early warning" and "feedback" systems are used and discussed in a management context by Geoffrey M. Bellman in *The Quest for Staff Leadership*, 1982, p. 82.

PART TWO

Nuclear Power

4

The Role of the States in Nuclear Regulation

Dan M. Berkovitz

The Atomic Energy Act[1] (AEA) differs from federal environmental statutes in the extent to which it displaces state regulation of matters addressed by the federal government. Under the AEA, the federal government has the exclusive authority to regulate the construction and operation of nuclear power plants for radiation hazards. The AEA also preempts states from regulating the radiological hazards from nuclear waste disposal facilities licensed by the Nuclear Regulatory Commission (NRC).

Most environmental statutes, such as the Solid Waste Disposal Act[2] (SWDA), the Clean Air Act[3] (CAA), the Safe Drinking Water Act[4] (SDWA), the Clean Water Act[5] (CWA), and the Comprehensive Environmental Response, Compensation, and Liability Act[6] (CERCLA), allow the states to regulate environmental hazards more stringently than the federal government.

The reasons for the differences in the federal-state relationship between these environmental statutes and the AEA are both historical and philosophical. The AEA was enacted just after World War II, when exclusive federal control of all nuclear materials was considered necessary to prevent the proliferation of nuclear materials and technology for weapons purposes. The states were not formally allowed to participate in the regulatory process until the 1950's, when concerns over secrecy had somewhat diminished. Even then, however, the states had no role in the regulation of radiation hazards from nuclear power plants. This federal-state relationship under the AEA has remained essentially unchanged since the late 1950's.

By contrast, most other environmental statutes were enacted or amended significantly in the late 1960's and the 1970's, a period in which environmental awareness was increasing and, correspondingly, the public was demanding stronger substantive protections for the environment and more elaborate procedural rights for states and individuals. Additionally, many environmental statutes have undergone significant revisions since their original enactment, and thus reflect a partnership-oriented philosophy towards state and public participation.

This paper will examine the reasons for the broad preemption under the AEA and whether the AEA should be modified to be more in conformance with the cooperative federal-state approach underlying the environmental statutes to protect the public health and safety from environmental hazards.

The analysis in this paper is based upon the principle that absent a compelling national interest states should not be preempted in areas of traditional state authority. Areas of traditional state authority include the protection of the public health and safety and the regulation of local utilities. An additional assumption underlying this approach is that public confidence in nuclear energy will be improved with greater state and local decisionmaking authority.

With respect to nuclear energy, this analysis then finds that two national interests may be compelling enough to justify state and local preemption: (1) to improve the safety and economics of new nuclear power plants by the use of standardized designs; and (2) to find a safe site for the permanent disposal of high-level nuclear waste and spent nuclear fuel. This analysis therefore concludes that the states should have the maximum amount of authority in areas of traditional state responsibility unless the authority would discourage the use of standardized designs or lead to the frustration of the federal program to find a repository for spent nuclear fuel and high-level nuclear waste.

Background

Legislative History of Preemption Under the Atomic Energy Act[7]

Congress first enacted legislation to provide for exclusive federal control of nuclear materials in 1946, shortly after the use of atomic weapons at Hiroshima and Nagasaki ended the Second World War. Because of the potential use of nuclear materials in nuclear weapons, Congress believed "an absolute Government monopoly [over nuclear materials] . . . is indispensable."[8] The Atomic Energy Act of 1946[9] created a governmental monopoly over the development and use of atomic energy as well as exclusive federal control over all nuclear materials. The 1946 Act established the Atomic Energy Commission

(AEC) to oversee the use of these materials and to promote the use of atomic energy.[10]

By 1954, the use of nuclear materials for peaceful purposes by private industry was no longer considered a threat to the national security. To promote the development of atomic power by private industry, the Atomic Energy Act of 1954 ended the governmental monopoly over nuclear materials. The 1954 Act authorized the AEC to issue licenses to private industry to construct and operate nuclear power plants.

Significantly, in the 1954 Act Congress intended only to control the nuclear aspects of nuclear power. Section 271 of the 1954 Act stated "Nothing in this chapter shall be construed to affect the authority or regulations of any Federal, State, or local agency with respect to the generation, sale, or transmission of electric power."[11] Senator Hubert Humphrey emphasized that section 271 was a "positive negation of any intent by [the 1954 Act] to interfere with the existing laws and the existing authorities, State and Federal, that have to do with electricity."[12]

The 1954 Act was successful in fostering the growth of the commercial nuclear power industry. Over the next few years, as the industry grew, the states began to exhibit interest in asserting regulatory authority over the health and safety issues that were arising. In 1959, Congress passed section 274 of the Act in order to clarify the authorities of the states in regulating source, special nuclear, and byproduct materials.

Section 274 authorized the AEC to enter into agreements with the states that would allow the states to regulate certain uses of source, special nuclear, and byproduct materials to protect the public health and safety from radiological hazards. The activities which the states would be allowed to regulate would be those that did not involve either the use or production of nuclear materials in nuclear reactors or the disposal of nuclear wastes that the Commission determined were required to be exclusively regulated by the Commission. Thus, for example, the states would be allowed to regulate the medical and industrial uses of nuclear materials.

Prior to entering into an agreement, the AEC was required to determine that the state program was "compatible" with the Commission's program for regulating such hazards, and that the state program was adequate to protect the public health and safety from the materials covered by the agreement. The AEA did not define the term "compatible."

Section 274 did not authorize these agreements with respect to the use or production of nuclear materials in nuclear power plants. The AEC retained exclusive authority over the regulation of the construction and operation of nuclear power plants for the purpose of protecting the public from radiological hazards. The AEC also was prohibited from discontinuing any exclusive regulatory authority over the disposal of nuclear wastes in facilities licensed by the Commission. The Joint Committee on Atomic Energy explained the division of responsibility as follows:

> Licensing and regulation of more dangerous activities—such as nuclear reactors—will remain the exclusive responsibility of the Commission. Thus a line is drawn between types of activities deemed appropriate for regulation by individual States at this time, and other activities where continued AEC regulation is necessary . . . . [T]his is interim legislation. *The committee believes that the uses of atomic energy will be so widespread in future years that states should continue to prepare themselves for increased responsibilities.*[13]

The 1959 amendments also affirmed Congress's desire in the 1954 Act to leave undisturbed traditional state authority over non-nuclear matters. Section 274(k) states that "Nothing in this section shall be construed to affect the authority of any State or local agency to regulate activities for purposes other than protection against radiation hazards."[14]

The federal-state division of regulatory responsibilities over nuclear power plant construction and operation has remained essentially unchanged since 1959. The only area in which Congress has expanded state authority to regulate the radiological hazards associated with the operation of nuclear power plants has been with respect to the regulation of radioactive air emissions.[15] In the Clean Air Act Amendments of 1977 Congress provided the states with authority to regulate more stringently than the federal government the emissions of radioactive air pollutants.[16] In all other respects, however, the scope of preemption under the Atomic Energy Act is the same today as it was in 1959.

Judicial Interpretations of the Scope of Preemption

In 1983, the United States Supreme Court addressed the scope of preemption under the AEA in the case of *Pacific Gas & Electric Co. (PG&E) v. State Energy Resources Conservation and Development Commission.*[17] In *PG&E*, two California utilities challenged the constitutionality of the State of California's moratorium on the construction of new nuclear power plants. The California law prohibited the construction of any new nuclear power plants within the state until the California Energy Commission finds that there is a demonstrated technology for the disposal of high-level nuclear wastes.[18] California stated that the moratorium was needed as an economic measure in order to ensure that the inability to permanently dispose of spent nuclear fuel would not disrupt or "clog" the nuclear fuel cycle, thereby causing unanticipated costs in the generation of electricity from nuclear power plants.

The utilities argued that the moratorium was motivated by safety concerns over the hazards posed by nuclear waste and therefore was preempted. Additionally, the utilities contended that the moratorium conflicted with the federal government's policy to continue licensing nuclear power plants in the absence of a waste disposal technology and also frustrated the federal goal of the promotion of nuclear power.

The Supreme Court upheld California's moratorium. First, the Court held that "Even a brief perusal of the Atomic Energy Act reveals that, despite its comprehensiveness, it does not at any point expressly require the States to construct or authorize nuclear powerplants or prohibit the States from deciding, as an absolute or conditional matter, not to permit the construction of any further reactors."[19] The Court then stated that federal preemption was confined to the matters of radiological safety: "Congress, in passing the [Atomic Energy Act of 1954] and in subsequently amending it, intended that the Federal Government should regulate the radiological aspects involved in the construction and operation of a nuclear plant, but that the States retain their traditional responsibility in the field of regulating electrical utilities for determining questions of need, reliability, cost, and other related state concerns."[20]

The Court refused to look behind California's assertion that the motivation for the moratorium was economic. The Court therefore concluded that the state statute was not an impermissible regulation of nuclear power for the protection of the public from radiation hazards.

The Court also concluded that the California moratorium did not frustrate any federal objectives regarding the promotion of nuclear energy. "The legal reality remains that Congress has left sufficient authority in the States to allow the development of nuclear power to be slowed or even stopped for economic reasons."[21]

The Court made it clear, however, that a state could not regulate the construction and operation of a nuclear power plant, "even if enacted out of nonsafety concerns."[22] The Court also added that "[a] state moratorium on nuclear construction grounded in safety concerns falls squarely within the prohibited field."[23]

In a concurring opinion that was joined by Justice Stevens, Justice Blackmun concluded that a state prohibition on the construction of new nuclear power plants would be constitutional even if motivated by safety concerns. "Rather than rest on the elusive test of legislative motive, therefore, I would conclude that the decision whether to build nuclear plants remains with the States. In my view, a ban on construction of nuclear powerplants would be valid even if its authors were motivated by fear of a core meltdown or other nuclear catastrophe."[24]

One year later, in *Silkwood v. Kerr-McGee Corp.*[25] the U.S. Supreme Court was faced with the question of whether the AEA preempts an award of punitive damages in a state tort action for activities presenting radiation hazards regulated by the NRC. An Oklahoma jury had ordered, pursuant to Oklahoma state law, the defendant Kerr-McGee Corporation to pay $10,000,000 in punitive damages for radiological injuries to Karen Silkwood, one of Kerr-McGee's employees. The jury found Silkwood's injuries to have been caused by Kerr-McGee's operation of its plutonium fuel fabrication facility. Kerr-McGee's facility was licensed and regulated by NRC. By a 5-4 margin, the Court upheld the state award of punitive damages.

Examining the legislative history of the AEA, the Court found:

> Congress's decision to prohibit the states from regulating the safety aspects of nuclear development was premised on its belief that the Commission was more qualified to determine what type of safety standards should be enacted in this complex area. As Congress was informed by the AEC, the 1959 legislation provided for continued federal control over the more hazardous materials because "the technical safety considerations are of such complexity that it is not likely that any State would be prepared to deal with them during the forseeable future."[26]

The Court discerned no intent by Congress to preempt state tort remedies in either the 1954 Act or the 1959 Amendments. The Court cited the Price-Anderson Act, which relies upon state tort law to provide compensatory damages to victims of nuclear accidents, as further support for this finding. In conclusion, the Court held that an award of punitive damages against a NRC licensee would not impermissibly conflict with any federal objective to promote the use of nuclear energy.[27]

In sum, both the statutory language and the judicial interpretations of the AEA demonstrate that the Act preempts state regulation of the radiological hazards from nuclear power plant operation and construction. The statute also preempts state regulation of nuclear waste facilities licensed by the NRC. However, the AEA does not preempt state decisions to prohibit the construction of nuclear power plants for reasons other than the protection of the public from radiological hazards.

The major reason for federal preemption is to ensure that there is adequate protection to the public health and safety from the use of nuclear materials in nuclear reactors. There is no preemptive federal objective to compel the states to choose nuclear energy rather than non-nuclear technologies to generate electricity.

Agreement State Program Status

Twenty-eight states have signed agreements with the NRC that allow those states to regulate the medical, industrial, and academic uses of nuclear materials within their borders. There are approximately 15,000 materials licensees in those states.

The NRC believes that the agreement state program has been successful. The NRC believes that the states and the NRC have worked well together, that the states have gained competence and maturity in the regulation of nuclear materials, and that both the states and the NRC have benefitted from the regulatory innovation that has occurred within the agreement states.[28]

Although the 1959 Amendments to the AEA specify that agreement state programs must be "compatible" with the NRC's program, the NRC has never formally and comprehensively defined compatibility. For example, the NRC has never formally determined whether agreement states should be permitted to establish standards more stringent than the NRC for the disposal of low-level radioactive waste. The NRC has established internal procedures for its own use in making compatibility determinations for agreement state programs, but these procedures do not constitute formal agency policy.

The NRC recently has solicited public comment on the compatibility issue.[29] For example, the NRC has requested public comment on the degree to which uniformity should be required in radiation protection regulations, and the degree to which states should be allowed to set radiation protection standards different from those of the NRC. The comments received by NRC indicate there is no consensus on the degree of uniformity that should be required.

Federal-State Relations Under Other Environmental Laws

Generally, under our federal system traditional state authority should be preempted only for clear and compelling national interests. Federal restraint in preempting state regulation is apparent in the Supreme Court's decisions. "The principle to be derived from [the Supreme Court's] decisions is that federal regulation of a field of commerce should not be deemed preemptive of state regulatory power in the absence of persuasive reasons—either that the nature of the regulated subject matter permits no other conclusion, or that the Congress has unmistakably so ordained."[30] This is particularly true where the Congress seeks to regulate in an area of traditional state authority, such as the protection of the public health and safety.[31]

In a number of other federal environmental statutes Congress has respected the traditional authority of the states to regulate for the protection of the public health and safety. These statutes generally provide for the establishment of minimum federal standards, and allow for the states to set more stringent requirements. In addition, these statutes frequently include citizen suit provisions, which allow both individuals and state and local governments to bring enforcement actions to compel compliance with the statute.

For example, the Solid Waste Disposal Act (SWDA) allows states to regulate the treatment, storage, and disposal of hazardous wastes more stringently than the federal government.[32] Section 3009 of the SWDA states that "Nothing in this title shall be construed to prohibit any State or political subdivision thereof from imposing any requirements . . . which are more stringent than those imposed by [regulations under this subtitle]."[33]

Subtitle C of the SWDA, commonly referred to as the Resource Conservation and Recovery Act (RCRA),[34] allows the Environmental Protection Agency (EPA) to authorize states to administer the RCRA program instead of the EPA. Section 3009 of RCRA requires that state regulations be no less stringent than the federal regulations.[35] The section specifically states that it does not prohibit state regulations that are more stringent than the federal regulations.[36] "In practice, many states have imposed more stringent requirements in one or more areas."[37]

The Clean Air Act (CAA) allows the states to regulate air pollutants more stringently than the federal government. Section 116 of the CAA states that, with limited exceptions, "nothing in this Act shall preclude or deny the right of any State or political subdivision thereof to adopt or enforce (1) any standard or limitation respecting emissions of air pollutants or (2) any requirement respecting control or abatement of air pollution . . . ."[38]

The Safe Drinking Water Act (SDWA) and the Clean Water Act (CWA) also allow the states to regulate more stringently than the federal government.[39]

The Superfund law, CERCLA, accommodates both the states' interest in protecting the public health and safety and the national interest in establishing a comprehensive system for the clean-up of hazardous materials. CERCLA allows the states to impose standards for the clean-up of contaminated sites that are more stringent than the federal standards, but it also requires that a state pay the incremental costs associated with any additional degree of clean-up that is imposed by that state.[40] The statute also prohibits the imposition of any state standard "which could effectively result in the statewide prohibition of land disposal of hazardous substances, pollutants, or contaminants."[41]

In addition, the Clean Water Act, the Clean Air Act, the Safe Drinking Water Act, CERCLA, and RCRA all have citizen suit provisions, which enable private citizens, local governments, and states to bring suit, under specified circumstances, to enforce compliance with the statute by either the government or by other private persons regulated by the statute.[42]

In sum, the Atomic Energy Act stands in stark contrast to most federal environmental statutes. The AEA preempts state authority to a much greater degree than the environmental statutes designed to protect the public health and safety. Whereas the environmental statutes have established a complementary federal-state regime for standard-setting and enforcement, the AEA provides that the federal government shall have the exclusive authority for standard-setting and enforcement for the construction and operation of nuclear power plants. The remainder of this paper discusses whether the scope of preemption under the AEA should be modified to be more in conformance with the environmental statutes.

Potential Changes to the Scope of Preemption

*Whether the States Should Be Permitted to Prohibit
the Construction of New Nuclear Power Plants for Safety Reasons*

There are several arguments for allowing the states to prohibit the construction of new nuclear power plants for safety reasons. First, it could be argued that the states should determine which sources of electrical generation are best for its citizens, taking into account all relevant factors, including both economics and public health and safety concerns. Both of these are areas of traditional state concerns.

Second, it could be argued that the states already have the *de facto* authority to prohibit nuclear power plants for safety reasons, even if they do not possess the *de jure* authority. Thus removing this authority from the scope of the AEA's preemption would merely be a formal legal recognition of the current reality. The cases in which state prohibitions on nuclear power plant construction or operation have been challenged demonstrate that it is not difficult for a state to avoid preemption even if safety concerns were a significant factor underlying the state prohibition.

Third, limiting the scope of preemption as much as possible could enhance the public's confidence in nuclear energy. Citizens who are able to participate in the decisionmaking process are more likely to have confidence in and respect for the process than citizens who are excluded from the process.

On the other hand, it could be argued that allowing the states to veto the construction of new nuclear power plants for safety reasons could lead to state regulation of nuclear power plant construction and design. This could undermine the federal government's attempts to standardize nuclear power plant design. It also could be argued that allowing the states to veto the construction of new nuclear power plants for safety reasons would frustrate federal objectives regarding the use of nuclear energy.

On balance, the arguments for preempting state authority to consider radiological safety in energy facility permitting decisions are not as persuasive as the arguments against preempting such authority.

It is clear from the legislative history and the judicial interpretations of the AEA that Congress never intended to preempt state regulation of the safety of nuclear power plants in order to force the states to rely upon nuclear energy. Rather, Congress preempted state regulation of nuclear safety in order to ensure that the public would be adequately protected from radiological hazards from nuclear power plants, which the Congress believed could only be accomplished through uniform regulation at the federal level. State actions that have prevented the construction of nuclear power plants therefore have not been, and cannot be, considered to frustrate any overriding federal objectives to promote the growth of the nuclear industry.

If the promotion of nuclear energy has never been considered a compelling enough motivation to preempt state economic vetoes of nuclear power plant construction, then it is difficult to consider the promotion of nuclear energy as a compelling enough motivation to preempt state safety vetoes of nuclear power plant construction. If the end result is the same, and no federal objective is frustrated by that result, then the state's motivation should not be an issue.

It may be argued that allowing state vetoes of nuclear power plant construction for safety reasons could lead to state regulation of nuclear power plant design, since, theoretically, a state could veto one particular design but allow another. Even assuming that states should not be allowed to regulate nuclear power plant construction and design, however, this objection does not prove fatal.

To preclude the use of veto authority by the states as a regulatory tool, states could not be allowed to conditionally veto nuclear power plant construction. The states could have the authority only to approve or disapprove of the proposed plant or a proposed site.

Furthermore, it could be clarified that any conditions insisted upon by the state as a prerequisite for state approval would have to be considered and approved by the NRC in the same manner as any other proposed change to the plant's design. Under the NRC's recently modified licensing procedures in 10 C.F.R. Part 52, there is a high threshold for approving changes to certified designs. A proposed change to a standardized design that already has been certified by the NRC may be approved only if the NRC determines, in a rulemaking proceeding, that the proposed modification is necessary "either to bring the certification or the referencing plants into compliance with the Commission's regulations applicable and in effect at the time the certification was issued, or to assure adequate protection of the public health and safety or the common defense and security."[43] For proposed changes that are plant-specific, the Commission must also find that "special circumstances," as defined in 10 C.F.R. Section 50.12(a), are present, and the Commission must consider whether the presence of such special circumstances "outweigh any decrease in safety that may result from the reduction in standardization caused by the plant-specific order."[44] This type of clarification would operate as a significant restraint upon the ability of a state to use the veto as a regulatory tool.

As a practical matter, amending the AEA so that it would no longer preempt states from considering radiological safety in deciding whether to permit nuclear power plant construction would not have much of an effect upon the ability of the states to prevent the construction of unwanted nuclear facilities within their borders. The states already possess substantial authority to prohibit nuclear power plant construction for non-safety reasons, such as economic concerns. They can refuse to co-operate in emergency planning activities due to nuclear safety concerns, including the evacuation of the population surrounding a nuclear power plant in the event of an emergency, and thereby create a significant additional obstacle to plant operation. Furthermore, it is not difficult for a state to blend its safety concerns with non-safety concerns, and the Supreme Court has shown extreme reluctance to overturn state decisions that have at least a plausible non-safety rationale. Thus, the states already possess a number of ways by which to prohibit nuclear power plant construction or operation based on safety concerns.

The California-type moratorium on new nuclear power plant

construction in the absence of a waste disposal technology is a good example of how a safety rationale can be intertwined with an economic one, and thereby escape preemption. In addition to California, at least six other states have prohibited the construction of new nuclear power plants in the absence of a demonstrated technology to dispose of high-level nuclear wastes.[45] A strong argument can be made that the motivation behind these moratoria, including California's, is as much safety as economic.

Although the asserted rationale of California's moratorium is to prevent the clogging of the fuel cycle, the absence of a permanent disposal technology has not forced the shutdown of any reactors. Expansion and reracking of spent fuel storage pools and the on-site use of dry cask storage has been available to ensure that spent fuel can be safely stored pending the availability of off-site storage or disposal capacity. If a state's concern with the accumulation of spent nuclear fuel were purely economic, it would make more sense to prohibit the construction of new nuclear power plants in the absence of adequate on-site or off-site storage capacity rather than to condition plant construction on the availability of off-site disposal capacity.[46]

In PG&E, the Supreme Court refused to "become embroiled in attempting to ascertain California's true motive."[47] It therefore "accept[ed] California's avowed economic purpose as the rationale for [the moratorium]."[48] This indicates that the courts will not overturn state prohibitions on nuclear power plant construction as long as the state articulates a reasonable non-safety rationale.

The history of the Rancho Seco nuclear power plant provides a good example of how a local government can even force the closure of an operating nuclear power plant for a combination of safety and economic concerns. Operated by the Sacramento Municipal Utility District (SMUD), Rancho Seco had been the target of public criticism for a number of years for both economic and safety reasons. The plant was frequently shut down in order to address safety issues. Finally, in 1989, as the plant lifetime's operating percentage hovered around 40%, a voter referendum forced SMUD to shut down the plant and to use alternative sources of electricity.[49] Although Rancho Seco's poor economic record probably was the main reason for its demise, undoubtedly nuclear safety also was a concern for many voters.[50]

Most state and local decisions on whether to object to nuclear power plant construction or operation would involve both safety and economic considerations. As the California moratorium case and the Rancho Seco case illustrate, it would not be difficult for a state to present any such decision largely in economic terms. At the very least, it would be very difficult for the courts to attempt to ferret out any impermissible safety motivations. The Supreme Court stated in the *PG&E* case that it would not look beyond a state's asserted motive in determining the state's rationale for its actions. Courts therefore will have difficulty ruling that state decisions to prevent nuclear power plant construction or operation are preempted because of an impermissible safety motive.

The saga of the Shoreham nuclear power plant on Long Island, New York, further demonstrates how a state can effectively block nuclear power plant operation due to nuclear safety concerns. The State of New York and Suffolk County, in which the Shoreham facility was located, had determined that in the event of a nuclear accident at the Shoreham facility it would be impossible to safely evacuate the population in a timely manner. Both the state and the county therefore refused to participate in off-site radiological emergency preparedness planning for the Shoreham facility.

The Long Island Lighting Company ("LILCO"), the licensee for Shoreham, contended in U. S. District Court that the county's refusal to participate was based on the county's perceived need to protect the public from the radiation hazards associated with the facility.[51] LILCO argued that the county's actions were preempted because the AEA preempts state and local regulation of radiological hazards from a nuclear power plant.

The court disagreed with LILCO. Although the court agreed that a state or local government may not regulate nuclear power or impose a moratorium on nuclear power plant construction due to radiological safety concerns, the court found that Suffolk County's actions did not amount to such a moratorium. The court found that the county merely had refused to participate in emergency planning. Examining the legislative history of the 1980 NRC Authorization Act,[52] which directed the NRC to issue emergency preparedness requirements for nuclear power plants, the court found that Congress contemplated the possibility that state or local governments might not cooperate in the development of such requirements. The court therefore held that "[u]nder these circumstances it cannot be said that the defendants have impermissibly entered the preempted area of nuclear power safety regulation."[53]

The strong objections of the state and local governments to the operation of Shoreham due to emergency planning concerns eventually forced LILCO to give up trying to operate the plant, even though the plant was fully constructed and LILCO had obtained a license from the NRC to operate the plant at low-power.

Thus, as Justice Blackmun noted in *PG&E*, "States retain many means of prohibiting the construction of nuclear plants within their borders."[54] States may prohibit the construction of nuclear power plants for economic reasons. States may prohibit nuclear power plant construction due to the absence of a safe technology for nuclear waste disposal. States and local governments may refuse to participate in nuclear emergency preparedness due to concerns over the ability to safely evacuate the population in the event of a radiological emergency.[55] To a large extent, therefore, the states already possess the authority to prevent or to erect significant barriers to the construction and operation of new nuclear power plants due to safety concerns.

Hence, amending the AEA so that it would no longer preempt the states from considering radiological safety in decisions whether to allow the construction of new nuclear power plants would not radically change the existing federal-state balance with respect to nuclear energy decisionmaking. In practice, the AEA has not preempted states from taking radiological concerns into account in decisions regarding nuclear energy supply.

Amending the AEA in this manner would not be an affirmative grant of any authority to the states. Such an amendment would merely state that to the extent that states already possess authority under federal and state laws governing the regulation of electricity to make decisions about the need for and type of electrical generating facilities, the AEA would not preempt the consideration of radiological safety under such authority. Whether in fact the states possessed this authority to consider radiological safety would depend upon those other federal and state laws.

This amendment would fully conform the AEA to the intent of Congress in the 1954 Act by clarifying that the AEA would not affect state authority over the regulation of electricity generation.[56] Thus, for example, to the extent that a state possessed the authority to consider environmental factors such as the potential for air pollution in determining whether to permit the construction and operation of a coal-fired plant, the state similarly would be able to consider environmental factors such as the potential for radiological emissions in determining whether to permit the construction of a nuclear power plant. The states would then have comparable authority to determine which sources of electricity were best for its citizens.

This amendment would also conform with the original intent of the Congress to provide the states with increased responsibilities over the use of atomic energy as the states became more familiar with this technology.[57] After almost forty years of experience with the generation of electricity from nuclear energy, state public utility commissions and other relevant state decisionmaking bodies have become thoroughly familiar with the pros and cons of this technology.

These state authorities now possess the necessary competence and expertise to make informed decisions on the appropriate mix of electricity generating technologies, including the appropriate role for nuclear energy. Accordingly, there is no longer a need for the AEA to continue to preempt the states from fully exercising this expertise.[58]

Although it is recommended that the AEA be amended in this manner, at this time this is not an urgent issue. This issue is significant only with respect to the approval process for new nuclear power plants, and it does not now appear that there will be a significant number of attempts—if any—to begin the construction of new nuclear power plants in the near future. Until such time as it appears that there will be any orders for new nuclear power plants, this issue would not appear to be a high legislative priority.[59]

Whether the States Should Be Provided With Authority to Regulate Nuclear Power Plants for Safety Reasons

There are two potential ways states could have authority to regulate nuclear power plant construction and operation for radiological hazards. The first is to allow a state to impose more stringent radiological safety requirements than the federal government. The second is to allow a state to regulate radiological safety requirements only as part of a federally approved state program to regulate such radiological hazards.

The major objection to either of these alternatives would be that state regulation would have the potential to create duplicative and conflicting safety regulations. Such duplication and conflict could be detrimental to safety. Additionally, state regulation could undermine the federal goal of the promotion of the development and use of standardized nuclear reactor designs.

It is generally agreed that one of the reasons for the cost overruns in nuclear power plant construction and the relatively poor operating performance of the U.S. industry in the early to middle 1980's was the failure of the industry to use standardized nuclear power plant designs. The use of customized designs made it difficult for both the regulators and the licensees to apply lessons learned at plants that already had been constructed to plants that were under construction or newly in operation. In France and Japan, where standardized designs have been used, nuclear power plant construction costs and schedules have been more predictable than in the United States. Generally, on average, nuclear power plants in France and Japan also have had better operating records than plants in the United States.

The NRC recently amended its licensing regulations in order to encourage the use of standardized designs for new nuclear power plants. The NRC regulations at 10 C.F.R. Part 52 allow for reactor vendors to submit standardized nuclear power plant designs for "design certification" by rulemaking. Any utility could then use the certified designs at a proposed or a pre-approved site without being required to relitigate the issues decided in the design certification proceeding.

Allowing unrestricted state regulation of nuclear power plant construction and design would clearly undermine the federal objective of the use of standardized nuclear power plant designs. Moreover, it could lead to the potential for conflict between federal and state regulation of nuclear power plant design and operation. Both of these results could be detrimental to nuclear safety.

The regulation of nuclear power plant design and operation is fundamentally different from other public health and safety matters which the states have traditionally regulated, such as, for example, agricultural goods, industrial practices, and product liability. Nuclear power plants are far more complex and must be regulated in a fundamentally different manner than these traditional matters of state regulation. Whether the need for national uniformity is compelling enough to preempt state authority often is a subjective determination. However, the need for national uniformity in nuclear power plant design and operation would appear to be far more compelling than in any of these other areas of traditional state authority. As the history of the nuclear industry demonstrates, both the safety and economics of nuclear power are enhanced by uniformity in design, construction, and operation. It would be impossible to achieve this uniformity without a single, national federal regulatory body. The safety and economic consequences of non-uniformity in nuclear power plant design and operation are far more significant than in areas of traditional state authority.

One method to avoid an ad hoc state-by-state undermining of standardization would be to require a state to have a federally approved regulatory program in order to regulate nuclear power plant construction and operation. One way to do this would be to extend the agreement state program to allow states to obtain the necessary authority to regulate nuclear power plant safety, provided that the state program was "compatible" with the NRC's and adequate to protect the public health and safety.

This option is far more attractive than allowing unrestricted state regulation of nuclear safety. Presumably, states with approved regulatory programs would be technically sophisticated enough not to impose additional safety requirements that undermined standardization in such a manner as to jeopardize public health and safety.[60]

It is unlikely, however, that many states would have the resources to develop a regulatory program that was "compatible" with the NRC's. Very few states would have sufficient budgetary or technical resources to regulate nuclear power plant safety, including a program to enforce state regulations. Thus, it is unlikely that many states would attempt to take advantage of an expansion of the agreement state program.

If less than a handful of states would be able to assemble the necessary technical and budgetary resources to develop a compatible regulatory program, it is unclear whether the practical results of allowing the states to possess this authority would be worth the costs. It would require considerable state and federal resources to develop compatible state programs, and the safety benefits—which would exist in only a few states, if at all—may not be that significant. Thus, it could be argued that expanding the state agreement program to include reactor safety would not be worthwhile.

On the other hand, it could be argued that this determination— whether the additional resources are worth the safety benefits— should be up to the states that would have to expend those resources.

State resources, however, are not the only resources that would be required to implement an expanded agreement state program. Considerable federal resources would be required to establish and oversee an expanded agreement state program. The NRC would have to determine how to define compatibility for an expanded agreement state program, something that it is only now doing for the existing agreement state program. For example, establishing such a program could require the NRC to review all of its regulations and technical guidelines to determine which were essential to safety, and which would be optional for the states to adopt. This would not be an easy task. Moreover, the NRC may be required to continually oversee the state program to ensure that it remained compatible with the federal program. This too would require considerable federal resources.

At present there is no consensus on the degree to which states should be allowed to impose more stringent regulations for matters within the agreement state program. It is certain that any proposal to both expand the agreement state program and to allow the states to regulate more stringently within that program would be even more controversial and would be strenuously opposed by the nuclear industry.

This analysis therefore concludes that in light of the very few states—if any—that could potentially take advantage of this type of program, it is highly questionable whether the benefits to the states or public health and safety from expanding the agreement state program to include nuclear power plant regulation would be worth the costs in attempting to establish or implement such a program. Accordingly, no change is recommended to the current federal preemption of state and local regulation of nuclear power plant construction and operation for the protection of the public health and safety from radiological hazards.

Removing from the scope of federal preemption the authority of the states to consider safety as well as economic reasons in determining whether to permit the construction of new nuclear power plants may ameliorate the intrusiveness of this otherwise exclusive federal regulatory structure. If the recommendations in this paper were adopted, the states would be provided the authority to determine whether or not to accept new nuclear power plants within the state and the exclusive federal regulation that would accompany the design and operation of those plants. In other words, the states would have the ultimate authority to decide whether the use of nuclear energy—as regulated exclusively by the federal government—posed acceptable risks to the public health and safety. The states would be allowed to decide whether any new plants should be built, but the federal government would retain the sole authority to regulate to protect the public health and safety from radiological hazards. This system would appear to accommodate both the state interest in retaining authority to protect the public health and safety and the national interest in the uniformity of nuclear power plant design, operation, and regulation.[61]

Relaxing the scope of preemption in this manner could serve to improve public confidence in nuclear energy. Citizens and states critical of the comparatively broad scope of preemption under the AEA would no longer be able to object to new nuclear power plants as an unsafe technology that is foisted upon an unwanting public in an undemocratic manner. This relaxation also could serve to address the criticism that nuclear energy is so dangerous a technology that it requires special federal regulation because the states cannot be trusted, or do not have the competence, to make rational decisions regarding the risks associated with its use.

Whether the States Should Be Provided With Authority to Regulate Nuclear Waste Storage or Disposal for Safety Reasons

High-Level Radioactive Waste and Spent Nuclear Fuel. The major objection to state authority to impose more stringent regulations for the storage or disposal of high-level nuclear wastes is that this authority could be used to prevent the siting of unwanted nuclear waste facilities. To prevent the siting of an unwanted facility a state would only have to enact a regulation that would be either impossible or too costly to meet.

It may be countered, however, that it should not be presumed that a state will abuse its delegated authority. It could be argued that fear of an improper use of state authority is not a sufficiently compelling reason to preempt that authority.

Additionally, it could be argued that states already possess this type of authority to some degree. For example, it could be argued that the states have the authority under the Clean Air Act to impose more stringent regulations than the federal government for the emissions of hazardous air pollutants, which includes radioactive air pollutants. Moreover, it could be argued that Congress expressly declined to preempt more stringent state regulation of radioactive air pollutants during the consideration of the Clean Air Act Amendments of 1990.[62] At the time it declined to preempt the states Congress was fully aware of the potential that this authority could be used to prevent the siting of unwanted facilities.

The Superfund law provides a model that could be used to prevent the abuse of state authority. CERCLA prohibits the imposition of any state standard that could "effectively result in the statewide prohibition of land disposal of hazardous substances, pollutants, or contaminants."[63] If the states had the authority to impose radiological standards for high-level nuclear waste storage or disposal, then a similar prohibition could be included to prevent this potential for abuse.

Although these arguments are not without considerable force in the abstract, they must be considered in the context of the current program to characterize Yucca Mountain, Nevada, as the site for the high-level waste repository. The question of whether the states should have any additional authority is likely to be viewed in terms of the issue of whether the State of Nevada should have any additional authority over the high-level waste program.

It is very unlikely that in the current political climate the Congress would seriously consider providing the states with any additional authority that could be used to delay or increase the costs of the current high-level waste program. In fact, it is much more likely that Congress would do just the opposite, probably by taking away the State of Nevada's existing authority that potentially could be used to delay the program.

During the consideration of the Energy Policy Act of 1992 the House of Representatives adopted a provision that would have preempted the State of Nevada's authority to issue non-radiological environmental permits to the Department of Energy for activities undertaken to characterize Yucca Mountain as a site for a high-level nuclear waste repository. The Senate Committee on Energy and Natural Resources approved a similar bill in the last Congress. Neither provision, however, was adopted.

Instead, in the Energy Policy Act of 1992 the Congress directed the EPA and the NRC to rewrite their high-level nuclear waste standards following a study by the National Academy of Sciences.[64] This provision was adopted largely as result of allegations by the DOE that the existing federal standards were too costly and might not be attainable.

It probably would be counterproductive to attempt to provide the states with any greater authority over the disposal or storage of high-level nuclear waste. Members of Congress and the nuclear industry are frustrated with the costs and pace of the current high-level waste program. Any proposal that would be perceived as providing the State of Nevada with additional authority to frustrate the high-level waste program is likely to fail, and may even result in more restrictions on state authority.

Low-Level Radioactive Waste. Under the Low-Level Radioactive Waste Policy Act and the Low-Level Radioactive Waste Policy Amendments Act of 1985[65] the states have the responsibility to provide disposal capacity for low-level radioactive waste. It can be argued that because the states have the responsibility for developing low-level radioactive waste disposal facilities, then at the least the agreement states should also be able to establish standards for those facilities that are more stringent than the federal standards.

Agreement states already have the technical expertise and authority to regulate the disposal of low-level nuclear waste. Providing these states with the authority to impose more stringent regulations than the NRC would not require any extensive additional technical expertise or resources within the state program.

The states already possess some authority to regulate low-level waste disposal more stringently than the NRC. In the Energy Policy Act of 1992 Congress gave the states the authority to regulate more stringently than the federal government the disposal of low-level radioactive waste that the NRC declares is below regulatory concern ("BRC").[66] This provision would allow a state, whether or not an agreement state, to determine whether BRC waste should be disposed of in a landfill or in a low-level radioactive waste disposal facility.

Additionally, two states already are attempting to regulate non-BRC low-level radioactive waste more stringently than the NRC. Illinois and Pennsylvania have adopted standards for low-level radioactive waste disposal that are more stringent than the NRC standards. Illinois adopted a release limit of one millirem from any disposal facility, and Pennsylvania has by statute authorized the imposition of more stringent disposal standards, to the extent allowable under federal law. The NRC has not yet formally determined whether either of these state provisions render the state program incompatible with the federal program.

There do not appear to be any compelling reasons why the more stringent standards of Illinois or Pennsylvania should be preempted. There is no indication that the Illinois or Pennsylvania actions will interfere with state responsibilities for low-level radioactive waste disposal or be detrimental to the public health and safety. Nor is there any indication of any interference with federal objectives.[67] There will be a loss of uniformity in regulation of low-level radioactive waste disposal standards, but it is not apparent why this should be objectionable.

Under RCRA, the states may regulate hazardous waste disposal more stringently than the federal government. The dangers to the public health and safety posed by low-level radioactive waste are not orders of magnitude different from the dangers posed by hazardous wastes. The level of technical expertise required to regulate hazardous waste disposal is comparable to the level of technical expertise required to regulate low-level radioactive waste disposal. It is not apparent why the states should be allowed to regulate more stringently than the federal government with respect to some of these materials but not the others.

In sum, there are no persuasive reasons why the regulation of low-level radioactive waste disposal would appear to require a different state-federal relationship from the regulation of other hazardous wastes. States with federally approved programs for the regulation of low-level radioactive waste should have the authority to regulate the disposal of those wastes more stringently than the federal government. The NRC therefore should interpret the AEA to permit such more stringent regulation by agreement states.

The NRC should address this issue in a relatively prompt manner. This is an issue of major concern to the states, and, if not resolved properly, could have a negative impact upon the siting process for low-level radioactive waste facilities.

Recommendations

The following legislative and regulatory changes are recommended:

A. Congress should amend the AEA to allow states to prohibit the construction of nuclear power plants for radiological health and safety reasons.

The federal government should retain the sole authority to regulate the construction and operation of nuclear power plants for the purpose of radiological protection. This would ensure that state regulatory action does not interfere with the federal goal to standardize the design of nuclear power plants or otherwise detrimentally affect nuclear safety.

Amending the AEA so that it would no longer preempt the states from considering radiological health and safety in decisions whether to allow the construction of a nuclear power plant could restore a significant measure of the traditional authority of the states in the areas of public health and safety regulation and electric utility regulation as applied to nuclear energy. Under this approach, the AEA would be a statute primarily devoted to the radiological regulation of nuclear power plant operation and construction, and would not affect state and local authority regarding the selection of electricity-generating technologies.

Amending the AEA in this manner would not be an affirmative grant of authority to the states to block nuclear power plant construction. Rather, such an amendment would merely remove any exercise of this authority from the AEA's sphere of preemption. Whether in fact a state or local government would have the affirmative authority, and under which conditions, to prohibit the construction of a nuclear power plant due to radiological safety or other considerations, would depend upon other relevant state and federal statutes.

This amendment to the AEA is not a practical urgency. In practice, if not in legal theory, the states already possess substantial authority to block the construction or operation of a nuclear power plant. Thus this amendment would not greatly enhance state authority. Moreover, no new plants are on the horizon. Hence, at least until it appears that there will be a genuine interest in the construction of new nuclear power plants, this amendment would not be a high legislative priority.

B. The NRC should interpret the AEA so that agreement states would not be preempted from regulating more stringently than the federal government the disposal of radioactive wastes for which the states have the responsibility for disposal (i.e. low-level radioactive wastes).

This would bring the AEA more into conformance with federal environmental statutes regulating the disposal of substances that pose hazards to the public health and safety.

The NRC should make this interpretation as soon as possible to remove any uncertainty within potential host states for low-level radioactive waste disposal facilities as to the validity of any state provisions that are more stringent than those of the NRC.

Notes

1. 42 U.S.C. §§ 2011-2296 (1988 & Supp. II 1990).

2. 42 U.S.C. §§ 6901-6992k (1988 & Supp. II 1990).

3. 42 U.S.C. §§ 7401-7671q (1988 & Supp. II 1990).

4. 42 U.S.C. §§ 300f-300j-10 (1988 & Supp. II 1990).

5. 33 U.S.C. §§ 1251-1387 (1988 & Supp. II 1990).

6. 42 U.S.C. §§ 9601-9660a (1988 & Supp. II 1990).

7. Much of this discussion is taken from Berkovitz, *California's Nuclear Power Regulations: Federal Preemption?*, 9 Hastings Const. L. Q. 623 (1982).

For a good history of nuclear regulation from 1946 through 1962, *see* George T. Mazuzan and J. Samuel Walker, *Controlling the Atom* (1984).

8. S. Rep. No. 1211, 79th Cong., 2d Sess. 14 (1946).

9. Ch. 724, 60 Stat. 755 (1946).

10. Atomic Energy Act of 1946, §2, 60 Stat. 756-58 (1946). Congress abolished the AEC in the Energy Reorganization Act of 1974, 42 U.S.C. §§ 5801-5891 (1988), transferred its promotional functions to the Energy Research and Development Administration (ERDA), *id.* at § 5814(c), and created the NRC to take over its licensing and regulatory authority, *id.* at § 5842. In 1977 ERDA's functions were transferred to the newly created Department of Energy (DOE). Department of Energy Organization Act, 42 U.S.C. §§ 7131, 7151 (1988).

11. Congress amended this section in 1965 by adding that "this section shall not be deemed to confer upon any Federal, State, or local agency any authority to regulate, control, or restrict any activities of the Commission." The report accompanying the 1965 amendment explained, however, that "[AEC licensees] are subject to AEC's control with respect to the common defense and security and protection of the health and safety of the public with respect to the special hazards associated with nuclear facilities, and otherwise to any and all applicable Federal, State, and local regulations with respect to the generation, sale, or transmission of electric power." H.R. Rep. No. 567, 89th Cong., 1st Sess 9-10, *reprinted in* 1965 U.S. Code Cong. & Ad. News 2775, 2784.

12. 100 Cong. Rec. 11709 (1954).

The following exchange also occurred in the Senate:

"MR. HICKENLOOPER . . . . We take the position that electricity is electricity. Once it is produced it should be subject to the proper regulatory bodies . . . . We feel that there is no difference and that it should be treated as all other electricity which is regulated by the public.

"MR. HUMPHREY. . . . I agree. . . . The fact is it becomes electricity. . . . I see no reason why electricity should be treated any differently because of the parentage of the generation." *Id.* at 11567.

13. S. Rep. No. 870, 86th Cong., 1st Sess. 8-9, *reprinted in* 1959 U.S. Code Cong. & Ad. News 2872, 2879-80 (emphasis added). As explained below, however, this legislation has been long-term rather than interim, and the states have not been given any substantially increased responsibilities.

14. 42 U.S.C. at § 2021(k).

15. The Clean Water Act allows the states to regulate more stringently than the federal government the discharge of pollutants into navigable waters, 33

U.S.C. § 1370 (1988), and defines the term "pollutant" to include, inter alia, "radioactive materials," *id.* at § 1362(6) (1988). In *Train v. Colorado Public Interest Research Group, Inc.*, 426 U.S. 1 (1976), the Supreme Court held that Congress did not intend in the Clean Water Act to alter the AEC's exclusive control over the discharge of source, special nuclear, or byproduct materials.

16. *See* H.R. Rep. No. 564, 95th Cong., 1st Sess. 143, *reprinted in* 1977 U.S. Code Cong. & Ad. News 1077, 1523 ("[R]adioactive pollutants, including source material, special nuclear material, and byproduct material are covered by section 116 of the Clean Air Act. Thus, any State, or political subdivision thereof, may establish standards more stringent than Federal, or where a Federal standards [sic] has not been established, may establish any standards they deem appropriate.")

It has been argued that section 116 of the Clean Air Act provides only for the retention of state authority, and hence can not be considered as an affirmative grant of any authority to the states. Thus, the argument proceeds, despite the language in the conference report, the Clean Air Act does not provide the states with authority in any areas in which the states are affirmatively preempted under other federal statutes, including the Atomic Energy Act.

This argument was severely undercut during Congressional consideration of the Clean Air Act Amendments of 1990. *See* note 62, *infra*, and accompanying text.

17. 461 U.S. 190 (1983). Prior to this case a number of lower courts had addressed the issue. *See, e.g., Illinois v. Kerr-McGee Chemical Corp.*, 677 F.2d 571 (7th Cir. 1982) (NRC has exclusive authority to regulate radiation hazards from materials and activities regulated under the AEA unless the state has assumed responsibility for such regulation; even absent such an agreement the state retains the right to regulate for non-radiation hazards); *Northern States Power Co. v. Minnesota*, 447 F. 2d 1143 (8th Cir. 1971), *aff'd mem.*, 405 U.S. 1035, 1154 (1972) ("federal government has exclusive authority under the preemption doctrine to regulate the construction and operation of nuclear power plants" for radiation hazards).

18. Cal. Pub. Res. Code § 25524.2 (West 1986).

19. 461 U.S. at 205.

20. *Id.*

21. *Id.* at 223.

22. *Id.* at 212.

23. *Id.* at 213.

24. *Id.* at 229.

Justice Blackmun explained that:

Congress did not compel States to give preference to the eventual product of that industry or to ignore the peculiar problems associated with that product. . . .

More recent legislation [the Energy Reorganization Act of 1974, which "demonstrates a desire to have the Federal Government 'place greater relative emphasis on nonnuclear energy'"; the NRC Authorization Act of Fiscal 1980, which preserves state authority regarding siting and land use requirements for nuclear power plants; and the Clean Air Act Amendments of 1977, which allows the states to regulate radioactive air pollutants more stringently than the NRC] makes it very clear that there is no federal policy preventing a State from choosing to rely on technologies it considers safer than nuclear power. . . .

In sum, Congress has not required States to "go nuclear," in whole or in part. . . . Congress simply has made the nuclear option available, and a State may decline that option for any reason. . . .

Id. at 227-229.

25. 464 U.S. 238 (1984).

26. *Id.* at 250.

27. The Court left open the question of whether a specific award of damages might be so large as to put a federal licensee out of business and therefore conflict with NRC's desire to avoid the imposition of penalties that would put a licensee out of business or otherwise affect a licensee's ability to safely conduct licensed activities. *Id.* at 257, n. 18. The Court also added that "We do not suggest that there could never be an instance in which the federal law would pre-empt the recovery of damages based on state law." *Id.* at 246.

28. *See* Memorandum from Harold R. Denton, Director, Office of Governmental and Public Affairs, For The Commissioners, U.S. Nuclear Regulatory Commission: Evaluation of Agreement State Compatibility Issues, SECY-91-039 (February 12, 1991).

29. NRC, Request for Comments on the Compatibility of Agreement State Programs With NRC Regulatory Programs, 56 Fed. Reg. 66457-59 (December 23, 1991).

30. *Florida Lime & Avocado Growers v. Paul*, 373 U.S. 132, 142 (1963).

31. The Supreme Court has stated that "in a field which the States have traditionally occupied . . . . we start with the assumption that the historic police powers of the States [are] not to be [ousted] by the Federal Act unless that was the clear and manifest purpose of Congress." *Rice v. Santa Fe Elevator Corp.*, 331 U.S. 218, 230 (1947).

32. Source, special nuclear, and byproduct materials regulated under the Atomic Energy Act are excluded from the definition of solid waste, and hence are similarly excluded from the definition of hazardous waste. 42 U.S.C. at § 6903 (27). Solid or hazardous wastes that are mixed with nuclear materials regulated under the Atomic Energy Act are considered "mixed wastes" and are not excluded from the scope of the SWDA. *See. e.g.*, H.R. Rep. No. 102-886, 102d Cong., 2d Sess. 23-27 (1992) (Federal Facility Compliance Act of 1992).

33. 42 U.S.C. at § 6929.

34. 42 U.S.C. §§ 6921-6979a (1988 & Supp. II 1990).

35. *Id.* at § 6929.

36. 42 U.S.C. at § 6929. In order to provide final authorization for a state program, the EPA must find that the state program is equivalent to the federal program, consistent with the federal program or other state programs, and will adequately enforce regulatory requirements. *Id.* EPA considers a state program to

be inconsistent with the federal program if any aspect of the state program either unreasonably restricts the interstate transport of hazardous wastes, has no basis in human health or environmental protection and acts as a prohibition on the treatment, storage, or disposal of hazardous waste in the state, or if the state manifest system does not meet the EPA's requirements. 40 C.F.R. § 271.4 (1991).

37. Richard C. Fortuna and David J. Lennett, *Hazardous Waste Regulation: The New Era* 336 (1986).

38. 42 U.S.C. at § 7416. This interpretation of the Clean Air Act is not universally shared. *See* note 16, *supra*.

39. 42 U.S.C. at § 300g-3(e) (retention of state authority under Safe Drinking Water Act); 33 U.S.C. at § 1370 (retention of state authority under Clean Water Act).

40. 42 U.S.C. at § 9621(d)(2)(C)(iii). The federal government retains the ultimate authority to select the appropriate remedial action. *Id.* at § 9621(d)(4); *see also* 42 U.S.C. at § 9620(g) (authority over clean-up of federal facilities may not be delegated).

41. *Id.* at § 9621(d)(2)(C)(ii).

42. *See* 33 U.S.C. at § 1365 (Clean Water Act); 42 U.S.C. at § 7604 (Clean Air Act); 42 U.S.C. at § 300j-8 (Safe Drinking Water Act); 42 U.S.C. at § 9659 (CERCLA); 42 U.S.C. at § 6972 (RCRA).

43. 10 C.F.R. § 52.63(a)(1) (1992).

44. *Id.* at § 52.63(a)(2). The NRC will consider "specific circumstances" to be present whenever either (i) application of a regulation will conflict with other requirements of the Commission; (ii) application of the regulation is not necessary or will not serve the purpose of the underlying rule; (iii) compliance would result in undue hardships or costs in excess of those contemplated when the regulation was adopted, or are significantly in excess of the costs incurred by those similarly situated; (iv) the exemption would result in a benefit to the public health and safety that would compensate for any decrease in public health and safety that may result from the exemption; (v) the exemption would provide only temporary relief where the applicant has made a good faith effort to comply with the regulation; or (vi) material circumstances are present that were not considered when the regulation was adopted and which make it in the public interest to grant the exemption. 10 C.F.R. § 50.12 (a)(2) (1992).

45. *See* Conn. Gen. State. Ann § 22a-136 (West 1985); Me. Rev. Stat. Ann. 35-A, §§ 4371-4376 (West 1988); Mass. Gen. Laws Ann. ch. 164, app. § 3-3 (West Supp. 1990); Mont. Code Ann. § 75-20-1203 (1987); Or. Rev. Stat. §§ 469.590 - 469.595 (1987); Wis. Stat. Ann. § 196.493 (West Supp. 1990).

46. The California moratorium legislation also prohibited the construction of any nuclear facility requiring either the reprocessing of spent fuel or the storage of spent fuel unless reprocessing or storage facilities would be in operation when required, "provided, however, that such storage of fuel is an offsite location to the extent necessary to provide continuous onsite full core reserve storage capacity." Cal. Pub. Res. Code § 25524.1(b) (West 1986). This provision, alone, would have been sufficient to prevent the clogging of the fuel cycle. For a more complete analysis of the California provision and its motivations, *see* Berkovitz,

supra note 7; *see also* Alan D. Pasternak and Robert J. Budnitz, *State-Federal Interactions in Nuclear Regulation* (Lawrence Livermore National Laboratory, UCRL-21090, December 1987)

47. 461 U.S. at 216.

48. *Id.*

49. The voter referendum was not legally binding upon SMUD. However, SMUD had pledged to abide by the results of the ballot initiative.

50. *See, e.g., Sacramento's Voters, in a First, Shut Down Atomic Power Plant,* N.Y. Times, A1, June 8, 1989.

51. *Citizens For An Orderly Energy Policy, Inc. v. County of Suffolk,* 604 F. Supp. 1084 (E.D.N.Y. 1985).

52. P.L. 96-295, 94 Stat. 780 (1980).

53. 604 F. Supp. at 1096.

54. 461 U.S. at 228.

55. Justice Blackmun's dissent also noted that states "may establish siting and land use requirements more stringent than those of the NRC," "and may impose more stringent [radioactive air] emission standards than those promulgated by the NRC," and thereby "prevent the construction of nuclear plants altogether." *Id.*

56. *See* notes 11 and 12 *supra* and accompanying text.

57. *See* note 13 *supra* and accompanying text.

58. A similar analysis could apply to the question of whether the AEA should preempt a state's ability to consider radiological safety when determining whether to allow continued operation or the relicensing of a nuclear power plant. The scope of the authority of a state to affect the operation of electrical generating facilities should be determined by the federal and state statutes governing public utility operation and the sale, transmission, and generation of electricity, and not the federal statute governing the protection of the public health and safety from radiological hazards.

However, any proposal to amend the AEA to remove from the scope of preemption state actions that affect nuclear power plant operation would have to be clear that such an amendment should not be interpreted to provide the state with any authority to actually regulate nuclear power plant operation.

59. It could be argued, on the other hand, that this issue is ripe for immediate consideration because, despite the lack of potential orders for new nuclear power plants, Congress has just legislatively amended the nuclear power plant licensing process, and that the amendment advocated in this paper should be no less of a priority than the licensing reform legislation just enacted. *See* Energy Policy Act of 1992, P.L. 102-446, §§ 2801-2807, *reprinted in* H.R. Rep. No. 102-1018, 102d Cong., 2d Sess. 360-361 (1992).

60. Another way to prevent this would be to provide the NRC with the veto authority over any state regulations that the NRC believed were detrimental to plant safety. This option, however, would divert NRC resources from its primary mission—to protect the public health and safety—into potentially unending reviews of proposed state regulations. This option, therefore, would seem to be too unwieldy to implement.

61. In 1983, the NRC proposed to Congress legislation that would have required the NRC, in a proceeding for the issuance of a combined construction permit and operating license, to conclusively rely upon a state's certification of need for the facility and upon the state's consideration of the alternative sources of generating capacity. This proposal would have transferred the responsibility for carrying out pre-licensing reviews mandated by the National Environmental Policy Act to the states. *See Nuclear Licensing and Regulatory Reform: Hearings Before the Subcommittee on Nuclear Regulation of the Senate Committee on Environment and Public Works on S. 893, S. 894,* 98th Cong., 1st Sess. 25-26, 41-42 (1983).

Commissioner Ahearne further stated, in part:

> What I would propose is a restructuring of the licensing process which basically removes the NRC from the environmental aspects of the plant, giving those to States, regional agencies, or other Federal agencies to resolve. The NRC would retain jurisdiction over all health and safety issues . . . To enable non-Federal agencies to adequately address the siting issues, total Federal preemption would be removed for certain parts of the radiation hazard issue. States would have to accept the operating characteristic envelope given by the NRC, basically that the plant would meet EPA standards for normal operation. . .

Id. at 11.

Commissioner Ahearne also stated that "In my view, [the states] are the ones who ought to be deciding what kind of power they will have," *id.* at 25.

Commissioner Asselstine stated that "I support a provision giving the Commission the authority to rely on need for power and choice of generating means decisions by appropriate Federal, State, or regional authorities," *id.* at 14.

It appears that the NRC's 1983 proposal would have provided the states with authority substantially similar to the authority recommended in this paper.

62. During the consideration of the Clean Air Act Amendments of 1990, the Senate voted 61-36 to strike a provision in the bill reported by the Committee on Environment and Public Works that would have eliminated the states' authority under the Clean Air Act to regulate radionuclide emissions more stringently than the federal government. *See* 136 Cong. Rec. 2253-2276 (daily ed. March 7, 1990).

63. 42 U.S.C. at § 9631(d)(2)(C)(iii).

64. Energy Policy Act of 1992, § 801, *reprinted in* H.R. Rep. No. 102-1018, at 153.

65. 42 U.S.C. §§ 2021b-2021d (1988 & Supp. II 1990).

66. Energy Policy Act of 1992, § 2901, *reprinted in* H.R. Rep. No. 102-1018, at 362.

67. Six low-level radioactive waste compacts and four non-compact states have prohibited the use of shallow-land burial. The NRC states that "[t]his prohibition has not been an impediment to making continuing compatibility determinations in those States in the past." NRC, Evaluation of Agreement State Compatibility Issues, *attachment to* SECY-91-039, *supra* note 28, at 24.

5

The Role of the Public in the Licensing of Nuclear Power Plants

Eric Glitzenstein

At the same time that the Chairman of the Nuclear Regulatory Commission ("NRC"), Ivan Selin, has extolled the value of public participation in NRC decisionmaking, and professed deep concern for the future of such participation, the Commission has—along with Congress and the courts—erected enormous legal and regulatory barriers to effective public access to, and participation in, NRC proceedings. At a June 1992 press conference, Chairman Selin proclaimed that public "openness and credibility" have been his "highest priority other than continued safety" and, when specifically questioned by a somewhat startled New York Times reporter about this pronouncement, the Chairman did not backtrack but, rather, further hailed public involvement in NRC proceedings:

> [W]e are set up as a quasi-judicial organization and quasi-judicial organizations really only work well when all parties are strongly represented. *I think that overall there's no question that the safety of American plants is greater or the risk is lower than it would have been had [there] not been active intervenors along the way.*[1]

In fact, Chairman Selin even went so far as to decry the budgetary problems plaguing many environmental groups, opining that "I would hate to see them in these days when it's really tough to raise money for all kinds of causes to back off the nuclear industry questions and just take on the broader questions of global warming, et cetera."[2]

To the environmental community, Chairman Selin's avowed ardor for public involvement is certainly welcome and represents a pronounced shift in attitude from other recent Commission chiefs.

Regrettably, however, NRC's real-world actions with regard to public access and participation have not matched the Chairman's rhetoric. To the contrary, the Commission has taken a series of steps that virtually guarantee that the public will not have a significant role in NRC licensing proceedings or in the Commission's efforts to ensure the safety of operating nuclear facilities.

While Chairman Selin's explicit recognition that the public has a vital part to play in NRC proceedings is laudatory and long overdue, it is simply not enough for the NRC to make such declarations and bemoan the resource constraints of environmental organizations. As we detail below, there are, at present, enormous legal and practical barriers to effective public involvement in NRC proceedings. If these barriers are not removed or at least lowered—either through legislative action, the NRC's own initiatives, or a combination of both—the public will have little meaningful input into Commission decisionmaking in the future, irrespective of the financial wherewithal of public-interest groups or the best intentions of the Commission's chairman.

Another, related reality is that the NRC and nuclear industry cannot cheaply purchase public confidence in the safety of nuclear power plants. The price for such confidence—without which there will be no new generation of nuclear plants—is genuine public scrutiny of, and input into, NRC decisionmaking. Proceedings which merely offer a pretense of public involvement will accentuate, rather than assuage, public suspicion and skepticism concerning the risks of nuclear power. It is, therefore, in the enlightened self-interest of the nuclear industry itself to ensure that there are legitimate opportunities for affected members of the public to have their say—*within* institutional channels—on issues that may impinge on their health and safety.

At the same time, however, drastic changes are not needed to facilitate meaningful public involvement in NRC proceedings. To the contrary, extremely modest reforms in the way NRC conducts business can help ensure genuine public input—and the increased agency credibility that goes along with it—*without sacrificing any legitimate interests of the nuclear industry or the Commission.* By the same token, relatively minor adjustments in the Commission's statutory charter—*i.e.,* the Atomic Energy Act—can help make the public a valuable adjunct to NRC enforcement efforts, comparable to the role that public groups play in other environmental statutory schemes, such as the Clean Water Act and the Clean Air Act.

In this paper and the two related papers that follow, we will discuss in detail existing obstacles to public involvement in all aspects of NRC decisionmaking. This paper will focus on legal and administrative barriers to public input in initial NRC licensing proceedings. The next paper will address the lack of effective avenues available to the affected public to ensure that health, safety, and environmental standards are enforced against operating nuclear facilities. The third paper will discuss recently enacted NRC rules which severely restrict the public's input into NRC decisions to renew licenses for nuclear power plants.

Legal and Administrative Barriers to Effective Public Participation in NRC Licensing Proceedings

Historical Overview: The Role of The Public in NRC Decisions Authorizing the Construction and Operation of Commercial Nuclear Facilities.

When Congress enacted the Atomic Energy Act in 1954, a fundamental compromise was struck with the fledgling nuclear power industry. As explained by former NRC commissioner Peter Bradford:

> The current NRC adjudicatory hearing process was developed as part of a bargain from which the nuclear power industry gained a great deal in the late 1950's. *In return for accepting extensive federal hearings, the industry was exempted from any state or local regulation of radiological health and safety and received the limitations of liability that are set forth in the Price-Anderson Act.* Thus, citizens in any community in which a nuclear facility was to be located - a facility with a remote but not nonexistent chance of destroying the community - gave up local regulation of the facility and the additional financial and safety assurances that normal insurance industry operations would have brought . . . *In return they got a commitment to the full panoply of trial-type procedures as part of the federal licensing process.*[3]

Hence, when Congress established a two-step process for the construction and operation of nuclear power plants—under which a utility was first required to obtain a construction permit and then, following construction, an operating license—it expressly provided, in Section 189 of the Act, that members of the affected public would have a right to be heard at both stages of the process. In seemingly unequivocal terms, therefore, Congress dictated that:

> [i]n any proceeding . . . for the granting . . . of any license or construction permit . . . the Commission shall grant a hearing upon the request of any person whose interest may be affected by the proceeding, and shall admit any such person as a party to such proceeding. . . .[4]

Similarly, in Section 185 of the Act, Congress set forth the specific post-construction "findings" that the Commission would have to make before allowing a plant to operate, and as to which the affected public should have an opportunity to be heard.[5] Thus, Congress mandated that the Commission find *both* that "the facility authorized has been constructed and will operate in conformity with the application as amended" *and* that the facility will operate "in conformity with the provisions of this chapter and of the rules and regulations of the Commission. . . ."[6]

In enacting Sections 189 and 185, therefore, Congress rejected a system under which the NRC's post-construction review, and the public's right to a hearing, would be limited to whether the plant had been built in accordance with the terms of the construction permit. Instead, as the NRC's predecessor agency, the Atomic Energy Commission ("AEC"), advised the Supreme Court in the first contested case resolved under the Act, Congress concluded that the NRC's pre-operation review, and the public's right to a hearing, should encompass all safety-related issues arising since the construction permit was issued, such as new and previously-unconsidered developments bearing on the design, siting, and environmental consequences of the plant.[7]

Shortly after passage of the AEA, the AEC adopted regulations which "elaborate[d] upon and describe[d] in fuller detail the step-by-step licensing procedure contemplated" by Congress.[8] Under the regulations—which, with minor revisions, remained in effect until 1989—the AEC and NRC first issued a construction permit after holding a public hearing on such matters as "the proposed design of the facility," "[w]hether the applicant is technically [and] financially qualified," and whether "construction of the facility will be inimical to the . . . health and safety of the public."[9] Members of the affected public could move to intervene in the hearing and thus participate in the resolution of those issues.[10]

After construction, the Commission was required to hold hearings, at the request of any affected member of the public, on whether an operating license should be issued.[11] This hearing focused on whether the plant, as actually constructed, was sufficiently safe to operate, including such matters as whether "[c]onstruction of the facility" has been "completed in conformity with the [construction] permit," whether there is "reasonable assurance [that the plant can be operated] . . . without endangering the health and safety of the public," and "whether plans for emergency evacuation in the event of an accident are adequate."[12]

While the legal "machinery for public participation" existed under the AEA and implementing regulations, "powerful forces subvert[ed] its effectiveness" as a practical matter.[13] As the Union of Concerned Scientists concluded following a comprehensive review of NRC licensing proceedings in 1985, "not only a general, institutional momentum within the NRC, but also specific instances of direct intervention by the Commission itself, act[ed] to undermine public participation."[14]

In a statement before Congress, former Commissioner Bradford candidly summarized the reasons for the NRC's traditional antipathy to public involvement in its proceedings, in the course of explaining the Commission's refusal to allow public intervenors to be heard on the adequacy of additional regulatory requirements imposed following the Three Mile Island accident:

> The Commission is poorly informed as to the history, motivations and consequences of citizens' groups intervenors. It seems to be basing its decisions instead on some hypothetical concept of a vampire intervenor with whose imagined potential transgressions it is obsessed to the point of curtailing all interventions to avoid a few abuses.
>
> The citizens whose right or privileges of inquiry are at stake here are not some crew of anti-nuclear crazies unless the Commission succeeds in driving three-fourths of the nation in that category . . . They are people raised on the American notion that they have a legitimate right to inquire into events affecting the fundamental nature of their communities. . . .[15]

According to public groups and their attorneys who sought to participate in licensing proceedings, the Commission's blatant hostility to public intervenors tainted the entire licensing system.[16] Not surprisingly, therefore, the NRC's Special Inquiry Group—which the Commission established following the Three Mile Island accident to provide it with a non-industry perspective—concluded that, "insofar as the licensing process is supposed to provide a publicly accessible forum for the resolution of all safety issues relevant to the construction and operation of a nuclear plant, it is a sham."[17]

The Commission employed a variety of specific means to minimize effective public involvement in its licensing proceedings. For example, the NRC structured its licensing process so that intervenors were required to file their "contentions"—i.e., the specific safety and environmental issues they wished to raise in hearings—before environmental and safety analyses had been prepared by the NRC staff. Thus, intervenors had to present their contentions months before the staff's safety evaluation report ("SER") and draft environmental impact statement ("DEIS") were available.[18] While public intervenors could, following preparation of SERs and DEIS's, file motions to amend or supplement their contentions, or to reopen discovery based on the matters discussed in those documents, such discretionary motions were resolved by licensing boards which, with rare exceptions, regarded their prime mission as that of completing licensing proceedings as rapidly as possible.

Another procedure used by the NRC to limit legitimate public involvement was the exclusion of evidence that intervenors could rely on to argue that safety problems had not been adequately addressed.[19] For example, in a 1983 proceeding involving whether an operating license should be issued for the San Onofre facility, the Licensing Board prohibited intervenors from presenting evidence showing that hospitals around the plant were not sufficiently equipped to treat the public in the event of a major accident.[20] Likewise, in proceedings concerning restart of Three Mile Island in the early 1980s, the Union of Concerned Scientists was precluded by the Licensing Board from introducing critical evidence gathered by the NRC's own staff with regard to whether the safety equipment could function under extreme accident conditions such as high heat, pressure and radiation.[21] The Licensing Board sustained the staff's position that its own safety evaluation report bearing on these issues was "outside the scope of the hearing," although the Board subsequently was forced to acknowledge that, without this evidence, it had "no basis" for determining how the accident equipment would hold up under harsh conditions.[22]

Yet another method that was used by the Commission to restrict effective public involvement was the postponement of safety issues raised by public intervenors to the operating license phase of the process. Obviously, once a utility has invested billions of dollars in constructing a plant, the public largely loses its ability to influence whether, and under what conditions, that plant should be permitted to operate. The classic example of this is the Seabrook debacle, which involved the public's futile effort to convince the Commission to consider, at the earliest feasible time, whether the Seabrook plant would violate NRC rules relating to emergency planning and evacuation in the event of an accident.

Shortly after the Three Mile Island accident, the NRC issued regulations providing that "no operating license for a nuclear power reactor will be issued unless a finding is made by NRC that there is reasonable assurance that adequate protective measures can and will be taken in the event of a radiological emergency."[23] At the time these regulations were published, a construction permit had already been issued for the Seabrook plant but construction of one unit was only 25% complete, and construction had barely begun on the other unit.[24] Public intervenors petitioned the NRC to consider whether adequate emergency protection could be afforded to the public, consistent with the Commission's recently-promulgated regulations.[25]

The Licensing Board, however, refused to consider the emergency planning issue at an early phase of construction but, rather, concluded that the issue should be deferred until the plant was built and the utility was seeking an operating license.[26] When the public intervenors, including the state of Massachusetts, raised the emergency evacuation issue at the operating license stage, the Commission gave the argument short shrift, refusing to even assess whether the evacuation plan that had been adopted would actually provide for adequate protection of the public—in terms of minimizing the public's exposure to radiation—in the event of an accident.[27] And, ironically, even though the NRC itself had deferred the emergency evacuation issue until the operating license stage, the public intervenors were widely accused by the nuclear industry and NRC of unduly delaying operation of the Seabrook plant.

Despite the Commission's longstanding animosity to public participation and the variety of ways in which this attitude manifested itself, intervenors in licensing proceedings still managed to make major contributions to the safe operation of a number of facilities. The former chief of the Atomic Safety and Licensing Board, B. Paul Cotter, Jr., outlined the value of public participation in 1981:

> (1) Staff and applicant reports subject to public examination are performed with greater care; (2) preparation for public examination of issues frequently creates a new perspective and causes the parties to reexamine or rethink some or all of the questions presented; (3) the quality of staff judgments is improved by a hearing process which requires experts to state their views in writing and then permits oral examination in detail . . . and (4) Staff work benefits from two decades of hearings and Board decisions on the almost limitless number of technical judgments that must be made in any given licensing application.[28]

Thus, in spite of the enormous obstacles to effective public participation that have existed under current law, public involvement in adjudicatory hearings contributed to the following safety-related improvements in specific nuclear plants, among others:

- Design and training improvements at St. Lucie (in Florida) to cope with offsite power grid instabilities;
- Safer storage for replaced steam generators at Turkey Point (in Florida);
- Improvements in the steam generator system at Prairie Island (in Minnesota);
- Additional requirements for turbine blade inspections and overspeed detection at North Anna (in Virginia);

- Improvement and conformation of the plume exposure pathway Emergency Planning Zone at San Onofre (in California);
- Upgraded effluent-treatment systems at Palisades (in Michigan) and Dresden (in Illinois);
- A total revamping of the NRC's site-review process as a result of contentions raised during the Pilgrim 2 proceedings (in Massachusetts);
- Upgraded requirements at Beaver Valley (in Pennsylvania) for steam generator tube-leakage plugging.[29]

In the case of the St. Lucie plant in particular, the Atomic Safety and Licensing Appeal Board went out of its way to stress the crucial role played in the licensing process by public intervenors:

We regret the necessity of having to state that the record of this case does not instill confidence in us that the staff always acts with that degree of care which would demonstrate its commitment to the vigorous enforcement of [the National Environmental Policy Act's] commands regarding alternate site inquiries . . .

There was need here for careful probing of the staff's efforts, *and the intervenors helped initiate and conduct that probe . . . [T]he intervenors clearly assisted in the search for truth. The contribution they made should not pass unnoticed.*[29]

The case of the Grand Gulf 1 reactor, where no members of the affected public intervened in the initial licensing process, illustrates the adverse effects that the lack of public participation has on the public's health and safety. After the plant was granted an operating license, the NRC staff discovered that the conditions specified in the reactor's license contained over a thousand errors, operators were unqualified, training records were apparently falsified, and there were design defects in a number of safety systems.[31] Obviously, public intervenors may not have prevented all of these problems, but there can be little doubt that critical scrutiny by public groups would have helped the situation enormously.

The Recent Erection Of Legal and Administrative Barriers To Effective Public Participation In The Licensing Process.

The NRC's Repeated Efforts to "Streamline" The Nuclear Licensing Process. Even though the licensing process was, in practice, already heavily tilted against public intervenors, the NRC and nuclear industry consistently insisted—since the early 1970s—that fundamental legislative change was needed to further "streamline" licensing proceedings, and that the public's invocation of the hearing rights guaranteed by the AEA had inappropriately delayed the operation of a myriad of nuclear power plants. This rationale for licensing reform was advanced, even though the NRC's own commissioners, when asked in Congressional testimony, were hard-pressed to point to any specific examples of how public hearing rights had improperly delayed the operation of nuclear facilities. As former Commissioner Bradford testified before the Senate Subcommittee on Nuclear Regulation in 1983:

> [C]ontrary to a popularly held myth, the public hearings aspects of the licensing process has *never delayed a single nuclear power-plant's operation by a single week.* Indeed, one reads the many pages of industry, NRC and DOE testimony in vain for a single specific illustration of a licensing delay . . . that this legislation would cure.[32]

Even former NRC Chairman Nunzio Palladino—a staunch supporter of efforts to "streamline" the licensing system—flatly admitted to Senator George Mitchell in 1983 that the Commission had no information "reflecting [any] specific instances where the hearing process has delayed a nuclear power plant's operation . . . ."[33]

Since the time that those concessions were made by the NRC, nuclear industry advocates have repeatedly pointed to the Seabrook and Shoreham licensing proceedings as their sole examples of how public participation has unduly delayed the process. In reality, as discussed earlier,[34] the experiences with those plants prove precisely the contrary—public intervenors attempted to raise and resolve serious emergency planning issues at a relatively early stage but the NRC refused to let them.

In addition to the unproven assertion that public intervenors had caused inappropriate and excessive delays in power plant operation, the nuclear industry and NRC proffered an additional rationale for licensing "reform" with which public advocates generally agreed, namely, the desirability of ensuring that the Commission would consider at an early stage of the process—*i.e.*, before vast sums of money had been invested in the plant—all of the safety and environmental issues that lent themselves to early resolution. Such issues would include the general appropriateness of a site for a nuclear power plant— *e.g.*, whether emergency evacuation is feasible—and whether the prospective design for the plant has any inherent safety defects.

At the same time, the NRC consistently recognized that certain crucial safety issues could not, by definition, be definitively resolved prior to power plant construction, and thus the public should not be foreclosed from being heard—following construction and prior to power plant operation—on previously unconsidered safety-related developments taking place during the construction process. As Commissioner James Asselstine observed, there are a number of issues "which can only be adequately litigated at the pre-operation stage," including whether environmental conditions at the site have radically changed since the site was initially approved, whether other plants with the same design have experienced unforseen problems, and whether emergency evacuation plans are deficient because the assumptions underlying them—such as population patterns and transportation conditions—have proven erroneous over the years.[35]

Thus, for over fifteen years, the NRC's own proposed legislation for "streamlining" the licensing system by authorizing the Commission to issue combined construction permits and operating licenses prior to construction endorsed the principle that the public should have a right to be heard on significant, previously unconsidered safety issues prior to power plant operation. For example,

- In **1974**, H.R. 11957 would have authorized the Atomic Energy Commission to issue a combined license but would have preserved the public right to be heard, prior to operation, on "(1) a specifically identified question substantially affecting the public health and safety, or the common defense and security, or the protection of the environment [which] was *left unresolved in connection with the most recent licensing action in the proceeding;* or (2) as a result of a *significant advance or change in the technology occurring after the most recent licensing action in the proceeding.*"[36]
- In **1977, 1978,** and **1979,** the NRC pushed the Nuclear Siting and Licensing Act, which would have preserved the public's right to a pre-operation hearing on "(1) *significant new information or a significant new issue,* or (2) a violation of a permit or license *or rule, regulation or order issued by the Commission.*"[37]
- In **1983,** the Commission's bill (H.R. 2512), would have authorized the issuance of combined licenses, but would have preserved the public's opportunity for a pre-operation hearing on "*issues that were not and could not have been considered and decided in a prior proceeding before the Commission*"—i.e., instances where "*significant new information* has been discovered since the prior proceeding and that *as a result thereof it is likely that the facility will not comply with this Act, other provisions of Federal law, or the Commission's regulations.*"[38]
- In **1985** and **1986,** the NRC supported S. 836, which would have allowed for public hearings where an "issue *was not and could not have been raised and resolved in any proceeding* for the issuance, modification or amendment of a license," as well as where "a showing has been made that . . . there has been nonconformance with the [combined] license."[39]

- In **1987** and **1988**—the same time frame that it was proposing its own licensing reform rules - the NRC was advocating the Nuclear Power Plant Standardization and Licensing Act of 1987, which would have, yet again, provided that the public could have a hearing not only where there is "nonconformance with the license," but also where "*the issue was not and could not have been raised and resolved*" in prior proceedings—in other words, significant new information.

In sum, the Commission itself routinely recognized the reasonableness and advisability of preserving the public's opportunity to be heard on significant new issues that, by definition, could not have been resolved previously. Nevertheless, perceiving no overriding rationale for amending the Atomic Energy Act, Congress refrained from adopting even these relatively modest proposals for change.

Believing that it had waited long enough for the "overdue . . . enactment of licensing reform legislation," the NRC chose to take matters into its own hands.[40] Hence, the Commission issued two related sets of regulations: first, new "rules of practice" for all of its licensing proceedings and, second, new regulations narrowing the substantive issues that the affected public may raise at various stages of the licensing process. Either set of regulations, standing by itself, would have been a serious blow to the public's ability to participate in nuclear licensing proceedings. Taken together, as demonstrated below, they created nearly insurmountable barriers to effective public participation.

The NRC's Adoption of New Part 2 Rules Substantially Raising the Threshold for Admissibility of Safety Contentions. The first set of regulations substantially amended the Commissions' Rules of Practice for Domestic Licensing Proceedings—known as Part 2 rules—for the ostensible purpose of "improv[ing] the hearing process with due regard for the rights of parties."[41] Among other changes, these Part 2 amendments—which were proposed in July 1986 and published in final form in August 1989—limit opportunities for discovery against NRC staff,[42] require parties to obtain permission of the presiding officer in order to conduct cross-examination,[43] and eliminate the ability of public intervenors to file proposed findings of fact and conclusions of law on safety issues other than those placed in controversy by the public intervenors.[44]

In addition—and most damaging of all to the affected public—the new Part 2 rules make it far more difficult for prospective intervenors to raise and pursue safety and environmental issues at all stages of the licensing process.[45] Prior to the Part 2 amendments, a prospective intervenor was, at the outset of the licensing proceeding, required to identify the "contentions" that he or she wished to litigate, setting forth the "bases" for each such contention with "reasonable specificity."[46] The legitimate purposes of this notice requirement were:

> (1) [to] assure that the contention in question raises a matter appropriate for adjudication in a particular proceeding, (2) to establish a sufficient foundation for the contention to warrant further inquiry into the subject matter addressed by the assertion, and (3) to put the other parties sufficiently on notice so that they will know at least generally what they will have to defend against or oppose.[47]

Thus, in order to pursue a particular safety issue—*e.g.*, through discovery directed at the NRC staff or the utility applying for a license—intervenors were not required to detail all of the evidence that would eventually be offered in support of the contention. Nor was the Licensing Board permitted to examine the merits of the contention in ruling on its threshold admissibility.[48] Any party that timely filed at least one admissible contention could participate in the hearing on whether a license should be awarded.

In revising its Part 2 rules, however, the Commission substantially raised the threshold requirement for the admissibility of safety and environmental contentions by intervenors. Thus, the Commission required intervenors—at the very outset of the licensing proceeding, *i.e.*, *before* any discovery or other fact-finding could be pursued—to identify the "alleged facts or expert opinion[s] which support the contention," as well as the "references to those specific sources and documents . . . on which the petitioner will rely to establish those facts or expert opinion."[49] In addition, members of the public were required to prove, simply to have contentions admitted for further consideration, that a "genuine dispute exists with the applicant on an issue of law, fact, or policy"—thus, in effect, requiring intervenors to prove that they could survive a summary judgment motion before even having the opportunity to take appropriate discovery, peruse the staff's SER and EIS, and engage in other appropriate factual investigation.[50]

Moreover, at the same time that it significantly heightened the threshold requirement for the admissibility of contentions, the Commission refused to revise its longstanding rules with regard to the admissibility of "late-filed contentions." Under those rules, parties advancing "untimely" contentions are not automatically granted access to a hearing even if their contentions would otherwise pass muster under the NRC's admissibility criteria. Instead, they are admitted on the basis of a nebulous, five-factor balancing test which vests near-total discretion in the Licensing Board to decide whether to allow a "late-filed" contention to be filed.[51] *This test applies even in cases where contentions are filed late only because the information on which they are based was not available until after the filing deadline.* The NRC's long-time position has been that, although the first of the five factors—good cause for filing late—is by definition met in such circumstances, one or all of the other four factors may nevertheless serve as a basis for rejecting public intervention.[52]

It is readily apparent why the Commission's heightened threshold for the admissibility of contentions may, in conjunction with the staff's delay in producing its SER and EIS and the late-filed contention rule, have a devastating impact on the ability of members of the public to raise and pursue serious safety and environmental issues in future licensing proceedings. Under the more relaxed admissibility standard that previously existed, members of the public could at least seek to file "anticipatory" contentions and thereby preserve their rights to be heard with regard to a particular issue. In other words, they could file timely contentions raising potential safety issues—but which could not be supported through the license application itself or through other materials available at the initial stage of the proceeding—and then seek to bolster the contentions when the SER or EIS became available. Obviously, this strategy would not work for potential issues that could not be gleaned at all from the licensing application or other available materials, but it would at least provide intervenors with an opportunity to preserve their right to litigate issues that they suspected, for one reason or another, that the staff might address in the SER, EIS, or other pertinent investigatory materials.[53]

As the NRC conceded to the United States Court of Appeals for the D.C. Circuit, however, "many of these 'anticipatory' contentions would be eliminated by the new rule's specificity requirements."[54] Thus, even where the affected public envisions that the staff will address a particular issue in the SER or EIS—but the license application itself or other then-available materials are not sufficient to satisfy the Commission's heightened admissibility requirements— the public will effectively be foreclosed from filing timely contentions, and thus ensuring their right to be heard, on potentially grave safety and environmental matters. And, if and when members of the public seek to raise such issues following the filing deadline, they will run up against the Commission's "late-filed" test, under which the Licensing Board may reject the contention for a host of reasons, including such vague factors as the "extent to which the petitioner's participation will broaden the issues or delay the proceeding"—which, of course, will almost invariably be true to some degree whenever a public intervenor seeks to pursue a "late-filed" contention on a serious safety or environmental issue that is publicly addressed for the first time when the staff issues its SER or EIS.[55]

When the Part 2 amendments were challenged by the Union of Concerned Scientists, a conservative panel of the D.C. Circuit (consisting of Reagan appointee Laurence Silberman, and Bush appointees Raymond Randolph and Karen Henderson) recognized that the NRC rules "of course *could be* applied so as to prevent *all* parties from raising a material [safety or environmental] issue."[56] Nevertheless, the Court rejected UCS's contention that the amendments violate the public's right to a hearing under the Atomic Energy Act, ruling that "the Act itself nowhere describes the content of a hearing or prescribes the manner in which this 'hearing' is to be run."[57]

The D.C. Circuit further found that "much of what those reports [SERs and EIS's] bring to light will . . . not be new *issues* but new *evidence* on issues that were apparent at the time of application," and were not raised because intervenors could not satisfy—based on the evidence then available—the Commission's more stringent criteria for admissibility of contentions.[58] While recognizing that, "in practice," the "concepts of new issues and new evidence . . . can converge," the Court held that it was not a violation of the AEA for the NRC to exclude contentions based on new "evidence."[59] At the same time, the Court suggested that, if the NRC applied its rules so as to "prevent all parties from raising material issues which could not be raised prior to release" of the SER or EIS, that "might transgress" the public's right to a hearing under the AEA.[60] Since those "hypothetical applications" had not yet taken place, however, the Court rejected UCS's facial challenge to the regulations.[61]

Thus, although the Court determined that the new Part 2 rules are not violative of the AEA on their face, it did suggest that the rules could be improperly applied so as to prevent any members of the affected public from being heard on new safety "issues." In any case, the question of whether the rules, from a policy standpoint, adequately protect the affected public's right to be heard is obviously a far different matter from whether the rules can survive judicial scrutiny by judges who believe that the NRC "'should be accorded broad discretion in establishing and applying rules for . . . public participation.'"[62]

In the course of the NRC's consideration of the Part 2 amendments, former Commissioner James Asselstine proposed a simple solution to the obstacles created by the heightened admissibility threshold together with the late-filed contention rule. Thus, Commissioner

Asselstine suggested a revision of the "Commission's rules governing the consideration of late-filed contentions to require the admission of any late-filed contentions upon a showing of good cause due to the institutional unavailability of the information which establishes the factual bases for the contention."[63]

In other words, under Commissioner Asselstine's proposal—which was not addressed at all by the full Commission when the Part 2 rules were adopted—if a prospective intervenor failed to raise a significant safety or environmental issue through no fault of her own, but, rather, because the SER or EIS pinpointing the issue was not yet available, then the contention could not be excluded because of the other discretionary factors contained in the Commission's late-filed contention standard. Obviously, under this approach, the Commission would retain the discretion to determine whether "good cause" excusing the failure to file truly was present because of the "institutional unavailability of the information" supporting the contention.

It is difficult to imagine any legitimate objection to such a modest modification in the Commission's Rules of Procedure. Certainly, if the Commission finds that a public intervenor only had a sufficient factual basis for raising a particular safety or environmental issue following publication of the SER, EIS or other relevant materials, then it is fundamentally unfair to preclude that intervenor from being heard with regard to the issue. Simply stated, the affected public should not lose its right to be heard on potentially serious issues because of circumstances that are completely beyond its control, *i.e.,* the Commission staff's own schedule for disseminating its safety and environmental analyses.

The Commission's "Streamlining" of the Licensing Process And Its Drastic Curtailment of the Public's Right To Be Heard Before Nuclear Power Plants Are Permitted To Operate. The NRC's second, and equally lethal, blow to public involvement came in the form of a new Part 52, which was added to Commission regulations. In August 1988, the NRC proposed regulations that mirrored the legislative proposals that the Commission had failed to convince Congress to adopt over the previous two decades.[64] Under the proposed rules, the Commission could issue, prior to construction, a "combined license for a nuclear power facility," but—consistent with its prior legislative proposals—the proposed rule at least recognized the public's right to a hearing on issues that had not been resolved prior to construction. Thus, the proposed rule provided that "[b]efore the facility may operate, the holder of the combined license shall apply for authorization of operation under the combined license," and that the affected public could seek a hearing on the "application for authorization" on two distinct bases:

> (1) that there has been a nonconformance with the [combined] license, the licensee's written commitments, the Atomic Energy Act, or the Commission's regulations and orders, which has not been corrected and which could materially and adversely affect the safe operation of the facility; or

> (2) that significant new information shows that some modification to the site or the design is necessary to assure adequate protection of the public health and safety or the common defense and security.[65]

On April 18, 1989, the NRC issued final rules which, in a number of crucial respects, went even further in dismantling the two-step licensing and hearing system than either the Commission's proposed rules or its prior, unsuccessful legislative initiatives would have gone. Most important, the Commission severely limited the right of the affected public to be heard before a nuclear power plant is allowed to begin operating for the first time. As explained by the NRC's General Counsel, the final rule is even:

> more strict than the proposed rule was on what issues can be raised in a hearing after construction is complete. The final rule permits such a hearing only if the petitioner makes a *prima facie* showing that one or more of the acceptance criteria [in the combined license] have not been met. . . .[66]

Moreover, even as to this narrow range of issues, the Commission erected a series of additional obstacles to the public's ability to obtain a hearing prior to operation, which are even more onerous than the Part 2 requirements imposed on all intervenors at other stages of the licensing process. Thus, instead of merely requiring prospective intervenors to "set[] forth with reasonable specificity the facts and arguments which form the basis for the request" for a hearing,[67] the NRC instead required members of the public to (1) show "prima facie, that one or more of the acceptance criteria in the combined license have not been met," (2) demonstrate that "as a result" of the failure to meet an acceptance criterion "there is good cause to modify or prohibit operation," (3) support their prima facie showing with materials which "include[], or clearly reference[], official NRC documents, documents prepared by or for the combined license holder," or similar materials, and (4) convince the Commission that they have raised a "genuine issue of material fact," and that "settlement or other informal resolution of the issues is not possible."[68] And, even if all of these threshold conditions could be satisfied with respect to contentions bearing on compliance with the combined license, the final rule suggests that the NRC may nevertheless decline to hold hearings on any or all material issues pursuant to 5 U.S.C. § 554(a)(3), a provision of the Administrative Procedure Act (APA) which exempts from formal hearing procedures adjudicatory "decisions [that] rest solely on inspections, tests, or elections. . . ."[69]

With respect to all issues other than compliance with the combined license, the Commission simply abolished the public's right to a hearing outright. Thus, "under the final rule, contentions alleging inadequacies in a combined license *are not admissible in a post-construction hearing"*—i.e., even where members of the public can satisfy the stringent procedural and evidentiary hurdles delineated above.[70] In contrast to its proposal, therefore, the Commission's final rule affords the affected public no right to a pre-operation hearing on "significant new information show[ing] that some modification to the site or the design is necessary to assure adequate protection of the public health and safety or the common defense and security."[71] The Commission further provided that the only way in which such matters could be brought to its attention would be through petitions filed under 10 C.F.R. § 2.206—the Commission's catch-all provision for the filing of "request[s] to . . . *modify, suspend or revoke a license* . . . ."[72]

The NRC's final rule also made other fundamental changes in the licensing system, which "in effect make possible the banking of designs and sites" years before a utility even applies for a combined license or, indeed, before it even has any concrete intention of constructing a nuclear power plant.[73] Along with the virtual elimination of the public's right to be heard prior to power plant operation, these other changes will also have a devastating, insidious impact on public participation in the licensing process.

Hence, the NRC provided that "any person may seek a standard design certification for an essentially complete nuclear power plant design," and that the entitlement to such certifications will be resolved in a generic rulemaking proceeding.[74] Under the provision, the Commission may certify designs for up to fifteen years and renew them for another fifteen years.[75]

Once a design has been "certified" by the Commission, any utility—including one with no prior involvement in the design certification proceeding—may "reference" that design in its application for a combined license.[76] In determining whether to issue to an applicant a combined license that references a certified design, the Commission will not allow intervenors to challenge or modify the basic design—because it was "certified" in a generic rulemaking proceeding that will have taken place up to thirty years earlier—but, rather, will restrict its review only to "those portions of the design which are site-specific" and were not resolved in the prior rulemaking proceeding.[77] On the other hand, the "applicant or licensee who references a standard design certification *may request an exemption* from one or more of the elements of the design certification."[78] In other words, in a licensing proceeding, the utility may seek to water down the certified design but intervenors may not seek to strengthen it or challenge it.

The other major change adopted by the NRC's rule allows the Commission to approve a site for a nuclear plant years before and "separate from the filing of an application for a construction permit or combined license for such a facility."[79] As the Commission has explained, "[w]hat design certification is to the early resolution of design issues, the early site permit is to the early resolution of site-related issues."[80] Under the rule, any utility may apply for a permit which would be valid for up to twenty years and could be renewed for another twenty years.[81] The permit would determine the general appropriateness of the site for a nuclear power plant, including the "environmental effects of construction and operation of . . . reactors[] which have characteristics that fall within the postulated site parameters."[82] In addition, the permit may be employed by a utility to obtain approval for emergency preparedness plans that must be triggered in the event of an accident.[83]

Any utility applying for a combined license may "reference" a previously granted early site permit.[84] If the utility does so, then the Commission will not consider in the licensing proceeding the general suitability of the site for a nuclear facility but, rather, will only decide whether the "design of the facility falls within the parameters specified in the early site permit. . . ."[85] In addition, intervenors in a licensing proceeding may not challenge or seek to strengthen emergency evacuation plans or any other matter previously "approved in connection with the issuance of the [early site] permit" issued years or decades earlier.[86] But, once again, the Commission's rule only works one way—the applicant who "references" an early site permit is free to seek a "variance from one or more elements of the permit," including any previously approved evacuation plan.[87]

Environmental organizations challenged several aspects of the Commission's revamped licensing process in the D.C. Circuit, on the grounds that they were contrary to the plain language of Sections 185 and 189 of the Atomic Energy Act and will completely deprive the affected public of a right to be heard on significant safety and environmental issues prior to operation of nuclear power plants. A panel of the Court of Appeals (consisting of Judges Patricia Wald, Clarence Thomas, and David Sentelle) unanimously held that the

Commission's rule illegally deprived the affected public of the right to be heard on significant new safety-related issues before nuclear power plants are permitted to operate.[88] The panel reasoned that the regulations:

> expressly provide[] a hearing opportunity regarding the plant's conformity with its license, but not regarding the plant's (and license's) conformity *with the Act* . . . Although many issues of a plant's eventual conformity with the Act could be heard at the combined-license hearing, some issues cannot - by definition - be heard at that time. During the lengthy construction process, new and safety-significant information about plant design, siting, or operation may arise. These intervening developments may in turn raise new issues about the conformity of the plant with the Act and thus about the propriety of authorization. *These developments might involve significant new experiences with the plant design or operation, significant new information about site seismology or meteorology, or significant changes in local population density or infrastructure.*[89]

The panel further found that the "availability of § 2.206 petitions" was an inadequate substitute for the right to a hearing under the Act, since such "petitions are treated as enforcement actions and may be decided by the Commission without briefing or a hearing."[90] Moreover, the NRC has convinced courts in other contexts to "treat[] § 2.206 petitions as enforcement actions [that are] presumptively unreviewable" under the Supreme Court's landmark decision in *Heckler v. Chaney*, 470 U.S. 821 (1985).[91] The panel concluded that, "[a]s these facts indicate, § 2.206 petitions are insufficient to satisfy the hearing opportunity requirements" of the AEA.[92]

By a 6 to 4 vote, however, this ruling was reversed by the full Court of Appeals. In an opinion written by Judge Sentelle—who switched his panel vote without providing any direct explanation for the change—and joined by five other Reagan and Bush-appointed judges, the Court of Appeals largely read the public's right to a hearing out of the AEA entirely. Thus, the Court asserted that, because the Atomic Energy Act "provides no unambiguous instruction as to *how* the 'hearing' is to be held," the Commission has nearly unfettered discretion to determine what issues should be heard at which stage of the licensing process.[93] Thus, in a ruling that has sweeping and dire implications for the public's hearing rights at *every* stage of licensing, the Court held that the Commission could rely on prior administrative determinations that a plant is safe as a basis for eliminating public hearing rights, *even with regard to entirely new safety issues that the Commission itself determines are significant and were not, and could not have been, raised in the prior administrative proceedings.*[94]

The *en banc* majority sought to soften the obviously harsh effect of its ruling by expressly holding that, "[a]fter additional consideration . . . we think that Commission action on § 2.206 petitions authorized by Part 52 is judicially reviewable."[95] In reaching this conclusion—which was based, in large measure, on the Commission's own about-face on the issue—the Court attempted to distinguish 2.206 petitions filed in the context of Commission decisions allowing plants to operate for the first time from those seeking "enforcement" action:

> True, the Commission also uses § 2.206 as a vehicle for entertaining requests for enforcement action where, of course, the petitions do fall within the unreviewability presumption of *Heckler v. Chaney*. Nonetheless, the choice to use the § 2.206 form cannot determine the reviewability question. Rather, we must look to the purpose to which the petition is put. Part 52 employs § 2.206 not as a means for requesting enforcement, but as an integral part of the licensing process itself.[96]

The Court thus glossed over the fundamental fact that, under Part 52 as constructed by the NRC itself, there is no qualitative legal difference between 2.206 petitions seeking modifications of previously issued combined licenses before power plants are permitted to begin operation and those which seek "enforcement" action against operating plants. In both instances, members of the public are asking the Commission to take action against a utility that has already been granted a license and to consider, based on new safety-related developments, to alter the terms and conditions under which the licensee will be allowed to operate its nuclear plant. In light of the lack of substance to the Court's newly discovered distinction between different kinds of 2.206 petitions, it is not surprising that the Court did not expound on the precise *standard* that a reviewing court would use to consider the Commission's denial of 2.206 petitions in the "licensing" context, other than to say that:

> Thus, even if potential new factual information might undermine the reasonableness of the Commission's reliance on its prior determinations, and even if the Commission reads §§ 52.103(b)(1)(ii) and (2)(ii) to deny arbitrarily a meritorious petition raising such information, a court may properly intervene to adjudicate the question.[97]

Finally, the majority found it unnecessary to rule on another rationale for Part 52 that was offered by the NRC for the first time in the *en banc* proceeding, and which carries ominous implications for the public's right to be heard in any and all future licensing proceedings. Thus, the Commission attempted to argue that section 2.206 is "not merely a mechanism to reopen closed hearings and require new findings, *but is also a hearing" itself* within the meaning of section 189 of the AEA.[98] Under this interpretation of section 189, the affected public receives a "hearing" whenever it sends a letter to the Commission raising a particular safety issue and receives a response back. If the Commission adheres to this interpretation in the future, it could theoretically eliminate formal hearings at *every* stage of the licensing process—including, for example, the combined license phase—and instead restrict the affected public to letterwriting as the sole mechanism for involvement in decisions about whether and where nuclear power plants will be built.

In a vehement dissent, Judge Wald—who had written the vacated panel decision—along with Chief Judge Mikva and Judge Edwards,[99] accused the majority of "misstat[ing] the petitioners' and the panel's position as one requiring a new hearing on request for any and all material safety issues, whether or not those issues were raised and resolved at the earlier hearing or at a prior rulemaking, and whether or not any material new information on these issues has surfaced since the first hearing."[100] As Judge Wald explained, the narrow though vital issue in the case—which the majority completely sidestepped— was whether members of the public should have a right to be heard, at the pre-operation stage, *once the NRC has determined that significant new information raises a previously unconsidered safety or environmental issue which goes beyond the acceptance criteria in the combined license.*[101] Thus,

> [i]n the final analysis . . . the majority and the NRC ask us to accept without more their assumption that in the present state of the art of nuclear design and plant siting, a finding that a design and a site are safe and secure at one point in time is invulnerable to later challenge on the basis of any new information, be it Chernobyl, Three Mile Island-type accidents, earthquakes, floods or changes in the cooperative stance of local communities who must implement evacuation plans in case of nuclear accidents. *I do not see how any newspaper reader in today's world can swallow that elephantine assumption.*[102]

The dissent further spelled out how the NRC's rule, when viewed in light of the Commission's commitment to developing "evolutionary" and "advanced" power plant designs that have never previously been employed, would work in such a fashion as to completely eliminate directly affected communities from the licensing process.[103] To hammer this point home, the dissent relied on the "following paradox raised during the congressional hearings," the fundamental validity of which has never been denied by the Commission or the nuclear industry:

> In December 1991, an engineering company requests a "standard design certification for an essentially complete nuclear plant design" which has never previously been tried and which no utility has expressed an intention or even an interest in using as the basis for a power plant at a particular site. The NRC "certifies" the design in a generic rulemaking proceeding;
>
> In 2001, a utility decides to construct a plant near Reno, Nevada. In its application for a combined license, the utility "references" the design that was "certified" by the Commission in December 1991; this is the first time that any utility has proposed to construct a power plant at a specific site with this design;
>
> Members of the public who are concerned about the construction of a nuclear plant in their community intervene in the licensing process and request a hearing on a number of issues, including the safety of the basic design of the proposed plant. They are told by the NRC, however, that it made a final decision on the design of the plant in a rulemaking proceeding over a decade ago. Obviously, none of the residents or the community participated in or had any reason to participate in the rulemaking proceeding which took place eleven years earlier and had no relationship to Nevada or any other specific location;
>
> In 2002, therefore, the NRC issues a combined license without ever allowing the residents of Reno to have a hearing on the safety of the basic design of the plant—a design, it should be emphasized, that is "evolutionary" and has never previously been tested in any commercial nuclear reactor;
>
> In 2006, five years into construction of the Reno plant, new scientific studies are published which raise serious, previously-unconsidered safety issues regarding the design of the plant. But when the residents of Reno request a hearing on these issues, prior to operation of the plant, they are told that they have no right to a hearing because they cannot demonstrate that the plant has not been built in accordance with the combined license;
>
> Consequently, the plant goes into operation in the absence of input by members of the affected public on the safety of the plant's underlying design in light of the most recent scientific data available.[104]

Finally, Judge Wald took issue with the majority's conclusion that the ability to file 2.206 petitions raising new issues may serve as a substitute for the right to a hearing under section 189. As characterized by Judge Wald, the 2.206 procedure "is not a hearing, nor has the majority treated it as such."[105] Judge Wald further pointed out that the standards for judicial review of 2.206 petitions are "murky" at best and, moreover, "if a hearing is denied by the Commission there will, of course, be no record for us to review."[106] Judge Wald concluded that "a discretionary petition combined with a possibility for judicial review without a record or any 'law to apply' is not an adequate substitute" for the affected public's right to be heard before nuclear power plants are permitted to operate.[107]

Congress's Codification of the NRC's Authority to Drastically Curtail Public Participation in the Nuclear Licensing Process. At essentially the same time that the D.C. Circuit was considering the legality of the NRC's Part 52 rules, the Commission was in the process of convincing Congress to adopt changes in the licensing process which overlap to a considerable degree those changes adopted by the NRC through rulemaking. To understand the extent to which the legislation as enacted permits—but does not *require*—the Commission to curtail public participation in the licensing process, it is necessary to review in some detail the complex evolution of the amendments to the AEA.

On the Senate side, the nuclear licensing "reforms" had their genesis in S. 340, a comprehensive energy package crafted by Senators Malcolm Wallop, a Republican from Wyoming, and Bennett Johnston, a Democrat from Louisiana, who is Chairman of the Senate Energy Committee. Title XIII of S. 340 as originally introduced would have stripped the public of a right to a pre-operational hearing unless "(i) a showing is made that a substantial dispute of material fact exists that has not been previously considered by the Commission and that cannot be resolved with sufficient accuracy except at a hearing; *and* (ii) a showing is made that there has been nonconformance with the combined license that has not been corrected and that could materially and adversely affect the safe operation of the facility."[108]

To underscore the narrow nature of the hearing contemplated by its drafters, the provision further provided that "any hearing held under this section after the granting of a combined license to construct and operate a facility *shall be limited to issues of nonconformance with the combined license*," i.e., a hearing "under this section" would not encompass significant new safety and environmental developments falling outside the four corners of the combined license.[109] The bill did not expressly address how the Commission should deal with such issues if raised through section 2.206 petitions, but Senators Johnston and Wallop made it clear that the drafters intended to preserve the Commission's discretion, as embodied in its Part 52 rules, to deal with such petitions as it saw fit:

Title XIII clarifies the Nuclear Regulatory Commission's authority to implement its licensing reform rule (10 CFR part 52) . . . Last November, the U.S. Court of Appeals for the District of Columbia Circuit upheld most of the rule but struck down the all-important provision restricting the post-construction hearing to conformance questions. *Title XIII amends existing law to make it clear that the NRC has the authority the court denied it.* The NRC has asked the court to rehear the case. *If the court agrees and reverses itself, title XIII will prove unnecessary.*[110]

Shortly after S. 340 was introduced, six members of the Senate Committee on Environment and Public Works wrote to Senator Johnston, indicating that that Committee properly had jurisdiction over various sections of the comprehensive energy bill and asking that Senator Johnston consent to the referral of those sections for consideration by the Environment Committee.[111] The Senate Environment Committee specifically requested referral of the nuclear licensing provisions on the grounds that "[t]he entirety of Title XIII, Nuclear Reactor Licensing, is within the sole jurisdiction of the Committee on Environment and Public Works," and "Nuclear reactor licensing has always been considered within this Committee's jurisdiction over the non-military environmental regulation of nuclear energy."[112]

Senator Johnston did not consent to this or any other referral. To the contrary, the Senate Energy Committee, at the urging of Senators Johnston and Wallop, rapidly proceeded to the markup of S. 340 in April 1991. At the markup, Senator Wallop proposed a substitute for Title XIII, which would have largely tracked nuclear licensing "reforms" contained in the Administration's own proposed comprehensive energy legislation.[113] With relatively minor revisions, this substitute was approved by the Senate Energy Committee and embodied in the comprehensive energy bill as reported out of that Committee.[114]

As reported out of the Senate Energy Committee, the Wallop substitute would have gone even further than the original Johnston-Wallop proposal and Part 52 in eviscerating public hearing rights, and would even have gone so far as to restrict the Commission's own discretion in determining when such hearings should be held and the effect that they should have on plant operation. For example, the substitute would have provided that, even where the NRC decides to hold a hearing on an apparent failure of the nuclear plant to comply with its own combined license, the Commission would have been required to allow the plant to operate unless the NRC made a separate, preliminary finding that the petitioners were "likely to succeed on the merits" of their contention, *i.e.*, they had more than a 50% probability of success.[115] Thus, if the Commission believed that the petitioners "only" had a 30% chance of prevailing on a claim that there was a serious flaw in power plant construction, then the

Commission would seemingly have been obligated, under the plain language of the Wallop substitute, to nevertheless allow the plant to operate while the public hearing proceeded.

The Wallop substitute would also have restricted the Commission's discretion in conducting any pre-operation hearings that are held, by providing that "[d]iscovery and cross-examination of witnesses *shall not be permitted*, unless the presiding official determines that discovery, cross-examination, or other procedure is *necessary* to the resolution of a substantial dispute of material fact."[116] Hence, the bill would have established an extremely heavy presumption against two of the most important truth-determining methods in our adjudicatory arsenal: cross examination of adverse witnesses and discovery into facts which may be known only to opposing parties.

The Wallop substitute would also have directly undermined the public's ability to obtain judicial review of *any* final decision made by the NRC to allow a plant to operate, even with regard to whether the plant had been constructed as previously contemplated. Rather than compel the Commission to make an explicit "finding" that the acceptance criteria have been satisfied—as does Part 52—the Wallop substitute merely provided that the NRC "shall *satisfy* itself that the prescribed acceptance criteria are met." The bill did not provide that the Commission's determination that it was "satisfied" would be subject to judicial review and, indeed, it would appear that such a statement would be entirely subjective and discretionary and thus, under the Administrative Procedure Act, "committed to agency discretion by law."[117]

Following the Senate Energy Committee's approval of the Wallop substitute, the Senate Subcommittee on Nuclear Regulation—a Subcommittee of the Senate Environment Committee which has jurisdiction over nuclear licensing matters—held two hearings on the Wallop substitute and other alternative nuclear licensing reforms. Two House subcommittees—the House Interior and Insular Affairs' Subcommittee on Energy and the Environment and the Energy and Commerce Committee's Subcommittee on Energy and Power—also held hearings on licensing reform. At these hearings, the NRC did not embrace the Wallop substitute that had been approved by the Senate Energy Committee, precisely because of the concern that it went beyond the codification of Part 52 and could be construed as restricting the Commission's own discretion to hold public hearings on significant safety issues before nuclear plants are permitted to operate. For example, Chairman Selin testified before the House Interior and Insular Affairs Subcommittee that "We believe we have enough authority currently" to implement one-step licensing and that:

[w]e do not welcome legislation that would restrict our authority. We'd prefer not to have a statute that says when certain conditions exist, you can't hold a hearing even when you want to. . . .[118]

Indeed, the NRC's "support" for the Wallop substitute was so half-hearted that the Department of Energy's Assistant Secretary for Nuclear Energy, William Young, wrote to the White House and Secretary of Energy James Watkins that "some action should be taken to obtain an unequivocal written or public statement from Chairman Selin supporting the specific provisions" of the Wallop substitute.[119] Assistant Secretary Young further complained that:

Chairman Selin is undermining the important provisions of S. 1220 even as he professes support for that legislation. I have no doubt that his concessions to Democratic legislators will be used against S. 1220 on the Senate floor and will make it more difficult for us to gain the support of Senator Graham (Chairman, Senate Subcommittee on Nuclear Reactor Regulation) for S. 1220.[120]

In fact, Senator Graham—a moderate Democrat and general supporter of nuclear energy—did become a staunch opponent of the nuclear licensing reforms embodied in the Wallop substitute. After holding two hearings at which DOE and NRC officials, nuclear industry representatives, and environmentalists testified, Senator Graham concluded that the Wallop substitute would gravely and unnecessarily undermine public participation in the licensing process. Accordingly, when the comprehensive energy bill was considered by the full Senate in February 1992, Senator Graham, along with Senator Wyche Fowler of Georgia, proposed an alternative to the Wallop substitute.[121]

Under the proposed Graham-Fowler amendment, the affected public would have been entitled to pre-operation hearings by showing either (1) that there was "nonconformance" with the combined license and such "nonconformance could materially and adversely affect the safe operation of the facility," or (2) that there was a serious issue falling outside the combined license which "was not and could not have been raised and resolved in any proceeding for the issuance, modification or amendment of a license, permit, or approval for that facility, its site, or design. . . ."[122] The Graham-Fowler amendment would also have provided that any hearing held on such an issue would be "on the record"—*i.e.*, it would involve formal hearing procedures such as cross-examination and discovery—"if the issue consists of a substantial dispute of fact, necessary for the Commission's decision, that cannot be resolved with sufficient accuracy except at a hearing. . . ."[123]

In response to the Graham-Fowler amendment and suggestions—including by the NRC itself—that their nuclear licensing "reforms" would go so far as to curtail the Commission's own discretion to hold hearings on safety issues, Senators Johnston and Wallop offered a new, more moderate amendment as a substitute for the provision that had been passed by the Senate Energy Committee. This amendment—which was eventually enacted into law as part of the comprehensive energy legislation passed by Congress—eliminated some of the harshest features of the Wallop substitute, and essentially vests in the NRC sweeping discretion to determine what sorts of pre-operation hearings are appropriate and what effect they will have on plant operation.

Thus, under the amended provision, the NRC is no longer required to find that an intervenor is "likely" to prevail on an issue in order to prevent "interim operation" while a hearing is being conducted on whether the plant has been constructed in accordance with the acceptance criteria in its combined license. Rather, the Commission has broad discretion to:

> determine, after considering petitioners' prima facie showing and any answers thereto, whether during a period of interim operation, there will be reasonable assurance of adequate protection of the public health and safety. If the Commission determines that there is such reasonable assurance, it shall allow operation during an interim period under the combined license.[124]

Similarly, the amendment no longer contains the presumption that formal hearing procedures should not be allowed in any pre-operation hearing and instead provides simply that the "Commission, in its discretion, shall determine appropriate hearing procedures, whether formal or informal adjudicatory, for any hearing under this subparagraph, and shall state its reasons therefore."[125]

The amendment is silent with respect to the Commission's consideration of significant new issues falling outside the combined license, and thus preserves the Commission's discretion to deal with such issues through the modified 2.206 procedure outlined in Part 52. However, in response to criticisms that the Wallop substitute could have been construed as foreclosing judicial review of the Commission's determination to allow plants to operate, the substitute amendment expressly provides that "any final order allowing or prohibiting a facility to begin operating under a combined construction and operating license . . . shall be subject to judicial review."[126] Consistent with the D.C. Circuit's *en banc* ruling in *NIRS*, this assurance of judicial review will presumably encompass the Commission's treatment of significant new issues raised by members of the public in pre-operation 2.206 petitions.

On the House side, the comprehensive energy bill reported out of the House Committee on Energy and Commerce did not contain any nuclear licensing provisions. The House Interior Committee, however, approved a bill which would have sought to safeguard public hearing rights by, in effect, codifying the panel ruling in the *NIRS* case.[127] This bill, which was authored by the Chairman of the House Subcommittee on Energy and the Environment, Rep. Peter Kostmeyer, would have provided for a public hearing "on the record" with respect to "significant new information previously unconsidered by the Commission" relating to whether the "facility will operate in conformity with this Act and the rules and regulations of the Commission" or "whether such facility has been constructed and will operate in conformity with any permit or license that has been issued for such facility by the Commission."[128] On the floor of the House, this proposal was rejected in favor of one that was identical to the provision that had been approved by the Senate, *i.e.*, the scaled-down version of the Johnston-Wallop proposal which essentially preserves the NRC's discretion to structure the timing and scope of its pre-operation proceeding in the manner that it deems appropriate.

The NRC Can and Should Revise Its Part 52 Regulations To Ensure that The Affected Public Has A Sufficient Opportunity To Participate in Nuclear Licensing Proceedings. As the foregoing recitation of the legislative history makes clear, however, the NRC has extremely broad latitude under the provision ultimately enacted by Congress to determine how its pre-operation proceeding should be run. Specifically, the NRC retains ample statutory authority to ensure that the public has an opportunity to be heard, before a nuclear power plant goes into operation, on any significant new safety or environmental issues that were not and could not have been considered at an earlier proceeding and which do not fall within the four corners of the combined license.

Moreover, as both Chairmen of the Congressional committees with NRC oversight responsibilities have already concluded, there are obvious and compelling policy reasons why the affected public should have the right to be heard on new safety and environmental issues *which the NRC itself deems to be significant and which were not and could not have previously been considered by the Commission in any prior proceeding.* Neither the NRC nor the nuclear industry has offered a persuasive reason as to why the NRC should not ensure that public has a right to be heard with respect to issues that the Commission itself agrees are of overriding safety or environmental significance and were not the subject of any prior NRC hearing.

Ensuring that the public has a right to be heard with respect to significant new issues would require only a modest amendment to the NRC's Part 52 rules. The NRC could continue to require the affected public to raise such issues through the modified 2.206 procedure set forth in section 52.103. In addition, however, the Commission should specify the standard that it will use in ruling on petitions pinpointing new safety or environmental issues that fall outside the combined license. One such standard is that which the NRC *itself* proposed when it issued its Part 52 rules in draft form, namely, that the affected public will be entitled to a hearing when it can point to "significant new information show[ing] that some modification to the site or the design is necessary to assure adequate protection of public health and safety or the common defense and security."[129] Consistent with its final Part 52 rules and the amendment enacted by Congress, the Commission could further specify that a hearing will only be granted under these circumstances when a member of the public is able to come forward with *"prima facie"* evidence raising a "significant" new safety or environmental issue not previously considered by the Commission.[130]

In addition, also paralleling the language contained in the AEA amendment adopted by Congress, the Commission should further modify its rules to provide that if, in response to a petition raising a significant new safety issue, it determines that there will not be "reasonable assurance of adequate protection of the public health and safety," it will not allow "interim" operation while the significant new issue is being resolved. This would replace the completely open-ended and essentially meaningless proviso in the current rules that the Commission will simply "consider the [modified 2.206] petition and determine whether any immediate action is required."[131]

The Commission's adoption of such modest changes in its rules would not only provide the affected public with some assurance that important, previously unconsidered safety issues will be resolved before nuclear plants are allowed to operate, but it will also greatly assist the Commission, the nuclear industry, and the courts by providing for a modicum of administrative and judicial certainty and consistency. Part 52 as currently written provides absolutely no sense as to how the Commission will rule on modified 2.206 petitions purportedly raising significant new developments. Moreover, as Judge Wald pointed out in her dissent in *NIRS v. NRC*, the Commission's

Solicitor was utterly unable at oral argument to articulate the standards that either the Commission itself or a reviewing court would employ in considering pre-operation 2.206 petitions.[132] Accordingly, it would be of enormous value to the affected public, reviewing courts, and the NRC itself if the Commission were to provide additional direction as to the standards that should be applied in assessing pre-operation 2.206 petitions.

The NRC should also explicitly provide in its licensing rules that, whenever it holds a pre-operation hearing—regarding either compliance with the combined license or significant new issues falling outside the license—it will use formal adjudicatory procedures, such as discovery and cross-examination, to resolve all *genuine issues of material fact*. As noted above, the licensing amendments enacted by Congress plainly preserve the NRC's discretion to "determine appropriate hearing procedures, whether informal or formal adjudicatory" for pre-operation hearings.[133]

While it has sought to raise the threshold for the admissibility of safety contentions at all stages of the licensing process, the NRC has never suggested that safety or environmental issues *which the Commission itself concludes involve genuine issues of material fact* should be resolved through other than formal adjudicatory proceedings. Indeed, if the NRC still intends to resolve genuine factual disputes through formal hearings at the combined license stage, as appears to be the case, then any such disputes which arise for the first time at the pre-operation stage—*i.e.*, those pertaining to compliance with the combined license or significant new issues—should, logically, also be resolved in formal hearings.

Of course, adoption of this proposal would not preclude the Commission from resolving non-factual disputes through more informal procedures, or from relying on its stringent summary disposition procedures to weed out the many factual issues that are not truly "material" or "genuine." But there is simply no plausible policy rationale for the Commission to refrain from using traditional, tested adjudicatory methods to resolve those relatively few but potentially crucial factual disputes that do not lend themselves to summary disposition.

The Energy Policy Act of 1992 required the NRC to issue regulations, by October 24, 1993, implementing the nuclear licensing reforms adopted by Congress. This rulemaking exercise could have afforded a perfect opportunity for the NRC to consider the proposals outlined above, as well as other suggestions for improving public participation in NRC proceedings. Ironically, however, in an action that embodies all too well the Commission's disdain for public participation, *the NRC decided to issue final rules without first bothering to solicit prior public comment on how it should carry out its responsibilities under the Energy Policy Act.* In a novel approach to administrative law, the Commission has told members of the public that they may comment on the rules only *after* the rules have been published in final form.

The new regulations make no effort to flesh out the standards and criteria that the Commission will employ in ruling on 2.206 petitions raising significant new issues. Thus, the Commission has decided to continue to force the public, the courts, and the industry to guess as to how these petitions will be resolved in the first instance by the Commission and, ultimately, by reviewing courts.

Likewise, the Commission has refused to even take a stab at defining whether, and under what circumstances, it will provide for formal hearings in post-construction proceedings. Rather, it has simply parroted the language of the statute, providing that it "shall determine appropriate hearing procedures, whether informal or formal adjudicatory, for any hearing under paragraph (a) of this section. . . ."[134] This means, of course, that the Commission may opt to use "formal adjudicatory" hearings in one set of licensing proceedings and "informal" hearings in other proceedings—even if, for example, both proceedings involve disputed issues of material fact, or even if both involve essentially identical issues. Aside from the impact on the affected public, it is impossible to see how this haphazard approach accomplishes certainty and predictability in the licensing process— one of the supposed rationales for the new licensing system.

In addition, as Commissioner Curtiss pointed out, the revised rules will undermine the "overall objective" of standardization—and undercut the public's right to be heard—in yet another way that has not previously been addressed. Thus, the NRC has now provided that the "Commission may issue and make immediately effective any amendment to a combined construction and operating license upon a determination by the Commission that the amendment involves no significant hazards consideration, notwithstanding the pendency before the Commission of a request for a hearing from any person."[135] This extension of the so-called "Sholly amendment" to combined licenses means that licensees may now seek to water down—before ever operating a nuclear facilty and without any prior public hearing—the safety conditions embedded in a previously issued combined license.[136]

Prior to enactment of the Energy Policy Act, the Commission's rules provided that amendments to combined licenses would not be permitted in the absence of a prior hearing, if such a hearing was requested by a member of the affected public. Moreover, the Commission expressly took the position before Congress that this approach was correct as a matter of policy. For example, in response to a question from the Senate Subcommittee on Nuclear Regulation, the Commission explained that it

> did not extend Sholly as a policy choice because it wanted to discourage late changes to combined licenses or to the [conditions] therein. Such changes could have the effect of undermining standardization or changing the scope of imminent or pending hearings on conformance issues.[137]

In the Energy Policy Act, Congress permitted, but did not require, the NRC to extend the Sholly rationale to combined licenses.[138] More specifically, there is absolutely nothing in the Act which requires the Commission to approve amendments weakening the safety conditions in combined licenses, in the absence of public hearings, *before the plant has even begun to operate*. And there is certainly nothing in the Act that requires the Commission to adopt this fundamental change in policy without first considering public comment.[139]

It is difficult to comprehend how Chairman Selin can talk in glowing terms about the value of public participation while, at the very same time, the Commission is *refusing to even consider public comment before it adopts basic policy changes that have the effect of further eviscerating public participation in nuclear licensing proceedings*. The gap between the Commission's real-world actions and its lofty rhetoric has grown to Grand Canyon-like proportions.

In sum, if the Commission wishes to be taken seriously in its professed commitment to public participation, it should propose for public comment licensing rules that address the reforms discussed previously and, most importantly, which establish standards and criteria for the pre-operation consideration of significant new safety issues. In addition, the Commission should reverse its effort to extend the Sholly amendment to combined licenses, at least in the pre-operation stage.

Notes

1. Transcript of June 22, 1992 Press Conference at 15 (emphasis added).

2. *Id.*

3. *Nuclear Licensing and Regulatory Reform: Hearings Before Senate Subcommittee on Nuclear Regulation of the Senate Committee on Environment and Public Works*, 98th Cong., 1st Sess. 562 (1983) (Testimony of Peter Bradford); *see generally English v. General Electric Company*, 110 S. Ct. 2270 (1990); *Pacific Gas & Electric Co. v. State Energy Resources Conservation and Development Comm'n*, 461 U.S. 190 (1983).

4. 42 U.S.C. § 2239(a)(1) (prior to 1992 amendment) (emphasis added).

5. 42 U.S.C. § 2235 (prior to 1992 amendment).

6. *Id.*

7. *See, e.g.*, Brief for Petitioners United States and Atomic Energy Commission, at 47-48, *Power Reactor Development Co. v. Electrical Union*, 367 U.S. 396 (1961).

8. *Power Reactor*, 367 U.S. at 407; *see* 21 Fed. Reg. 355 (Jan. 19, 1956).

9. 10 C.F.R. § 2.104(b)(1)(ii).

10. *Id.* at § 2.714(a).

11. *See* 42 U.S.C. § 2239(a)(1).

12. 10 C.F.R. § 2.104(c); 10 C.F.R. § 50.47.

13. Union of Concerned Scientists, *Safety Second: A Critical Evaluation of the NRC's First Decade* 66 (February 1985) ("Safety Second").

14. *Id.* at 66.

15. Statement of Peter Bradford, *House Subcommittee on Environment, Energy and Natural Resources, House Committee on Government Operations* (July 2, 1980).

16. *See* Safety Second at 66.

17. Regovin *et al., Three Mile Island: A Report to the Commissioners and to the Public* 139 (Jan. 1980).

18. *See* Safety Second at 66-67.

19. *Id.* at 68.

20. *See Southern California Edison Company, et al.* (San Onofre Nuclear Generating Station, Units 2 and 3), LBP-83-47, 18 NRC 228.

21. *See* Safety Second at 68.

22. *Metropolitan Edison Co.* (Three Mile Island Station, Unit No. 1) LBP-81-59, 14 NRC 1211, 1401-04 (1981).

23. 10 C.F.R. § 50.47(a)(1).

24. *See* Safety Second at 69.

25. *Id.*

26. *See Director's Decision*, 14 NRC 279, 286 (1981).

27. *See Commonwealth of Massachusetts v. NRC*, 924 F.2d 311, 326 (D.C. Cir. 1991).

28. B. Paul Cotter Jr., *Memorandum to Commissioner Ahearne on the NRC Hearing Process*, p. 8 (May 1, 1981).

29. Safety Second at 78-79.

30. *In the Matter of Florida Power & Light Company* (St. Lucie Nuclear Power Plant Unit No. 2), at 5, 6, 7 (ALAB-435) (Oct. 7, 1977) (emphasis added).

31. Safety Second at 82.

32. *NRC Licensing Reform: Hearing Before the House Subcommittee on Energy Conservation and Power of the Committee on Energy and Commerce*, 98th Cong., 1st Sess. 120 (1983) (emphasis added).

33. *Id.* at 121.

34. *See* text accompanying notes 25-28 *supra.*

35. *Nuclear Facility Standardization Act of 1986: Hearing Before the Senate Committee on Energy and Natural Resources*, 99th Cong., 2d Sess. 395 (1986).

36. *See Nuclear Powerplant Siting and Licensing: Hearings Before the Joint Committee on Atomic Energy*, 93d Cong., 2d Sess. 580 (1974) (emphasis added).

37. *See Hearings Before the House Subcommittee on Energy and the Environment*, 95th Cong., 2d Sess. 18 (1978).

38. *See NRC Licensing Reform: Hearing Before the House Subcommittee on Energy Conservation and Power of the Committee on Energy and Commerce*, 98th Cong., 1st Sess. 43 (1983).

39. *Nuclear Regulatory Reform: Hearings Before the Senate Subcommittee on Nuclear Regulation of the Committee on Environment and Public Works*, 99th Cong., 1st Sess. 216-17 (1985).

40. *Nuclear Licensing Reform: Hearing Before the House Subcommittee on Energy and Commerce*, 100th Cong., 2d Sess. 7 (1988) (Testimony of NRC General Counsel William Parler).

41. 54 Fed. Reg. 33168 (Aug. 11, 1989).

42. *Id.* at 33173; 10 C.F.R. § 2.720.

43. 54 Fed. Reg. at 33173; 10 C.F.R. § 2.743.

44. 54 Fed. Reg. at 33177; 10 C.F.R. §§ 2.754, 2.762.

45. *See* 54 Fed. Reg. 33168 (August 11, 1989); 51 Fed. Reg. 24365 (July 3, 1986).

46. 10 C.F.R. § 2.714(b) (1989).

47. *Vermont Yankee Nuclear Power Corp.* (Vermont Yankee Nuclear Power Station), LBP-90-6, 31 NRC 85, 91-92 (1990) (footnote omitted), *quoting Philadelphia Electric Co.* (Peach Bottom Atomic Power Station, units 2 and 3), ALAB-216, 8 AEC 13, 20 (1974).

48. *See Mississippi Power & Light Co.* (Grand Gulf Nuclear Station, Units 1 and 2), ALAB-130, 6 AEC 423, 426 (1973); *Houston Lighting and Power Co.* (Allens Creek Nuclear Generating Station, Unit 1), ALAB-590, 11 NRC 542, 548 (1980).

49. 10 C.F.R. § 2.714(b)(ii); 51 Fed. Reg. at 24371.

50. 10 C.F.R. § 2.714(b)(iii); *compare* Rule 56(f) of the Fed. R. Civ. P. (allowing a party opposing a summary judgment motion to "seek a continuance to permit affidavits to be obtained or depositions to be taken or discovery to be had").

51. 10 C.F.R. § 2.714(a). The five factors are (i) "good cause, if any for failure to file on time," (ii) the "availability of other means whereby the petitioner's interest will be protected," (iii) the "extent to which the petitioner's participation may reasonably be expected to assist in developing a sound record," (iv) the "extent to which the petitioner's interest will be represented by existing parties"; and (v) the "extent to which the petitioner's participation will broaden the issues or delay the proceeding."

52. *See Duke Power Co.* (Catawba Nuclear Station, Units 1 and 2), CLI-83-19, 17 NRC 1041, 1045-50 (1983).

53. *See Union of Concerned Scientists v. U.S. Nuclear Regulatory Commission*, 920 F.2d 50, 53 (D.C. Cir. 1990).

54. *Id., citing* NRC Brief at 27-28.

55. *See* 10 C.F.R. § 2.714(a).

56. 920 F.2d at 56.

57. *Id.* at 53.

58. *Id.* at 55 (emphasis added).

59. *Id.*

60. *Id.* at 56, 57.
61. *Id.* at 56.
62. *Id.* at 54, *quoting Cities of Statesville v. Atomic Energy Comm'n*, 441 F.2d 962, 977 (D.C. Cir. 1969) (*en banc*).
63. 51 Fed. Reg. at 24,370 (July 3, 1986).
64. 53 Fed. Reg. 32069 (August 23, 1988).
65. 53 Fed. Reg. 32076 (emphasis added).
66. SECY-89-036 at 4 (emphasis added); *see* 10 C.F.R. § 52.103(b)(1)(i).
67. 53 Fed. Reg. 32077.
68. 10 C.F.R. § 52.103(b).
69. 5 U.S.C. § 554(a)(3); 10 C.F.R. § 52.103(b)(2)(i).
70. 54 Fed. Reg. 15381 (J.A. 10) (emphasis added).
71. 53 Fed. Reg. 32077.
72. *Id.* (emphasis added); *see* 10 C.F.R. § 52.103.
73. 54 Fed. Reg. 15378.
74. 10 C.F.R. §§ 52.45, 52.54.
75. *Id.* at §§ 52.55(a), 52.59(a), 52.61.
76. *Id.* at § 52.73.
77. *Id.* at §§ 52.63(a)(4), 52.79(b).
78. 54 Fed. Reg. 15392 § 52.63(b)(1) (emphasis added).
79. *Id.* at § 52.11.
80. 54 Fed. Reg. 15378.
81. 10 C.F.R. §§ 52.27(a), 52.33.
82. *Id.* at § 52.18.
83. *Id.* at § 52.17(b).
84. *Id.* at § 52.73.
85. *Id.* at § 52.79(a)(1)).
86. *Id.* at § 52.79(d)(1)).
87. *Id.* at § 52.39(b).
88. *Nuclear Information and Resource Service v. NRC*, 918 F.2d 189 (D.C. Cir. 1990) ("*NIRS*").
89. 918 F.2d at 195 (first emphasis in original; second emphasis added).
90. *Id.*
91. *NIRS*, 918 F.2d at 196, *citing Safe Energy Coalition v. NRC*, 866 F.2d 1473 (D.C. Cir. 1989) and *Massachusetts v. NRC*, 878 F.2d 1516 (1st Cir. 1989).
92. 918 F.2d at 196.
93. *Nuclear Information and Resource Service v. NRC*, 969 F.2d 1169, 1173 (D.C. Cir. 1992) (*en banc*).
94. *Id.* at 1179-80.
95. *Id.*
96. *Id.* at 1178.
97. *Id.*
98. *Id.* at 1180.
99. Judge Buckley did not join in Judge Wald's opinion but separately dissented on the grounds that "neither the potential post-construction hearing on conformity with the license's acceptance criteria nor the section 2.206 proceeding

is a permissible substitute for the pre-operational hearing mandated by section 189(a)(1) when read in conjunction with section 185. . . ." *NIRS*, 969 F.2d at 1187.

100. *Id.* at 1183.

101. *Id.*

102. *Id.*

103. *Id.* at 1184.

104. *Id., quoting National Energy Security Act of 1991: Hearing Before the Senate Committee on Energy and Natural Resources*, 102d Cong., 1st Sess. 123 (1991) (Testimony of Eric R. Glitzenstein, on behalf of the Union of Concerned Scientists and Nuclear Information and Resource Service).

105. *NIRS*, 969 F.2d at 1187.

106. *Id.*

107. *Id.*

108. 137 Cong. Rec. § 1542 (Feb. 5, 1991).

109. *Id.*

110. *Id.* at S. 1512 (Statement of Senators Johnston and Wallop) (emphasis added).

111. February 20, 1991 Letter from Senators John H. Chafee, Dave Durenburger, Quentin Burdick, Max Baucus, Frank Lautenberg, and Bob Graham, to Senator Bennett Johnston.

112. *Id.* at 3.

113. The Administration proposal in the Senate was initially introduced as S. 570.

114. When the bill was reported out of the Senate Energy Committee it was renumbered S. 1220.

115. Wallop Substitute to Title XIII of S. 340, as approved by the Senate Energy Committee on April 24, 1991.

116. *Id.*

117. 5 U.S.C. § 701.

118. *Inside NRC* at 1 (July 29, 1991).

119. *Memorandum for Admiral Watkins from William H. Young, Subject: Chairman Selin and Nuclear Licensing Reform Legislation*, at 4 (Sept. 24, 1991).

120. *Id.*

121. When the energy bill came before the full Senate in February 1992 it was designated S. 2166 and was called the National Energy Security Act. The marked up version of S. 340 did not come before the Senate for a vote in 1991 because of a successful filibuster on a provision, which was subsequently removed, that would have opened up the Arctic National Wildlife Refuge to oil drilling.

122. Proposed Graham-Fowler Amendment to Nuclear Reactor Licensing Provisions of S. 2166, § 9101(b) (February 4, 1992).

123. *Id.*

124. S. 2166 at § 9103.

125. *Id.*

126. *Id.* at § 9106.

127. H.R. 3629 (introduced on Oct. 24, 1991).

128. *Id.* at § 102.

129. 53 Fed. Reg. 32077 (August 23, 1988).

130. 10 C.F.R. § 52.103(b)(1)(i).

131. 10 C.F.R. § 52.103(b)(2)(ii).

132. *NIRS*, 969 F.2d at 1187 ("The standards for such review, however, are murky as extended colloquies at oral argument demonstrated all too well.").

133. 42 U.S.C. § 2239(B)(iv).

134. Revised section 52.103(d).

135. Revised Rule at § 52.97(b)(2)(ii).

136. The "Sholly amendment," 42 U.S.C. § 2239(A)(2), was enacted in 1983 in response to a D.C. Circuit ruling that the NRC was "required under section 189(a) to hold a hearing on a license amendment whenever interested parties request one." *Sholly v. United States Nuclear Regulatory Commission*, 651 F.2d 780, 791 (D.C. Cir. 1980). Believing that this ruling excessively restricted the Commission's administrative flexibility with respect to *operating* nuclear plants, Congress provided that the NRC could dispense with a hearing before making an amendment "immediately effective" upon a "determination by the Commission that such amendment involves no significant hazards consideration." 42 U.S.C. § 2239(a)(2)(A).

137. *Hearing Before the Senate Subcommittee on Nuclear Regulation of the Committee on Environment and Public Works, on the Nuclear Licensing Provision in S. 1220, the National Energy Security Act of 1991*, 102d Cong., 2d Sess. 56 (1992).

138. *See* Energy Policy Act at § 2804.

139. *See* Commissioner Curtiss' Separate Views on Final Rules Amending 10 CFR Part 52 to Incorporate Provisions of the Energy Policy Act.

6

Public Participation in the Oversight of Nuclear Power Plant Operations

Eric Glitzenstein

Over the past two decades, new and serious safety and environmental concerns have arisen with regard to the operation of already-licensed nuclear plants. Examples of such problems which have received considerable publicity in recent years have involved reactor operators found sleeping on the job at Peach Bottom; the occurrence of an earthquake more severe than the plant was designed for at Perry; improper maintenance practices resulting in non-functioning safety equipment at Three Mile Island, Davis-Besse and many other plants; inadequate operator training at Seabrook and elsewhere; the tardy discovery of serious design flaws at Diablo Canyon and Grand Gulf; and the clear inadequacy of emergency evacuation plans at Pilgrim, Seabrook, Davis-Besse, and Indian Point.[1] In light of these and many other serious incidents, it is apparent that persons who live in the vicinity of nuclear plants should have some reasonably reliable means by which they can raise, and participate in the resolution of, genuine safety and environmental issues pertaining to such plants. Unfortunately, it is equally clear that such means simply do not exist.

This paper discusses the enormous hurdles to effective public participation in the oversight of ongoing operation of commercial nuclear facilities. In the course of this discussion, I will propose administrative and legislative reforms that would greatly facilitate public involvement and confidence in the process without adding significant administrative costs or otherwise impairing NRC's oversight functions.

Legal and Administrative Barriers to Effective Public Participation in NRC's Ongoing Oversight of Operating Nuclear Facilities

The Section 2.206 Process Is Not An Adequate Vehicle Through Which The Affected Public Can Ensure Consideration of Serious Safety and Environmental Issues That Arise With Regard To Operating Nuclear Facilities.

The NRC's Own Treatment of 2.206 Petitions. Section 2.206 provides that any member of the public may "file a request to institute a proceeding ... to modify, suspend, or revoke a license, or for such other actions as may be proper."[2] The NRC's Executive Director for Operations is required to refer the request to the "Director of the NRC Office with responsibility for the subject matter of the request for appropriate action . . . ."[3] In turn, "[w]ithin a reasonable time," the sole responsibility of the relevant NRC director is to "either institute the requested proceeding or . . . advise the person in writing that no proceeding will be instituted in whole or in part, with respect to the request, and the reasons for the decision . . . ."[4] The NRC regulations also provide that the Commission may on its own initiative review for an "abuse of discretion" a Director's decision not to institute a proceeding in response to a 2.206 petition, but the Commission will not entertain requests by the public that it undertake such review.[5]

Measured by virtually any objective standard, the 2.206 device has not been an effective vehicle for public participation in the ongoing oversight of nuclear plants. Thus, in the seven years between the beginning of 1985 and the end of 1991, the NRC failed to hold a *single* hearing in response to 93 2.206 petitions raising safety and environmental issues.[6] In only one such instance, involving the Yankee Rowe reactor, the Commission itself took jurisdiction over a 2.206 petition and reviewed the staff's determination.

Moreover, in recent testimony before the House Subcommittee on Energy and Power, the Commission conceded that it has allowed a total of *two* hearings in response to 321 requests under section 2.206 it has received in the more than ten years since the procedural device was established.[7] Both of the hearings were completed in the early 1980s[8] and *thus it has been approximately a decade since the Commission has held a formal public hearing in response to a 2.206 petition.* At the risk of understatement, it is difficult to view a procedural device that has, in its lifetime, resulted in public hearings less than 1% of the time as being an effective vehicle for public participation.

In view of these bleak statistics, the NRC has apparently

recognized that it cannot plausibly defend its section 2.206 process as an effective vehicle for public participation, *i.e.*, as a process which affords the affected public an opportunity to participate in the consideration and resolution of serious safety problems. Rather, in response to Congressional and public criticism, the Commission has simply—and not very subtly—defined the purpose of its 2.206 process in an artificially narrow fashion so that it can be characterized as "successful." Thus, while admitting that it almost never actually "institutes a proceeding" against a licensee in response to a 2.206 petition—which is what the public is expressly authorized to seek under the NRC's regulations—the Commission nevertheless maintains that such petitions have been "granted in whole or in part" approximately "ten percent" of the time because, in such instances, "some regulatory action was taken" in response to the petition.[9]

The Commission's explanation of its dismal record with regard to 2.206 petitions is, to borrow a phrase from economists and pollsters, a classic case of "torturing the data until it confesses." It is also a transparent way of avoiding serious Congressional and public scrutiny of the 2.206 process, since the Commission's after-the-fact assertion that it took some "regulatory action" *because* of a 2.206 petition is—in the absence of a public hearing record—virtually impossible to prove or disprove. Moreover, the fact that the Commission's most self-serving defense of its 2.206 process still means that the public's requests are "denied" in at least 9 out of ten cases itself speaks volumes about the inadequacies in the process, at least from the vantage point of the affected public.

In any event, even if, as the NRC maintains, it has indeed taken some substantive action in response to a small fraction of 2.206 petitions, that hardly transforms the 2.206 process into an effective vehicle for *public participation* in NRC consideration and resolution of serious safety and environmental problems. To the contrary, the Commission's record in those uncommon cases where it has deemed it necessary to take *some* action in response to a safety or environmental issue raised by a 2.206 petition merely confirms the extraordinary lengths to which the NRC will go to *avoid* involvement by the affected public in the resolution of such issues, even where they are raised by the public.

In an April 1992 report, the Union of Concerned Scientists carefully scrutinized the manner in which the Commission had treated and responded to a number of 2.206 petitions. One of UCS's central findings was that, in the unusual case in which the NRC did not simply deny a 2.206 petition outright, it instead followed a "usual pattern of delaying ruling on the petitioners' requests for hearings until it could make a plausible claim that its own, private interactions with the licensee had yielded sufficient improvement to justify denial of the hearing requests."[10] In none of the cases studied by UCS—with the single exception of Yankee Rowe—did the NRC involve, to any significant degree, the person or organization which filed the 2.206 petition in the actual process of determining what sort of regulatory response was needed.[11] Rather, the Commission staff simply informed the petitioner that the NRC had taken whatever steps it deemed to be appropriate and thus it considered the matter closed.[12]

And, even with regard to the Yankee Rowe petition—which has been invoked by Chairman Selin as the shining example of the Commission's new-found commitment to public participation[13]—the Commission nevertheless imposed stringent constraints on the petitioner's ability to participate effectively in the Commission's resolution of the issues. In that case, the NRC partially granted a June 1991 emergency enforcement petition brought by UCS and the New England Coalition on Nuclear Pollution against the Yankee Rowe nuclear power plant in western Massachusetts.[14] Relying on the NRC staff's own studies, the petitioners maintained that the plant's pressure vessel, which holds the radioactive core and its primary cooling water, had become seriously embrittled and thus posed an unacceptable threat of rupturing and causing a core meltdown.[15] The Commission ordered an investigation of mitigating measures, and set a schedule for the submission of a plan to resolve uncertainties regarding the degree of pressure vessel embrittlement.

With respect to participation by the 2.206 petitioners, the Commission ordered the NRC staff and licensee to serve their correspondence on the petitioners and to open their meetings to the public.[16] In addition, UCS and NECNP were permitted to address the Commissioners in public briefings on the issue.[17] On the other hand, the Commission refused to hold a formal adjudicatory proceeding, and thus UCS and NECNP never had the opportunity to pursue discovery or cross-examination in an effort to buttress their argument that the plant should be shut immediately, because the safety risks were even graver than the staff had previously acknowledged.[18]

The Refusal By Courts To Review The Commission's Treatment of 2.206 Petitions. It is not surprising that the NRC acts as if has unfettered freedom to treat 2.206 petitions and petitioners in any manner it chooses. In reality, there are virtually no legal restraints on the Commission's consideration of 2.206 petitions for a simple reason— the courts have almost uniformly viewed 2.206 petitions as tantamount to enforcement requests and thus presumptively unreviewable under the Supreme Court's landmark ruling in *Heckler v. Chaney*.[19]

In *Chaney*, the Supreme Court held that an agency decision *not* to take sought-after enforcement action is presumptively unreviewable because, in the Court's view, there is no "meaningful standard against which to judge the agency's exercise of discretion."[20] Thus, the Court ruled that, ordinarily, an agency's refusal to take enforcement action falls within the second exception to judicial review set forth in section 701(a) of the Administrative Procedure Act, *i.e.*, the government's refusal constitutes "agency action [that] is committed to agency discretion by law."[21]

The Supreme Court further held, however, that the presumption against review could be rebutted through a showing that the agency's organic statute restricted its discretion not to take enforcement action under particular circumstances.[22] In addition, the Court declined to address the question of whether a properly adopted agency rule "might under certain circumstances provide courts with adequate guidelines for informed judicial review of decisions not to enforce," although the Court did suggest that an agency "policy statement," standing by itself, would not sufficiently circumscribe the agency's discretion to afford a basis for judicial review.[23] Finally, the Court noted that it was not presented with a "situation where . . . the agency has 'consciously and expressly adopted a general policy' [of non-enforcement] that is so extreme as to amount to an abdication of its statutory responsibilities."[24] The Court intimated, but did not expressly state, that the presumption against reviewability would be inapplicable in such circumstances.[25]

In applying *Chaney* to NRC denials of 2.206 petitions, the courts of appeals have generally regarded such denials as "enforcement" decisions to which the presumption of unreviewability applies.[26] In addition, the courts have not found that this presumption was rebutted by anything in the AEA itself or, for that matter, any self-imposed restraint adopted by the NRC through rulemaking or otherwise.[27] For example, in *MassPIRG*, the First Circuit declined to review NRC's denial of a 2.206 petition, which had asked the Commission to issue an order to show cause why the Pilgrim Nuclear Power Station—which had been shut down "voluntarily" by its owner as a result of management and emergency planning problems identified by NRC— should not remain closed or have its operating license suspended until it took specific steps to protect the public health and safety.[28]

In reaching its conclusion, the First Circuit observed that "[t]he general enforcement provisions of the Act [itself] are all framed in permissive language," and thus "[t]hey provide no guidance as to how the agency should exercise its discretion."[29] Consequently, the Court focused its analysis on whether the agency's own pronouncements established adequate criteria for judicial review of the denial of the 2.206 petition. However, while the Court agreed with the D.C. Circuit that "agency regulations *may* provide a standard to apply within the meaning of *Chaney*," the Court did not believe that the Commission had, in fact, imposed sufficient "restraints upon agency discretion so as to establish a standard for judicial review. . . ."[30]

Thus, the Court held that "NRC regulations concerning section 2.206 petitions are entirely permissive" because they simply provide that the relevant Commission Director "shall *either* institute a proceeding as requested or deny the request in writing," and they provide no criteria by which the Director is to make this determination.[31] Next, the Court ruled that the NRC's policy statements regarding enforcement did not, in light of *Chaney*, provide a sufficient basis for judicial review, particularly since the particular statements issued by the NRC simply "underline the vast discretion of the agency. . . ."[32]

Finally, the First Circuit analyzed a Commission ruling which, at first blush, would appear to establish a sufficient standard for judicial review of denials of 2.206 petitions. Thus, in *Consolidated Edison Co. of New York*[33] the NRC discussed the standard of review that the *Commission* should apply in considering a Director's denial of a section 2.206 petition, and stated that "[t]he Director correctly understood that a show cause order *would have been required* had he reached the conclusion that *substantial health or safety issues had been raised*."[34] In *Lorion*, the Supreme Court cited this ruling for the proposition that "[t]he Commission *interprets § 2.206 as requiring issuance of an order to show cause when a citizen petition raises 'substantial health or safety issues.'*"[35]

Nevertheless, the First Circuit refused to read this seemingly nondiscretionary standard as establishing a basis for judicial review, primarily because "[n]o indication exists that the agency *intended* to bind itself to a standard of 'substantial health or safety issues.'"[36] Ironically, the Court relied heavily on the fact that the *Consolidated Edison* ruling had been issued *before Chaney* was handed down, when the Commission and other "agencies *presumed* that courts could review all nonenforcement decisions. . . ."[37] Since the *Consolidated Edison* language had not been crafted with the *Chaney* presumption in mind, the First Circuit reasoned, it did "not reflect an intent to restrict [the Commission's enforcement discretion" and thus "[w]e do not find that this informal agency ruling creates a meaningful standard under *Chaney*."[38]

In *Safe Energy Coalition*, the D.C. Circuit applied and extended the First Circuit's analysis in the context of considering the NRC's denial of a 2.206 petition requesting that the NRC take certain actions with respect to an "employee concern" program established by Detroit Edison Company, the licensee of the Fermi-2 nuclear power plant.[39] In essence, the petitioners asked the NRC, first, to determine that its regulations requiring all nuclear plants to establish "quality assurance program[s]" applied to the "employee concern" program instituted by Detroit Edison and, second, that NRC should take specific enforcement action against the utility on the grounds that its program did not satisfy the strictures of the NRC regulations.

The D.C. Circuit ruled that the NRC's denial of both of these requests was unreviewable. Thus, the Court rejected the petitioners' effort to sidestep *Chaney* entirely by arguing that they were not seeking "enforcement action" but, rather, were simply asking a "legal determination" on the application of the NRC's regulations to a particular set of facts.[40] In addition, the Court held that, even if the NRC's refusal to apply its regulations here was conceded to be "part of a general policy applicable to all voluntary 'employee concern' programs," that would *still* not be enough to render its decision presumptively reviewable because it would not rise to the level of a "'general policy' of non-enforcement" or a total "abdication" of statutory responsibilities within the meaning of *Chaney*.[41]

In addition, mirroring the analysis of the First Circuit, the D.C. Circuit held that the petitioners could not rebut the presumption against judicial review by pointing to anything in the AEA itself or in NRC pronouncements that would establish sufficient standards for assessing the Commission's response to 2.206 petitions. Following Circuit precedent, the Court held that "[i]t is clear that 'regulations promulgated by an administrative agency in carrying out its statutory mandate can provide standards for judicial review of agency action,'"[42] yet the Court could discern no such standards in section 2.206 itself or the substantive, quality assurance regulations relied on by the petitioners.[43]

Finally, the D.C. Circuit suggested, as did the First Circuit, that the Commission's 1975 ruling in *Consolidated Edison*—which states that a show cause order is "required" when the NRC finds that there is a "substantial health or safety issue"—*would* afford an adequate standard for judicial review *if* there were sufficient indicia that the NRC intended itself to be bound by this standard. Agreeing with the First Circuit that the NRC did not intend itself to be so bound, the D.C. Circuit also did "not view that NRC opinion as a binding norm for the treatment of section 2.206 petitions."[44]

In light of these and other decisions construing and applying *Chaney* in the 2.206 context, there is no realistic prospect—in the absence of statutory or regulatory reform—that courts will, in the future, entertain judicial review of garden-variety 2.206 petitions, *i.e.*, those which seek license amendments or other enforcement action against particular features of operating nuclear plants. It is still conceivable that a future court might exercise review of a 2.206 petition if the NRC were to adopt a general policy of non-enforcement of a statutory or regulatory requirement, but it is unlikely that the Commission would be foolish enough to announce that it had such a policy and, lacking such an announcement, it is extremely improbable that a petitioner could persuade a reviewing court that such a policy existed. For all practical purposes, therefore, the Commission is free to deny most 2.206 petitions for any reason or no reason, with no concern that it will be called to account for its actions under even the most deferential standard of judicial review.

As noted in the preceding paper, to sustain the NRC's Part 52 rules, the *en banc* D.C. Circuit did expressly hold that there would be judicial review of denials of 2.206 petitions raising significant new safety issues in the pre-operation context.[45] In reaching this result, the Court went to great pains to distinguish section 2.206 petitions that make "requests for enforcement action"—and which "do fall within the unreviewability presumption of *Heckler v. Chaney*"—from Part 52's "employ[ment] [of] § 2.206 not as a means for requesting enforcement, but as an integral part of the licensing process itself."[46] According to the Court, therefore, because *pre-operation* 2.206 petitions will be considered in the context of "licensing" decisions, courts will have an adequate basis for "interven[ing] to adjudicate the question" of whether the Commission has "den[ied] arbitrarily a meritorious petition raising [new factual] information. . . ."[47]

On close inspection, however, the Court's "distinction" between different kinds of 2.206 petitions—particularly in terms of the appropriateness or availability of judicial review—completely disintegrates. Relegation of the public to the 2.206 process for the consideration of significant new information in the pre-operation context was more than merely a "convenient . . . procedural cross-reference," as the NRC characterized it for the Court.[48] Rather, it embodied the NRC's view that, since combined licenses would henceforth be issued prior to construction, the only recourse available to the public for challenging "inadequacies" in that license,[49] would be through the same basic route that had been established for challenging "inadequacies" in *any* operating license, *i.e.*, the 2.206 process.[50]

In short, there is no coherent conceptual reason why a 2.206 petition in the pre-operation context should be any more or less subject to judicial review than 2.206 petitions filed at any other time, particularly petitions that simply ask the Commission to institute proceedings to modify, amend, or rescind a license. In both contexts, the petitioner is asking for essentially the same thing, namely, a determination by the Commission as to whether the terms of a previously-issued license should be reassessed in order to bring the licensee into compliance with the Atomic Energy Act or the NRC's implementing regulations. Simply put, if a reviewing court can discern and apply sufficient standards to determine whether the Commission has "arbitrarily" denied a meritorious petition in the pre-operation context—as the *en banc* D.C. Circuit has held—it makes absolutely no sense for the Commission to continue to maintain, as it has in the past, that courts cannot make precisely the same judgment with regard to petitions filed after plants have begun operating.

Moreover, the Commission cannot legitimately argue that, if its denials of all 2.206 petitions were subject to judicial review under an extremely deferential "arbitrariness" standard, such as that suggested by the D.C. Circuit in *NIRS*, this would unduly infringe on the Commission's administrative prerogatives. As the First Circuit emphasized in *MassPIRG*, prior to *Chaney*, the Commission *assumed* that its denials of 2.206 petitions could be reviewed by courts,[51] and it never complained that this interfered with its ability to carry out its statutory responsibilities. Indeed, it appears that there are no cases in which a reviewing court even *remanded* a Commission ruling on a 2.206 petition for a fuller explanation, let alone one in which a Court ordered the agency to take an action which it did not regard as appropriate. When *Chaney* was decided, the NRC's lawyers predictably latched onto it as a way of avoiding even the highly solicitous review that the Commission had been subjected to in the past, but that hardly bespeaks a considered Commission judgment that immunity from judicial review was truly integral to, or even consistent with, the Commission's ability to carry out its vital task of safeguarding the public health and safety.

On the other hand, as both the D.C. Circuit's and the Commission's own shift of position on the issue in *NIRS* suggest, there is a compelling rationale for ensuring that courts can review the Commission's denials of 2.206 petitions, if only under an extremely deferential "arbitrariness" standard. The simple awareness by Commission Directors that their rulings on 2.206 petitions would be subjected to judicial scrutiny would necessarily lead them to take such petitions more seriously than would otherwise be the case.

In this regard, it is plainly not mere coincidence that the few occasions where the NRC did agree to hold formal hearings in response to 2.206 petitions occurred *before* the principle of nonreviewability was established. By the same token, even with regard to those situations in which the NRC maintains that it took "some types of regulatory action" in response to 2.206 petitions, virtually every one of the examples on which the Commission has relied took place prior to its determination to rely on *Chaney* as a basis for circumventing judicial review entirely.[52] The circumstantial evidence is strong, therefore, that the prior possibility of judicial review at least had the modest value of encouraging the Commission to pay enough attention to 2.206 petitions so that it could show to reviewing courts that it had not responded to the petition in an entirely "arbitrary" fashion. Thus, there are persuasive policy reasons to restore the prospect of judicial review, and few, if any, legitimate reasons not to do so.[53]

As the earlier discussion of *Safe Energy* and *MassPIRG* suggests, it would be a simple matter for the NRC itself to afford an adequate basis for some judicial review under a highly deferential standard. All the Commission need do is issue a rule clarifying that it did indeed intend to be bound by the norm embodied in its *Consolidated Edison* ruling, as construed by the Supreme Court in *Lorion, i.e.*, "The Commission interprets § 2.206 as requiring issuance of an order to show cause when a citizen petition raises 'substantial health or safety issues.'"[54] If the Commission were to reaffirm its prior ruling in that manner, then a reviewing court plainly would, as suggested in *NIRS*, *Safe Energy* and *MassPIRG*, have an adequate basis for determining whether the Commission has "arbitrarily" declined to institute a show cause proceeding in response to a 2.206 petition. Indeed, as discussed above, such judicial review of whether the Commission had arbitrarily ignored new "substantial health or safety issues" bearing on whether the operating license should be modified or revoked would be functionally identical to the judicial review that will be forthcoming after the Commission passes on pre-operation 2.206 petitions raising significant new safety or environmental issues.

If the Commission continues to adhere to its intellectually inconsistent and indefensible position that some of its 2.206 petitions should be subject to judicial review while others may escape such review entirely, Congress should amend the Atomic Energy Act to remedy this anomaly. In fact, the nuclear licensing amendment authored by Rep. Kostmayer and approved by the House Environment Committee would have accomplished this result by establishing the following basis for judicial review of all 2.206 petitions:

> (d)(1) IN GENERAL - Any person may petition the Commission to institute a proceeding to modify, suspend, or revoke a license, or for such other action as may be proper.

(2) STANDARDS FOR GRANTING - The Commission shall grant any request under paragraph (1) if there is material evidence to suggest that the holder of the license with respect to which a request has been made under paragraph (1) is in significant non-compliance with the terms of its license, this chapter, or the Commission's regulations, or that conditions at the licensed facility may present undue risk to the public health and safety, or common defense and security.

(3) JUDICIAL REVIEW. - Any Commission order denying a request under paragraph (1) shall be subject to judicial review in accordance with chapter 158 of title 28, United States Code and chapter 7 of title 5, United States Code.[55]

This provision, if enacted into law, would largely return the NRC to the situation as it existed prior to *Chaney* and its progeny. However, there are several potential problems with the proposal. First, by providing merely that the NRC "shall grant" any request that satisfies the criteria set forth in subsection (2), the provision might allow the NRC to continue its practice of claiming that it has "granted" a 2.206 petition simply by looking at the problem raised in the petition and taking whatever action it regards as appropriate. Consistent with the *Consolidated Edison* ruling, it would be preferable for Congress to specifically provide that the Commission must "grant" a 2.206 proceeding by actually instituting a "show cause" proceeding whenever it concludes that the pertinent criteria are satisfied.

In addition, while the Kostmayer proposal would clearly manifest Congress's intent that there be judicial review and would suggest the relevant standard of review by cross-referencing the Administrative Procedure Act, it would be better to spell out the appropriate standard in the provision itself. This is especially true in the current judicial climate, in which the federal appellate courts are generally dominated by conservative jurists who will resolve any ambiguity in Congress's enactments in favor of the NRC and the regulated industry and against the interests of the affected public. Thus, any provision enacted by Congress should specifically provide that Commission denials of 2.206 petitions may be reviewed for whether they are "arbitrary or capricious" or an "abuse of discretion," consistent with the basic standard of review set forth in section 10 of the APA.[56]

The Absence of a Citizen Suit Provision In The Atomic Energy Act Seriously Impairs The Ability Of the Affected Public To Raise and Pursue Legal Violations By NRC Licensees and The Commission Itself

The NRC's cavalier approach to 2.206 petitions might not pose such a serious problem if the Atomic Energy Act, like most modern day environmental and public health statutes, contained a citizen suit provision. But largely due to the fact that the AEA was enacted long before the citizen suit concept became commonplace, the statute does not authorize members of the affected public to bring enforcement actions directly against private statutory violators. To the contrary, the AEA expressly provides that:

> [N]o action shall be brought against any individual or person for any violation under this Chapter unless and until the Attorney General of the United States has advised the Commission with respect to such action *and no such action shall be commenced except by the Attorney General of the United States.*[57]

As we discuss below, however, there is no persuasive reason why Congress should not bring the AEA into line with more contemporary environmental laws, such as the Clean Water Act, Clean Air Act, and Resource Conservation and Recovery Act.

Congress has recognized a number of rationales for citizen suits against private violators, all of which would appear to be fully applicable to the nuclear regulation context. First, Congress has concluded that persons whose health, safety, and environment may be directly affected by legal violations may be better situated than distant federal regulators to assess the need for, and then to initiate and pursue, enforcement actions.[58] Second, citizen suits can save an agency considerable money and time by allowing the government to pursue only those enforcement actions that would not otherwise be pursued by the affected public.[59] Third, and of particular value in the NRC context, Congress has concluded that the availability of citizen suits can spur the federal agency into taking its enforcement responsibilities more seriously.[60] As Judge Wald of the D.C. Circuit has explained:

> There is also a notion that over time enforcers and polluters, who deal with one another constantly, may work out "agreements" that are not necessarily true to the spirit of the environmental law in question. The citizen outsider acts as a goad in such cases.[61]

Some commentators have criticized citizen suit provisions on the grounds that they may "undermine prosecutorial discretion," and, as a related proposition, lead to inconsistent and unfair enforcement against regulated entities.[62] Congress, however, has soundly rejected these criticisms and thus "citizen suit provisions are now fixtures in the landscape of federal environmental law."[63] At least twelve federal environmental statutes now include citizen suit provisions, including the Toxic Substances Control Act,[64] the Endangered Species Act,[65] the Surface Mining Control and Reclamation Act,[66] the Clean Water Act,[67] the Clean Air Act,[68] the Resource Conservation and Recovery Act,[69] the Energy Policy and Conservation Act,[70] and the Safe Drinking Water Act.[71] In fact, citizen suit provisions have been "included in *all* new federal environmental statutes or major statutory amendments to existing federal environmental statutes in the 1970's," except for the Federal Insecticide, Fungicide, and Rodenticide Act.[72]

For the most part, the various citizen suit provisions created by Congress are quite similar in form and function. They allow members of the public to bring suit against regulated entities for failures to comply with the organic statute itself, as well as for violations of implementing regulations, orders, and permit and license conditions established in accordance with the underlying statute.[73] Citizen suit provisions also generally authorize members of the public to sue the federal agencies charged with implementing the statutory schemes, on the grounds that they have failed to perform "non-discretionary" duties required by the law.[74] Such suits are frequently brought to compel agencies to issue overdue regulations or standards that are subject to specific statutory deadlines.

Citizen suit provisions have other standard features. Thus, a person contemplating bringing an enforcement action must generally provide written notice to the pertinent federal agency, as well as to any private party that is asserted to be in violation of the statute, regulations, or permit conditions.[75] In some statutes, however, Congress created an exception to the notice requirement for emergency situations that may pose imminent hazards to public health or the environment.[76]

The function of the notice requirement is to give the federal agency an opportunity to cure any violation, or to initiate enforcement action on its own, once it has been informed that a citizen suit is imminent. Consistent with this design, most environmental statutes provide that, if the agency is pursuing its own enforcement action against the target of a citizen suit, then the citizen suit may not proceed.[77] If the agency is not pursuing such enforcement action, or if the affected public is charging that the agency itself is violating the law, then the public may, after expiration of the requisite notice period—usually sixty days—file an action in federal district court.

The citizen suit provisions crafted by Congress differ somewhat in terms of the kinds of relief that district courts may award, but all authorize the issuance of injunctions compelling the violator to comply with the applicable statutory or regulatory requirement.[78] In addition, to encourage the filing of suits in appropriate circumstances, Congress has included in most federal environmental laws provisions authorizing courts to order defendants, including the government, to pay attorney fees and costs to prevailing plaintiffs.[79]

As suggested above, when Congress first contemplated authorizing citizen suits, a number of legislators and commentators predicted that the provision would burden the courts and unduly infringe on the government's prosecutorial discretion.[80] The near-universal consensus now is that such dire forecasts have proven to be baseless, and that citizen suits have not had a deleterious effect on either court dockets or agency enforcement priorities.[81] Rather, citizen suits have, as Congress anticipated, effectively supplemented agency enforcement efforts, particularly in the Clean Water Act area,[82] and have also been instrumental in remedying a number of "gross departures from the law" by federal agencies themselves.[83]

In theory, there is no apparent reason why Congress should not incorporate into the AEA a citizen suit provision that would follow the pattern which has been set in numerous other public health and environmental statutes. Such a provision should authorize citizen suits in U.S. district courts against (1) the NRC itself where the Commission has failed to carry out a nondiscretionary duty imposed on it by Congress, and (2) licensees which are in violation of license conditions, regulations, or orders issued by the Commission. Since there are somewhat different benefits and potential difficulties associated with these two kinds of citizen suits, I will discuss each of them separately.

Congress Should Authorize Citizen Suits Against The NRC Where The Commission Has Failed To Carry Out A Nondiscretionary Duty Imposed On It By Congress

A citizen suit provision could greatly assist members of the public to ensure that the NRC carries out its nondiscretionary responsibilities. While the AEA is "hallmarked by the amount of discretion granted the Commission in working to achieve the statute's ends,"[84] Congress has imposed mandatory duties on the Commission to issue regulations and standards,[85] and it will presumably do so again. A citizen suit provision authorizing the filing of nondiscretionary duty claims in district court would help to ensure that Congress's directives are carried out in a timely manner.

In contrast to claims against private parties that violate the AEA—which, as noted above, have been expressly precluded by Congress—members of the public may currently seek judicial relief against the NRC itself where the Commission has failed to comply with a legislative command. Nevertheless, in the absence of a citizen suit provision, persons complaining about the failure of the NRC to fulfill a nondiscretionary duty must plow through a heavy jurisprudential thicket just to figure out which court has jurisdiction over their claims. Under the Hobbs Act, the courts of appeals have jurisdiction to review "all final orders" of the NRC made reviewable by section 189(a)(1) of the AEA.[86] Section 189(a)(1), in turn, provides for review of orders entered in "any proceeding for the issuance or modification of rules and regulations dealing with the activities of licensees. . . ."[87]

On their face, therefore, the AEA and Hobbs Act only provide for court of appeals' review of "final orders" and "rules and regulations dealing with the activities of licensees" which have actually been issued. After reading the plain language of the relevant statutes, members of the public (and lawyers not steeped in administrative law) might reasonably conclude that jurisdiction over the Commission's *failure to take required action* has not been vested in the courts of appeals, and thus the only way to obtain relief would be through a petition for mandamus or other appropriate remedy in the district court.[88]

This judgment, however, would certainly be wrong in the D.C. Circuit, and perhaps in other circuits as well. In *Tele-communications Research and Action Center v. FCC ("TRAC")*,[89] the D.C. Circuit held that, in the absence of a citizen suit provision such as that discussed above, "where a statute commits review of agency action to the Court of Appeals, any suit seeking relief that might affect the Circuit Court's future jurisdiction"—such as a claim that the agency is unlawfully delaying the action at issue—"is subject to the *exclusive* review of the Court of Appeals."[90] As noted earlier, in the context of the AEA in particular, the Supreme Court has also taken an expansive view of the court of appeals' jurisdiction, although it has not specifically commented on whether such courts would have review over NRC failures to take required action.[91] Other circuits may follow *TRAC* in determining whether they have initial jurisdiction over NRC failures to comply with nondiscretionary duties, or they may decide that exclusive jurisdiction is vested in the district courts under the plain language of the Hobbs Act. Or other circuits may adhere to the view that the D.C. Circuit seemed to follow prior to *TRAC, i.e.,* that the courts of appeals and district courts have *concurrent* jurisdiction over claims of unlawful or unreasonable delay.[92]

Assuming that members of the public can, under the current complex state of the law, ascertain the court in which they belong in any particular circuit, there are other compelling reasons to enact a citizen suit provision authorizing nondiscretionary duty claims against the NRC in district court. The central reason why Congress has elected to assign such claims to the district courts in other environmental statutes is that the courts of appeals are ordinarily restricted to reviewing a record that has already been compiled by the administrative agency. Indeed, when an agency *has* taken action, it is textbook law that "[t]he focal point for judicial review should be the administrative record already in existence, not some new record made initially in the reviewing court."[93] Since the "factfinding capacity of the district court is thus typically unnecessary to judicial review of agency *decisionmaking*," Congress has reasonably determined that "[p]lacing initial review in the district court" of final agency actions would have the "negative effect . . . of requiring duplication of the identical task in the district court and in the courts of appeals," namely, a determination of "whether the action passes muster under the APA standard of review."[94]

On the other hand, where the agency is charged with violating a nondiscretionary duty—*e.g.*, where it has failed to meet a statutory deadline—there typically is, by definition, no record for a court to review. In such cases, Congress has determined that jurisdiction should be vested in the district court so that any appropriate "factfinding" can be undertaken and a record can be compiled for review purposes. For example, the agency may submit affidavits explaining the reasons for its delay in issuing regulations and the consequences if it were required to promulgate them within a particular time frame. Likewise, the plaintiff may pursue discovery in an effort to demonstrate that the agency can meet and therefore should be held to a strict timetable.

In any event, Congress's judgment that such nondiscretionary duty claims typically belong in the district court applies with full force to statutory responsibilities imposed on the NRC. There is simply no good reason why Congress should not expressly authorize such claims with regard to all nondiscretionary statutory duties that it imposes on the Commission.

Congress Should Authorize Citizen Suits Against Private Parties For Violations of NRC Regulations, License Conditions, and Orders

The question of whether Congress should amend the AEA to authorize citizen suits against licensees is, at least on the surface, more problematic. On the one hand, it can be argued that utilities who violate the AEA, implementing regulations, and license conditions, are not fundamentally different from other regulated entities who place the public health and safety at risk and are therefore subject to citizen suits. In addition, even if denials of 2.206 petitions are made judicially reviewable through administrative or legislative reform, courts will be loathe to second-guess the NRC's judgment as to whether it should be expending its limited resources on enforcement action in a particular case.[95] Thus, a persuasive case can be advanced that the *only* effective way in which Congress can afford the public a meaningful role in the ongoing oversight of nuclear facilities is by authorizing members of the public to initiate their own enforcement actions against licensees and others who violate the Act.

On the other hand, it is also clear that there are singular problems in crafting a citizen suit provision that would provide meaningful private enforcement opportunities in the nuclear power context. As noted above, the courts have commented time and again that the AEA "'is virtually unique in the degree to which broad responsibility is reposed in the [Commission], free from close prescription in its charter as to how it shall proceed in achieving the statutory objectives.'"[96] Since the AEA vests such broad discretion in the NRC to determine when regulated entities are satisfying the Act's standards, a citizen suit provision authorizing members of the public to bring actions to enforce the statute *itself* would be largely ineffectual. Indeed, since the courts have already determined that the "general enforcement provisions of the Act are *all* framed in permissive language," and thus "provide *no guidance* as to how the *agency* should exercise its discretion,"[97] it is difficult to envision these same courts feeling comfortable making initial determinations that the statute *itself* is being violated—at least in the absence of a major Congressional overhaul of the Act, which is unlikely any time in the near future.

Such a significant revamping of the statute would not be needed, however, to create a citizen suit provision that simply authorized members of the public to initiate actions against licensees that are violating standards, license conditions, and orders issued by the Commission itself. Indeed, a number of other environmental laws define "actionable violations" in this manner.[98] For example, the Resource Conservation and Recovery Act authorizes citizen suits for any "violation of any permit, standard, regulation, condition, requirement, or order. . . ."[99] Similarly, the Surface Mining Control and Reclamation Act allows any "person having an interest which is or may be adversely affected" to bring suit against any person "who is alleged to be in violation of any rule, regulation, order or permit issued pursuant to this subchapter."[100]

One potential criticism of this approach in the nuclear power context is that many of the NRC's regulations and standards are highly complex and that courts may therefore misconstrue or misapply them in analyzing whether particular licensees are in "violation" of them. The same sort of argument, of course, could be advanced with regard to the technically complicated environmental statutes mentioned above, but this has certainly not dissuaded Congress from incorporating citizen suit provisions into them. Moreover, if the Commission perceives a risk that a court may misconstrue or misapply one of its rules or orders in a particular case, there is nothing to prevent it from apprising the Court of its interpretation or analysis by intervening in the lawsuit or through the submission of an *amicus* brief.

Another possible, and more substantive, criticism is that some license conditions may have only an indirect bearing, if any, on the public's health and safety, and thus citizens should not be permitted to haul licensees into federal court whenever there is any deviation from the terms of a highly detailed license. Once again, the same argument could be directed at other statutory schemes in which Congress has authorized federal agencies to issue detailed permits or licenses for inherently dangerous activities, such as the transportation and disposal of hazardous wastes, the surface mining of coal, and the emission of toxic pollutants into the air and water. Since Congress has already determined that members of the public may bring citizen suits for violations of licenses or permits in these contexts, irrespective of whether the specific license or permit condition at issue is demonstrably related to public health and safety, then Congress should logically make the same judgment with regard to the nuclear regulation framework.

Moreover, there are built-in institutional barriers to the filing of citizen suits over trivial or inconsequential license violations. To begin with, years of experience with other citizen suit provisions should be sufficient to belie any suggestion that citizen groups and individuals will expend their limited resources rushing to bring federal lawsuits over license violations that have no bearing on the public health and safety.[101] Indeed, if anything, the overall *"paucity* of citizen suits against polluters—at least under federal laws—has frequently been remarked."[102]

In addition, if members of the public were authorized to file actions over license violations, they would, of course, have to show that they have "standing," as is true for any lawsuit filed in federal court. Thus, even where Congress has authorized "any person" to bring a citizen suit, the suit is nevertheless barred by the Constitution unless the complaining party can satisfy the traditional three-part test for standing, *i.e.*, he or she can show that (1) there is an "'injury in fact'"; (2) there is a "causal connection between the injury and the conduct complained of"; and (3) the injury is likely to be redressed by a favorable decision.[103]

If the violation of a particular license condition is truly unrelated to the public health and safety, then the licensee should have little difficulty convincing a court to dismiss the case on standing grounds, particularly in view of recent Supreme Court rulings that have made it more difficult for plaintiffs in environmental cases to establish standing.[104] And even if a plaintiff can overcome the threshold standing barrier and demonstrate that there is in fact a violation of a permit or license condition, the reviewing court will still have broad flexibility to take the severity of the violation into account in fashioning appropriate equitable relief.[105]

In any event, Congress could easily draft a citizen suit provision that takes into account any legitimate concerns that licensees will be sued over trivial violations. For example, Congress could require the NRC to designate in each license it issues those conditions or requirements that it regards as being of fundamental public health and safety significance. Congress could further provide that violations of only such terms and conditions may serve as a foundation for citizens suits. Any other violation would have to be raised through the filing of a 2.206 petition, with the prospect of judicial review, as discussed above.

This sort of hybrid approach would ensure that citizen suits are only pursued in cases of overriding importance to the public and, moreover, it would build an additional layer of NRC discretion into the designation of "fundamental" license conditions, *i.e.*, it would allow the Commission effectively to control what kinds of violations could be used as a basis for citizen suits. On the other hand, such an approach would ensure that the public could initiate legal action to ameliorate serious damage or risks to the public health and safety, in the event that the NRC fails to take such action.

Any citizen suit provision along these lines should be accompanied by requirements that licensees issue public reports describing in detail the extent to which they are complying with their licenses. One of the key factors in whether particular citizen suit provisions work as Congress contemplated is the relative ease or difficulty of developing cases from readily-available public records.[106] Unfortunately, as a result of recent court rulings and NRC actions, there are now severe restrictions on the public's ability to monitor problems at the nation's nuclear facilities.

For example, until recently utilities were required to submit to NRC detailed responses to Commission enforcement documents such as bulletins and generic letters.[107] The Commission has now told licensees, however, not to submit detailed documentation in response to such notices, but, rather, simply to retain such documents at the plant site and to send only conclusory letters to the NRC.[108] The effect, and apparent purpose, of this change in policy is to shield detailed enforcement-related information from public scrutiny, as it is no longer available in either the NRC's Public Document Room, nor pursuant to the federal Freedom of Information Act ("FOIA").[109]

In addition, as explained further below, the NRC recently won another sweeping decision from the *en banc* D.C. Circuit, which allows the Commission to withhold from the public, in response to FOIA requests, vast amounts of information bearing directly on the degree to which nuclear facilities are complying with NRC regulatory requirements.[110] Accordingly, if Congress contemplates incorporating a citizen suit provision into the AEA, as recommended in this paper, it should also take the necessary steps to ensure that the public has sufficient access to the kinds of proof that would be needed to make citizen suits feasible.

The Affected Public Should Be Permitted To Intervene When The NRC Itself Institutes Enforcement Proceedings Against Licensees

In exceptional circumstances, the NRC itself initiates formal enforcement proceedings against licensees. Unfortunately, in an extraordinary 1983 ruling, *Bellotti v. NRC*,[111] the D.C. Circuit essentially held that the affected public has no right whatsoever to intervene in such proceedings in order to argue for different or more demanding remedies than those being contemplated by the Commission itself.

At issue in *Bellotti* were "serious deficiencies in Boston Edison's management" of the Pilgrim Nuclear Power Station in Plymouth, Massachusetts.[112] The NRC's Office of Inspection and Enforcement had issued to Boston Edison an order amending the utility's license to require development of a plan for reappraisal and improvement of management functions. In addition, the Commission imposed civil penalties of $ 550,000 on the utility. The Attorney General of Massachusetts sought to intervene in the enforcement proceeding in order to address the "adequacy of Boston Edison's reappraisal plan, the nature of necessary improvements at the plant and the adequacy of Boston Edison's implementation of required changes."[113]

The NRC refused to allow the state to intervene on the remarkable ground that its interest was not "affected by the proceeding" within the meaning of section 189(a) of the AEA, and, in a split decision, the D.C. Circuit sustained this position.[114] Thus, in an opinion authored by Judge Robert Bork and joined by Senior Circuit Judge George MacKinnon, the D.C. Circuit held that the Massachusetts Attorney General "would be an affected person only if he opposed issuance of the

Order, which he does not. . . ."[115] Since the state "only" wished to argue that the enforcement order should be modified and strengthened in
order to further improve management at Boston Edison—and thus further safeguard the public and safety—the state was not, under the
Court's contorted reasoning, "affected" by the Commission's enforcement proceeding and had no right to intervene in the proceeding.[116]

Ironically, the Court stated that it was "reinforced in this view" by
the fact that "[p]etitioner Bellotti is in no sense left without recourse
by the NRC's denial of intervention in the Boston Edison
proceeding."[117] Thus, in this pre-*Chaney* case, the NRC argued and
the Court held that, since 2.206 petitions could be filed and were
judicially reviewable, they could provide an adequate substitute for
the right to intervene in the enforcement proceeding:

> Commission regulations provide for public petitions to modify a license,
> which may lead to license modifications proceedings if the Commission
> finds that appropriate. 10 C.F.R. § 2.206 (1983). *Moreover, Commission
> denials to institute proceedings under section 2.206 are subject to judicial
> review* . . . The issues petitioner seeks to raise through intervention he may
> seek to raise by this alternative route. It is true that the Commission need
> not hold a hearing on the section 2.206 request [] and that the decision
> whether or not to begin proceedings is *reviewable under deferential
> standards*. But, given the fact that members of the public cannot be allowed
> to litigate before the Commission any and all issues that occur to them
> without demolishing the regulatory process, *it is appropriate that the
> Commission be reviewed under an 'arbitrary and capricious' standard. That
> ensures that only serious issues need be addressed.*[118]

In dissent, Judge Skelly Wright agreed with two members of the
NRC—former Commissioners Bradford and Gilinsky—who had
registered vehement opposition to the Commission's bizarre
interpretation of section 189. Thus, Judge Wright maintained that the
position upheld by the majority was a "'pell mell retreat from
meaningful public inquiry . . . [that] suggests to the . . . outside world
that the agency is run by people living in fear of their own
citizenry.'"[119]

Judge Wright also harshly criticized the Commission's basic
philosophy regarding public participation in its proceedings:

> [u]nderlying the Commission's position seems be a view that public
> participation in decisionmaking is an enforcement weapon for the agency
> to use or not as it attempts to influence licensee behavior. It thus argues
> that 'by drawing the scope of the enforcement hearings narrowly, . . . [it
> can] encourag[e] the licensee to consent to, rather than contest, enforcement

actions[.]' . . . *But the congressionally bestowed right of the public to participate in the making of enforcement policy is not a tool to be traded off by an agency as part of its enforcement discretion.* The Commission's position presents the public with an image of behind-the-scenes decision-making and licensee-agency collusion. *The public might rightly ask why, if a public proceeding might convince the Commission that there is a need for more drastic remedies, a public proceeding is not held. The Commission position seems to envision no legitimate and independent public interest in participation.*[120]

In short, if Chairman Selin is serious about adopting concrete measures to increase public participation in NRC proceedings, then one obvious such step is to reverse the Commission's draconian and counterintuitive policy that affected members of the public have no right to intervene in enforcement proceedings in order to argue for stronger and more effective enforcement action. If the Commission refuses to do so, Congress should adopt amendments that would accomplish this essential change in policy.

At an absolute minimum, the Commission should not continue to have it both ways. Thus, it cannot defend its refusal to allow for public intervention in enforcement proceedings on the grounds that there is judicial review of 2.206 denials, as it did in *Bellotti*, and then turn around and continue to maintain that there should be no judicial review whatsoever of such denials in the aftermath of *Chaney*. If the Commission wishes to continue to adhere to the position that it convinced the D.C. Circuit to adopt in *Bellotti*—*i.e.*, that the public may be excluded from enforcement proceedings because it may seek additional enforcement measures in judicially reviewable 2.206 petitions—then it should at least take the minimal steps necessary to ensure that the public may in fact secure judicial review when such petitions are denied.

The NRC and Congress Should Ensure That The Public Has Access To Information That Is Essential To Monitoring Threats to the Public Health and Safety At The Nation's Nuclear Facilities.

The preceding sections described major obstacles to the public's ability to affect nuclear regulatory decisions through administrative proceedings and the courts. Obviously, if the public cannot have input through established legal channels—*i.e.*, through intervening in licensing hearings, filing enforcement actions, and the like—it can at least attempt to influence governmental policy through other means, such as providing publicly-significant information to the news media or Congressional representatives. These alternative vehicles for affecting nuclear regulatory policy, however, are dependent on the public's ability to obtain timely, pertinent information regarding conditions at nuclear facilities that may bear on the public's health, safety, and environment. Indeed, as suggested above, the efficacy of formal institutional mechanisms for ensuring the safe operation of nuclear plants—such as, for example, a citizen suit provision—is also contingent on the public's ability to obtain up-to-date, reliable information regarding conditions at nuclear plants.

Unfortunately, the public's access to crucial information bearing on the safety of nuclear facilities, as well as the significant extent to which the NRC's own regulatory responsibilities have been delegated to the nuclear industry, has been greatly compromised by another devastating decision by the conservative majority of the *en banc* D.C. Circuit, *Critical Mass Energy Project v. NRC.*[121] As a consequence of this case, the public can no longer even count on using the federal Freedom of Information Act ("FOIA")[122]—the nation's premier "open government" statute—to monitor the extent to which the NRC is carrying out its vital mission of safeguarding the public health and safety. In fact, as explained below, *Critical Mass* fundamentally—and adversely—alters the rules of public access to records throughout the federal government.

Critical Mass involved a request by a public-interest group for a series of reports about the safety of nuclear power plants which were submitted to the NRC by the Institute of Nuclear Power Operations ("INPO"). INPO is a non-profit organization that was established in the wake of the Three Mile Island accident. Following the accident, the Kemeny Commission concluded that, unless the industry immediately embarked on a program of self-improvement, the NRC would be required to greatly tighten its regulatory grip on the industry. Based on the Kemeny Commission's report and other analyses of the Three Mile Island accident, the NRC developed a comprehensive set of requirements, known as TMI Action Plan Requirements, that were designed to avoid serious mishaps in the future. One of these requirements, as clarified in a subsequent NRC directive, is that nuclear utilities must develop "procedures to assure that operating information pertinent to plant safety originating both within and outside the utility organization is continually supplied to operators and other personnel. . . ."[123]

In order to assist it in satisfying the TMI Action Plan requirements, as well as to avoid more stringent federal regulation of its practices, the nuclear industry created INPO in October 1979. INPO is chartered as a non-profit corporation, and its members include all domestic utilities that operate or have nuclear plants under construction.[124]INPO performs a wide array of functions for its members, many of which are designed to discharge its members' responsibilities under the TMI Action Plan.

One of these functions involves the preparation and dissemination of reports regarding safety-related events and conditions in nuclear plants—referred to by INPO as the "SEE-IN" program.[125] As INPO has explained, the SEE-IN program is used by utilities "in meeting most of the requirements detailed in Item I.C.5 [of the TMI Action Plan Requirements],"[126] and, in fact, the NRC has specifically "endorse[d] utility use of the program" as a means of fulfilling the requirements of TMI Action Plan Item I.C.5.[127]

As part of its SEE-IN program, INPO prepares Significant Event Reports ("SERs") and Significant Operating Experience Reports ("SOERs"). These reports analyze safety-related "events" at nuclear plants, using a broad range of sources including technical literature, NRC records, and interviews with plant employees. INPO distributes the reports to every utility operating a nuclear power plant, to engineering and construction firms, and to consultants and contractors.

In 1982, the NRC entered into an agreement with INPO, under which INPO agreed to provide the SEE-IN reports to the Commission, and the Commission agreed to keep the documents secret. The NRC made this commitment even though it routinely uses the INPO reports in its regulatory and oversight functions, *e.g.*, to make sure that licensees are in fact making their employees aware of new safety information, and also to verify the completeness and accuracy of other, similar reports that nuclear licensees are required to submit to the NRC, which are known as Licensee Event Reports ("LERs").[128] As a consequence of the Commission's commitment to keep the SEE-IN reports out of the public's hands, these documents are available to everyone who has any interest in the safety of nuclear power plants—the Commission, utilities, contractors, and consultants—with the single exception of the American public.

Critical Mass submitted an FOIA request to the NRC for the SEE-IN reports in 1984. The Commission withheld the records under Exemption 4 of the FOIA,[129] which exempts from disclosure "trade secrets and commercial or financial information obtained from a person and privileged or confidential."[130] The Commission did not argue that the reports reflected trade secrets or privileged information, but instead asserted that they contain "commercial . . . confidential" information even though they are shared with everyone in the nuclear industry.

In a 1974 case, *National Parks & Conservation Ass'n v. Morton*,[131] the D.C. Circuit established a test for determining whether information obtained from a regulated business is "confidential." Under this test, which has now been adopted in every federal circuit, records may be withheld by an agency only if it demonstrates that "disclosure of the information is likely . . . to impair the Government's ability to obtain necessary information in the future; or . . . to cause substantial harm to the competitive position of the person from whom the information was obtained."[132] Since the INPO reports were widely distributed to the nuclear industry, the NRC obviously could not argue that they would cause "competitive" harm to INPO or its members. Instead, the Commission sought to rely on the "impairment" prong of the *National Parks* test, arguing that disclosure of the records would impair its ability to obtain them in the future.

Two panels of the D.C. Circuit, however, held that the Commission had completely failed to show that release of the INPO reports to the public would significantly interfere with the Commission's ability to obtain them and thus rejected the Commission's invocation of Exemption 4. Thus, in 1987, the Court explained that "INPO has *not* suggested that it would discontinue either production of the reports here at issue, dissemination of those reports to its members or any other aspect of its SEE-IN program - let alone that INPO itself would disband - were we to reject definitively the NRC's FOIA exemption plea."[133] Moreover, while the NRC had asserted that, "[i]f INPO knows that the reports will be publicly disclosed, its reports are *less likely to be entirely candid* and, therefore, helpful to the NRC,"[134] the Court found the "record barren . . . of any support for this assertion . . . ."[135] The Court, however, remanded to the district court to give the Commission another opportunity to show that public access would cause some "'impairment . . . significant enough to justify withholding the information.'"[136]

When the case came back up to the Court of Appeals in 1991, another panel (consisting of Carter appointee Harry Edwards, Reagan appointee Stephen Williams, and Bush appointee Raymond Randolph) again found that "*there is no evidence whatsoever* to support" the Commission's position that "disclosure of the INPO reports will significantly impair the effectiveness or efficiency of the agency by virtue of anticipated antagonism in the relationship between NRC and INPO."[137] The Court explained that:

[w]hatever the ultimate disposition of this case, the Commission and INPO will still share a common goal of promoting nuclear power plant safety. Moreover, INPO, as the representative of the nuclear power industry, will continue to possess a powerful incentive to cooperate with the Commission in the pursuit of this goal. Through such concerted efforts, INPO has a first-

hand opportunity to demonstrate the efficacy of industry self-regulation to the Government agency responsible for regulating nuclear power.[138]

The Court further found that, once again, the NRC had failed to demonstrate that disclosure of the INPO reports to the public would impair the quality of the reports and thus their value to the Commission:

> INPO reports are distributed not only to the Commission, but also to all domestic nuclear utilities, plant suppliers and an occasional consultant or contractor. Thus, while these records are not generally available to the public-at-large, they do receive wide distribution through the nuclear energy community. Moreover, *employees seem perfectly willing to talk with INPO investigators even though it is understood that their comments will be reviewed by their employees and by federal regulators.*
>
> . . . *The record contains absolutely no testimony from working-level employees regarding the importance of confidential treatment of INPO reports to their willingness to speak to INPO analysts.* In fact, the record fails to demonstrate whether the employees interviewed by INPO analysts are even informed or aware of INPO's current limited distribution policy.[139]

However, Judge Randolph, joined by Judge Williams, wrote a concurring opinion in which he criticized the *National Parks* test itself on the grounds that the government should not have to show that any discernible harm will befall anyone in order to withhold the INPO reports or any other documents submitted by the regulated industry to the government:

> I see no legitimate basis for a court's adding some two-pronged 'objective' test relating to the government's need for the data and the consequences of destroying its confidential nature. Information not customarily revealed to the public is no less confidential *when disclosing it would cause only discomfort rather than objectively measurable harm. In business affairs, as in personal affairs, there are many things people simply prefer to keep to themselves or to reveal to others only on a confidential basis.*
>
> . . . The argument against this is that parties, by designating the information they provide as confidential, would wind up controlling whether it is publicly revealed. One may reasonably ask what is wrong with such a system.[140]

Not surprisingly, the government then asked for *en banc* review on whether *National Parks* itself should be overruled and the Court granted such review. In its *en banc* decision, the Court found that the government had "failed to demonstrate any of the considerations that would justify our overturning the *National Parks* test."[141] The conservative majority of the Court nevertheless proceeded to adopt an entirely new rule for most Exemption 4 cases, which allows the regulated industry to essentially control the public's access to records under the FOIA. Under this new rule, when records are "voluntarily" submitted to an agency, the government need no longer show that *any* discernible harm will occur if the records are disclosed. Instead, such records may now be withheld for any reason or no reason so long as they are of a type that the business asserts "would customarily not be released to the public by the person from whom it was obtained."[142] Since INPO does not "customarily release" its safety reports to the public, and since they have been provided to the Commission "voluntarily," the *en banc* Court held that they are "confidential within the meaning of Exemption 4 and therefore protected from disclosure."[143]

Judge Ruth Bader Ginsburg, a moderate Carter appointee who had written the first panel decision, wrote the dissent, which was joined by fellow Carter appointees Judges Wald, Mikva, and Edwards. Judge Ginsburg protested that the "guiding purpose" of the FOIA—to "shed light on an agency's performance of its statutory duties"—has not "been well served by the en banc disposition."[144] Judge Ginsburg further opined that the "public interest that the FOIA was enacted to serve" is "centrally at stake," as well-illustrated by the public's failure to obtain access to the INPO reports:

> Critical Mass Energy Project seeks access to comprehensive reports, prepared by a consortium comprised of the entire nuclear utility industry, concerning the causes and potential hazards of 'significant' safety-related events at nuclear power plants. *Disclosure of these reports, and the response of the Nuclear Regulatory Commission to the information contained in them, would undoubtedly shed light on the character and adequacy of the Commission's pursuit of its mission to 'encourage . . . the development and utilization of [nuclear] energy for peaceful purposes to the maximum extent consistent . . . with the health and safety of the public.'* 42 U.S.C. § 2013(d). The FOIA request we face seeks no 'information about *private* citizens that happens to be in the warehouse of the Government'; *disclosure is sought 'not primarily in the commercial interest of the requester,' but to advance public understanding of the nature and quality of the NRC's oversight operations or activities.*[145]

As Judge Ginsburg's opinion suggests, the *en banc* ruling will have a sweeping and devastating impact on the public's right to gain access to, among other materials, records bearing directly on the safety of nuclear power plants. Thus, it is obvious that any such records which reflect risks to the public's health, safety, and environment are not "customarily" disclosed by the very licensees that may be responsible for such threats, and thus—under the new D.C. Circuit test—such information can and will be withheld from the public whenever it is "voluntarily" supplied to the Commission.

An equally disturbing aspect of the Court's ruling—which the Court expressly recognized—is the degree to which it allows (indeed, encourages) "government agencies and industry to conspire to keep information from the public by agreeing to the voluntary submission of information that the agency has the power to compel."[146] In a transparent display of disdain for the underlying purposes of the FOIA, the Court simply dismissed this problem outright by saying that the Court could not "see *any reason* to interfere with the NRC's exercise of its own discretion in determining how it can best secure the information it needs."[147]

One solution to the enormous problems caused by the *Critical Mass* ruling is for Congress to overrule it legislatively and instead direct federal agencies and the courts to again follow the *National Parks* test. In the past, Congress has rejected judicial constructions of the FOIA when they would subvert the pro-disclosure thrust of the Act,[148] and there is no legitimate reason why it should not so here as well. An even superior alternative, at least from the vantage point of the public, would be an FOIA amendment that goes even further and provides unqualifiedly that the government must disclose to the public, in response to FOIA requests, all records which reflect risks to the public health, safety, and environment.

If a general amendment to the FOIA proves problematic, the Congressional committees with jurisdiction over the NRC should consider more narrow legislation that compels the Commission to make available to the public all documents, including those obtained from INPO, which reflect safety or environmental problems at the nation's commercial nuclear facilities. There is simply no justification for precluding the affected public from gaining access to such information, which is essential, as Judge Ginsburg pointed out in *Critical Mass*, to the public's ability to monitor the NRC's performance of its regulatory responsibilities.

In addition, the Commission should, of its own accord, take a more enlightened approach to public access to INPO records and other vital documents. Instead of exploiting the *Critical Mass* ruling to the maximum extent possible—for example, by arranging to obtain crucial records from licensees on a "voluntary" basis so that it can avoid providing them to members of the public[149]—the Commission should adopt a policy of full disclosure of such information. Since the FOIA exemptions are, for the most part, discretionary rather than mandatory—*i.e.*, an agency may claim an exemption but is not required to do so—there would appear to be nothing in *Critical Mass* that would preclude the Commission from announcing that it will refrain from invoking exemption 4 to withhold INPO and related records, at least where—as in *Critical Mass* itself—disclosure would cause no demonstrable harm to the Commission's regulatory functions or the competitive position of a particular licensee.

Notes

1. Curran, *The Public as Enemy: NRC Assaults on Public Participation in the Regulation of Operating Nuclear Plants (A Report by the Union of Concerned Scientists)* 5 (April 1992) (hereafter "*The Public As Enemy*").

2. 10 C.F.R. § 2.206(a).

3. *Id.*

4. *Id* at § 2.206(b).

5. *Id.* at §§ 2.206(c)(1) and (2).

6. *The Public as Enemy* at 24.

7. *Hearings Before the House Subcommittee on Energy and Power of the House Committee on Energy and Commerce*, 102d Cong., 1st Sess. 743-44 (May 8, 1991).

8. *See Consolidated Edison Company of New York, Inc.* (Indian Points Units 1 and 2); *Power Authority of New York* (Indian Point Unit No. 2), DD-80-5, 11 NRC 351 (1980); *see also* LBP-83-68, 18 NRC 811 (1983); *Dairyland Power Cooperative* (La Crosse Boiling Water Reactor), DD-80-9, 11 NRC 392 (1980); *see also* LBP-81-7, 13 NRC 257 (1981), *aff'd* ALAB 733, 18 NRC 9 (1983).

9. *Letter from Dennis K. Rathbun, Director, NRC Congressional Affairs Office, to Chairman Philip R. Sharp of the House Subcommittee on Energy and Power, Answering Subcommittee Questions and Enclosing Insert for the Record of May 8, 1991 Hearing*, at 3 (May 31, 1991).

10. *The Public As Enemy* at 15.

11. *Id.* at 7-24.

12. *Id.* (discussing NRC's treatment of 2.206 petitions raising safety and environmental issues with regard to Babcock and Wilcox reactors, the Pilgrim plant near Plymouth, Massachusetts, and the Perry Nuclear Power Plant near Cleveland, Ohio).

13. Transcript of June 22, 1992 Press Conference at 15.

14. Memorandum and Order, CLI-91-11 (July 31, 1991). The petition was originally brought before the Commission, which referred it to the staff. The staff denied the petitioners' request for immediate shutdown. Subsequently, the Commission on its own initiative reasserted jurisdiction over the petition and granted some relief in response to it.

15. *Id.*

16. *See The Public As Enemy* at 24.

17. *Id.*

18. *Id.* Several months later, after further investigation disclosed that uncertainties concerning the embrittlement issue were far greater than the staff

had previously recognized, Yankee Rowe shut down voluntarily, pending testing
of the vessel materials. In February 1992, as a result of the huge expense that
would be associated with testing and repair of the vessel, the utility decided to
shut the facility down permanently. *Id.*

19. 470 U.S. 821 (1985).

20. *Id.* at 830.

21. *Id., citing* 5 U.S.C. § 701(a)(2). The NRC has never argued, and no court
has ever suggested, that the first exception to judicial review—where "statutes
preclude review," *id.* at § 701(a)(1)—has any applicability in the context of
2.206 petitions.

22. *Id.* at 835.

23. *Id.* at 836.

24. *Id.* at 833, *quoting Adams v. Richardson*, 480 F.2d 1159, 1162 (D.C. Cir.
1973) (*en banc*).

25. 470 U.S. at 833 n. 4.

26. *See Massachusetts Public Interest Research Group v. U.S. NRC*, 852 F.2d 9
(1st Cir. 1988) ("*MassPIRG*"); *Safe Energy Coalition v. U.S. Nuclear Regulatory
Commission*, 866 F.2d 1473 (D.C. Cir. 1989). On the same day that it decided
Chaney, the Supreme Court also handed down a ruling in *Florida Power and Light
Co. v. Lorion*, 470 U.S. 729 (1985), which established that the courts of appeals,
rather than the district courts, have subject matter jurisdiction over challenges to
NRC denials of 2.206 petitions. The Supreme Court expressly noted that no party
had raised the distinct question of whether denials of section 2.206 petitions are
unreviewable under the reasoning in *Chaney*, and the Court declined to address
that issue on its own. *Id.* at 735 n. 8. On remand, the D.C. Circuit also declined to
resolve the issue definitively, and instead affirmed the NRC decision on the
merits. *See Lorion v. NRC*, 785 F.2d 1038, 1040 (D.C. Cir. 1986).

27. *Id.*

28. *MassPIRG*, 852 F.2d at 10.

29. *Id.* at 15.

30. *Id.* at 17 (emphasis added).

31. *Id.* at 17.

32. *Id.* at 17, *citing* 10 C.F.R. Part 2, App. C ("General Statement of Policy and
Procedure for NRC Actions").

33. (Indian Point, Units 1, 2, and 3), 2 NRC 173 (1975).

34. *Id.* at 176 (footnote omitted) (emphasis added).

35. *Lorion*, 470 U.S. at 732 (emphasis added).

36. 852 F.2d at 18 (emphasis added).

37. *Id.* (emphasis added).

38. *Id.*

39. 866 F.2d at 1474.

40. *Id.* at 1466.

41. *Id.* at 1477, *quoting Chaney*, 470 U.S. at 833 n. 4.

42. 866 F.2d at 1478, *quoting Center for Auto Safety v. Dole*, 846 F.2d 1532,
1534 (D.C. Cir. 1988).

43. 866 F.2d at 1478.

44. 866 F.2d at 1480.

45. *NIRS v. NRC*, 969 F.2d at 1178.

46. *Id*.

47. *Id*.

48. *En banc* Brief of NRC, at 56, *NIRS v. NRC*.

49. *See* 54 Fed. Reg. 15381 (April 18, 1989).

50. *Id*.

51. 852 F.2d at 18.

52. *Letter from Dennis K. Rathburn, Director, NRC Congressional Affairs Office, to Chairman Philip R. Sharp of the House Subcommittee on Energy and Power, Answering Subcommittee Questions and Enclosing Insert for the Record of May 8, 1991 Hearing*, at 2-5 (May 31, 1991).

53. *See generally* Stewart, *The Reformation of American Administrative Law*, 8 Harv. L. Rev. 1667, 1702 (1975) ("A requirement that agencies articulate and consistently pursue policy choices may have only a modest effect on outcomes, but it can serve as a useful, selective judicial tool to force agency reconsideration of questionable decisions and to direct attention to factors that may have been disregarded.").

54. *Lorion*, 470 U.S. at 732, *quoting Consolidated Edison Co.*, 2 NRC at 176.

55. H.R. 3629, 102d Cong. 1st Sess. 301 (1991).

56. 5 U.S.C. § 706(2)(A).

57. 42 U.S.C. § 2271 (emphasis added).

58. Marshaw, *Private Enforcement of Public Regulatory Provisions: The "Citizen Suit"*, 4 Class Action Rep. 29, 33 (1975); J. Marshaw & R. Merrill, *Introduction to The American Public Law System* 892 (1975).

59. Fadil, *Citizen Suits Against Polluters: Picking Up the Pace*, 9 Harv. Env. L. Rev. 23, 24 (1985).

60. *See* Wald, *The Role of the Judiciary in Environmental Protection*, 19 B.C. Env. Aff. L. Rev. 525 (1992); *Proffitt v. Rohm & Haas*, 850 F.2d 1007, 1011 (3rd Cir. 1988).

61. Wald, *supra* n. 60, at 525. In his influential law review article, *The Reformation of American Administrative Law*, Professor Richard Stewart extensively discusses the agency "'capture' scenario, in which administrations are systematically controlled, sometimes corruptly, by the business firms within their orbit of responsibility, whether regulatory or promotional." Stewart, *The Reformation of American Administrative Law*, 8 Harv. L. Rev. 1667, 1685 (1975). Professor Stewart notes that "many legislators, judges, and legal and economic commentators have accepted the thesis of persistent bias in agency policies," and, while he did not subscribe to this "thesis" in its "crudest" form, he set forth a number of "more subtle explanations of industry orientation . . .." *Id.; see also* G. Schubert, *The Public Interest* 119 (1960); Green & Nader, *Economic Regulation vs. Competition: Uncle Sam the Monopoly Man*, 82 Yale L.J. 871, 876 (1973); Landis, *The Challenge to Traditional Law in the Rise of Administrative Law*, 13 Miss. L.J. 724, 725 (1941).

62. Marshaw, *supra* n. 58, at 33; *see also* R. Posner, *Economic Analysis of Law* 461-478 (2d ed. 1977).

63. Fadil, *supra* n. *59*, at 25.

64. 15 U.S.C. § 2619.

65. 16 U.S.C. § 1540(g).

66. 30 U.S.C. § 1270.

67. 33 U.S.C. § 1365.

68. 42 U.S.C. § 7604.

69. 42 U.S.C. § 6972.

70. 42 U.S.C. § 6305.

71. 42 U.S.C. § 300j-8.

72. Miller, *Private Enforcement of Federal Pollution Control Laws: Part I,* 13 Envtl. L. Rep. (Envt'l. L. Inst.) 10,309, 10,311 (1983).

73. Fadil, *supra* n. 59, at 26.

74. *See, e.g.,* 15 U.S.C. § 2619 (Toxic Substances Control Act); 33 U.S.C. § 1365(a)(2) (Clean Water Act); 42 U.S.C. § 6972(a) (Resource Conservation and Recovery Act).

75. *See, e.g.,* 16 U.S.C. § 1540(g)(2)(A)(i) (Endangered Species Act); 33 U.S.C. § 1365(b)(1)(A) (Clean Water Act).

76. *See* 42 U.S.C. § 6972(c) (RCRA); 42 U.S.C. § 7604(b) (Clean Air Act).

77. *See, e.g.,* 42 U.S.C. § 300j-8(b)(1)(B) (Safe Drinking Water Act); 42 U.S.C. § 6604(b)(1)(B) (Clean Air Act).

78. Fadil, *supra* n. 59, at 27-28.

79. *See, e.g.,* 15 U.S.C. § 2619(c)(2) (under Toxic Substances Control Act, court may award costs and reasonable fees to successful plaintiffs); 33 U.S.C. § 1365(d) (under Clean Water Act, court may award costs, including fees, to any prevailing party whenever court determines award is appropriate).

80. *See, e.g.,* 116 Cong. Rec. 32,924-27 (1970), *reprinted in* 1 A Legislative History of the Clean Air Act Amendments of 1970, at 273-81 (1974).

81. *See, e.g.,* Wald, *supra* n. 60, at 525.

82. Fadil, *supra* n. 59, at 34; Envt'l. Law Inst., *Citizen Suits: An Analysis of Citizen Enforcement Actions Under EPA-Administered Statutes,* at III-10 (Sept. 1984).

83. Wald, *supra* n. 60, at 526 n. 30.

84. *Siegel v. AEC,* 400 F.2d 778, 783 (D.C. Cir. 1968).

85. *See, e.g.,* 42 U.S.C. § 10226 (provision of the Nuclear Waste Policy Act of 1982 requiring the NRC, within twelve months, to "promulgate regulations . . . for the training and qualifications of civilian nuclear powerplant operators"); § 2803 of the Comprehensive National Energy Policy Act (requiring NRC to adopt conforming amendments to its Part 52 rules within one year).

86. 28 U.S.C. § 2342(4).

87. 42 U.S.C. § 2239(a)(1).

88. *See, e.g.,* 13 C. Wright, A. Miller & E. Cooper, *Federal Practice & Procedure* § 3522, at 44 (1975 ed.) (federal courts of appeals are courts of limited jurisdiction "empowered to hear only those cases . . . entrusted to them by a jurisdictional grant of Congress").

89. 750 F.2d 70 (D.C. Cir. 1984).

90. *Id.* at 75 (emphasis in original) (footnote omitted).

91. *See Lorion, supra,* 470 U.S. at 737 (holding that courts of appeals have jurisdiction to review NRC denials of 2.206 petitions because "Congress intended to provide for initial court of appeals review of all final orders in licensing proceedings whether or not a hearing before the Commission occurred or could have occurred").

92. *TRAC,* 750 F.2d at 75 n. 23, 77 n. 37.

93. *Camp v. Pitts,* 411 U.S. 138, 142 (1973).

94. *Lorion,* 470 U.S. at 744.

95. *See Lorion v. NRC,* 785 F.2d 1038, 1041 (D.C. Cir. 1986) (upholding the NRC's denial of a 2.206 petition on the merits, the D.C. Circuit explained that "[b]ased on the record, we cannot say that the Commission abused its discretion in refusing to consider Lorion's concerns 'substantial,' or to institute a licensing procedure").

96. *NIRS, supra,* 969 F.2d at 1177, *quoting Siegel v. Atomic Energy Comm'n,* 400 F.2d 778, 783 (D.C. Cir. 1958); *see also BPI v. Atomic Energy Comm'n,* 502 F.2d 424, 428 n. 3 (D.C. Cir. 1974); *Cities of Statesville v. AEC,* 441 F.2d 962, 977 (D.C. Cir. 1969).

97. *MassPIRG, supra,* 852 F.2d at 15 (emphasis added).

98. *See* Miller, *Private Enforcement of Federal Pollution Control Laws: Part I,* 13 Envt'l L. Rep. (Envt'l. Law Inst.) 10,309, 10,319-21 (1983).

99. 42 U.S.C. § 6972(a)(1).

100. 30 U.S.C. § 1270(a)(1).

101. Fadil, *supra* n. 59, at 29.

102. *Id.* (emphasis added); *see also* Feller, *Private Enforcement of Federal Anti-Pollution Laws Through Citizen Suits: A Model,* 60 Den. L.J. 553, 564-65 (1983); R. Stewart and J. Krier, *Environmental Law and Policy* 547-48 (2d ed. 1978).

103. *Lujan v. Defenders of Wildlife,* 112 S. Ct. 2130 (1992), *quoting Allen v. Wright,* 468 U.S. 737, 751 (1984).

104. *Id.; Lujan v. National Wildlife Federation,* 497 U.S. 871, 883-889 (1990).

105. *See, e.g., State of New Mexico v. Watkins,* No. 91-5387 (D.C. Cir. July 10, 1992) ("a federal court is obliged to fit each equitable remedy ordered to the nature of the violation found"), *citing Amoco Production Co. v. Village of Gambell,* 480 U.S. 531, 541-46 (1987); *see also Weinberger v. Romero-Barcelo,* 456 U.S. 305, 314 (1982).

106. Fadil, *supra* n. 59, at 66 & n. 242.

107. *The Public As Enemy,* at 50.

108. *Id.*

109. 5 U.S.C. § 552.

110. *Critical Mass Energy Project v. NRC,* 975 F.2d 871 (D.C. Cir. 1992) (*en banc*).

111. 725 F.2d 1380.

112. *Id.* at 1381. In particular, the "NRC had found that over a period of two and a half years there had been a 'series of breakdowns' in a wide variety of management functions relating to the operations of the nuclear facility. Management's ability to control engineering and design review activities, revise operating procedures, conduct facility maintenance activities, notify NRC about

safety problems, and conduct onsite safety committee activities had all deteriorated." *Id.* at 1384, *quoting* Order Modifying License.

113. *Id.* at 1381.

114. *Id.* at 1381, *citing* 42 U.S.C. § 2239(a).

115. 725 F.2d at 1382.

116. *Id.*

117. *Id.*

118. *Id.* at 1382-83 (emphasis added) (citation omitted).

119. *Id.* at 1383, *quoting Wisconsin Electric Power Co. (Point Beach, Unit 1)*, 12 NRC 547, 550 (1980) (dissenting view of Commissioner Bradford with Commissioner Gilinsky concurring).

120. *Id.* at 1388 (emphasis added) (citations omitted).

121. 975 F.2d 871 (D.C. Cir. 1992) (*en banc*).

122. 5 U.S.C. § 552.

123. *Clarification of TMI Action Plan Requirements,* NUREG 0737, Item I.C.5.

124. *See INPO at Age Five,* Nuclear News (March 1984).

125. *See Significant Event Evaluation and Information Network (SEE-IN) Program Description,* INPO, p. 30 (May 1984) ("SEE-IN Program Description").

126. *Id.*

127. NRC Generic Letter No. 82-04, at 1 (1982).

128. *See* 10 C.F.R. §§ 50.72, 50.73; 48 Fed. Reg. 33850 (1983).

129. 5 U.S.C. § 552(b)(4).

130. *Id.*

131. 498 F.2d 765 (D.C. Cir. 1974).

132. *Id.* at 770.

133. *Critical Mass Energy Project v. NRC,* 830 F.2d 278, 283 (D.C. Cir. 1987).

134. Brief for the NRC, at 22 (emphasis in original), *Critical Mass v. NRC,* 830 F.2d 278.

135. 830 F.2d at 285.

136. *Id.* at 286, *quoting Washington Post Co. v. HHS,* 690 F.2d 252, 269 (D.C. Cir. 1982).

137. *Critical Mass Energy Project v. NRC,* 931 F.2d 939, 944 (D.C. Cir. 1991) (emphasis added).

138. *Id.* at 944.

139. 931 F.2d at 946 (emphasis added).

140. *Id.* at 948. (emphasis added).

141. 975 F.2d at 876.

142. *Id.* at 879.

143. *Id.* at 880.

144. *Id.* at 882.

145. *Id.* at 885 (emphasis added), *quoting U.S. Dep't of Justice v. Reporters Committee for Freedom of the Press,* 489 U.S. 749, 774, 775 (1989).

146. 975 F.2d at 880.

147. *Id.*

148. For example, in 1976, Congress amended Exemption 3 of the Act in order

to overturn the Supreme Court's overly broad construction of it in *Administrator, FAA v. Robertson*, 422 U.S. 255 (1975).

149. This risk is very real, as demonstrated by NRC decisions in the past. In 1980-81, the NRC considered instituting a greatly expanded mandatory reporting system that would have required licensees to file reports about component failures at their plants. *See* 46 Fed. Reg. 3541 (1981); 45 Fed. Reg. 6793 (1980). The NRC discarded its proposal for a mandatory reporting system when INPO volunteered to manage a similar system privately and assured the NRC that it would have access to the system. *See* 46 Fed. Reg. 49134 (1981). Under *Critical Mass*, the public would have been able to obtain any reports that the NRC *required* to be submitted, but it has no access to the identical information on the INPO-operated system, simply because INPO has objected to such disclosure. As a legal matter, there is nothing to preclude the NRC from foreclosing public access in a similar fashion in the future simply by agreeing to obtain information "voluntarily" rather than through mandatory means.

7

The Re-licensing of
Nuclear Power Plants

Diane Curran

In 1954, when Congress enacted the Atomic Energy Act, it imposed a 40-year limit on the license term for any nuclear power plant, with provision for renewal. However, at that early stage in the life of the nuclear power industry, Congress made no provision for the manner in which renewal of those licenses should be considered. The oldest facilities in the current generation of nuclear power plants have now reached or are approaching thirty years of operation. In response, in 1991, the NRC promulgated regulations that establish a process for considering license renewal applications.[1] In the absence of any direction from Congress, the NRC used that rulemaking to make a number of important policy decisions that seriously undermine Congress' original purpose in the Atomic Energy Act of assuring that operation of nuclear power plants will not pose an undue risk to the public health and safety. The rule also places severe limitations on the types of issues that can be raised by citizen intervenors in license renewal proceedings, thereby thwarting Congress' intent that the public should be given a meaningful opportunity to participate in important regulatory decisions made by the NRC.

Standard for Renewal

The most fundamental consideration in license renewal is what standard the NRC should use in deciding whether to renew a license: should existing plants be brought into compliance with current standards for new plants, or should they be allowed to continue to operate under the much laxer standards to which they were licensed decades ago? Instead of using license renewal as a logical opportunity to bring operating plants up to current safety standards, the Commission has chosen a very low standard: a plant need only comply with its "current licensing basis" or "CLB," *i.e.*, the plant's original licensing basis, plus whatever requirements have been imposed on the licensee over the operating life of the plant.[2] Thus, for each plant, the rule grandfathers all exemptions and excuses for noncompliance that are unrelated to aging, regardless of why or when they were granted.

The fire protection rule is an example of important safety requirements that look strong on the books, but which are substantially weakened in their application—largely due to generous grandfathering and exemptions. In 1980, in response to an enforcement petition decrying the lack of effective fire protection standards, the NRC promulgated a rule setting forth preventative measures that would be required of licensees.[3] While the rule itself was impressive, the NRC was reluctant to apply or enforce it. Plants licensed to operate before January 1, 1979, were required to meet only three of the rule's fifteen standards. In addition, the loopholes were so large that a plant technically could meet all the fire-protection regulations without actually having any means of preventing a major accident. The rule also contained liberal provisions for granting exemptions and long schedules for installing the necessary protection features. In a fourteen-month period, the NRC granted 234 technical exemptions to various parts of its fire-protection regulations, as well as numerous schedule exemptions.[4] Over five years later, NRC's Executive Director for Operations reported that:

> The requirement of separation of the redundant trains of safe shutdown equipment prescribed by 10 CFR 50, App. R cannot be met in many control rooms. The rule requires in such cases that an alternative or dedicated shutdown capability be provided. Whether in the event of a credible control room fire the operator will have time enough and the physical ability to transfer control of the reactor to the alternative or dedicated shutdown panel is at issue. There is also the question of how much of the control equipment will survive and whether and when control room operation can be resumed.[5]

The NRC's lax enforcement of its fire protection program is illustrated by its treatment of the Pilgrim nuclear power plant. In 1988, the NRC notified Boston Edison Company that it would "exercise enforcement discretion" and not issue a Notice of Violation or a civil penalty concerning the "extensive number of fire barrier deficiencies" at Pilgrim.[6] The reasons given for this act of forbearance was that the utility had devoted "significant resources" to identify and resolve fire protection deficiencies. Thus, the standard applied by the NRC was not whether an acceptable level of safety was achieved, but whether the licensee had made an effort to achieve it. The same day, the NRC issued a license amendment exempting the utility from the fire barrier requirements.[7]

Under the license renewal rule, exemptions to important requirements like the fire protection rule will be grandfathered into renewed licenses, without any opportunity for public challenge unless the public can demonstrate that the exemption would have detrimental effects related to aging. This is not an acceptable standard. Economic considerations do not justify asking the public to continue to accept higher risks from a plant than would be presented by a new plant in the same location. If it is going to permit operation beyond 40 years, the NRC should at a minimum require plants to meet current new plant safety standards to qualify for license renewal. The burden should be on the licensees to justify the appropriateness of continuing grandfather clauses and exemptions which excuse them from complying with these fundamental requirements.

Refusal to Examine Adequacy of or Compliance with Current Licensing Basis

Even assuming the safety of operating nuclear plants, an additional twenty years could be assured without bringing them up to current standards. The license renewal rule fails to provide any means for either evaluating the adequacy of the CLB, or whether it has been complied with. It is inescapable that the major objective of the license renewal rule is to minimize the scope of any license renewal proceeding. The NRC concededly intends the scope of license renewal proceedings to be "much narrower" than construction permit and operating license proceedings.[8] The bulwark of this effort is the declaration that the CLB of a plant is off-limits in a license renewal proceeding. Under the rule, members of the public may not challenge either the sufficiency of a plant's CLB or the plant's compliance with its current licensing basis in the license renewal proceeding unless it relates to aging.[9]

Moreover, the general public will lack the means even to verify whether a licensee has adequately defined the scope of equipment subject to license renewal review or to identify non-aging related issues that should be raised under an exemption to the rule, as provided for in 10 C.F.R. § 2.758. This is because the NRC requires submittal of *only* those parts of the CLB that are related to aging; other portions of the CLB may be stored at the plant or elsewhere, where the public has no access to it.

As an additional limitation on the scope of license renewal proceedings, the rule requires that citizen intervenors who seek hearings on age-related degradation issues must demonstrate that the degradation is "unique" to license renewal.[10] If the degradation has occurred during the term of the current operating license, it must be shown to be "different in character or magnitude" during the license renewal term; or that it was "not explicitly identified and evaluated by the licensee for the period of extended operation and the evaluation found acceptable by the NRC;" or that it "occurs only during the period of extended operation."[11] While this provision is somewhat unclear, it is apparently intended to require that, in order to obtain a hearing on aging issues, prospective intervenors must show that some marked change in the nature or degree of degradation will occur after the original license term expires—a virtually impossible task that will effectively exclude most aging issues from public hearings.

The NRC's refusal to consider the adequacy of or compliance with the CLB in the license renewal proceeding amounts to a fundamental abdication of the Commission's responsibility to safeguard public health and safety. As the NRC conceded in the proposed rule, the adequacy of the current licensing basis is absolutely key to the validity of a license renewal. If the CLB is not sufficient, or if the licensee does not in fact comply with it, then obviously the NRC lacks a basis for finding a reasonable assurance of continued safe operation of the plant during the term of the renewed license. However, the license renewal rule is carefully worded to prevent the NRC Staff or the public from determining if these essential safety criteria are met.

CLB Is Unknown for Most Plants

The NRC's motivation for shielding the adequacy of the CLB from review or attack is clear: it simply does not know what the CLB is for most, if not all, plants. In 1979, the Commission was unable to comply with Congress' mandate in the "Bingham Amendment" that it specifically identify regulations applicable to each operating nuclear power plant, and which of those regulations were complied with.[12] The license renewal rule provides no indication that 13 years later, either the NRC or licensees know what the licensing basis is for each plant. In fact, licensees are spending hundreds of millions of dollars trying to "reconstitute" the licensing basis for many of the older plants.[13] The NRC has acknowledged that it is "concerned" that some plants may not have sufficiently documented their ability to ensure that they are operating "within the design bases envelope."[14] Accordingly, the Commission has issued a policy statement stating its "expectation" that licensees will compile and maintain their CLB's.[15] However, the NRC studiously avoided making this a mandatory requirement; moreover, the records may be kept by the licensee at the plant, thus effectively blocking access by the public.

The NRC's refusal to reexamine the adequacy of a plant's licensing basis is especially egregious in light of the fact that approximately 55 operating plants received their operating licenses from the old Atomic Energy Commission, which had the dual mission of regulating and promoting nuclear power. These old plants are, of course, the first that will be eligible for potential renewal. Congress concluded in 1974 that this inherent conflict of interest did or could cause regulatory considerations to be tainted by promotional considerations. Consequently, it abolished the AEC and attempted, not entirely successfully, to divide the regulatory and promotional functions between the Nuclear Regulatory Commission and the Energy Research and Development Administration (now the Department of Energy), respectively.[16] Because licensing decisions by the AEC may have been improperly influenced by undue promotional considerations, renewal of licenses issued by the AEC should receive special scrutiny.

Refusal to Review Compliance With Safety Standards

The license renewal rule also forbids consideration of whether an applicant for license renewal complies with its current licensing basis unless the non-compliance relates to aging of the plant.[17] In support of this prohibition, the Commission reasons that, aside from age-related degradation, "current regulatory processes are sufficiently broad and rigorous" to ensure the safety of extended operation.[18] The NRC's determination that general NRC oversight provides a reasonable assurance that plants comply with their licensing basis is utterly irrational in light of the abundant evidence that NRC does not know whether plants comply with all relevant safety requirements, is sometimes given false information about compliance by its licensees, and consciously refuses to enforce compliance with crucial safety regulations that it knows are not met.

First, as evidenced by its failure to comply with the Bingham Amendment, NRC has admitted that it does not know whether licensed plants meet its regulations. The NRC's own former director of regulation, Harold Denton, has explained that "using an audit process, it is simply not possible for the NRC to state, based on its own knowledge, that every rule and regulation has been met for every applicable action by the applicant."[19] The NRC's attempt to do precisely that in the license renewal rule flies in the face of the Commission's own history. The NRC has not even seriously tried to find out for itself whether plants meet all requirements, and has repeatedly said that it is up to licensees to make sure that the regulations are met.

Second, the NRC often refuses to enforce compliance with its regulations even when it knows about noncompliance. Following are a few examples among dozens:

Motor-Operated Valves—Boiling water reactors contain numerous motor-operated valves (MOVs) which are depended on to satisfy the General Design Criteria (GDC) for containment isolation following steam line break accidents. Testing and analyses have indicated that these valves will probably be unable to close as required to serve their safety function.[20] Yet, the NRC permits plants with these valves to operate, knowing they do not meet the GDC for containment isolation.[21]

Indian Point—In the early 1980's, the Indian Point plants in New York missed four deadlines over a three year period for complying with new, strengthened emergency planning requirements promulgated following the TMI accident. Indian Point is surrounded by the highest population density in the country. Instead of shutting the plants down pending the development of adequate plans, as virtually every public official connected with them urged the NRC to do, the Commission issued an order, with two dissenting votes, to permit them to operate notwithstanding their non-compliance on the grounds that "adequate compensating measures" had been taken or were "planned to be taken."[22]

Equipment Qualification—The NRC counts among its "fundamental" requirements the rule requiring licensees to demonstrate that electrical safety equipment is "environmentally qualified," *i.e.*, that it can function in an accident environment.[23] Yet the NRC has tolerated a long history of noncompliance by licensees. The deadline for compliance with the NRC's 1980 requirements has been extended twice, first until 1982, then until March 1985 or the second refueling outage after March 1982, whichever came later. Even now, the NRC continues to discover instances of substantial noncompliance with its equipment qualification rule, by the very licensees who were thought to be in compliance years ago. For instance, on August 28, 1990, the NRC issued a notice of violation and a hefty penalty to the Farley nuclear power plant for failure to environmentally qualify electrical equipment important to safety.[24]

Finally, the NRC's purported assurance that plants meet their licensing bases is untenable because it is based in part on false information provided by licensees. For example:

Station Blackout Rule—The station blackout issue was a category A Unresolved Safety Issue for more than a decade. NRC published a rule which utilities have several years to meet. In 1989 the NRC Staff conducted an audit of the responses of ten utilities to the requirements of the rule. The audit found that in many cases the utility responses had been misleading, inaccurate, and nonsensical. Among the deficiencies found in the "misleading" category was a utility reference to an analysis that was never performed.[25] It is beyond question that the NRC Staff considered that the station blackout rule was *not being complied with* (the plants were not in compliance with their licensing basis), and that utilities were intentionally submitting incorrect information to the NRC in an attempt to mislead it into thinking that compliance existed where it did not.

Pilgrim—In a 1982 Report to Congress on Abnormal Occurrences, the NRC describes three occurrences of safety significance at Pilgrim Unit 1 "indicating continuing serious deficiencies in management control. . . ."[26] Two of the occurrences involved time periods of several years. One of those occurrences included material false statements by the licensee over a two-and-a-half year period concerning its compliance with requirements to control combustible gas mixtures in containment.[27] The utility simply claimed full compliance in a 1979 letter without checking whether its existing system complied or not, then failed to inform NRC when it discovered its non-compliance in 1980.

Three Mile Island—In 1983, the licensee of this plant was indicted on eleven criminal counts for falsifying the results of leak-rate tests for its primary coolant system for many months. In 1984 the company pleaded guilty to one count and no contest to six others.[28]

In sum, contrary to the assumption in the NRC's license renewal regulation, noncompliance with the Commission's safety requirements appears to be as much the rule as the exception among licensees. The examples noted here are just a small fraction of those which have been identified and publicized in recent years. In light of the spotty nature of NRC oversight and the many instances of licensee non-disclosure and false reporting that have been revealed, it is indisputable that there are many instances of noncompliance which are not known for each one that is known.

Abuse of National Environmental Policy Act

Not only has the NRC drastically limited the scope of safety issues that may be considered in a license renewal proceeding, but it has proposed to virtually eliminate the preparation of Environmental Impact Statements ("EIS's") for license renewal decisions on individual plants. Such EIS's would address such important issues as the potential environmental impacts of license renewal (for example, given a plant's history and the aging of its components, how much has the risk of an accident increased?), the need for and relative cost of the energy to be produced by the plant, and the availability of less costly energy sources.

The NRC has attempted to eliminate the need for individual EIS's by issuing a draft generic EIS that concludes, for all plants, that the benefits of going forward with license renewal generally outweigh the costs.[29] The NRC claims that these conclusions apply to 118 nuclear power plants, which include not only those plants that are licensed for operation, but also plants which hold construction permits issued between 13 and 15 years ago and are still not in operation. Thus, even if it is unrealistically assumed that these plants will be licensed for operation in 1992, the NRC claims that it can not only assess the economic, safety and environmental impacts of continuing to operate aging nuclear power plants until the year 2052 (*i.e.*, a 40-year original license term plus a 20-year renewal term), but that these impacts are acceptable and preferable to every alternative to renewal of the operating licenses. This generalization is not only grossly premature, but is belied by recent decisions to shut down several aging plants— Yankee Rowe, Rancho Seco, and Trojan—because continued operation was deemed impractical and uneconomical.

It is simply absurd to expect that neighbors of nuclear power plants, whose license renewal applications may not be filed for another five to twenty years, will seek to comment on—or even know about—the sweeping conclusions that are intended to bind them years down the road. Yet the NRC has declared that it will refuse to allow these issues to be examined closely at the time of license renewal.[30] In proceeding in this manner, the Commission is not only defeating NEPA's goal of encouraging widespread and effective public participation, but it is also seriously eroding any confidence that the public might have in the openness and accountability of the NRC.

The Rule Contains Virtually No Substantive Standards

The preamble to the proposed version of the license renewal rule stated that the rule would establish the requirements for nuclear power plant license renewal and the information that must be submitted to the NRC for review.[31] Unfortunately, aside from defining the scope of equipment that is subject to review in license renewal proceedings, the license renewal rule does no such thing. Instead, the NRC has placed all of its substantive criteria for license renewal in regulatory guides. As the NRC well knows, these guides are unenforceable.[32] The NRC should be required to promulgate substantive standards that can be enforced by the agency and the public.

Twenty Years Prior to License Expiration Is Too Early to Consider Renewal

The license renewal rule permits application for a renewed license up to 20 years prior to expiration of the existing license.[33] This is too early. Although aging begins before a plant ever operates, there is simply too much about the age-related degradation of a plant that will still be unknown when it is only half-way through its 40-year life. The Yankee Rowe plant is a good example. In 1981, when it was twenty years old—the point at which the NRC proposes to permit an application for renewal—a license renewal review would not have revealed the serious reactor vessel embrittlement problem that led to the plant's shutdown in 1992.

Of course, utilities need lead time to plan for and implement alternatives if licenses are not renewed, but that need does not dictate or justify a 20-year lead time. The *earliest* that a license renewal application should be accepted is about thirteen years prior to license expiration. That leaves three years for the license renewal proceeding, plus ten years for the utility to implement alternatives if the renewal is denied. Thus, the renewal decision could have the benefit of the knowledge gained from at least two-thirds of the plant's initial operating term, and utilities would still have ample time to implement alternatives.[34]

The Timely Renewal Doctrine Should Not Be Abused

The license renewal rule also includes a "timely renewal" provision which allows the indefinite extension of the original license term while a renewal application is pending.[35] The timely renewal doctrine should not be abused in the context of license *renewal* as it has been in the context of operating licenses. There should be a firm limit—perhaps four or five years—on the time an applicant has to satisfy the requirements for renewal. It should not be possible to operate a reactor for 17 years following license expiration the way it has been possible to operate on a provisional operating license for that long.

Notes

1. Final Rule, Nuclear Power Plant License Renewal, 56 Fed. Reg. 64,943 (December 13, 1991).

2. Moreover, as discussed below, aside from those aspects of the CLB that are affected by aging of the reactor, licensees need not even demonstrate compliance with the CLB.

3. 10 C.F.R. § 50.48, 45 Fed. Reg. 76,610 (November 19, 1980).

4. SECY-83-269, "Fire Protection Rule for Future Plants (SECY-82-267)" (July 5, 1983).

5. Memorandum from Victor Stello, Jr., EDO, to Samuel Chilk, NRC Secretary, re: Report Requested by Commissioners Asselstine and Bernthal, Enclosure: Impact of Budget Cuts on NRC's Ability to Assure Safety (Overview), at 18 (April 30, 1986).

6. Letter from William T. Russel, Region I Administrator, to Boston Edison Company, re: Exercise of Enforcement Discretion Relative to Fire Barrier Deficiencies" (October 13, 1988).

7. Letter from Daniel G. McDonald, Senior Project Manager, to Ralph G. Bird, Boston Edison Co., re: Issuance of Amendment No. 123 to Facility Operating License No. KPR-35 (TAC# 69026) Pilgrim Nuclear Power Station (October 13, 1988).

8. Proposed rule, 55 Fed. Reg. 29,053.

9. 10 C.F.R. § 54.29.

10. 10 C.F.R. § 54.29.

11. 10 C.F.R. § 54.3(1).

12. *See* Letter from NRC Commissioner John F. Ahearne to Hon. Morris Udall (December 17, 1979).

13. *See, e.g.*, Maize, "Commonwealth Edison Says it Will Try Harder," *The Energy Daily* (September 25, 1990); Nelson, "NRC Willing to Let NUMARC Regulate Industry on Design Reconstitution," *Inside NRC* (August 13, 1990); Jordan, "Hundreds of Millions Expected to be Spent on Design Reconstitution," *Nucleonics Week* (April 26, 1990).

14. Policy Statement, "Availability and Adequacy of Design Bases Information at Nuclear Power Plants," 57 Fed. Reg. 35,455 (August 10, 1992).

15. *Id.*

16. Energy Reorganization Act of 1974, Pub. L. 93-438, 88 Stat. 1233.

17. 10 C.F.R. § 54.29.

18. 56 Fed. Reg. at 64,950.

19. Harold Denton, memorandum to the Commission (July 23, 1980), at 5. When it licenses nuclear power plants, the NRC conducts only "audit reviews" of design and construction. In an operating license proceeding, the NRC Staff reviews, at most, forty percent of the design for one-of-a-kind plants. For plants whose designs are more familiar, the staff reviews significantly less. NRC inspectors physically review less than one percent of the completed plant to determine compliance with NRC regulations. *See Nuclear Licensing Reform: Hearing Before the House Subcommittee on Energy Conservation and Power, House Committee on Energy and Commerce*, 98th Cong., 1st Sess. 450 (1983). As noted by Mr. Denton, it is impossible for the Commission to state, based on these audit reviews, that all requirements are met.

20. Generic Letter No. 89-10, June 28, 1989, Attachment 20.

21. *Id.*

22. *Consolidated Edison Company of New York* (Indian Point, Unit No. 2), *Power Authority of the State of New York* (Indian Point, Unit No. 3), CLI-83-16, 17 NRC 1006, 1014 (1983).

23. *Petition for Emergency and Remedial Action*, CLI-80-21, 11 NRC 707, 710 (1980).

24. 55 Fed. Reg. 35203 (August 28, 1990).

25. "NRC Staff Unhappy with Industry Responses to Station Blackout Resolution," *Inside NRC* (November 6, 1989). The NRC Staff was preparing a generic letter on the issue that would have required utilities to submit sworn statements as to the accuracy and sufficiency of their previously submitted analyses and documentation. Under pressure from the industry, the NRC decided not to issue the letter. *See* "NUMARC Convinces NRC to Scrap Generic Letter on Station Blackout," *Inside NRC*, January 1, 1990.

26. Report to Congress on Abnormal Occurrences, NUREG-0090, Vol. 5, No. 1, August 1982, Item 82-3.

27. 10 CFR § 50.44.

28. *TMI-1 Restart: An Evaluation of the Licensee's Management Integrity as It Affects Restart of Three Mile Island Nuclear Station Unit 1*, NUREG-0680, Supp. 5 (1984).

29. NUREG-1437, Draft Generic Environmental Impact Statement for License Renewal of Nuclear Plants (August 1991). As of this writing, no final EIS has been issued.

30. 56 Fed. Reg. 47,016, 47018-19 (Sept. 17, 1981).

31. 55 Fed. Reg. 29,043.

32. *Gulf States Utilities Co.* (River Bend Station, Units 1 & 2), ALAB-444, 6 NRC 760 (1970).

33. 10 CFR § 54.17(c).

34. The inappropriateness of the 20-year lead time is highlighted by the re-renewal provision, proposed 10 CFR § 54.31(d). That provision permits a renewed license to be renewed again subject to the same requirements. If the second renewal can also be applied for 20 years ahead of its expiration, that application can be submitted the day after the initial license would have expired. In other words, when the plant has been operating for 40 years plus 1 day, the utility can immediately apply for a second renewal that would extend the plant's life from 60 to 80 years. This makes no sense whatsoever.

35. 10 C.F.R. § 2.109.

8

Nuclear Oversight by Congress

Henry R. Myers

The focus of this discussion of Congressional oversight of nuclear matters is on what is and is not practical, the reasons for ineffectiveness in the oversight process, and recommendations for improvements.

Nuclear oversight seeks to (1) determine whether agencies are carrying out Congressional mandates as specified in the Atomic Energy Act and related legislation; (2) prod these agencies into fulfilling their responsibilities; and (3) determine the need for new legislation.

Oversight is the last link in the chain of institutional checks that is supposed to protect the public against health hazards resulting from nuclear malfunctions. This last link is not a superfluous activity having only theoretical value. Occurrences of dangerous, costly and confidence eroding episodes (the accident at Three Mile Island (TMI), design defects at Diablo Canyon, quality assurance breakdowns at such plants as Zimmer (Ohio) and Watts Bar (TVA), safety and contamination problems at DOE facilities, etc.) have been all too real and cannot be denied or wished away as the most ardent proponents of the technology would like. Such episodes arise from licensee and regulatory failures which, in some cases, would not have occurred if Congressional oversight had been adequate.

A review of the record of nuclear oversight reveals that many issues deserving of oversight were not taken up; some issues were delved into when it should have been apparent beforehand that they were matters not amenable to oversight; in other cases, investigations were called off prior to completion of what should and could have been done. Initial good intentions, accompanied by declarations that the bottom of the matter would be uncovered, have all too often given way to reelection imperatives.

Moreover, it is a fact that Congress' primary concern is not with seemingly abstract issues of regulatory compliance, but rather with assuring a near-term absence of serious accidents. Because there is a long interval between regulatory failures and the occurrence of dangerous situations rooted in such failures, Congressional oversight usually happens too late in the game after an accident or when the cost of remedial action is so great that a natural tendency to rationalize the existing situation is allowed to prevail.

Owing to the tediousness of the process that must be followed in order to establish whether a regulatory breakdown has created a real danger, the interest of oversight committee members tends to wane well before the investigatory process has run its course. This waning takes place even when the event triggering the oversight is dramatic, as in the use of incorrect engineering drawings at Diablo Canyon. Interest wanes in such cases because what begins as a clear cut regulatory failure calling for a remedy develops into a morass of sufficient complexity that Congressional overseers find the easiest path is not to intervene. In place of pursuing investigations, the overseers are disposed to hope and trust that the regulators themselves will learn the necessary lessons and take the appropriate corrective actions.

The multi-billion dollar regulatory breakdown at TVA is but one example of a case where Congress went on to other matters before assuring that the causes and consequences of the breakdown were determined, and the resulting safety issues resolved. Here, over a several year period—as indications of management mis- and malfeasance grew, and evidence of faulty design and construction mounted—Committee members' interest in the inquiry simply faded. In the absence of Congress members' interest and support, staff investigators were unable to continue their inquiry, and the investigation ended without pinpointing the specific origins of the debacle, much less determining those responsible for it. Far from assuming the micromanagerial posture that it is accused of doing in many areas, Congress has often ignored the need to insist upon accountability, thereby allowing the NRC itself to decide how to deal with the costly failings of its staff and licensees, and the dangers resulting therefrom.

Although there have been occasional bursts of determination, energy and enthusiasm directed at the oversight job, these have withered in the face of tedium and complexity and the eruption of unrelated crises calling for members' time. Even the accident at TMI—which, if anything, should have been able to sustain Congressional interest—was abandoned, leaving important facts about this near-catastrophe (which changed the course of nuclear development) locked within the heads of a small number of NRC and utility employees. For example, there is no public record describing measurements of a reactor coolant sample taken early in the accident; we do not know the specifics of the NRC's failure to act on Carl Michelson's pre-TMI analysis indicating the need for measures that might have prevented the accident; there are outstanding questions concerning modification of General Public Utilities' accident investigation report; the circumstances of the disappearance and reappearance of thermocouple data are not known; etc.

Other examples abound in which oversight was deficient or non-existent: e.g. operating deficiencies at Pilgrim, electrical system problems at Nine Mile Point, power oscillations in Boiling Water Reactors, the NRC's use of risk analysis in seeming contradiction to the Commission's position, the inability of the Commission to take strong actions in the face of licensee material false statements, etc.

At bottom, Congressional oversight of the nuclear enterprise, while having some success at the margins, has been largely ineffective. The failure of the oversight process has caused the risks and costs of nuclear power to be substantially greater than they would have been had oversight obligations been fulfilled.

Background

There is a forty year history of the NRC and its predecessor agencies pulling punches in fulfilling responsibilities to assure protection of the public health and safety. Until the NRC came into being in 1975, this punch pulling, in my view, was rooted in the regulators' deep-seated belief that a thriving nuclear enterprise was necessary to assure the nation's economic well-being. The regulators thought the risks were low; many of them really did believe that the dangers associated with the use of fission energy to boil water were not all that different from the problems associated with other energy sources used for this purpose. As stated by Rasmussen *et al.* in the Reactor Safety Study,[1] the regulators believed the probability of being injured by a nuclear accident was on the order of the probability of being hit by a meteor.

The regulators also had a tendency to believe that their critics were acting on the basis of irrational fears. At times the regulators made known their belief that, for reasons unspecified, the nuclear critics' real purpose was to disable the nuclear enterprise in order to cause an erosion of the national security. Believing they were on the side of the good, and because they had little respect for the critics, whom they sometimes considered un-American and nearly always loose with facts, the regulators themselves did not feel a particular compunction to be truthful. In essence, truth was not an important element in the nuclear regulators' value system.

While it was and is supposed to carry out its safety mandate by issuing and enforcing appropriate regulations, the NRC sometimes simply failed to do so. The agency also got into the habit of making its regulations comport with conditions in the field rather than requiring that activities and facilities comply with regulations.

Moreover, the regulators' prevailing views have always been shared by strong forces within the Congress. Until the mid-1970's, the Joint Committee on Atomic Energy (JCAE) exercised practically full control over nuclear affairs within the Congress. While the JCAE almost certainly had much more complete access to agency information than did the JCAE's successors, the Committee members had a booster mindset that seemed to filter out data on nuclear risks that could threaten public acceptance of nuclear power or nuclear weapons production facilities.

Around 1973, Jonathan Bingham, Morris K. Udall and others got concerned enough with the Joint Committee's lax oversight and unabashed support for the commercial nuclear establishment that they were able to persuade their colleagues first to dilute the JCAE's authority and later to abolish it. In 1974, nuclear oversight authority was assigned to the House Interior Committee and in late 1976, the JCAE was disestablished and its oversight and legislative powers were assigned to other standing committees.[2]

With the disestablishment of the JCAE, Congressional jurisdiction shifted to committees chaired by members who were not prone to accept at face value information conveyed to them by nuclear regulators and their industrial cohorts. This Congressional skepticism, along with serious nuclear mishaps and evidence of misfeasance (e.g. the Browns Ferry fire, the misuse of risk analysis for propaganda purposes, the after-the-fact appearance of design and construction errors at numerous plants) led to more serious but still deficient Congressional oversight. The post-JCAE oversight arrangements, while less effective than had been hoped by the proponents of the reassignment of responsibility, nevertheless did bring into the public domain much more information concerning the safety status of the commercial nuclear enterprise.

The change in Congressional jurisdiction, which resulted in numerous Committees having authority to conduct nuclear oversight, seemed to cause a change in regulatory attitudes. While the regulators continued to present an overly optimistic evaluation of the inherent safety of nuclear reactors, I believe that in the post-JCAE era the regulators were not primarily motivated by a desire to protect an industry whose virtues and safety they postulated. Rather, the regulators' behavior, in important respects, could be explained by a desire to avoid having to account for whatever might go wrong.[3] (For example, *there is no clear evidence of NRC officials being held accountable* for the billion dollar regulatory lapses that occurred at Three Mile Island, Zimmer, Watts Bar, etc.)

The new era and associated attitudinal changes notwithstanding, the regulators continued to coverup problems that were figuratively, if not actually, buried in concrete, (i.e. the regulators sought to conceal design, construction, and operations deficiencies at existing facilities). They acted this way because, in my view, they perceived (correctly) that it would not be good for their careers if they were seen as disposed to raise questions that might jeopardize huge investments. The regulatory conventional wisdom was that regulations were so conservative that strict compliance was not necessary to assure safety.

In the post-JCAE era, however, the regulators' apologia for the industry did have limits; NRC officials would move quickly to throw a licensee over the side if an obviously dangerous situation arose. And the regulators would not protect the industry at the price of appearing foolish in defending the indefensible.

The purportedly stricter oversight that followed the JCAE had a narrow success at best in exposing the coverup of regulatory noncompliance. The coverup was so successful that the extent of the gap between what is required by regulation and what is installed in the field is unknown and perhaps unknowable. For example, the NRC cannot enumerate the extent to which reactors comply with current regulations, and in some cases, the NRC has difficulty in determining the extent to which plants comply with regulations applicable to their own operating licenses.

The pipe welds at the Seabrook Nuclear Power Station (New Hampshire) exemplify a situation in which, owing to a disarray in records and the practical difficulties of re-inspection, the quality of a small but unknown number of welds is now indeterminate and is likely to stay so. The Seabrook licensee certified that the plant had been built and designed as required by NRC regulations; the NRC then accepted this certification as valid and issued an Operating License. When investigators found that the weld records did not comply with NRC regulations, the Commission at first disputed and then ignored the finding. The House Interior Committee Subcommittee on Energy and the Environment dropped its investigation of the matter, apparently deciding whatever violation of NRC regulations might have occurred, including issuance of an Operating License on the basis of a false certification, was a *de minimis* matter. This does not mean the Seabrook welds are unsafe; it does mean that confidence in safety derives from faith that the people who approved the welds during construction did the job properly; confidence in safety does not derive from the document trail that is required by NRC regulations.

In sum, regulatory dissembling persisted in the post-Joint Committee era. The primary purpose of the new Congressional overseers should have been to determine whether reactor safety was adequate. Although this was a relatively tractable task, the Congress was up and down (but mostly down) in its demand for accurate and complete information, and for holding accountable officials who failed to fulfill their regulatory responsibilities. Congress did not confront the significance of the failure of regulation manifest in such events as inadequate seismic design calculations at Maine Yankee et al., the Three Mile Island accident, quality assurance breakdowns at Zimmer. These and other episodes would not have occurred if regulators' assertions as to the adequacy of the regulatory process had been valid.

With so little understanding of the safety status of nuclear operations, the overseers were unable to address adequately the question of whether existing statutes were being observed. And the need for new legislation was even more difficult to address than were questions of adherence to existing law. Nevertheless, in spite of so little knowledge of whether the existing law had brought about the desired level of safety, Congressional oversight during the period 1976–1992 dealt at tedious length with legislative proposals for "reforming" the nuclear licensing process, a reformation which advocates said was necessary in order to reduce regulatory inefficiency, and which opponents argued would lead to reduced safety. During this time, proponents of reform, in my view, never developed a plausible justification for it. Such legislation was finally enacted in 1992, notwithstanding that it was founded on flawed arguments and unreal scenarios as to why the commercial nuclear enterprise had foundered.[4]

What Oversight Can and Cannot Achieve

A properly managed Congressional oversight process would play a critical role in keeping the nuclear risk at or below the level that the majority of Congresspeople believe to be acceptable. Some in Congress would of course set much stricter standards than would others.

There is undoubtedly a great variance among members as to what in their minds constitutes the tolerable risk level, and there is probably a difference between their private and public views as to what this level should be. For example, the publicly stated position of many members (after having been presented with various safety goal options) might be that the probability of a major accident should be less than one per million reactor years. But of the members that state this position, I suspect that, in private, few believe it to be necessary, or to be the level of safety that has been achieved or that is even achievable. I suspect that in their hearts, most Congresspeople would consider nuclear safety to be adequate at a level of risk much greater than one severe accident per million reactor years; i.e. safety, in their minds, would be adequate if during their lifetimes significant off-site releases of radiation did not occur, thus alleviating them of the need to explain why they had not exercised stricter oversight.

The conventional Congressional wisdom appears to be that reactors are safe enough and that concern about a serious nuclear accident can be safely relegated to the bottom of the in-box. This conventional wisdom may or may not be correct; no one really knows. But whether it is or not can be determined through the oversight process, which can also be a major force in bringing about remedial actions. The goal of making sure that safety is at the level set by the Congressional conventional thinking is a limited and achievable oversight goal. If the NRC fulfills its regulatory obligations, the likelihood of a severe accident would be sufficiently low to satisfy the large majority of Congresspeople and their constituents.

It is not the purpose of this discussion to delve into questions such as: how safe is safe enough; how many plants would be uneconomic if regulations were rigorously enforced; or what the impact of a strict regulatory process would be upon decisions to construct additional plants. I do not know the answers to these questions. The best that can be done in arriving at a judgement about such matters is to make as much sense as possible from an analysis of experience to date and the disparate expert interpretations of this experience.

Notwithstanding differences as to what ultimately constitutes adequate safety, oversight committees can take specific actions that would exert pressure upon regulators to act in a way that will assure that accidents are rare and their consequences limited. Such specific actions do not include involvement in establishing regulations; e.g. radiation exposure limits, seismic standards, emergency core cooling requirements, etc. While Congress can set the overall tone, it should suppress tendencies to become directly involved in regulation writing; to do so creates confusion, leading sometimes to a strengthening of regulations and sometimes to making them weaker, depending on which Congressional committees are acting and depending upon the personalities of the Chairmen. In fact, regulations addressing a particular issue can be both strengthened and weakened as a result of micromanagement by disparate committees; Congressional micro-management of regulations and regulators creates considerable uncertainty as to Congressional intent and sets the groundwork for the regulators to go off in directions determined by their own biases.

The following is a listing of the specifics of what I believe can and cannot be accomplished by the oversight process.

Oversight Can Extract Truth

Whatever the specific objective of an oversight activity, its primary function is to extract truth. The oversight process can and should overcome the nuclear regulators' historic tendency to present information in a way that seeks to obscure data that could be viewed as indicating a threat to the public safety. By insisting upon full disclosure, the Congressional nuclear overseers would help assure that the nuclear industry performance actually matched the level of protection nominally mandated by law and regulation.

The idea is that if the truth is laid out, safety will take care of itself; i.e. since accident avoidance is a shared and pervasive goal, the managers of the nuclear enterprise, once forced to face facts, can in principle be counted upon to do whatever is necessary to assure safety. One problem, of course, is that in many situations there is no single or simple truth; e.g. there is no unique truth concerning levels of radiation exposure that regulations should allow; there is no single truth about what constitutes a best reactor design; etc.

On the other hand, there is close to a unique truth as to whether reactor construction was done in accord with design; the problem arises when attempts are made to determine the extent to which safety has been degraded as a result of the divergence between design and construction, and whether the amount of degradation was significant. The difficulty of resolving the question of the significance of decreased safety margins is enhanced by the likelihood that utility managers might accept for a particular facility a higher level of risk than the NRC would accept as the average plant risk. This owes to the fact that for a particular plant, a utility might accept an accident risk of 1 per 10,000 reactor years rather than spend hundreds of millions to reduce the risk to the level of 1 per 1,000,000 reactor years, which the NRC might seek in order to keep within tolerable bounds the overall risk from all plants.

In any case, in the real oversight world, truth is elusive and Congressional overseers are confronted with dissembling that which typically they are reluctant to challenge even though they have the powers and ability to do so. Oversight must deal with false statements made directly to the Congress by the NRC or its licensees, as well as such statements made to the NRC by its licensees or employees thereof.

During the course of oversight, situations will be encountered where the NRC has not dealt forthrightly with the licensee's failure to provide accurate and complete information. In such situations, rather than take enforcement action specified by regulations, the NRC officials have accommodated the licensee by invoking canards as: "It was not a lie because we already had other information indicating they were not telling the truth." [Zimmer welds.] Or: "The false statement was made knowing it was false but not with intent to mislead." [Licensee reporting on the TMI accident.] Another tack is to interpret licensee deficiencies in specious ways: "Yes, the records documenting weld quality were defective, but they did not contain evidence that the welds were bad." Hence the suggestion was that there is no problem because the records do not document a problem; the NRC simply ignored the fact that the records are defective and for this reason may not show the existence of problems. At Seabrook, the NRC disregarded the fact that its regulations require accurate records showing that the welds were properly inspected.

In sum, misrepresentations, dissembling, lies and simple unintentional error are susceptible to investigation because contrary facts generally reside in documents which can be brought forward by regulatory or licensee employees willing to risk their jobs in order to put the truth in the open. Moreover, relevant documents can be subpoenaed by oversight committees.

Oversight Can Expose the Existence of an Issue and,
Thereby, Cause Corrective Measures to be Instituted

The need to prepare testimony helps to assure that agency managers address problems that would otherwise be ignored or relegated to relatively low level staff. For example, Congressional oversight activities caused the Commission to focus on the quality assurance breakdown at Zimmer, the widespread failure of regulation at TVA, accident reporting failures at TMI, emergency planning deficiencies at Pilgrim, abuses of power by the Commission's Inspector and Auditor, and weld program deficiencies at Seabrook.

In some such situations, agency and/or industry management are ignoring or minimizing expert opinion suggesting the existence of a safety problem that would be costly to remedy. In these circumstances, where all parties may believe they are telling the truth (and, therefore, by definition, they are not lying) the Congress can convene an oversight hearing for the purpose of listening to diverse expert views. While it is likely that Congresspeople and staffs will not be able to reach valid conclusions as to the correctness of one argument or another (e.g. arguments for and against the adequacy of the Pressurized Thermal Shock [PTS] regulations), the fact that the arguments had to be prepared, approved by agency management, and presented in public, cause the matter to be taken more seriously.

This is what happened with PTS. Demitreos Basdekas, an NRC engineer, persisted in encouraging oversight committees (which did not always welcome such encouragement) to examine his assertion that a PTS could lead to a major accident. Over the years, PTS was the subject of hearings and several written inquiries from committee chairmen. While, during this time it is unlikely that any Congressperson or staff truly understood the technical merits of the disparate arguments, Congressional interest served to keep the matter before the Commission. Notwithstanding their lack of comprehension of details, several Congresspeople did develop the view that PTS was an unresolved problem that could lead to disaster. The Commission came to realize that the Congress did grasp the importance of the issue even though it might not comprehend the metallurgical details. As a result, PTS became a subject of regulatory directives that led to a reduced probability that a catastrophe would follow a PTS that caused pressure vessel failure. While the NRC did not do all that Basdekas thought needed doing, the oversight process did lead to corrective actions that would probably not have been taken otherwise.

Oversight Can Expose and Discredit Projects that are Fraudulent and/or Serving of Narrow Agendas

Zealous promotion sometimes gains backing for implausible and/or bizarre policies and projects: e.g. excavation of a sea-level Panama canal using nuclear explosives; implementation of a "plutonium economy;" the nuclear-powered airplane and rocket; laser isotope separation of plutonium from nuclear waste, etc. The exposure that comes from proper oversight can lead to the termination of endeavors that, like the supersonic transport, do not serve the overall public good and which may contain within them the potential to cause great harm.

Oversight Can Help Congress Determine the Need for and Shape of Legislation

Oversight can define the nature of an issue and provide the information necessary to craft the legislation that will help resolve the problem. Oversight should have been instrumental in leading to resolution of the various nuclear waste issues. This is an area where there has been no shortfall in oversight activity. That nuclear waste issues remain unresolved owes more to unshakable opinions (mostly pertaining to the dangers rightly or wrongly perceived to be inherent in the waste problem) than it does to lack of attention by Congress.

Oversight should also be effective in determining the need and character of legislation affecting the path taken by reactor technology. That is, the oversight process could help to determine the need for legislation requiring or encouraging standardization of reactor designs. Oversight also can help determine the need for legislation that would establish goals to be achieved by standardized designs. In my view, however, it is not productive for Congressional committees to seek to resolve through legislation such things as disputes as to which reactor designs best satisfy Congressional safety goals.

Oversight Can Provide an Overview of the Safety and Economics of Nuclear Technology, and a Picture of the Status of Public Acceptance

The House Interior Committee periodically convened hearings to examine the nuclear big picture. While the resulting record was comprehensive, it is unclear what, if any effect, it had upon nuclear decision makers or interested citizens. I suspect the greatest impact of these hearings resulted from the need to prepare testimony. This caused the preparers and approvers of such testimony to think through their positions, to organize their thoughts, and, possibly, to exorcise a certain amount of hyperbole, thus (maybe) making them more effective at their jobs. For example, requesting the Secretary of Energy to present views on the state of the nuclear enterprise should initiate a testimony preparation process that leads to a clarification and refining of positions. Presenting testimony, and engaging in the give and take that sometimes occurs at hearings, has the potential to bring about a modification of official views and agency spending priorities.

Oversight Can Develop a Public Record of the Circumstances of Serious Accidents and Significant Regulatory Lapses

While nuclear oversight has had only limited success in pinpointing the causes of and responsibility for accidents and regulatory failings, Congressional hearings have led to a more complete and public exposition of the facts than would have otherwise occurred.

Oversight is Unlikely to Resolve Controversy
Founded on Honest Differences of Opinion

Situations in which oversight is not likely to lead to a useful outcome are those where a matter is already being considered in a fairly forthright manner, where there is no attempt to avoid facts, and there is honest disagreement among experts; i.e. there are no hidden analyses or concealed experiments which, if revealed, would lead to a particular decision. An example is the High Temperature Gas Cooled Reactor (HTGR). I once believed strongly (I now have some doubts) that the HTGR had significant safety advantages over water reactors. More important than my believing this, however, was that there were real experts who held this view. There were also experts, who believed that improved LWRs would be safe enough. [There are of course those who believe existing designs are fully adequate.] As a result, periodic hearings aimed at ferreting truths that might have given a boost to the HTGR led to nothing other than modest appropriations, keeping alive the shadow of the concept while its substance withered. Meanwhile, the nuclear mainstream went about the business of promoting safer and more reliable light water reactors.

Reasons for Ineffectiveness

Congresspeople are generally suited neither by temperament nor talent to conduct successful oversight; there is probably little overlap between the traits necessary for winning elections and those needed for oversight. In fact, in certain ways, the attributes that lead to electoral success may work against doing effective oversight.

Success in the legislative part of the Congressional job tends to come in part from an ability to accommodate disparate views and a temperament that avoids confrontation. On the other hand, success in oversight requires dealing with unpopular realities, often involving the misdeeds or stupidity of prominent and well-respected individuals. Oversight, by its nature, requires confrontation of the very kind that many successful legislators tend to disdain.[5]

Effective oversight requires substantial dedication to a small number of issues, a dedication that some might consider obsessive. Winning and holding office requires attention to so many issues that few members of Congress are able to gain more than a superficial understanding of most matters that come before them. On any particular day, attention to oversight issues tends to be deferred to allow time for legislative, constituent, media and fund-raising matters.

Former House Interior Committee Chairman Udall held the view that there was generally enough legislation on the books, and that Congress should focus on making sure that the missions specified by existing legislation were carried out in the manner Congress intended. (Chairman Udall, however, was himself unable to escape the prevailing Congressional currents, and for the most part ignored his own advice, directing his most serious efforts toward legislation.)

During 15 years as a Congressional staff person, I observed that the intrinsic complexity of most matters subject to oversight (it is not always immediately clear why a particular investigation is important) causes Congressional eyes to glaze over. Congresspersons' impatience with presentations of investigatory facts leads, in general, to indifferent support of staff investigators and, in particular, to poor preparation for hearings. One result is that members can appear foolish at hearings; while often displaying ignorance of the basics, they probably think they are being clever, a perception that comes from not knowing what they don't know. In my view, the great majority of questions are not relevant, and when questions that might lead to eliciting important information are asked, the questioners are unable to follow up.

In addition to not knowing what they don't know, Congresspeople often don't know what they do know. This is because most have little understanding of scientific and engineering matters and many, I believe, have mind blocks that lead them to believe themselves simply incapable of comprehending nuclear issues. This mindset need not exist; many and perhaps most members are capable of understanding what is necessary for the nuclear oversight job. They need not get into engineering detail. It is sufficient to be able to parse the nuclear jargon, and to understand that the language used in witness' conclusory statements is often intended to soothe. One need not have a physics Ph.D. to know that Three Mile Island was a near disaster and not an "incident," or to perceive a big difference between "no evidence" and "no conclusive evidence," or to appreciate the absurdity of claims that the Browns Ferry Fire demonstrated the inherent safety of nuclear technology.

Witnesses at oversight hearings have in fact exploited Congressional engineering insecurity by posing as paragons of scientific objectivity who take offense when their testimony is questioned. They portray themselves as workers dedicated to the national good, forced to take time from the important business of protecting the public safety in order to answer stupid questions posed by publicity seeking politicians. Witnesses use their technical expertise to evade answering questions or to redirect questions to more comfortable territory. Experts will seek to intimidate questioners; e.g.: "I have been a nuclear engineer all my life, and I know there was no meltdown at Three Mile Island."[6]

Members' overall hearing performance can sometimes make staff appear to be loose cannons acting in the name of egocentric politicians whose interest in substance is minimal. The hearing atmosphere created by uninformed and bored members begets an accurate perception among the overseen that stonewalling and obfuscation will cause investigations to end in a premature and indeterminate manner; even if the investigators don't tire, their bosses will.

The subjects of oversight correctly come to understand that complaints of harassment made to committee chairmen or their colleagues will have a good chance of causing the rug to be pulled from under the investigators. Chairmen are prone to do this in part because they are insecure with regard to their understanding of the facts. The Chairman also are driven to give up out of a sense of concern that investigations are open-ended and that they will be accused of wasting taxpayer dollars on what appears to be endless wrangling over details that do not relate to the pressing needs of ordinary citizens.

It is also noteworthy that there are not many staff who do well at oversight. On the surface this is surprising since there is no shortage of bright and energetic people who, prior to Congressional employment, declare with great confidence their enthusiasm for oversight work. But once ensconced in a Congressional staff position charged with oversight responsibilities, such people tend to work in a half-hearted manner, unable or unwilling to do what is necessary to achieve results. In these circumstances, staff tend to be rewarded on the basis of getting headlines featuring their bosses. This is not so good for oversight work, since a preoccupation with headlines undermines investigations by making it appear that they are being conducted for the purpose of enhancing the Chairman's prominence. Since investigations tend to be interminable and run a high risk of an indeterminate outcome, staff do better for themselves by focusing on legislative or constituent matters that yield more clear cut political benefits.

Apart from elements peculiar to the Congressional environment, there are also certain features common to all aspects of the government milieu that lead to reluctance to get into important matters calling for oversight. Such matters involve situations where persons with relatively distinguished careers appear to have engaged in behavior which, while apparently inappropriate, does not warrant an inquiry that might reveal feet of clay or, perhaps, perjury.

It is as though, within the government, there is a tacit understanding among the great majority of officials above the junior staff level, that one should not raise questions that might reveal chinks in an official's armor, except in circumstances that require the apparent wrongdoing to be confronted. A prerequisite for success in government is probably the ability to recognize not only what is to be ignored, but also the point at which the high threshold has been reached and wrongdoing can no longer be ignored.

In such an environment, the NRC has gone to extremes to protect officials from bearing responsibility for actions that revealed incompetence, irresponsibility, or mal-feasance. As indicated by participants in NRDC's December 1992 Graves Mountain Conference, NRC officials "circled the wagons" in the face of Congressional inquiries that NRC officialdom believed to be unfairly directed at "dedicated" NRC staff. In effect, NRC management assigned itself the decision as to what would or would not be an appropriate matter for Congressional oversight.

Acting under the "high-threshold" rule for defining wrongdoing, the Commission seemed to have no compunction as it generated smoke in defense of high agency and licensee officials with regard to such matters as evidence of a diversion of nuclear explosive material, false reports on the TMI accident, the safety status of TVA reactors, harassment of NRC staff by management, and descriptions of weld quality at Seabrook. Congressional overseers, showing their own tacit acceptance of the high threshold for chasing after miscreant officials, failed not only to pursue apparent wrongdoing but tolerated the Commission's coverup of same.

As noted above, there are numerous instances where Congressional committees ended investigations prior to the achievement of their objectives. We do not know about many significant NRC lapses pertaining to Three Mile Island, the Reactor Safety Study, Seabrook, Browns Ferry, Watts Bar, Nine Mile Point, Pilgrim, etc. The Congress could (but did not) deal with situations where the NRC says, for example, that the Sequoyah cables (Seabrook welds, Zimmer records) are o.k. cables (welds or records) when it later turns out that NRC and licensee documents, contemporaneous with NRC approval, reveal significant questions about the safety of cables (welds or records). Or Congress could and should have hammered the NRC for its use of the Reactor Safety Study in misrepresenting the risk of a nuclear accident; it did not do so. Our not knowing about these things, and the failure to hold miscreant officials accountable owes largely to a lack of Congressional perseverance in the face of the ability of the NRC and its supporters to derail investigations by stonewalling, "limited hangouts," and clever obfuscatory actions.

While the bottom line here is that, in general, Congressional overseers of the commercial nuclear enterprise have all too often been ineffective, there are exceptions to the norm. One group to which certain of these critical views do not apply is the House Energy and Commerce Committee's Subcommittee on Oversight and Investigations. This Subcommittee, when it has taken on issues involving civilian nuclear affairs, has been much more thorough in its conduct of hearings and investigatory work than the typical oversight committee. But even here, because of the large number of issues within its purview, it has had insufficient resources to apply to nuclear regulatory matters; it has had little effect in steering the NRC in the direction of being a rigorous regulator that can be counted upon to provide accurate and complete information to the Congress and public.

What Might Be Done to Improve the Process

Notwithstanding that nuclear oversight, at best, has achieved only limited success, a much better job could be done if the responsibility for such activities were assigned to members who believed in its importance, who had a good sense of where their resources should be applied and who were willing and able to expend the effort necessary to do the job. In my view the performance of the NRC could be upgraded considerably were a motivated and energetic Committee Chairman to commit a few (e.g. four) hours per week to the task.

If this is to happen, it is necessary that the Committee Chairman recognize the types of issues that are and are not tractable subjects of oversight. It is necessary that Committee members not fall victim to NRC and industry representatives who, knowing they know more than does the average politician, seek to intimidate by acting as though they have been dragged away from work on safety matters to satisfy Congressional egos, or by appearing more knowing about issues than in fact they are. Adequate oversight would require that the oversight Committee chairman have a grasp of what he or she does and does not know, and that he or she not be subdued by any sense of intellectual inadequacy in dealing with nuclear issues.

Successful oversight also requires that Committees not spend undue amounts of time in areas where the risk to public health and safety is relatively insignificant. For example, when the Congress gets intimately involved in the manner in which very low level radioactivity should be regulated (i.e. Below Regulatory Concern [BRC]), it is allowing itself to be diverted from issues where the potential threat to the public safety is real; e.g. the House Interior Committee diverted its principal oversight energies to BRC during a period when significant safety questions about Pilgrim, Nine Mile Point, and Seabrook had come to the fore.

The oversight task does not require that the overseers understand engineering details; it does require an ability to extract nuggets of truth from a sea of nuclear jabber. To do this requires intelligence, not an engineering degree. Perhaps, most of all, the oversight job requires persistence, the willingness to stick with the issue in the face of NRC stonewalling, questions by colleagues as to the worth of the endeavor, and nagging doubt as to whether the oversight goal is reachable (or even suspicion that the goal is simply a mirage).

Many Congresspeople possess the inherent capabilities necessary to do the oversight job. If it is to be done, however, there needs to be an understanding of the history of the nuclear enterprise and the reasons for the historic failure of Congress to do its share in confronting the issues. The question is whether there are capable Congresspeople who possess both the requisite understanding and a willingness to take on the task.

Christopher Paine has proposed a process that should lead to improved Congressional oversight. This would involve decisions by the Congressional leadership as to certain matters that should be subject of "special" oversight investigations. Along with such leadership decisions would be an assignment of resources to the job. The leadership could convene periodically or following the occurrence of an extraordinary event for the purpose of launching such "special" inquiries. Matters calling for this type of inquiry would include severe nuclear accidents (e.g. TMI), potentially dangerous situations (the Davis-Besse feedwater failure), major NRC lapses (the Grand Gulf Mark II/Mark III mixup), failings of the regulatory process leading to large economic losses (the failure of the NRC to detect in timely fashion the nuclear management breakdown at TVA), and significant NRC management failures (the misuse of internal investigatory resources to rid the agency of staff who happened to be disliked by management).

The 1992 election opened the door to changes in the way oversight is handled. This is a time when long-standing deficiencies might be corrected. The next NRDC conference on these matters will provide an opportunity to review and assess whether nuclear oversight will have been more effective in the future than it has been to date.

Notes

1. Reactor Safety Study—An Asssessment of Accident Risks in Commercial U.S. Power Plants, WASH 1400 (NUREG-75/014) NRC October 30, 1975.

2. Paul Parshley notes that commercial nuclear power plants were overseen by the JCAE for a time period that approximates the length of time that such

plants have been overseen by the JCAE's successors. The JCAE, being in charge at the beginning, established the process and culture that governed the use of fission energy to generate electricity. There is no way of knowing whether the history of the nuclear enterprise would have been significantly different had the JCAE not been disestablished following the 1976 elections.

3. For example, after finding that a licensee had used sub-standard electrical components, the NRC might impose a relatively modest penalty, implying that the use of such components was an isolated regulatory violation without serious safety implications. The NRC would not delve into questions of whether there might be a widespread use of such components, whether the violation was willful, and who was responsible. But the NRC would have done enough such that, in the event of an accident resulting from the use of sub-standard components, it could claim that it had in fact found an instance of such use and that, through the imposition of a penalty, had called the matter to the licensee's attention. The NRC could then go on to claim that it did not have sufficient resources to inspect all electrical components, and that this was the licensee's responsibility. The blame would thereby be shifted to the licensee, which is where it should go; but lost from view would be the fact that the accident might have been avoided had the NRC, located at the next level of the safety hierarchy, been diligent in pursuing the implications of its original finding. In such circumstances the NRC officials who failed to seek answers as to root causes, generic implications, and responsibility would escape being held accountable.

4. An interesting project for a student of government would be to compare statements made in the 1992 Congressional debate on nuclear licensing reform with the actual situations these statements addressed.

5. A Congressional staff member, in reference to this paper, stated that in his oversight work he and his colleagues had used a conciliatory approach in dealing with agency officials and that this had led to success in working out problems in a manner acceptable to all parties. He seemed to suggest that the investigations referred to in this paper might have gone better if the investigators had been less confrontational. My experience has been to the contrary: minor matters might have gotten resolved satisfactorily through discussion without confrontation, but when it came to major issues (e.g. whether Seabrook had been licensed on the basis of a false certification), the NRC viewed Congressional amiability as a sign of weakness that opened the door to seeking to overwhelm the investigators with irrelevant and inaccurate information. The usual result of trying the conciliatory approach was angry investigators and the NRC plaint that it was being criticized because the agency's position did not agree with that of the investigators. In situations in which I was involved, the investigators were angry because they believed (correctly, in my view) that the NRC was not interested in the truth, that it believed these investigations to be unwarranted meddling in its affairs, and it sought only to do whatever was necessary to terminate the Congressional the inquiries. "Whatever was necessary" often encompassed seeking to discredit the investigators and other actions that were clearly not appropriate regulatory behavior and which sometimes entered the gray area between what was legal and what was criminal.

6. This is an allusion to NRC testimony before the House Interior Committee on March 29, 1979, the second day of the TMI accident. The evidence indicates that at that time, high level NRC officials did not know that a significant portion of the TMI-2 reactor core had melted. The dialogue became testy in response to a member's expressions of doubt as to whether NRC officials were presenting the whole truth as they understood it on the morning of March 29.

9

An Investment Community Perspective on Nuclear Power

Paul Parshley

Investors must make individual risk-reward decisions as they choose among alternative investment opportunities. For electric utility investors, we believe the risk-reward determination should require consideration of a variety of risks associated with the ownership and operation of nuclear power plants. The cost of capital for those companies with above average nuclear risk should be higher than for those companies with average or below average risk. In other words, investors should demand to be compensated for taking on incremental nuclear risk. We have seen some evidence in recent years that investors move along a nuclear risk learning curve as the current generation of reactors ages. The progression has been from construction risk to operating risk, and now seems to be moving in the direction of discounting uncertainties associated with economic viability, early shutdowns and decommissioning.

If the financial community adequately understands the risks associated with individual nuclear utilities, those companies with above average risk will be forced to pay higher financing costs and therefore will have an economic incentive to improve their operations.

Nuclear Construction Risk

Comanche Peak 2, the last of the current generation of light water reactors being built by an investor owned utility in the U.S., is expected to enter commercial service in 1993. We are unaware of any electric utility CEO seeking to be first in line to order the next nuclear power plant.

An impediment to future expansion of domestic nuclear generating capacity is that many investors have clear recollections of the substantial financial distress experienced during the 1980s by those companies with large nuclear plant construction schedule slippages and cost overruns. One utility, Public Service Company of New Hampshire, was forced into bankruptcy by the economic burden of building the Seabrook plant, and now is a subsidiary of Northeast Utilities. The failure of another company, El Paso Electric, which still operates under the protection of the Federal Bankruptcy Court, was due in part to the cost of building the Palo Verde plant. Long Island Lighting, PSI Resources (formerly Public Service of Indiana) and Gulf States Utilities were brought to the brink of bankruptcy and had to suspend payment of preferred stock dividends for extended periods of time. Since 1984, financial pressures largely attributable to nuclear plant construction have caused 24 investor-owned electric utilities—nearly a third of the industry—to cut their common stock dividends (see table). Many companies also experienced credit quality erosion and bond rating downgrades.

Related problems (such as Commonwealth Edison's continuing inability to charge customers for construction costs incurred years ago at Byron 2 and the two Braidwood units) continue to depress the value of certain companies securities today. We expect in the foreseeable future that the market would react very negatively to any announced plans by investor-owned utilities to undertake the construction of an advanced reactor in the U.S.

Large Accident Risk

Electric utility investors implicitly are making the judgment that a large accident will not occur in the domestic nuclear utility industry while they are holding the securities of any company that has an ownership share in an operating commercial reactor. Other institutional and retail investors have adopted investment policies which allow them to invest only in non-nuclear utilities.

From time to time, we have reported to investors on risk assessment work being done by the NRC, and we have tried to say something meaningful about how the results should be perceived and integrated into utility investment decisions. While we will attempt to continue to monitor and interpret available information on this subject, it remains very difficult to factor low-probability/high-consequence events into daily investment decisions.

TABLE 9.1 Common Stock Dividend Cuts Attributable to Nuclear Construction Problems

Company	Nuclear Plant	Dividend Cut Date	From	To	Dividend Growth Restored	Restored Dividend Rate	12/1/92 Rate
Centerior	Beaver Valley 2 Perry 1	1988	$2.64	$1.60	—	—	$1.60
Central Hudson	Nine Mile Pt 2	1987	$2.96	$1.70	1988	$1.76	$2.00
Central Maine Power	Seabrook	1984	$1.96	$1.40	1987	$1.48	$1.56
CMS Energy	Midland	1984	$2.52	$0.00	1989	$0.04	$0.48
Commonwealth Ed	Byron 2 Braidwood 1 & 2	1992	$3.00	$1.60	—	—	$1.60
DQE	Beaver Valley 2	1986	$2.06	$1.20	1988	$1.28	$1.60
El Paso Electric	Palo Verde	1989	$1.52	$0.00	—	—	$0.00
Entergy	Grand Gulf	1985	$1.78	$0.00	1988	$0.80	$1.60
Gulf States Utils	River Bend	1986	$1.64	$0.00	—	—	$0.00
Illinois Power	Clinton	1989	$2.64	$0.00	1991	$0.80	$0.80
Kansas City P&L	Wolf Creek	1986	$1.18	$1.00	1987	$1.12	$1.44
Kansas G&E	Wolf Creek	1985	$2.36	$1.18	1986	$1.36	$1.72
Long Island Lighting	Shoreham	1984	$2.02	$0.00	1989	$1.00	$1.74
NY State E&G	Nine Mile Pt 2	1988	$2.64	$2.00	1989	$2.04	$2.16
Niagara Mohawk	Nine Mile Pt 2	1987	$2.08	$1.20			
		1989	$1.20	$0.00	1991	$>064	$0.80
NIPSCO Industries	Bailly	1985	$1.56	$0.00	1987	$0.60	$1.24
Ohio Edison	Beaver Valley 2 Perry 1	1990	$1.96	$1.50	—	—	$1.50
Pacific Gas & Elec	Diablo Canyon	1988	$1.92	$1.40	1990	$1.52	$1.76
Philadelphia Elec	Limerick 2	1990	$2.20	$1.20	1991	$1.30	$1.40
PSI Resources	Marble Hill	1984	$2.88	$1.00			
		1986	$1.00	$0.00	1989	$0.80	$1.00
PS New Hampshire	Seabrook	1984	$2.12	$0.00	—	—	—
PS New Mexico	Palo Verde	1988	$2.92	$1.52			
		1989	$1.52	$0.00	—	—	$0.00
Rochester G&E	Nine Mile Pt 2	1987	$2.20	$1.50	1989	$1.56	$1.68
United Illuminating	Sea Brook	1984	$3.08	$2.00	1985	$2.32	$2.56

Nuclear Operating Risk

Electric utility investors should attempt to evaluate the current risks associated with nuclear power plants and to differentiate among the nuclear plant operating performance of individual utilities.

There are now about 100 operating commercial power reactors which are owned or operated by U.S. investor-owned electric utilities. The trends in industry-wide nuclear operating performance for these plants, as measured by the operating statistics—or "Performance Indicators"—which are monitored by both the industry and the NRC, have improved over the past five years. Nevertheless, there is still a wide range of nuclear operating performance within the industry, and some plants continue to experience deteriorating performance and significant operating problems. As a result, investors should expect to see additional plants added to the Nuclear Regulatory Commission's "Problem Plants" list from time to time and, in extreme cases, some plants with performance problems will continue to experience extended forced shutdowns. A relatively recent phenomenon is the emergence of significant operating problems at some nuclear plants which previously had established reputations within the industry for successful nuclear operating performance.

Once operating performance deteriorates to the point at which an extended plant shutdown is required, the operating utility faces a substantial challenge in correcting the poor safety culture and operating problems at the plant. In these cases, regaining the NRC's confidence in the Company's ability to operate the plant safely often requires senior management changes at the utility and extensive programs lasting several years to correct the personnel performance, equipment condition, procedure problems, and design problems which contributed to the performance decline at the plant. The costs of an extended plant shutdown can have a significant adverse effect on a utility's financial condition, ability to pay dividends and credit quality. These costs can total several hundred million dollars and typically include replacement power costs, costs of plant refurbishment and upgrade programs, and, in some instances, return on equity penalties. State economic regulators are likely to scrutinize these expenditures carefully, and utilities may face disallowances for substantial portions of these costs. In addition, a number of state rate commissions are setting long-term nuclear performance standards for the electric utilities which they regulate. Although most of these standards use plant reliability performance measures as their key criteria, at least one state has also used plant operating statistics and NRC regulatory evaluations as criteria as well.

Public information is now available which helps investors to differentiate among the nuclear operating performance of individual plants and utilities. If properly interpreted, this information can be used to identify plants with strong and stable performance as well as those that are declining and, therefore, face a higher risk of being labeled as a problem plant or experiencing an extended plant shutdown.

Information in the public domain which can be useful in identifying the good and not so good nuclear plant operators include the following:

- Plant-by-plant capacity and availability factors
- NRC Systematic Assessment of Licensee Performance (SALP) Reports
- NRC notifications of regulatory violations and fines
- NRC Performance Indicators
- NRC "Problem Plant" list notifications
- NRC Licensee Event Reports
- INPO inspection reports (not generally available)

At Lehman Brothers, we have established a rating scheme intended to convey to investors our assessment of the relative nuclear operating performance of individual plants. Each plant is ranked in one of the following five categories: top performers, above average performers, average performers, below average performers, and poor performers.

Our nuclear operating performance rankings for each plant are based upon an evaluation of four factors: NRC Performance Indicators, or key plant operating statistics, which are compiled by the NRC on a quarterly basis; NRC regulatory performance, including significant operating events, NRC SALP evaluations, and NRC fines and violations; plant reliability performance as measured by recent annual and lifetime plant capacity factors; and insights gained from our own direct inspection and observation of these plants and their utility operators and management.

Nuclear Plant Economics

Key Issues for Investors

Half of the nuclear plants in the United States now are "middle aged", and important questions are beginning to arise about their ongoing ability to produce electricity at a price that is competitive with available alternatives. The questions cut widely across the utility industry because over two-thirds of the 75 largest investor-owned electric companies in the United States have an ownership stake in one or more of the 110 power reactors now in operation. Recent decisions by utilities in New England, southern California, and the Pacific Northwest to shutdown the Yankee Rowe, San Onofre 1 and Trojan nuclear units years before the expiration of their operating licenses have brought the matter into the national spotlight. There are increasing prospects that a number of additional plants will be permanently shutdown while substantial unamortized investment remains on their owners' books. Will the companies be allowed to recover the unamortized balance from customers? Can they continue to earn a return on assets that have become unproductive before the end of their originally presumed service life? How will the accrual of funds for decommissioning be affected? Will large write-offs be required which could effect an owner's dividend policy?

Our investment research has led us to the following conclusions and advice for investors.

- Evidence suggests the average operating costs of nuclear power plants are now higher than those of conventional plants and other power supply alternatives.
- On average, it appears that older as well as newer plant safety and operational performance has improved substantially in recent years. But, averages do not tell the whole story.
- There seems to be great variation in these costs from plant to plant. The most expensive plants are several times as expensive to operate as the most economical ones.
- Older plants as a class do not exhibit poorer safety or operational performance than newer plants. And, there is a positive correlation between plant safety performance and operational performance.
- Utilities must have effective maintenance programs in place at their nuclear units in order to help assure they remain safe, reliable and economic. Investors should be aware of the relative effectiveness of these programs.
- Generally, utilities should be allowed to recover such costs for prudently built and well run nuclear plants which are shutdown early, but this may not be possible in some states.
- It can be difficult and expensive to demonstrate to the NRC that older plants, are in compliance with today's key safety requirements.

Different utilities confronting these issues have handled them differently. Two recent case studies are worth reviewing because they show how utility management can affect the relative risk of an investment.

CASE 1: Nine Mile Point 1

On November 20, 1992, Niagara Mohawk submitted a noteworthy report to the New York Public Service Commission (NYPSC) containing the results of an economic analysis of continued operation of the Nine Mile Point Unit 1 nuclear plant (NMP1). We view the analysis as significant both for its conclusions, and for the innovative process it established and left in place to monitor the ongoing economic viability of NMP1.

The analysis determined that operating NMP1 for the remaining 17 years of its licensed lifetime probably would have a "negative value for ratepayers." In other words, the economic interest of Niagara Mohawk's customers is likely to be best served by the early shutdown of NMP1. At the same time, the company's study indicated it would be less costly to operate the unit through its next fuel cycle which ends in 1995, than to retire the plant immediately. The fundamental reason cited for this conclusion was the recognition that "retiring a nuclear generating unit before the end of its anticipated useful life is a momentous event with significant consequences, some predictable and many more unpredictable." Although Niagara Mohawk has not made an irrevocable commitment to the early retirement of NMP1, the transition period proposed by the company appears similar in concept to the phase-out plan submitted earlier this year by Portland General for the Trojan nuclear plant.

This new economic study is the first indication from Niagara Mohawk of the potentially negative economics for NMP1 over the long term. The company's previous report to the NYPSC in 1990 indicated a positive value of about $340 million would accrue to ratepayers if the unit operated until its current NRC operating license expires is 2009. The report submitted on November 20, 1992 concludes customers likely would lose between $100 million and $140 million if NMP1 remains in service for the full remaining term of the license.

We are favorably impressed by the process established to monitor and evaluate the economic viability of continuing to operate NMP1. Niagara Mohawk notes that a considerable effort was made throughout the past year to involve the staff of the NYPSC and other interested parties (including the Consumer Protection Board, Multiple Intervenors and the Albany Peace & Energy Council) in the study process leading up to the November 20th report. We believe this effort to exchange ideas on a continuing basis with key stakeholders from outside the ranks of the company's senior management will prove to be in the common interest of Niagara Mohawk's customers, employees and shareholders.

Moreover, the NMP1 monitoring process remains in place and includes specific "triggers" for measuring the unit's performance relative to alternative means of meeting the energy needs of Niagara Mohawk's ratepayers, while specific tasks are undertaken by the company to ready the plant for an orderly shutdown in 1995. The "triggers," targeted for completion by the first quarter of 1993, will include such items as schedule performance in the upcoming refueling outage, the possibility of major equipment failure, performance against Niagara Mohawk's current business plan for reducing NMP1 staffing levels, forecasted non-utility generation and fossil fuel prices, and resolution of certain environmental issues. The company has committed to reassess promptly the decision to continue operating the unit through the next fuel cycle if there is a significant negative change in any of the triggers. Niagara Mohawk also has pledged to complete, as soon as possible, the engineering and planning necessary to be fully prepared to retire the unit, should retirement be deemed prudent in 1995, or thereafter.

Niagara Mohawk contends that circumstances could change between now and the end of the next fuel cycle for NMP1, and that continued operation of the unit could become the preferred alternative. For example, the current economics of NMP1 are determined, in large measure, by the forecast of non-utility generation that will be available to the company over time. The new study anticipates a substantially higher level of power will be available from independent power producers than was projected in the 1990 study, but Niagara Mohawk has doubts about the actual amount and cost of non-utility generation which will be brought on line in the next couple of years. The company's report to the NYPSC also expresses some concern about the possibility of escalation in natural gas prices, uncertainties about the relative environmental attractiveness of nuclear and fossil fuel electric generation, and the value of a diversified fuel mix.

While Niagara Mohawk maintains that developments in these areas may tip the balance in favor of continued operation of NMP1, we currently doubt that will happen. And, we do not sense that the company harbors some deep-rooted, ego-involved, drive to keep NMP1 in service until its NRC operating license expires. In any event, the NMP1 monitoring process should guard against such uneconomic behavior, because as the company stated in its November 20th report: "We expect to keep the (NYPSC) and other parties fully informed of changes, as they occur, in the event the economic viability of the unit improves or declines significantly. A collaborative relationship will ensure that ratepayers and shareholders receive optimal value over the remaining life of the unit."

We agree with Niagara Mohawk's comment about the merits of a "collaborative relationship" which is consistent with out view that openness and candor should be inversely related to the cost of capital for nuclear utilities.

CASE 2: Trojan

On January 5, 1993, Portland General's management briefed securities analysts on the previous day's surprise decision by the company's Board to immediately and permanently shut down the Trojan nuclear plant. The Board's decision was an abrupt departure from the plan announced by the company last August to close Trojan in 1996. The new decision also is surprising in light of the fact that the company spent several million dollars in recent months to defeat an initiative on the November ballot calling for the immediate closing of Trojan.

On January 5th, the price of Portland General's common shares dropped and closed down more than five percent. We believe this erosion in the value of Portland General's common shares is justified because of new questions raised by the Board's decision, and the process leading up to it. Following is our initial assessment of the changed circumstances now surrounding Portland General.

- From an operating risk standpoint, immediate shutdown of Trojan is a good decision. The plant has been a chronic poor performer since it was placed in service in 1976, with a lifetime capacity factor of about 50%, which is among the lowest of the 110 nuclear plants now operating in the U.S. The tube leak which caused the unit to shut down on November 9 is further evidence that the facility was likely to continue to be unreliable if operated, as planned, until 1996.
- However, the process which led to Board's January 4th decision may complicate the company's ability to obtain favorable consideration from the Oregon PUC of its request to recover associated costs which include:
  1) $350 million of unamortized investment in Trojan, with an equity return on that amount;
  2) $115 million in unfunded decommissioning liability, which is not being fully recovered, and probably is a low estimate and probably does not include certain low level waste disposal and site restoration costs;

3) incremental replacement power costs, which the company estimates to be about $60 million in 1993, net of the assumed $60 million in savings from immediate closing of Trojan; and,

4) accelerated capital spending needs for long-term replacement power, the magnitude of which has yet to be determined.

- Evidence of the complications which may have been created by the Board's action include public statements of "surprise" about the decision from a key state regulator, and indications the PUC may review the prudency of the decision in public hearings. Also, in the wake of the Board's decision, we have seen expressions of concern from the company's customers about the wisdom of expenditures made to defeat the November initiatives.

- Portland General may face a credibility problem in explaining the significant changes since last August in its assumptions about the availability of replacement power for Trojan and the costs of running the plant until 1996.

- A number of other uncertainties are likely to face the company through 1993 including:

  1) development of a management plan to guide the accelerated transition of Trojan from an operating to a shut down facility;

  2) development of a decommissioning plan by Portland General, and the winning of its approval from the NRC;

  3) successful management of a rapid and substantial reduction in the 1300-person workforce at Trojan, and perhaps staff reductions in other parts of the company; and,

  4) resolution of long-term replacement of capacity issues, such as whether to accelerate the 1996 in-service date for the Coyote Springs project, and whether to take an equity position in the Smurfit project.

- On dividend policy, a senior company manager told analysts on January 5th that he cannot envision a situation resulting from the Board's decision to shutter Trojan that would lead to impairment of the current $1.20 common dividend, he also said that it would be imprudent of the company to increase the dividend before pending ratemaking issues are settled. We believe investors should pay close attention to the pending cases to help avoid regulatory surprises.

Decommissioning Issues

The future economic viability of existing nuclear power plants is an issue which has received increasing attention in the financial community in the past year. Beginning in the late 1980s, several reactors have been shut down prematurely because they cannot compete on the basis of cost with alternative means of meeting electric utility customer needs. In the next few years, we expect that economic pressure will continue to grow on marginal nuclear units due to enactment of the Energy Policy Act of 1992, which is intended to promote development of an independent power industry and competition in the wholesale electric market. Also, nuclear plants must continue to pass economic muster as more states implement integrated resource planning processes that put utilities with high operating costs at a competitive disadvantage.

These factors have led us to the conclusion that, of the 110 commercial nuclear plants now operating in the U.S., as many as 25 of them could face premature shutdown in the next several to 10 years. This raises some interesting issues for their utility owners related to the timing, cost and financial impact of decommissioning these units, and storage and eventual disposal of their low-level waste and spent fuel.

Among investors, a commonly-held view has been that, while decommissioning costs could grow well above current estimates, they are not likely to be incurred for many years and, therefore, are not particularly relevant to today's investment decisions. In our opinion, investors should begin paying closer attention to matters related to nuclear plant decommissioning for several reasons. First, an increasing number of companies are facing decommissioning questions sooner than previously had been expected as they contemplate early shutdowns of uneconomic nuclear plants. Second, the projected costs of decommissioning appear to be rising significantly. Third, early nuclear plant closings may create a shortfall between accrued decommissioning trust funds and the actual costs incurred for defueling, stabilizing, and maintaining these units in a long-term safe shutdown condition.

Key Issues for Investors

Investors should be concerned about rising nuclear plant decommissioning costs and should become knowledgeable about issues affecting the decommissioning of nuclear power plants in the U.S.

- The decommissioning issue has been something of a "sleeper," but now a number of electric utilities are likely to confront it sooner than had been expected.
- Since NRC regulations assume each plant's decommissioning fund

will accrue over the life of its operating license, prematurely closed units probably will not have accumulated sufficient funds at the time of shutdown to pay for the clean-up of the site.

- Investors should be concerned about the adequacy of the current defueling and decommissioning cost estimates, which are likely to rise.
- PS Colorado's experience at Fort St. Vrain indicates that defueling and decommissioning issues can be successfully managed in a way that provides an equitable solution for both customers and investors.
- Under NRC's existing decommissioning regulations some utilities could be pushed in the direction of uneconomic strategies. For example, we can envision situations occurring in which some plants are too expensive to run, but also too expensive to shut down.

Nuclear plant decommissioning costs are uncertain, probably higher than those estimated by the NRC, and probably going up.

- The decommissioning cost estimates in the NRC rule are generic, and they are minimum values. There is widespread consensus that current NRC estimates will go up over time.
- NRC decommissioning estimates are different for pressurized water reactors than for boiling water reactors, because the boiling water reactors tend to be a little bit more contaminated. The generic minimum value set forth in the rule for a PWR is $100 million. And the minimum generic value set forth in the rule for a BWR, boiling water reactor, is $135 million. These numbers are important, because they are the base against which utilities have to begin accumulating decommissioning funds.
- Currently, NRC's decommissioning cost estimates do not include significant items such as low-level waste storage and disposal, spent fuel storage and disposal, and restoration of the site to "green field" condition.
- Low-level waste disposal costs are going to be a significant component in the decommissioning area. Some have estimated $500 a cubic foot, and higher, which is several times current levels. Ironically, longer onsite low-level waste storage ultimately might lower waste disposal costs because of radioactive decay.

Federal and state nuclear plant decommissioning policy objectives are not clear, and may be inconsistent, which could have significant financial implications for certain electric utilities.

- NRC was for some years (and may still be) enthusiastic about extension of existing operating licenses for another 20 years. This orientation may have distracted the agency from focusing on near-term decommissioning issues.
- Unlike some state environmental regulators, NRC does not assume demolition of structures and a return of the reactor site to its original state beyond what is needed for decontamination of the reactor for radiological purposes.
- The underlying issue is "how clean is clean?" Today, utilities and their investors cannot be sure what will be required by the different regulatory bodies to establish when a site has been properly decontaminated.

For the foreseeable future, NRC determination of the adequacy of utility decommissioning plans, and state public service commission treatment of associated costs will be handled largely on a case-by-case basis.

- In 1992, the NRC adopted a rule to codify Commission policy that, for those power reactor licensees that shut down their facilities before the expected end of operating life, the agency will determine an appropriate decommissioning funding schedule on a case-by-case basis.
- In addition, as NRC gains experience with implementation of its 1988 decommissioning rule there likely will be continuing mid-course corrections. The 1988 rule established several acceptable methods by which utilities may provide assurances that they will have sufficient funds to decommission their plants by the time the plants are permanently shut down.
- Due to concerns about rising low-level waste disposal costs, there appears to be some preference within the NRC for early dismantlement, as opposed to long-term SAFSTOR, at least for utilities that have single unit sites.
- If a utility has multiple unit sites (e.g. Southern California Edison at San Onofre) it may be preferable to delay decommissioning until all plants at the site are permanently shut down.
- For prematurely shut down reactors, we expect state public

utility commissions to determine the recoverability from customers of unamortized investment, and various clean-up costs on a case-by-case basis.
- State environmental regulators are likely to establish differing standards for nuclear site clean-up and restoration.

Effective utility management can make a big difference in the financial impact on a company resulting from nuclear plant decommissioning, particularly for prematurely shut down facilities. To the benefit of their investors, we expect some companies will do a better job than others of meeting the technical, regulatory and political challenges of nuclear decommissioning.

- Both Public Service of Colorado at Fort St. Vrain, and SCEcorp at San Onofre 1, have made tough decisions in a timely manner and devised sound strategies for handling the challenges that accompany their respective decisions to close those facilities.
- In particular, much can be learned from the Fort St. Vrain experience that is applicable to the industry as a whole. For example, the two years that Public Service of Colorado spent in discussion with the NRC staff and the NRC commissioners has provided an opportunity for the industry and its regulators to learn a lot about the decommissioning effort that many other companies are likely to face in the next few years.
- The transition from an operating site into a decommissioning site should be planned and managed since there are some significant costs during that period which should be carefully considered.
- Also important to the success of a utility's ongoing operations is the managing of the downsizing of the labor force as a nuclear plan is shut down.
- Experience shows us that different utilities respond to NRC requirements differently. So, for example, the staffing levels and O&M expenses tend to vary from plant to plant for essentially the same set of regulatory requirements.
- Because of the great uncertainty now surrounding the Department of Energy's effort to site and build a repository for commercial reactor spent fuel and other high-level radioactive waste, utilities should be planning now for long-term onsite storage of spent fuel.

Some characteristics of good utility management practices for nuclear plant shut down and decommissioning.

- Contingency plans are important. One of Public Service of Colorado's key strategic moves at Fort St. Vrain was the decision early in the process to never operate with a single plan. Every plan the company developed for defueling and decommissioning also had a backup plan.
- Fixed-price decommissioning contracts, if obtainable, are desirable because they generally should reduce financial risk for utilities.
- Utilities should be conservative in their estimates and collection of funds for nuclear plant retirement and decommissioning costs. SCEcorp, for example, has made the following clean-up funding assumptions for its three San Onofre reactors: complete dismantling and full site restoration; $330 per cubic foot allowance for low level waste disposal; 25% contingency allowance; seven percent escalation rates; 5.25% decommissioning fund growth; and, a 30-year operating life for units 2 and 3, although their operating licenses are for 40 years.
- In addition to technology and financing considerations, labor issues should be addressed in company plans. An important objective should be managing the workforce reduction that naturally accompanies plant closings so, for example, a utility does not prematurely lose the very work force which is essential for maintaining NRC licenses. Public Service Company of Colorado spent about two years putting together a human resource plan to manage the downsizing activity at Fort St. Vrain.

Utilities can choose from three basic decommissioning methods provided under NRC rules (SAFSTOR, DECON and ENTOMB). We expect that most utilities, with some exceptions for special cases, will prefer to close their nuclear plants and then postpone actual decommissioning for up to 60 years, which is allowed under current NRC rules.

Recommendations

- NRC should increase its current decommissioning cost estimates, and also reflect low-level waste and spent fuel storage and disposal costs.

- NRC should clarify its policy on clean-up steps which can be taken by a utility prior to Commission approval of a decommissioning plan for the facility.
- State regulators (perhaps through the National Association of Regulatory Utility Commissioners), in collaboration with NRC and others, should seek to assure that utilities do not have an unintended incentive to keep uneconomic nuclear units in operation because they are too expensive to shut down.
- Congress should establish a clear national policy and minimum standards for nuclear plant decommissioning and site restoration.

Some Implications of a Clinton Presidency

The Clinton-Gore national energy policy is clear in its opposition to increased reliance on nuclear power. Our impression is that Clinton's objection to an expanded role for nuclear power is rooted in economic considerations rather than a concern that the technology is not sufficiently safe. The campaign's position paper on energy policy states "there is good reason to believe that we can meet future energy needs—with conservation and the use of alternative fuels—without having to face the staggering costs, delays and uncertainties of nuclear waste disposal." Clinton's thinking on the economics of nuclear power probably was influenced significantly by his experience as Arkansas' Attorney General and Governor battling Entergy and the Federal Energy Regulatory Commission during the 1980s over the allocation of costs for the Grand Gulf nuclear plant.

The future role of nuclear power may be the point of sharpest contrast between the energy policies of Bill Clinton and George Bush. The National Energy Strategy championed by President Bush strongly supports the building of new nuclear plants and the new Energy Policy Act contains time-worn licensing reform legislation intended to make it easier for utilities to get regulatory approval to order, construct and operate standardized reactors on pre-approved sites. Bush also has committed a substantial part of the Department of Energy's annual budget to R&D intended to foster another round of nuclear plant expansion. Our expectation is that Clinton's use of energy R&D dollars will be redirected away from nuclear and toward conservation and renewables. In Governor Clinton's first term in 1979, he created a state Department of Energy in Arkansas which emphasized renewable resource development, reduced institutional barriers to energy conservation and encouraged the development of new energy sources.

One of Clinton's specific proposals is to reduce federal spending by indexing for inflation the annual nuclear waste disposal fees that utilities must contribute to support the development of a federal repository for spent reactor fuel and other high-level nuclear waste. We would expect state regulators to pass any such incremental charges through to utility customers, thereby making them more directly aware of the all-in costs of nuclear, and perhaps less inclined to support wider use of the technology.

Had he won, we would have expected George Bush to try and use the Tennessee Valley Authority to demonstrate the viability of advanced reactors in order to stimulate future orders from investor-owned utilities. Bill Clinton is not likely to follow this course. In fact, his running mate, Senator Al Gore, was the sponsor of an amendment (added to the 1992 Senate energy bill) that would require the TVA to conduct a least-cost planning analysis of energy supply and demand requirements in its region. We would not be surprised to see that process, if carried out by the Clinton Administration, lead to the conclusion that Browns Ferry 1 not be restarted and that the two Bellafonte units not be completed.

Future Commercial Nuclear Power in the United States

Currently, it is difficult to imagine new orders for nuclear power plants in the U.S., particularly of the type we have now. At the same time, taking a longer-term view, the environmental impact of continued and increased burning of coal, and other fossil fuels may prove unacceptable to society.

I tend to agree with those who believe that any new commitment to nuclear power generation in this country will occur only if a widespread consensus emerges that nuclear power provides some major environmental advantages when compared with other sources. It cannot be pushed on people anymore. It has to be demand-driven. It may or may not get there, but that is what it will take.

PART THREE

Nuclear Waste

10

The Regulation of
Radioactive Pollution

David P. O'Very

The Environmental Protection Agency ("EPA"), Nuclear Regulatory Commission ("NRC"), Department of Energy ("DOE"), and state agencies regulate radioactive pollution pursuant to the Atomic Energy Act ("AEA"),[1] and federal and state environmental laws.[2] These agencies regulate radioactive pollution by limiting the discharge of radioactive effluent to the water and air, managing and cleaning up radioactive waste and radioactively contaminated sites and facilities, and disposing of radioactive waste. Often, there is uncertainty as to whether the AEA or a particular environmental law governs these operations, which can lead to confusion over which agency has ultimate regulatory authority. The resulting regulatory gaps or overlaps along with lack of oversight and inadequate enforcement can slow pollution control efforts, raise costs, and lead to further environmental contamination and public health risks.

This paper highlights some of the difficult issues involved with the regulation of radioactive pollution pursuant to the AEA and federal and state environmental laws.[3] The first part outlines the evolution of federal and state regulation of radioactive pollution from 1946 to the present. The paper then goes on to analyze the regulation of radioactive water and air pollution, the management of radioactive and mixed wastes, and the problems with radiation cleanup standards and low-level radioactive waste and naturally occurring radioactive material disposal standards.

The paper concludes with some recommendations for improving the regulation of radioactive pollution. Overall, Congress should strengthen EPA, state, and citizen regulation of radioactive pollution and promote greater EPA/NRC cooperation. This can be done by increasing the applicability of the environmental laws to radioactive pollution and by amending the AEA to give EPA, states, and citizens greater oversight and enforcement authority.

Regulation of Radioactive Pollution from 1946 to the Present

The regulation of radioactive pollution has changed significantly over the last forty years. The following section traces this history from the enactment of the AEA and creation of the Atomic Energy Commission ("AEC") to the creation of the EPA, NRC, and DOE and the rise of environmental law. It provides a background for some of the current problems with the regulation of radioactive pollution.

The Atomic Energy Act and Exclusive Atomic Energy Commission Regulation of Radioactive Pollution

Congress first enacted the AEA in 1946.[4] The "paramount objective" of the AEA, which was substantially amended in 1954,[5] is the development of atomic energy for the "common defense."[6] Although the AEA recognizes the importance of securing the "health and safety of the public,"[7] protection of the environment from radioactive pollution is not a stated goal of the law.

The AEA created the AEC[8] giving it broad authority to research and produce atomic weapons[9] and safeguard nuclear information and material for the common defense.[10] The AEA also directed the AEC to regulate and encourage atomic energy to "maximize scientific and industrial progress."[11] Although the AEA directed the AEC to establish health and safety criteria for licensing commercial uses of atomic energy,[12] it explicitly did not require licenses for nuclear weapons activities.[13]

In 1959, Congress amended the AEA[14] to "recognize the need, and establish programs for cooperation between the states and the Commission . . . with respect to control of radiation hazards[.]"[15] Specifically, the AEA allowed "agreement states" to assume the AEC's regulatory authority over "source,"[16] "special nuclear"[17] (in quantities not sufficient to form a critical mass), and "byproduct"[18] material to protect "the public health and safety from radiation hazards."[19] However, state standards had to be "compatible" with AEC regulations.[20]

Importantly, the AEA prohibited the AEC from giving agreement states its regulatory authority over the "construction and operation of any production or utilization facility" including nuclear power plants.[21] In 1971, the 8th Circuit Court of Appeals in *Northern States Power Company v. State of Minnesota*[22] held that this provision precluded the AEC from delegating to agreement states its authority to regulate the discharge of radioactive pollutants from nuclear power plants and other production and utilization facilities. The court also held that the AEA preempted independent state regulation of radioactive effluent discharged from nuclear power plants including state power to impose stricter standards than the federal government:

> Were the states allowed to impose stricter standards on the level of radioactive waste releases discharged from nuclear power plants, they might conceivably be so overprotective in the area of health and safety as to unnecessarily stultify the industrial development and use of atomic energy for the development of electrical power.[23]

The Creation of the Environmental Protection Agency, Nuclear Regulatory Commission, and Department of Energy

In the 1970's, Congress and the President terminated the AEC's monopoly over radiation regulation. In 1970, President Nixon created the EPA and transferred to it the authority of the AEC's Division of Radiation Protection Standards and the Federal Radiation Council, to establish:

> applicable environmental standards for the protection of the general environment from radioactive material. As used herein, standards mean limits on radiation exposures or levels, or concentrations or quantities of radioactive material, *outside the boundaries of locations of persons possessing or using radioactive material.*[24](emphasis added).

The AEC retained exclusive authority under the AEA to administer and enforce these standards at its nuclear facilities.[25]

In 1974, Congress adopted the Energy Reorganization Act ("ERA")[26] which abolished the AEC and transferred its functions to the NRC and the Energy Research and Development Administration ("ERDA").[27] The law gave NRC the AEC's licensing and regulatory authority over all commercial applications of atomic energy, including management and disposal of commercial radioactive waste.[28] Consequently, NRC also assumed the AEC's oversight of agreement state radiation programs.[29] The law did not, however, alter the requirements that agreement state regulations and standards be "compatible" with NRC's.

The ERDA assumed the AEC's non-regulatory functions, including nuclear weapons production activities and energy research and development.[30] The ERA established an ERDA Assistant Administrator in charge of environment and safety.[31] The Assistant Administrator was responsible for establishing and enforcing public health, safety, and environmental protection standards, including radioactive waste management standards, for all ERDA nuclear weapons production activities.[32] The ERA did not give NRC any regulatory authority over ERDA activities, except for its breeder and other demonstration nuclear reactors and high-level radioactive waste disposal facilities.[33]

The 1977 Department of Energy Organization Act[34] subsequently transferred all of ERDA's nuclear weapons and national security functions to DOE.[35] The Act enumerated DOE's broad defense nuclear waste management authority, including its power to establish programs and facilities for nuclear waste treatment, storage, and disposal.[36] Like the 1974 ERA, the 1977 law did not give NRC licensing or oversight authority over nuclear weapons production. The 1977 law did not require any specific action by DOE for managing its own radioactive waste, and DOE retained virtually complete discretionary authority in this area subject to no independent regulatory oversight.[37]

Thus by the end of the 1970's there were three federal agencies sharing responsibility for control of radioactive pollution under the AEA: EPA had authority to set but not enforce radiation protection standards outside of nuclear facilities; NRC had regulatory and licensing authority at non-military nuclear facilities; and DOE possessed control over nuclear weapons production. No single agency possessed complete authority over radioactive pollution and there was no formal legislative or policy framework to facilitate inter-agency cooperation or resolve possible inter-agency disputes over establishing, administering, or enforcing radioactive pollution control regulations.

The Rise of Federal Environmental Law

Federal regulation of radioactive pollution also changed in the 1970's and 1980's with the enactment of federal environmental laws, all of which apply in some way to radioactive pollution. These laws include: the Federal Water Pollution Control Act ("FWPCA"),[38] the Clean Air Act ("CAA"),[39] the Safe Drinking Water Act ("SDWA"),[40] the Uranium Mill Tailings Radiation Control Act ("UMTRCA"),[41] the Resource Conservation and Recovery Act ("RCRA"),[42] the Comprehensive Environmental Response, Compensation and Liability Act

("CERCLA" or "Superfund"),[43] the Nuclear Waste Policy Act ("NWPA"),[44] and the Low-Level Radioactive Waste Policy Act ("LLRWPA").[45] Unlike the AEA, the primary purpose of these laws is to protect human health and the environment.[46] For example, a primary "objective" of RCRA is to "promote the protection of health and the environment" by assuring that "hazardous waste management practices are conducted in a manner which protects human health and the environment."[47]

Many of these environmental laws give "authorized" states substantial implementation and enforcement authority, including the explicit right, unlike AEA "agreement states," to set more stringent standards than federal requirements.[48] States and citizens also have substantially more authority to enforce the requirements of environmental laws than to enforce the AEA.[49]

Thus, since 1946 the federal regulatory scheme has changed from a single law, single agency framework, to a more complex structure with several laws and federal and state agencies sharing authority for controlling radioactive pollution.

Radioactive Water Pollution and
the Federal Water Pollution Control Act

Congress enacted the Federal Water Pollution Control Act ("FWPCA") to "restore and maintain the chemical, physical, and biological integrity of the Nation's waters."[50] The FWPCA controls water pollution by prohibiting the discharge of any pollutant without a permit.[51] EPA or states authorized by EPA to run their own programs[52] issue permits pursuant to the National Pollutant Discharge Elimination System ("NPDES").[53] The NPDES permit program limits the discharge of pollutants by an "end-of-the-pipe" approach. This approach requires permittees to apply "technology based standards" to control the amount of pollution discharged from their facilities.[54] The FWPCA allows states to set standards more stringent than those of the federal government[55] and applies equally to private and federal facilities.[56]

EPA enforces FWPCA provisions against private parties through compliance orders and administrative penalties.[57] EPA may also initiate a civil action in federal district court against an individual for a FWPCA violation.[58] The FWPCA citizen suit provision gives any "affected" person or state[59] the right to bring an enforcement action for violations of the law and its regulations and standards.[60] However, a citizen may not bring an enforcement action if EPA or an authorized state is "diligently prosecuting" the violation in court.[61] The FWPCA also enables a citizen to bring an action to compel the Administrator of the EPA to perform a non-discretionary duty.[62]

The FWPCA defines pollutant broadly to include, among other things, "radioactive materials."[63] The FWPCA also states,

> Notwithstanding any other provisions of this chapter it shall be unlawful to discharge any radiological, chemical, or biological warfare agent, any *high-level radioactive waste*, or any medical waste into the navigable waters.[64] [emphasis added].

Despite this clear statutory language, in 1976 the U.S. Supreme Court in *Train v. Colorado Public Interest Research Group*[65] held that the FWPCA does not apply to radioactive materials regulated under the AEA, namely source, special nuclear, and by-product material. The Court analyzed the legislative history of the FWPCA and found that Congress intended these materials to be regulated exclusively by the AEC pursuant to the AEA:

> [R]eliance on the "plain meaning" of the words "radioactive materials" contained in the definition of "pollutant" in the FWPCA contributes little to our understanding of whether Congress intended the Act to encompass the regulation of source, special nuclear, and byproduct materials. To have included these materials under the FWPCA would have marked a significant alteration of the pervasive regulatory scheme under the AEA.[66]

However, the Court acknowledged that any radioactive materials not covered by the AEA are subject to regulation by EPA or authorized states under the FWPCA including "radium and accelerator-produced isotopes."[67] As a result, most radioactive pollutants discharged into state waters by NRC-licensed or DOE facilities are exempt from EPA or state regulation under the FWPCA.

Two problems result from the FWPCA's inapplicability to most radioactive discharges. First, since the AEA prohibits states from regulating the discharge of most radioactive pollutants from NRC-licensed and DOE facilities,[68] and because the FWPCA does not apply to radioactive materials regulated by the AEA, states have no enforcement authority under federal law with respect to discharges of radioactive effluent from NRC-licensed nuclear power plants and DOE facilities.

DOE's record at its K Reactor at the Savannah River Site in South Carolina provides an example of the problems states have in controlling radioactive water pollution. In 1991, the K Reactor discharged thousands of curies of radioactively-contaminated cooling water into the Savannah River.[69] As a result, a number of drinking water plants, food processors, and oyster beds on the Savannah River were shut down until tritium concentrations had diminished. This spill followed dozens of other tritium releases from the Savannah River Site over the past eight years.[70] Because of the inability of states to regulate the discharge of radioactive waste into state waters under the FWPCA and the AEA, the State of South Carolina has no legal authority under federal law to prevent or control these significant radioactive releases.

Second, states and citizens have almost no right under the AEA to bring enforcement actions to compel facilities to comply with AEA radioactive pollution standards. The AEA states:

> [N]o action shall be brought against any individual or person for any violation under this Chapter unless and until the Attorney General of the United States has advised the Commission with respect to such action and *no such action shall be commenced except by the Attorney General of the United States. . . .*[71][emphasis added].

The only remedy a person has under the AEA against the owner or operator of an NRC-licensed facility violating AEA requirements is to institute a proceeding under NRC regulations requiring the licensee to "show cause" why its license should not be "modified, suspended, or revoked."[72] The Director of Nuclear Reactor Regulation has complete discretion concerning whether to institute the proceeding,[73] and the rule is clear that "[n]o petition . . . for Commission review of a Director's decision . . . will be entertained by the Commission."[74] The Director's unfettered discretion to deny petitions combined with the lack of right to NRC review effectively eliminate the citizen's ability to enforce AEA requirements or standards against NRC-licensees. In addition, at least three federal circuits[75] have held that NRC denials of license proceedings are presumptively unreviewable.[76] No courts have ruled to the contrary.

A challenge to potentially illegal activities at DOE facilities is even more difficult, because there is no administrative remedy akin to the NRC petition process to enforce AEA safety standards. The problem is exacerbated by the fact that DOE safety standards are in the form of Department "Orders," which are vague, often permissive, and generally not adopted pursuant to the notice and comment procedures of the Administrative Procedure Act ("APA").[77]

In light of these problems, Congress should do two things. First, Congress should amend the FWPCA's definition of "pollutant" to explicitly include source, special nuclear, and byproduct material at DOE and other federal facilities not licensed by NRC. Second,

Congress should amend the AEA to permit NRC agreement states to assume NRC's regulatory authority over the discharge of radioactivity into U.S. waters and explicitly allow agreement states to set stricter standards than NRC's. Congress should also add a citizen suit provision to the AEA to allow citizens to enforce the AEA and agency regulations at NRC and agreement state licensed nuclear facilities.

These changes would give EPA, authorized states, and citizens regulatory authority over the discharge of radioactivity from DOE's nuclear weapons facilities under the FWPCA. Agreement states and citizens would be able to regulate the discharge of radioactivity to the water from commercial nuclear facilities pursuant to the AEA. Regulation of NRC-licensed facilities would not change drastically, since agreement states already may assume many of NRC's regulatory functions at facilities other than nuclear power plants, including managing and disposing of radioactive waste and cleaning up or decommissioning civilian nuclear facilities. A disadvantage to these changes would be a possible lack of uniform radiation standards, since different laws, agencies, and regulations would govern the discharge of radioactive pollution from DOE and NRC-licensed nuclear facilities.

Congress could solve this problem by directing EPA and NRC to work together to issue minimum radiation standards that are consistent, uniform, and that protect the environment and public health from radioactive pollution discharged to waters. EPA and NRC already have an informal "Memorandum of Understanding" regarding the regulation of radioactive materials under the AEA, NWPA, and CAA designed to "foster cooperation" between the agencies, avoid "duplicative or piecemeal regulatory requirements," and reduce "risk to the public health and safety and the environment" from radiation.[78] The problem with this kind of solution is that it is legally difficult for citizens and other interested parties to enforce an informal memorandum of understanding to ensure that EPA and NRC are fulfilling their regulatory responsibilities. Under the APA, where a statute calls for judicial review of agency action, a court can compel agency action required by statute, including agency rulemaking, that is "unlawfully withheld" or "unreasonably delayed."[79] The APA, however, generally does not apply to "interpretive rules, general statements of policy, or rules of agency organization, procedure, or practice."[80] The EPA/NRC memorandum of understanding would seem to fall into this second unenforceable catagory. Therefore, it would be necessary for Congress to enact legislation directing EPA and NRC to cooperate in issuing regulations for the discharge of radioactive pollution under the AEA and FWPCA that are uniform, consistent, and protective of human health and the environment.

Radioactive Air Pollution and the Clean Air Act

Congress enacted the Clean Air Act ("CAA") to "protect and enhance the quality of the nation's air resources so as to promote the public health and welfare and the productive capacity of its population."[81] Section 112 of the CAA requires the EPA to regulate hazardous air pollutants which "present or may present . . . a threat of adverse health effects"[82] and directs the EPA to issue national emission standards for hazardous air pollutants ("NESHAPs").[83] States may assume responsibility for implementing and enforcing NESHAP standards through EPA-authorized state programs.[84] The CAA specifically authorizes states to adopt standards that are more stringent than federal standards,[85] and the CAA applies equally to federal and private facilities.[86]

EPA enforces the CAA through compliance orders and administrative penalties and may also bring a civil action against an individual for a CAA violation.[87] The CAA citizen suit provision gives any person or state[88] the right to bring an enforcement action for violations of the law or its associated regulations and standards.[89] However, a citizen may not bring an enforcement action, if EPA or a state is "diligently prosecuting" the violation in court.[90] Citizens may also sue the Administrator of the EPA to perform a non-discretionary duty.[91]

The 1977 CAA Amendments[92] directed EPA to issue NESHAPs for radioactive air pollutants, if EPA determined that their emission "into the ambient air will cause, or contribute to, air pollution which may reasonably be anticipated to endanger public health."[93] Although EPA listed radionuclides in 1979,[94] it did not issue final NESHAPs until 1989[95] after several missed deadlines and law suits brought by environmental organizations.[96]

The 1990 CAA amendments[97] allow EPA to exempt NRC-licensed facilities from CAA regulation, if EPA determines that NRC standards under the AEA provide "an ample margin of safety to protect public health."[98] In April 1991, EPA stayed the application of radionuclide NESHAPs for NRC-licensed facilities other than nuclear power reactors pending its decision to exempt such facilities from the radionuclide emission standards.[99] In August 1991, EPA proposed the same action for NRC-licensed nuclear power reactors.[100]

If EPA ultimately decides to exempt NRC-licensed facilities from CAA regulation, NRC may have complete regulatory authority over radioactive air emissions from commercial nuclear facilities under the AEA. Although the CAA states that, "Nothing in this subsection shall preclude or deny the right of any state . . . to adopt or enforce any standard or limitation respecting radionuclides which is more stringent than the standard or limitation in effect under . . . this section,"[101] it does not explicitly give states authority to regulate radioactive air emissions from NRC-licensed facilities independent of the AEA. Therefore, it might be claimed that any attempt by states to regulate radioactive air emissions from NRC-licensed facilities, including nuclear power plants, is preempted by NRC's authority under the AEA to regulate the "construction and operation of any production or utilization facility."[102]

Ironically, because the 1990 CAA provision applies only to NRC-licensed facilities, DOE facilities will continue to be regulated by EPA or states under the CAA.[103] Therefore, exempting NRC-licensed facilities from CAA regulation may result in a double standard. States will clearly be able to regulate radioactive air emissions from DOE facilities and also set emission standards more stringent than those of the federal government. In addition, citizens and states will be able to enforce the provisions of the CAA at DOE facilities through the CAA citizen suit provisions. States and citizens may not enjoy such rights with respect to all NRC-licensed facilities.

The problem could be resolved by amending the AEA to clarify NRC agreement-state authority under the AEA to regulate radioactive air emissions from all facilities, including nuclear power plants, and set emission standards that are more stringent than NRC's. Alternatively, Congress could encourage NRC to allow agreement states to regulate radioactive air emissions and interpret the term "compatible" under the AEA[104] to allow states to set stricter standards than NRC. Under either option, it would be necessary to amend the AEA to provide citizens and states with enforcement authority equivalent to the CAA's citizen suit provision. Finally, since NRC radiation standards are much less stringent that EPA's, Congress should enact legislation directing EPA and NRC to cooperate in setting uniform, consistent radioactive emission standards.[105]

Management of Radioactive and Mixed Wastes and the Resource Conservation and Recovery Act and the Atomic Energy Act

The Resource Conservation and Recovery Act ("RCRA") governs the management of hazardous wastes from "cradle to grave," including their generation, transportation, treatment, storage, and disposal. Pursuant to RCRA, EPA sets strict standards for the treatment, storage, and disposal of hazardous waste.[106] Owners and operators of treatment, storage, or disposal ("TSD") facilities must apply for a permit[107] from the EPA or from a state authorized by EPA to run its own hazardous waste program.[108] However, if an existing facility qualifies for "interim status," it may continue to operate until a final permit is issued.[109]

RCRA directs EPA to set "corrective action" or cleanup standards for hazardous waste and requires TSD facilities to clean up any releases that occur at a site.[110] RCRA also requires TSD facilities to include a written "closure plan" in a permit application. The plan must identify the steps necessary to perform a partial or final closure of the facility at any point during its operation.[111] State promulgated hazardous waste regulations may be more stringent than those of the federal government,[112] and RCRA expressly states that all federal facilities are subject to its provisions to the same extent as private facilities.[113]

EPA enforces RCRA provisions against private parties through compliance orders and civil penalties.[114] EPA may also initiate a civil action in federal district court against an individual for a RCRA violation.[115] Private citizens and states may bring civil suit against any "person," including a government agency, for a RCRA violation.[116] However, a citizen may not bring an enforcement action if EPA or an authorized state is "diligently prosecuting" the violation in court.[117] Citizens and states may also sue EPA for failing to perform a non-discretionary duty,[118] or may petition EPA to promulgate, amend, or repeal a RCRA regulation.[119]

RCRA defines hazardous waste broadly as solid waste[120] that may,

> Cause, or significantly contribute to an increase in mortality or an increase in serious irreversible, or incapacitating reversible illness; or pose a substantial present or potential hazard to human health or the environment when improperly treated, stored, transported, or disposed of or otherwise managed.[121]

However, RCRA excludes from this definition source, special nuclear, and byproduct materials as defined by the AEA.[122] Hence, these materials are generally subject to DOE and NRC regulation under the AEA.

Several problems result from RCRA's inapplicability to the management of source, special nuclear, and byproduct materials. First, DOE is essentially self-regulating under the AEA with respect to the management of radioactive wastes not containing RCRA-regulated materials at its nuclear weapons facilities,[123] and the AEA does not give EPA, states, or citizens enforcement authority over DOE's nuclear waste management practices.[124]

DOE self-regulation has resulted in extensive contamination at its nuclear weapons facilities that will likely cost more than $100 billion and take decades to clean up.[125] In its comprehensive evaluation of the complex, the United States Congress Office of Technology Assessment ("OTA") concluded that:

> Poorly contained hazardous and radioactive wastes from weapons production have contaminated ground water, soil, sediments, and surface water . . . . Factors contributing to contamination include . . . a history of emphasizing the urgency of weapons production . . . to the neglect of health and environmental considerations; ignorance of, and lack of attention to the consequences of environmental contamination; and *decades of self-regulation, without independent oversight or meaningful public scrutiny.*"[126] [emphasis added].

Second, RCRA's exemption for source, special nuclear, and byproduct material also eliminates potential state and citizen RCRA authority over radioactive materials at NRC-licensed facilities. Although the AEA allows agreement states to assume the NRC's regulatory authority over some radiation hazards,[127] state radiation standards must be "compatible" with NRC's. NRC has interpreted "compatible" as meaning "essentially identical" to NRC's standards[128] implying that agreement states may not, in contrast with RCRA, generally adopt standards more stringent than NRC's.[129] Also, in contrast with RCRA, the AEA does not give citizens the power to sue to enforce its provisions at NRC or agreement state-licensed nuclear facilities.[130]

Third, when source, special nuclear, and byproduct material at either DOE or NRC/agreement state-licensed facilities are in combination with RCRA-regulated hazardous wastes, these "mixed wastes" are subject to joint regulation.[131] RCRA gives EPA or authorized states authority over the hazardous components of the mixed waste, and the AEA gives DOE and NRC or agreement states power over the radioactive portions. Although most of the mixed wastes have been generated at DOE facilities, nearly 10% of all low-level radioactive waste at NRC-licensed facilities are mixed wastes.[132]

This distinction between the chemical and radioactive components of the same wastes results in burdensome regulatory complexity. It means that two agencies—DOE and EPA/authorized states in the case of defense mixed wastes, and EPA/authorized states and NRC/agreement states in the case of commercial mixed wastes—share authority over the *same* wastes. DOE and NRC have argued that meeting RCRA requirements to control chemical hazards may exacerbate the risks from radioactivity. EPA has argued that existing

DOE and NRC radiation requirements may not adequately control chemical hazards.[133] The agencies have attempted to resolve their differences, but they argue that existing statutory and regulatory requirements make this difficult.

RCRA's exemption for source, special nuclear, and byproduct materials thus unnecessarily restricts state and citizen authority over radioactive wastes and may result in complex joint regulation of mixed wastes. Congress should eliminate the exemption for source, special nuclear and byproduct material for facilities not licensed by NRC thereby subjecting radioactive and mixed wastes at DOE facilities to complete RCRA regulation. This would enable EPA, authorized states, and citizens to regulate the management of radioactive and mixed wastes at DOE facilities.

There is arguably less of a problem over the management of purely radioactive and mixed wastes at NRC-licensed facilities for two reasons. First, agreement states may assume NRC's regulatory authority over purely radioactive wastes. Second, there is much less mixed waste at NRC-licensed facilities as compared to DOE facilities. Regarding the regulation of purely radioactive waste, Congress should either amend the AEA to define "compatible" to explicitly allow agreement states to set standards that are more stringent than NRC's or encourage NRC to do so in its regulations. Under either option, it would also be necessary to amend the AEA to allow citizens to enforce the AEA at NRC-licensed facilities.

The solution for the problems involved with the regulation of mixed wastes at NRC-licensed facilities is less clear. Giving one agency, either EPA or NRC, sole jurisdiction would resolve the joint regulatory problems and might lead to a more efficient and economical management of mixed wastes. But neither agency (nor their agreement or authorized state agencies) may be qualified to handle the often different problems involved with the other agency's waste. In other words, NRC is not experienced in regulating hazardous wastes, and EPA is not as qualified as NRC to protect against the hazards posed by the regulation of radioactive waste. Presumably, there would also be significant political and bureaucratic opposition to removing either NRC jurisdiction over the radioactive parts or EPA jurisdiction over the hazardous parts of the mixed wastes.

A better solution would be to preserve joint regulation of the mixed wastes but direct EPA and NRC to resolve the current conflicts and inconsistencies that exist between their two sets of regulations. Congress could accomplish this by enacting legislation establishing an interagency task force to develop joint rulemaking on mixed wastes. To ensure that EPA and NRC are moving expeditiously, the task force would be subject to Congressional oversight which would set a strict schedule for EPA and NRC to resolve their regulatory differences.[134] Citizens could enforce the legislative schedule for the rulemaking through the APA.[135]

Radiation Cleanup Standards

According to an EPA contractor report, there are more than 45,000 sites in the U.S. with actual or potential radioactive contamination.[136] In 1980, Congress enacted the Comprehensive Environmental Response, Compensation, and Liability Act ("CERCLA")[137] to expedite the cleanup of hazardous waste sites.[138] Whenever there is an actual or threatened *release*[139] of hazardous substances, *including radioactive materials*,[140] CERCLA directs the EPA[141] to take "removal" or "remedial" actions[142] consistent with the National Contingency Plan ("NCP").[143] Pursuant to the NCP, EPA, or a contractor hired by EPA, performs a Remedial Investigation and Feasibility Study ("RI/FS") for each site to determine the nature and extent of the threat posed by the release, and to select a remedy that protects human health and the environment.[144] CERCLA applies equally to private and federal hazardous waste sites.[145]

CERCLA, however, does not require EPA to promulgate cleanup standards for chemically hazardous and radioactive wastes. Instead, CERCLA requires that cleanups comply with all legally "applicable or relevant and appropriate requirements" ("ARARs") set by *other* federal and state laws.[146] CERCLA gives EPA discretion to determine which standard is "relevant and appropriate," and EPA selects the standards on a case-by-case basis.[147]

The only promulgated federal standards that specifically apply to the cleanup of radioactive waste—and thus the only potential federal ARAR—are EPA's uranium mill tailings standards[148] issued pursuant to the Uranium Mill Tailings Radiation Control Act ("UMTRCA").[149] Importantly, although EPA has discretion under CERCLA to use UMTRCA standards as a guide for the cleanup of any radioactively contaminated site, these standards were promulgated specifically to apply to the control, cleanup, and disposal of radioactive "tailings"[150] at active and inactive uranium milling sites.[151] In other words, they were not promulgated to address the broad range of radioactive contamination that EPA will encounter at thousands of U.S. civilian and defense waste sites.

In 1986, EPA issued an advance notice of proposed rulemaking indicating its plans to develop radiation cleanup standards pursuant to its AEA authority.[152] These standards were never finalized, however, and it is unlikely that EPA will promulgate cleanup standards in the near future.[153]

EPA's failure to promulgate radiation cleanup standards impedes cleanup efforts at both DOE and NRC-licensed facilities. In its comprehensive evaluation of radioactive contamination at the complex, the U.S. Congress Office of Technology Assessment ("OTA") emphasized the critical need to develop radiation cleanup standards.[154] In its 1989 report on the nuclear weapon complex, the National Academy of Sciences ("NAS") agreed stating that one of the "most important" questions in cleaning up DOE sites is how to establish "acceptable levels of cleanup (or, conversely, what levels of contamination may remain at a site after cleanup). . . ."[155] DOE officials have gone further and blamed the current lack of standards for delays in its cleanup activities.[156]

EPA's failure to promulgate radiation cleanup standards also frustrates cleanup or "decommissioning" efforts at NRC and agreement state-licensed nuclear facilities.[157] Currently, NRC's 1981 "Branch Technical Position"[158] guides cleanup operations. In 1988, NRC stated the urgent need for EPA to develop "residual radioactivity limits" to facilitate decommissioning efforts, and expected that an inter-agency working group headed by EPA would soon promulgate these standards.[159] However, in the absence of significant progress by the working group, NRC is considering amending its current regulations[160] to include "radiological criteria" for decommissioning its facilities.[161] NRC's action, however, will not necessarily solve the current cleanup standards problem. According to the General Accounting Office, NRC licensees who are currently decommissioning their facilities may have to conduct additional cleanup activities if EPA's final radiation standards end up being more stringent than NRC's. Conversely, if EPA's standards are less stringent than NRC's, the licensees would have incurred unnecessary cleanup costs.[162] Additionally, NRC standards for commercial facilities would not be binding and also may not be sufficient for the often greater and more complex contamination problems at DOE facilities.

Congress could fill the current regulatory gap by removing RCRA's exemption for source, special nuclear, and byproduct material at DOE and other federal facilities not licensed by NRC. Thus RCRA would direct EPA to set "corrective action" (cleanup) standards not only for hazardous waste, but also for radioactive waste. It would also be necessary to set a strict deadline in RCRA for EPA to issue corrective action standards for radioactive waste.[163]

Regarding the decommissioning of NRC-licensed facilities, Congress could enact legislation codifying EPA authority to set radiation cleanup standards under the AEA, setting a strict schedule for EPA to issue the standards, and directing NRC to incorporate these standards into its decommissioning regulations. Congress may also want to consider a less intrusive and politically palatable approach which recognizes NRC's regulatory experience with radiation but also supports EPA's authority under the AEA to establish radiation protection standards. Under this second approach, Congress would adopt EPA's earlier idea of an inter-agency work group or task force, but strengthen it by providing for Congressional oversight and setting strict, enforceable legislative deadlines for EPA and NRC to issue the cleanup standards.

Low-Level Waste and Naturally Occurring Radioactive Material Disposal Standards

The U.S. is currently faced with the task of disposing of over one million cubic feet of low-level radioactive waste ("LLW")[164] generated annually.[165] In addition, the nation must deal with the dangers of naturally-occurring radioactive material ("NORM"). Natural radioactivity occurs everywhere on earth, primarily in elements like uranium, thorium, radium, potassium, and radon gas. EPA estimates that industrial activities like oil and gas extraction, water treatment, mining, fossil fuel production, and aluminum production generate tens of billions of metric tons of NORM wastes annually.[166] This section analyzes EPA and NRC conflict over LLW and NORM disposal standards.

Environmental Protection Agency and Nuclear Regulatory
Commission Conflict Over Low-Level Waste Disposal Standards

Although EPA is responsible for promulgating radiation protection standards under the AEA,[167] NRC is the only agency that has promulgated LLW regulations[168] pursuant to its AEA authority to license LLW disposal facilities.[169]

In 1989, EPA produced draft standards for the disposal of LLW.[170] However, the standards were not finalized or even published in the Federal Register, because NRC convinced EPA to consider organizing an EPA/NRC interagency task force to address the "differences that have arisen between the two agencies related to regulatory initiatives of the EPA directed at activities licensed or otherwise regulated by NRC."[171] NRC cited the draft rules as an example of EPA/NRC conflict, presumably because NRC did not want to revise its licensing regulations based on EPA's disposal standards. Currently, EPA does not intend to issue final LLW standards until December 1994,[172] and it is unlikely that the agency will actually meet this schedule.

As with the problem over decommissioning standards at NRC-licensed facilities, Congress could prompt EPA and NRC to issue LLW disposal standards in two ways. First, Congress could amend the AEA codifying EPA authority to set standards for the disposal of low-level radioactive waste, setting strict legislative deadlines for EPA to issue the standards, and specifying that NRC adhere to these standards in its licensing regulations. Alternatively, Congress enact legislation setting up an EPA/NRC inter-agency task force to promulgate LLW disposal standards subject to Congressional oversight and strict, enforceable legislative deadlines.[173]

Environmental Protection Agency and Nuclear Regulatory Commission Conflict Over Naturally Occurring Radioactive Material Disposal Standards

Federal regulation over naturally-occurring radioactive material ("NORM") is incomplete and disorganized at best, in part because NORM is not classified as source, special nuclear or byproduct material subject to AEA regulation. The Radon Gas and Indoor Air Quality Act of 1986[174] directed EPA to study the dangers of NORM and radon gas in particular. In 1989, EPA proposed rules[175] for NORM pursuant to the Toxic Substances Control Act ("TSCA").[176] EPA also issued a report for lower activity NORM wastes.[177]

Although NRC had acknowledged that its jurisdiction under the AEA does not extend to NORM,[178] it convinced EPA to stay the proposed rules, as it did EPA's LLW disposal standards, pending an inter-agency study.[179] EPA does not currently intend to issue final standards for NORM until December 1994,[180] and it is unlikely that the agency will actually meet this schedule.

EPA already has statutory authority to regulate NORM pursuant to RCRA as well as TSCA. TSCA empowers EPA to regulate the manufacture, use, and disposal of any "chemical substance" that may present an "unreasonable risk of injury to health or the environment.[181] TSCA defines chemical substance to include any "organic or inorganic substance" including any combination of substances "occurring in whole or in part as a result of a chemical reaction or occurring in nature."[182] RCRA already gives EPA broad authority to regulate all types of hazardous wastes, including radioactive wastes that are not source, special nuclear, or byproduct material, i.e. NORM.[183]

Congress could rectify this problem by directing EPA to set minimum federal NORM standards under either RCRA or TSCA and specifying a strict date for their issuance.[184] States would then be free to set standards more stringent than the federal government.[185]

Recommendations

The federal government regulates radioactivity differently from almost any other pollutant. The AEA gives EPA, states, and citizens little oversight or enforcement authority over radioactive pollution. Moreover, Congress and the courts have exempted radioactive materials from regulation under federal and state environmental laws. This anomaly has contributed to regulatory gaps and overlaps, lack of oversight, and inadequate enforcement which has frustrated radioactive pollution control and cleanup efforts and lead to further environmental contamination and public health risks. Therefore, Congress should amend the environmental laws and the AEA to give EPA, states, and citizens more regulatory authority over radioactive pollution.

The recommendations in this chapter preserve, for the most part, the separate regulation of military and civilian applications of nuclear energy. The most fundamental change involves the termination of DOE self-regulation under the AEA which has been a primary cause of the extensive radioactive contamination at DOE's nuclear weapons facilities. The recommendations propose to end DOE self-regulation by giving EPA, authorized states, and citizens regulatory authority over radioactive materials at defense nuclear facilities pursuant to key environmental laws, namely the FWPCA and RCRA. The proposed changes to NRC regulation over the commercial applications of atomic energy are less dramatic and involve increased agreement state and citizen involvement under the AEA and greater EPA/NRC cooperation.

Arguably, it might make better sense to abolish the civilian/military distinction and have either the federal environmental laws or the AEA give one agency comprehensive regulatory authority over all applications of nuclear energy. For example, Congress could amend the AEA to give NRC complete authority to regulate radioactive pollution from both civilian and military nuclear facilities, thereby subjecting DOE to NRC or agreement state oversight. Alternatively, Congress could amend the environmental laws to give EPA and authorized states regulatory authority over both DOE and NRC-licensed facilities. Both options are attractive, because they simplify the current regulatory framework and avoid the problems associated with dual or joint and overlapping regulation of radioactive pollution. This argument is especially persuasive in the case of the management of mixed waste containing both radioactive and non-radioactive elements subject to joint regulation under the AEA and RCRA.

In addition, it should be noted that NRC might have more enforcement success than EPA at DOE and other federal facilities. As stated above, EPA has the power to bring civil judicial suits, issue unilateral administrative orders, and assess civil and administrative penalties against private individuals for violations of the FWPCA, CAA, RCRA, and other federal environmental laws.[186] However, EPA generally limits its enforcement actions at federal facilities to voluntary consent orders and compliance agreements.[187] This policy is primarily a result of the Justice Department's "unitary executive" theory.[188] This theory posits that the President, as Chief Executive, already has mechanisms within the executive branch to solve inter-agency environmental enforcement disputes.[189] Thus it is Justice's view that the President has a right to resolve inter-agency conflicts internally without court interference.[190] Further, Justice argues that suits between federal agencies would result in a situation where the President was, in effect, suing himself. Thus a court could not hear the case, because the case would present no "case or controversy" as is required by Article III of the Constitution.

Since EPA and NRC are both technically organizations within the executive branch, the unitary executive theory may apply equally to both bodies.[191] However, there is an important distinction between NRC and EPA that may improve NRC enforcement at federal facilities. Unlike EPA, NRC is an "independent regulatory commission."[192] NRC members are appointed by the President with the advice and consent of the Senate and may only be removed for "inefficiency, neglect of duty, or malfeasance of office."[193] In addition, no more than three of the five members of the NRC may be of the same political party as the President.[194] Thus the NRC is arguably less subject to political pressure than EPA. In fact, another "independent regulatory commission," namely the Federal Energy Regulatory Commission ("FERC")[195] was involved in a suit with the Commerce Department over the issuance of an environmental impact statement prior to the relicensing of a hydroelectric dam.[196] In the suit, the Commerce Department was represented by the Justice Department and FERC was defended by its own general counsel.[197] The degree of NRC's political insulation is weakened, however, by the fact that the President appoints the Chairman of the NRC, who serves at the "pleasure" of the President.[198]

Upon closer scrutiny, however, having either EPA or NRC regulate both the civilian and military applications of nuclear energy becomes less appealing. Although NRC has experience dealing with radioactivity at civilian facilities, it is not necessarily qualified to handle the greater and more complex radioactive pollution problems at DOE's nuclear weapons complex. Decommissioning a commercial nuclear power plant, for example, is quite different from overseeing the extensive and more complex radioactive cleanup operations at DOE's nuclear weapons facilities. Over the years, EPA has gained experience with DOE cleanups pursuant to its authority under CERCLA and is arguably better qualified than NRC in this area. EPA, on the other hand, does not have the resources, experience, or personnel to oversee the various operations at thousands of NRC licensees that include not only power plants but many other types of facilities like universities and hospitals.

Finally, it is probably not politically viable to propose to give one agency, whether it be NRC or EPA, comprehensive regulatory authority at the expense of the other. Congress showed its intent to maintain the separation between civilian and military applications of nuclear energy in the 1990 CAA Amendments where it proposed to exempt NRC-licensed facilities from CAA radionuclide emissions standards, if EPA finds that NRC's standards provide an "ample margin of safety to protect public health."[199]

A better way to improve the regulation of radioactive pollution at both civilian and military nuclear facilities preserves the current dual regulatory scheme but improves it by increasing EPA, state, and citizen authority under both the federal environmental laws and the AEA. The following summarizes the recommendations for each of the regulatory problems highlighted in this chapter:

Regulation of Radioactive Water Pollution

Currently, EPA, states, and citizens have no authority to control the discharge of radioactive waste to the nation's waters under either the FWPCA or the AEA. Congress should end DOE self-regulation over the discharge of radioactive pollution to water by amending the definition of pollutant under the FWPCA to include source, special nuclear, and byproduct materials at DOE and other facilities not licensed by NRC. This would give EPA, authorized states, and citizens authority over DOE facilities under the FWPCA. Congress should also amend the AEA to permit NRC agreement states to assume NRC's regulatory authority over the discharge of radioactivity to U.S. waters, allow agreement states to set stricter standards than NRC's, and provide for stronger citizen enforcement. Finally, Congress should also enact legislation requiring EPA and NRC to work together in setting minimum radioactive effluent standards that are consistent and uniform.

Regulation of Radioactive Air Pollution

States may not have clear authority to regulate radioactive air emissions from NRC-licensed facilities as they do at DOE facilities under the CAA. Therefore, Congress should either amend the AEA to clarify NRC-agreement state authority to regulate radioactive emissions from nuclear facilities and to set standards that are more stringent than NRC's or encourage NRC to permit agreement states to do so in its regulations. It would also be necessary to amend the AEA to allow citizen enforcement at NRC or agreement state licensed facilities. As with the FWPCA, Congress should also direct EPA and NRC to cooperate in setting consistent radioactive air emission standards pursuant to the CAA and the AEA.

Management of Radioactive and Mixed Wastes

Congress should end DOE self-regulation over the management of radioactive waste by eliminating RCRA's exemption for source, special nuclear, and byproduct material at DOE and other facilities not licensed by NRC. This would give EPA, authorized states, and citizens the power to regulate radioactive and mixed wastes at DOE facilities. Management of purely radioactive waste at NRC-licensed facilities could be improved by either clarifying agreement state authority under the AEA to set standards more stringent than NRC's or encouraging NRC to do so in its regulations. Under either option, it would also be necessary to amend the AEA to provide for stronger citizen enforcement at NRC-licensed facilities.

Congress could improve the management of mixed wastes at NRC-licensed facilities by establishing an EPA/NRC inter-agency task force to resolve overlapping and inconsistent radioactive and hazardous waste regulations subject to Congressional oversight and strict, enforceable legislative deadlines.

Radiation Cleanup Standards

Congress should require EPA to set radiation cleanup standards at both DOE and NRC-licensed facilities. For DOE facilities, this can be done by eliminating RCRA's exemption for source, special nuclear, and byproduct material at DOE and other facilities not licensed by NRC and setting a strict schedule for EPA to issue RCRA corrective action standards for radioactive contamination. Congress could require EPA to promulgate radiation cleanup standards for the decommissioning of NRC-licensed facilities in two ways. First, Congress could codify EPA authority under the AEA to set radiation cleanup standards for NRC-licensed facilities, set a strict schedule for EPA to issue radiation cleanup standards, and direct NRC to incorporate these standards in

its decommissioning regulations. Alternatively, Congress could set up
an EPA/NRC task force to set cleanup standards for NRC-licensed
facilities subject to Congressional oversight and strict legislative
deadlines.

Low-Level Radioactive Waste Disposal Standards

Congress should require EPA to set disposal standards for low-level
radioactive waste generated at NRC-licensed facilities. This could be
accomplished by codifying EPA authority under the AEA to set LLW
disposal standards, setting a strict schedule for EPA to issue these
standards, and directing NRC to incorporate these standards in its
low-level waste disposal facility licensing regulations. Alternatively, Congress could set up EPA/NRC task force to set LLW disposal
standards subject to Congressional oversight and strict legislative
deadlines.

TABLE 10.1 Selected Federal Radiation Protection Standards

Agency	Regulation	Law	Annual Dose Limits (millirem)	Other Limits
NRC	10 CFR 20	AEA	100	Effluent concentration limits (see Table 10.2)
NRC	10 CFR 61	AEA	25 (any organ) 75 (thyroid)	NA
DOE	Order 5400.5	AEA	100	Effluent Concentration Guides (see Table 10.3)
EPA	40 CFR 190	AEA	25 (body) 75 (thyroid)	Fuel cycle emissions krypton-85: 50,000 Ci iodine-129: 5 mCi Transuranics: 0.5 mCi
EPA	40 CFR 191 (being revised)	AEA, NWPA	25 (body) 75 (critical organ)	Groundwater: 4 mrem per year Radium-226: 5 pCi/l Radium-228: 5 pCi/l Radionuclides: 15 pCi/l
EPA	40 CFR 192	AEA, UMTR-CA	NA	Radium-226 in soil: <15 cm: 5 pCi/g >15 cm: 15 pCi/g Radon-222 into the air: 20 pCi/m^2/s release rate or 0.5 pCi/l above background
EPA	40 CFR 141 (being revised)	SDWA	4 (water pathway only)	Radium-226: 5 pCi/l Radium-228: 5 pCi/l Gross alpha: 15 pCi/l Tritium: 20,000 pCi/l
EPA	40 CFR 61	CAA	10 (air pathway only)	NA

TABLE 10.2 Selected NRC Effluent Concentration Limits: 10 CFR 20 (effluent concentrations in pCi/l)

Radionuclide	Air	Water
Tritium	1×10^2	1×10^6
Strontium-90	6×10^{-3}	5×10^2
Cesium-137	2×10^{-1}	1×10^3
Radium-226	9×10^{-4}	6×10^1
Thorium-230	2×10^{-5}	1×10^2
Uranium (natural)	9×10^{-5}	3×10^2
Uranium-238	6×10^{-5}	3×10^2
Plutonium-239	2×10^{-5}	2×10^1
Americium-241	2×10^{-5}	2×10^1

TABLE 10.3 Selected DOE Concentration Guides Order 5400.5 (effluent concentrations in pCi/l)

Radionuclide	Air	Water
Tritium	1×10^2	2×10^6
Strontium-90	9×10^{-3}	1×10^3
Cesium-137	4×10^{-1}	3×10^3
Radium-226	1×10^{-3}	1×10^2
Thorium-230	4×10^{-5}	3×10^2
Uranium (natural)	1×10^{-4}	6×10^2
Uranium-238	1×10^{-4}	6×10^2
Plutonium-239	2×10^{-5}	3×10^1
Americium-241	2×10^{-5}	3×10^1

Naturally Occurring Radioactive Material Disposal Standards

Although EPA has clear jurisdiction over the regulation of NORM under both RCRA and TSCA, EPA has not promulgated minimum federal standards for the disposal of NORM. Congress should therefore direct EPA to set NORM disposal standards pursuant to its RCRA or TSCA authority and set a strict schedule for their issuance.

Notes

1. 42 U.S.C. §§ 2011-2296 (1988 & Supp. II 1990).
2. *See infra* text accompanying notes 38 to 45.
3. There are several other problems with the regulation of radioactive

pollution that this paper does not consider including federal preemption of state regulation over the siting and construction of nuclear power plants and the siting, construction, and funding problems with the proposed high-level waste repository at Yucca Mountain, Nevada.

4. Atomic Energy Act of 1946, ch. 724, 60 Stat. 755.

5. Atomic Energy Act of 1954, ch. 1073, 68 Stat. 919.

6. 42 U.S.C. § 2011(a).

7. *Id.* §§ 2012(d), (e), 2013(d).

8. *Id.* § 2031.

9. *Id.* § 2121(a).

10. *Id.* §§ 2013(b), 2161-2168.

11. *Id.* § 2013(a), (d).

12. *Id.* §§ 2073(b), 2093(b), 2134.

13. *Id.* § 2140.

14. Pub. L. No. 86-373, 73 Stat. 688.

15. 42 U.S.C. § 2021(a)(2).

16. The term "source material" means "(1) uranium, thorium, or any other material which is determined by the Commission pursuant to the provisions of section 2091 of this title to be source material; or (2) ores containing one or more of the foregoing materials, in such concentration as the Commission may by regulation determine from time to time." *Id.* § 2014(z).

17. The term "special nuclear material" means "(1) plutonium, uranium, uranium enriched in the isotope 233 or in the isotope 235, and any other material which the Commission, pursuant to the provisions of section 2071 of this title, determines to be special nuclear material, but does not include source material; or (2) any material artificially enriched by any of the foregoing, but does not include source material." *Id.* § 2014(aa).

18. The term "byproduct material" means "(1) any radioactive material (except special nuclear material) yielded in or made radioactive by exposure to the radiation incident to the process of producing or utilizing special nuclear material and (2) the tailings or wastes produced by the extraction or concentration of uranium or thorium from any ore processed primarily for its source material content." *Id.* § 2014(e).

19. *Id.* § 2021(b). *See* G. Mazuzan and J. Samuel Walker, *Controlling the Atom: The Beginnings of Nuclear Regulation 1946–1962* (1984), 277-303.

20. 42 U.S.C. §§ 2021(d)(2), (g).

21. *Id.* § 2021(c)(1). A production facility is any "equipment or device" that *produces* special nuclear material in such quantities as to be "of significance to the common defense and security" or affects "the health and safety of the public[.]" 10 C.F.R. §§150.3(h). A utilization facility is any "equipment or device" capable of *making use* of special nuclear material in such quantity to be "of significance to the common defense and security" or affects "the health and safety of the public[.]" *Id.* § 150.3(l).

22. 447 F.2d 1143, 1149 (8th Cir. 1971), *sum aff'd*, 405 U.SD. 1035 (1971). *See also* 10 C.F.R. § 150.15(a)(1)(ii).

23. 447 F.2d at 1154.

24. Reorganization Plan No. 3 of 1970, §2(a)(6), (7), *reprinted in*, 5 U.S.C.A. app. 1 (West Supp. 1992).

25. *Id*. Since EPA standards under the AEA apply only at the boundary or "fencelines" of nuclear facilities, NRC and DOE have argued that they may allow radioactive discharges within their facility boundaries greater than EPA limits assuming that the radiation levels will decrease before reaching the general environment. *See* U.S. Congress, Office of Technology Assessment, *Complex Cleanup: The Environmental Legacy of Nuclear Weapons Production*, (OTA-O-484) (1991) at 54 [hereinafter referred to as "Complex Cleanup"]; 10 C.F.R. § 20.106(d).

26. 42 U.S.C. §§ 5801-5891.

27. *Id*. § 5814.

28. *Id*. § 5841.

29. *See* 10 C.F.R. pt. 150.

30. 42 U.S.C. §§ 5801(b), 5814(c), 5817(a).

31. *Id*. § 5812(d).

32. *See* S. Rep. No. 980, 93d Cong., 2d Sess. 30 (1974), *reprinted without appendices in*, 1974 U.S. Code Cong. & Admin. News 5470, 5492-93.

33. 42 U.S.C. § 5842.

34. *Id*. §§ 7101-7353.

35. *Id*. §§ 7112(18), 7151(a).

36. *Id*. § 7133(a)(8).

37. *See* B. Finamore, *Regulating Hazardous and Mixed Waste at Department of Energy Nuclear Weapons Facilities: Reversing Decades of Environmental Neglect*, 9 Harvard Envt. L. Rev. 83, 91-92, (1985).

38. 33 U.S.C. §§ 1251-1387 (1988 & Supp. II 1990).

39. 42 U.S.C. §§ 7401-7671q (1988 & Supp. II 1990).

40. 42 U.S.C. §§ 300f to 300j-26 (1988 & Supp. II 1990).

41. 42 U.S.C. §§ 7901-7942 (1988 & Supp. II 1990).

42. 42 U.S.C. §§ 6901-6992k (1988 & Supp. II 1990).

43. 42 U.S.C. §§ 9601-9675 (1988 & Supp. II 1990).

44. 42 U.S.C. §§ 10101-10226 (1988 & Supp. II 1990).

45. Pub. L. No. 96-573, 94 Stat. 3347 (1980) (amending 42 U.S.C. §§ 2021b-2021d). The LLRWPA was amended in 1985 by Pub. L. No. 99-240, 99 Stat. 1845 (1985).

46. *See, e.g.*, FWPCA, 33 U.S.C. § 1251(a); CAA, 42 U.S.C. § 7401(b); SDWA, S.Rep. No. 99-56, 99th Cong., 2d Sess. (1986), 1-2, *reprinted in*, 1986 U.S. Code Congress & Admin. News 1566-1567; CERCLA, 42 U.S.C. § 9604(a); NWPA, 42 U.S.C. § 10131(7).

47. 42 U.S.C. §§ 6902(a)(4).

48. *See infra* text accompanying notes 55, 85, 112, 146, 185.

49. *See infra* text accompanying notes 59–62, 71–77, 88–91, 116–119.

50. 33 U.S.C. § 1251(a).

51. *Id*. § 1311(a).

52. *Id*. § 1342(b); 40 C.F.R. pt. 123.

53. 33 U.S.C. § 1342; 40 C.F.R. pt. 122.

54. 33 U.S.C. § 1311(b); 40 C.F.R. pt. 125.

55. 33 U.S.C. §§ 1311(b)(1)(C), 1370.

56. *Id.* § 1323. However, the President may exempt any facility if he deems it to be in the "paramount interest" of the United States. *Id. See Weinberger v. Romero-Barcelo,* 456 U.S. 305 (1982). In 1992, the Supreme Court held that federal agencies were immune from state civil penalties for federal facility violations of the FWPCA. *See State of Ohio v. DOE,* 118 L. Ed. 2d 255 (1992). *But see, Sierra Club v. Lujan,* 728 F.Supp. 1513 (D.Colo. 1990), *aff'd,* 931 F.2d 1421 (1991).

57. 42 U.S.C. §§ 1319(a)(1), (g). A person who knowingly violates the FWPCA may also be subject to criminal penalties. *Id.* § 1319(c).

58. *Id.* § 1319(b).

59. The FWPCA defines "citizen" as a person and defines person as, among other things, a state or political subdivision of a state. 42 U.S.C. §§ 1362(5), 1365(g).

60. *Id.* § 1365(a)(1).

61. *Id.* § 1365(b)(1)(B).

62. *Id.* § 1365(a)(2).

63. *Id.* § 1362(6).

64. *Id.* § 1311(f).

65. 426 U.S. 1 (1976).

66. *Id.* at 23-25.

67. *Id.* at 8. *See also,* 40 C.F.R. § 122.2 at note.

68. *See supra* text accompanying notes 21-23.

69. Watkins, James D., Secretary of Energy, Press Conference Transcript; Augusta Sheraton, Augusta, Georgia, January 8, 1992.

70. Energy Department records indicate that DOE has released more than 3.5 million curies of tritium from the Savannah River Site since 1984. *See* DOE, Report of the Task Group on Operation of Department of Energy Tritium Facilities (DOE/EH-0198P) (1991). From 1980 to 1984, onsite surface streams at Savannah River contained tritium concentrations up to 750 times greater than EPA's public drinking water standard. *See* U.S. General Accounting Office, *Nuclear Waste: Impact of Savannah River Plant's Radioactive Waste Management Practices* (GAO/RCED-86-143) (1986) at 4-5.

71. 42 U.S.C. § 2271.

72. 10 C.F.R. § 2.206.

73. *Id.* § 2.206(b).

74. *Id.* § 2.206(c)(2).

75. *See Safe Energy Coalition of Michigan v. NRC,* 866 F.2d 1473 (D.C. Cir. 1989); *Arnow v. NRC,* 868 F.2d 223 (7th Cir. 1989); *P.I.R.G. v. NRC,* 852 F.2d 9, 16 (1st. Cir. 1988).

76. *See Heckler v. Chaney,* 470 U.S. 821 (1985).

77. 5 U.S.C. § 553(c). For example, unlike EPA and NRC standards, DOE's effluent standards for radioactivity are not limits in the sense that radioactive discharges from DOE facilities may never exceed a certain amount. Instead, DOE refers to its standards as "derived concentration guides" (DCGs) and states that "DCGs are not release limits, but rather screening values for considering [further

treatment] for these discharges and for making dose estimates." *See* DOE Order 5400.5, P. II-6. DOE is proposing to codify these orders at 10 CFR Part 834. *See* 58 Fed. Reg. 16268 (1993).

78. *See* Memorandum of Understanding Between the Environmental Protection Agency and the Nuclear Regulatory Commission (March 16, 1992). The memorandum was intended to apply primarily to EPA and NRC regulations under the CAA and NWPA but not RCRA or CERCLA.

79. 5 U.S.C. § 706. *See also, TRAC v. FCC,* 750 F.2d. 70, 76–77, C.D.C. (ir. 1984).

80. *See* 5 U.S.C. § 553 (b) (3) (a).

81. 42 U.S.C. § 7401(b)(1).

82. *Id.* § 7412(b)(2).

83. *Id.* § 7412.

84. *Id.* § 7412(l).

85. *Id.* §§ 7412(r)(11), 7416.

86. *Id.* § 7418(a). The President may exempt any federal facility from complying with the CAA if he determines it in the "paramount interest" of the U.S. *Id.* 7418(b). *See, U.S. v. South Coast Air Quality Management Dist.,* 748 F.Supp. 732 (C.D.Cal. 1990) (holding that the CAA waives sovereign immunity with respect to a federal facility's obligation to pay air pollution regulatory fees imposed pursuant to a local air pollution district's rules and regulations); *Ohio ex rel. Celebrezze v. United States Dept. of the Air Force,* 17 Envtl. L. Rep. (Envtl. Law Inst.) 21,210, 21,212 (S.D. Ohio 1987) (holding that federal facilities are subject to civil penalties for violations of air pollution laws).

87. 42 U.S.C. § 7413(a)(3).

88. The CAA allows any person to commence a suit to enforce the CAA, and defines person as including a state, municipality or political subdivision of a state. 42 U.S.C. §§ 7602(e), 7604(a)(1).

89. *Id.* § 7604(a)(1).

90. *Id.* § 7604(b)(1)(A).

91. *Id.* § 7604(a)(2).

92. Pub. L. No. 95-95, 91 Stat. 685 (1977).

93. 42 U.S.C. § 7422(a).

94. 44 Fed. Reg. 76,738 (1979).

95. 54 Fed. Reg. 51,654 (1989); 40 C.F.R. pt. 61. At the same time, however, EPA stayed the implementation for NRC-licensed facilities citing concerns that the standards would duplicate and clash with existing NRC standards. 54 Fed. Reg. 51,667-68 (1989). Since the initial three month stay, EPA has stayed the final standards for NRC-licensed facilities three additional times. *See* 55 Fed. Reg. 10,455-56; 29,205-06; 38,057-58 (1990).

96. EPA did not issue proposed regulations until April 1983, 48 Fed. Reg. 15,076 (1983), after the Sierra Club filed suit. *Sierra Club v. Gorsuch,* 551 F. Supp. 785-89 (N.D. Cal. 1982) (ordering EPA to issue proposed regulations within 180 days). EPA published final regulations in February 1985, 50 Fed. Reg. 5,190 (1985), after another successful Sierra Club suit and contempt order, *Sierra Club v. Ruckelshaus,* 602 F.Supp. 892-900, 900-904 (N.D. Cal. 1984) (ordering

EPA to publish final regulations within 90 days and a subsequent contempt order). These final standards were then litigated in the D.C. Circuit. While several petitions for review were pending, EPA sought a voluntary remand of the standards for consideration of the decision in *NRDC v. EPA*, 824 F.2d 1146 (D.C. Cir. 1987).

97. Pub. L. No. 101-549, 104 Stat. 2399 (1990).

98. 42 U.S.C. § 7412(d)(9). *See* 57 Fed. Reg. 56877 (1992). NRC's standards for radiation protection are at 10 C.F.R. Part 20.

99. 56 Fed. Reg. 18735 (1991). Recently, the D.C. Circuit vacated the EPA stay for NRC-licensed facilities other than nuclear power reactors holding that it violated § 112(q)(1) of the CAA, 42 U.S.C. § 7412(q)(1). *See NRDC v. Reilly*, 976 F.2d 36 (D.C. Cir. 1992).

100. 56 Fed. Reg. 37158, 37196 (1991).

101. 42. U.S.C. § 7412(d)(9).

102. *See supra* text accompanying notes 21-23. This argument is weakened by the fact that during Congressional consideration of the CAA amendments, the Senate voted to strike a provision that would have eliminated state authority under the CAA to regulate radionuclide emissions more stringently than the federal government. *See* 136 Cong. Rec. 2253-2276 (daily ed. March 7, 1990).

103. 40 C.F.R. pt. 61, subpts. H, Q.

104. 42 U.S.C. § 2021. *See* notes 128–129 *infra*.

105. *See* Table 10.1 *infra*.

106. 42 U.S.C. §§ 6924, 6925; 40 C.F.R. pts. 264, 265.

107. 42 U.S.C. § 6925; 40 C.F.R. pt. 270.

108. 42 U.S.C. § 6926(b); 40 C.F.R. pts. 123, 271.

109. A TSD facility may qualify for interim status if it was in existence on November 18, 1980 or on the date of a statutory or regulatory change requiring the facility to obtain a hazardous waste permit. 42 U.S.C. § 6925(e); 40 C.F.R. §§ 270.10(e)(1), 270.13.

110. 42 U.S.C. § 6924(u). RCRA also requires corrective action for hazardous waste releases beyond the waste facility boundary. *Id.* § 6924(v). RCRA authorizes EPA to issue administrative orders to interim status facilities when the Administrator of the EPA believes there has been a release of hazardous waste from the site. An order may require "corrective action or such other response as [the Administrator] deems necessary to protect human health or the environment[.]" *Id.* § 6928(h).

111. 40 C.F.R. pt. 264, subpt. G; 40 C.F.R. pt. 265, subpt. G. RCRA closure requirements allow TSD facilities two options for remediation. First, the facility may select the "clean closure" option, where virtually all contamination is removed and the site is returned to pre-operation condition. The facility is then absolved from all further obligation. The facility can also choose the "landfill closure" option by closing or "capping" the hazardous waste unit as a landfill. "Capping" involves sealing off the top of the unit with an impermeable synthetic cover, grading the unit and the surrounding area to prevent migration of hazardous wastes, and providing 30 year post closure monitoring. *Id.* §§

264.228, 265.228. *See* S. Smith, *CERCLA Compliance With RCRA: The Labyrinth*, 18 Envtl. L. Rep. (Envtl. L. Inst.) 10518, 10530-10531 (1988). EPA also has technical standards and corrective action requirements for owners and operators of underground storage tanks. 40 C.F.R. pt. 280.

112. 42 U.S.C. § 6929.

113. *Id.* § 6961. However, the President may exempt a federal facility from compliance if he determines it to be "in the paramount interest of the United States." *Id.* In 1992, the Supreme Court held that federal agencies are immune from state civil penalties for violations of RCRA at federal facilities. *See State of Ohio v. DOE*, 118 L. Ed. 2d 255, 264 (1992). However, in 1992, Congress enacted the Federal Facilities Compliance Act, Pub. L. 102-386, 106 Stat. 1505, which expressly allowed states to assess civil penalties against federal facilities for violations of RCRA.

114. 42 U.S.C. §§ 6928(a), (g). A person who knowingly violates RCRA may also be subject to criminal penalties. *Id.* § 6928(d).

115. *Id.* § 6928(a). EPA may also bring suit where a situation presents an "imminent and substantial endangerment to health or the environment." *Id.* § 6973(a).

116. 42 U.S.C. §§ 6903(15), 6972(a).

117. *Id.* § 6972(b)(1)(B).

118. *Id.* § 6972(a)(2).

119. *Id.* § 6974.

120. RCRA defines solid waste as "any garbage, refuse, sludge . . . and other discarded material, including solid, liquid, semisolid, or containing gaseous material[.]" *Id.* § 6903(27). *See also* 40 C.F.R. § 261.2.

121. 42 U.S.C. § 6903(5); 40 C.F.R. § 261.3. *See also American Mining Congress v. Environmental Protection Agency*, 824 F.2d 1177 (D.C. Cir. 1987).

122. RCRA specifically excludes source, special nuclear, and byproduct material from the definition of solid waste. 42 U.S.C. § 6903(27). RCRA also states that, "Nothing in this chapter shall be construed to apply to . . . any activity or substance which is subject to the . . . Atomic Energy Act of 1954." *Id.* § 6905(a).

123. *See supra* text accompanying notes 13, 34-37. *See also* Complex Cleanup *supra* note 25 at 4.

124. *See supra* text accompanying notes 24, 25, 71, 77. *See also* Complex Cleanup *supra* note 25 at 4.

125. *See* U.S. General Accounting Office, *Dealing with Problems in the Nuclear Defense Complex Expected to Cost over $100 Billion*, (GAO/RCED-88-197BR) (1988); U.S. General Accounting Office, *Improving DOE's Management of the Environmental Cleanup* (GAO/T-RCED-92-43) (1988), at 1. For estimates of cleanup costs at Department of Defense facilities see U.S. General Accounting Office, *Hazardous Waste: DOD Estimates for Cleaning Up Contaminated Sites Improved but Still Constrained* (GAO/NSIAD-92-37) (1992).

126. Complex Cleanup *supra* note 25 at 15.

127. *See supra* text accompanying note 29.

128. *See* NRC Review of Agreement State Radiation Control Programs: Final

General Statement of Policy, 57 Fed. Reg. 22495, 22498 (1992). This policy statement generally applies only to state low-level waste disposal programs.

129. However, NRC is currently reviewing its policy on agreement state programs and considering whether agreement states may impose radiation standards more stringent than NRC's. *See* 56 Fed. Reg. 66457 (1991).

130. *See supra* text accompanying notes 71-76.

131. *See* Federal Facility Compliance Act of 1992, Pub. L. 102-386, § 3021(b), 106 Stat. 1505, 1512; U.S. Congressional Office of Technology Assessment, *Partnerships Under Pressure: Managing Commercial Low-Level Radioactive Waste* (OTA-O-426) (1989) at 5 (hereinafter referred to as "Partnerships Under Pressure").

132. Partnerships Under Pressure, *supra* note 131 at 5.

133. *See id* at 5; 53 Fed. Reg. 37048 (1988).

134. *See* Partnerships Under Pressure, *supra* note 131 at 22-23. Task forces have been used in the past to resolve overlapping regulations. For example, the Mine Safety and Health Administration has overlapping jurisdiction with the Occupational, Safety, and Health Administration in developing health standards for workers in the mining industry. The two agencies formed an agreement to develop joint rulemaking. *See* 44 Fed. Reg. 22827 (1979).

135. *See* text accompanying notes 78–80 *supra*.

136. U.S. EPA Office of Radiation Programs, Sites Contaminated and Potentially Contaminated with Radioactivity in the United States, (1991), at 1-6 (draft). The contractor included in its study all private and federal sites that may, either currently or in the future, require the removal of radioactive contamination to a level that would allow unrestricted use.

137. 42 U.S.C. §§ 9601-9675. Congress strengthened the CERCLA cleanup program in 1986 through the Superfund Amendments and Reauthorization Act (SARA); Pub. L. No. 99-499, 100 Stat. 1613 (1986).

138. H.R. Rep. No. 1016, 96th Cong., 2d Sess. 17, *reprinted in*, 1980 U.S. Code Cong. & Admin. News 6119-6120.

139. CERCLA defines "release" as "any spillage, leaking, pumping, pouring, emitting, emptying, discharging, injecting, escaping, leaching, dumping, or disposing into the environment (including the abandonment or discarding barrels, containers, and other closed receptacles containing any hazardous substance or pollutant or contaminant)." 42 U.S.C. § 9601(22).

140. CERCLA defines hazardous substance to include any hazardous air pollutant listed by the CAA. *Id.* § 9601(14). The CAA lists radionuclides as a hazardous air pollutant. *Id.* § 7412(b)(1). *See*, S. Miller, *The Applicability of CERCLA and SARA to Releases of Radioactive Materials*, 17 ELR 10071 (Envt'l L. Rep.) (1987).

141. The President's authority over remedial actions under CERCLA has been delegated to the Administrator of the EPA. *See* Executive Order 12580, §4(d)(1), 52 Fed. Reg. 2923 (1987).

142. CERCLA defines "remove" or "removal" as short-term, risk-minimization actions. 42 U.S.C. § 9601(23). "Remedial" actions are intended to effect more nearly permanent remedies. 42 U.S.C. § 9601(24).

143. The NCP established procedures and standards for responding to hazardous waste releases. It includes, for example, methods and criteria for discovering and investigating contaminated facilities, and procedures for coordinating response actions between federal, state, and local governments. *Id.* § 9605(a).

144. *Id.* §§ 9604(a), 9622.

145. *Id.* § 9620(a)(1). However, to protect the "national security interests" of the U.S., the President may exempt a site or facility from CERCLA. *Id.* § 9620(j)(1). Federal facilities are cleaned up pursuant to inter-agency agreements (IAGs) between EPA and the appropriate federal agency. *Id.* § 9620(e)(2).

146. *Id.* § 9621(d)(2)(A). States may impose stricter cleanup standards than the federal government but must pay the incremental costs associated with the greater degree of cleanup. *Id.* § 9621 (d)(2)(c)(iii).

147. *Id.* § 9621(d)(1). *See* S. Smith, *supra* note 111 at 10522.

148. 40 C.F.R. pt. 192.

149. 42 U.S.C. §§ 7901-7942.

150. The term "tailings" means the remaining portion of a metal-bearing ore after some or all of such material, such as uranium, has been extracted. 42 U.S.C. § 7941(8).

151. *Id.* § 2022(a).

152. 51 Fed. Reg. 22264 (1986).

153. EPA intends to issue a notice of proposed rulemaking for cleanup standards by May 1994. *See* 58 Fed. Reg. 25032 (1993).

154. *See* Complex Cleanup, *supra* note 25 at 10, 134-135.

155. The Nuclear Weapons Complex: Management for Health, Safety, and the Environment (National Academy Press, 1989), at 38.

156. Statement of Roger P. Whitfield, Deputy Assistant Secretary, Office of Environmental Restoration, DOE Programmatic Environmental Impact Statement Implementation Workshop, Washington, D.C., March 31, 1992. EPA's own Radiation Advisory Committee recently urged EPA Administrator, William K. Reilly, to develop remediation standards for radioactively contaminated sites and facilities. *See* Letter to William K. Reilly from Science Advisory Board, Radiation Advisory Committee, U.S. EPA (January 9, 1992).

157. *See* NRC, General Requirements for Decommissioning Nuclear Facilities, 53 Fed. Reg. 24018 (1988).

158. *See* NRC, Branch Technical Position Regarding Disposal or On-site Storage of Thorium or Uranium Wastes from Past Operations, 46 Fed. Reg. 52061-63 (1981).

159. 53 Fed. Reg. 24038 (1988).

160. 10 C.F.R. pt. 20.

161. 57 Fed. Reg. 17740 (1992). *See* NRC, Proposed Rulemaking to Establish Criteria for Decommissioning Issues for Discussion at Workshops (April 28, 1992) (Draft).

162. *See* U.S. General Accounting Office, *NRC's Decommissioning Procedures Need to be Strengthened*, (GAO/RCED-89-119) (1989) at 27.

163. Congress has enacted this type of legislation before. For example, the

NWPA required EPA to issue standards for the disposal of high-level radioactive waste by January 1983. 42 U.S.C. § 10141 (a). *See NRDC. EPA*, 824 F. 2d 1258 (1st cir. 1987). More recently, the Waste Isolation Pilot Plant Withdrawal Act, Pub. L. 102–579 (1992), required EPA to set disposal standards for transuranic wastes at DOE's Waste Isolation Pilot Plant by April 30, 1993. The 1992 Energy Policy Act, Pub. L. 102–486, requires EPA to set high-level waste disposal standards for Yucca Mountain, Nevada by December 31, 1994.

164. Low-level radioactive waste is radioactive waste other than high-level waste, spent nuclear fuel, transuranic waste, uranium or thorium mill tailings. 42 U.S.C. § 10101(16); 10 C.F.R. § 61.2.

165. *See* U.S. General Accounting Office, *Nuclear Waste: Slow Progress Developing Low-Level Radioactive Waste Disposal Facilities* (GAO/RCED-92-61) (1992) at 2.

166. *See* U.S. EPA, Diffuse NORM Wastes: Waste Characterization and Assessment (May 991) (draft); J. Egan and J. Seymour, *Disposing of Naturally Occurring Radioactive Material Wastes: A Legal Strategy*, 22 Envtl. L. Rep. (Envtl. L. Inst.) 10433 (1992).

167. *See supra* text accompanying note 24.

168. 10 C.F.R. § 61.41.

169. *See supra* text accompanying note 28.

170. U.S. EPA, Environmental Standards for the Management, Storage, and Disposal of Low Level Radioactive Waste and Naturally Occurring and Accelerator Produced Radioactive Waste (1989) (to be codified at 40 C.F.R. pts. 193, 764 respectively). (hereinafter referred to as "EPA LLW and NORM Standards").

171. Letter from Kenneth M. Karr, U.S. NRC, to William K. Reilly, U.S. EPA (June 21, 1990). *See* A. Thompson, and M. Goo, *Naturally Occurring Radioactive Material: Regulators Should Look Before They Leap*, 22 Envtl. L. Rep. (Envtl. L. Inst.) 10052, 10056 n. 46 (1992).

172. 58 Fed. Reg. 25032 (1993).

173. *See* text accompanying notes 134–135 *supra*.

174. 42 U.S.C. § 7401 note.

175. *See* EPA LLW and NORM Standards, *supra* note 170. EPA also issued suggested guidelines for disposal of naturally occurring radionuclides in drinking water treatment plants. EPA, *Suggested Guidelines for the Disposal of Naturally Occurring Radionuclides Generated by Drinking Water Treatment Plants*, (1988). *See* Thompson and Goo, *supra*, note 171 at 10052, 10057.

176. 15 U.S.C. §§ 2610-2671 (1988).

177. *See* U.S. EPA, Diffuse NORM Wastes: Waste Characterization and Assessment ES-1 (Draft, May 1991).

178. U.S. NRC, *1987 Review of Naturally Occurring and Accelerator-Produced Materials. See* Thompson and Goo, *supra* note 171 at 10052.

179. *See supra* note 171.

180. 58 Fed. Reg. 25032 (1993).

181. 15 U.S.C. §§ 2601(a)(2), 2605.

182. *Id.* § 2602(2)(A).

183. *See supra* text accompanying notes 120–122.

184. *See* note 163 *supra*.

185. Both RCRA and TSCA allow states to set more stringent standards than the federal government. *See* text accompanying note 112 *supra*; 15 U.S.C. § 2617 (b)(2).

186. *See* text accompanying notes 57-58, 85, 112-113.

187. *See* EPA, *Federal Facilities Compliance Strategy*, at VI-3, App. I (1988).

188. *See, Federal Facility Compliance With Environmental Laws: Hearings Before the Subcommittee on Oversight and Investigations of the House Committee on Energy and Commerce*, 100th Cong., 1st Sess. 211 (1987) (statement of F. Henry Habicht II, Assistant Attorney General, Land and Natural Resources Division, U.S. Dept. of Justice). Some see the "unitary executive" theory as a growing threat to Congress' policy-making prerogative and the rule of law. *See*, M. Rosenberg, *Congressional Research Service Report to Congress - Congressional Control of Agency Decisions and Decision Makers: The Unitary Executive Theory and the Separation of Powers* (1987).

189. Under Executive Order 12146, 44 Fed. Reg. 42652 (1979), when two executive agencies are unable to resolve a legal dispute, they must submit the dispute to the U.S. Attorney General before going to court. Executive Order 12088, 43 Fed. Reg. 47707 (1978), states that if EPA and another federal agencies cannot resolve a conflict regarding the violation of a particular environment law, EPA must request that the Director of the Office of Management and Budget resolve the conflict.

190. Under Article II of the U.S. Constitution, the President, as Chief Executive, "shall take care that the laws be faithfully executed." To support the unitary executive theory, Justice relies on this clause and on the U.S. Supreme Court's declaration that the executive power be exercised in a "unitary and uniform" way, *Myers v. U.S.*, 272 U.S. 52, 161-64 (1926).

191. *see* D. Reicher, *Conflicts of Interest in Inspector General, Justice Department, and Special Prosecutor Investigation of Agency Heads*, 35 Stan. L. Rev. 975, 981–82 (1983).

192. 42 U.S.C. § 5841(a).

193. *Id.* §§ 5841(b), (f).

194. *Id.* § 5841 (b)(2)

195. *Id.* § 7171 (a)

196. *See, Confederated Tribes and Bands v. FERC*, 746 F.2d 466 (9th Cir. 1984).

197. Both FERC and NRC may choose to have their own staff attorneys represent them in court. *See* 28 U.S.C. § 2348; 42 U.S.C. § 7171 (i).

198. 42 U.S.C. § 5841 (a)(1).

199. *See supra* text accompanying notes 97-103.

11

Decommissioning Nuclear Power Plants

Martin J. Pasqualetti

Although the term "decommissioning" may not be in everyone's working vocabulary, people routinely "decommission" things like shoes, appliances, and cars when they wear out or become unsafe or too costly to keep. Such decommissioning is relatively mindless with ordinary items, but it becomes more complicated with materials and equipment that pose threats to the environment and the health of present and future generations. The decommissioning of nuclear power plants falls into this category.

The 21st century will witness large-scale terminations of nuclear power plant licenses raising many questions regarding the decommissioning of these plants. A cursory examination of this issue arguably leads to the conclusion that nuclear power plant decommissioning is better addressed as a social matter with a technical component rather than the other way around.[1]

The goals of this paper are to identify unrecognized and under-studied ramifications of decommissioning, to warn against complacency in the knowledge of these ramifications, to examine the ethics of current approaches to decommissioning, to stimulate wider discussion of decommissioning, and to develop recommendations for future decommissioning policy.

The Contextual Framework of Decommissioning

Since the beginning of military and civilian applications of nuclear energy in the 1940s and 1950s, most attention was directed toward the generation of nuclear power and the production of nuclear weapons rather than the disposal of nuclear waste. Only recently has there been any interest, effort, and money devoted to the task of disposing of the nuclear power plants. The US Nuclear Regulatory Commission states that the goal of decommissioning is "to remove nuclear facilities safely from service and to reduce residual radioactivity to a level that permits release of the property for unrestricted use and termination of license".[2] This definition masks a huge and never-ending duty involving not only technical but social problems.

Decommissioning activities so far have focused primarily on research and demonstration reactors and, to a much more limited degree, on government and commercial power reactors (Table 11.1).[3] One from this latter category, the Shippingport power plant near Pittsburgh, was recently fully dismantled. Several power plant decommissionings are also under way in other countries, such as the Berkeley station in England.

These projects are just the beginning. Several dozen commercial reactors will be eligible for decommissioning by the end of the century, and most of more than 500 commercial power plants now in operation or under construction worldwide will be eligible for decommissioning within the first quarter of the 21st century (Figure 11.1).[4] Unfortunately, there is no adequate policy to deal with the many consequences of nuclear power plant decommissioning.

A cursory examination of the implications of decommissioning reveals many problems: a large commercial nuclear power plant has not been decommissioned anywhere in the world; there are insufficient funds in most cases to carry out the task; there are no firm plans for safely removing each plant; there are no transport routes or identified sites for the disposal of dismantlement debris; there are no limits for

Table 11.1 Permanently Closed Commercial Reactors (as of the end of 1992)

	State	MWe	First	Last
Peach Bottom 1	PA	46	1967	1974
Indian Point 1	NY	275	1962	1974
Humboldt Bay 3	CA	65	1963	1976
Dresden 1	IL	220	1960	1978
Three Mile Island 2	PA	961	1978	1979
Shippingport	PA	72	1957	1983
LaCrosse	WI	65	1968	1987
Rancho Seco	CA	963	1974	1989
Fort St. Vrain	CO	343	1976	1989
Yankee Rowe	MS	175	1961	1991

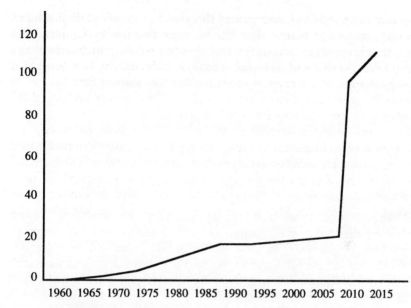

Figure 11.1 - The Rise in Expected Decommissionings

the release of sites for unrestricted use; and there has been no thorough consideration of the environmental impact of dismantlement and removal of each power plant.

The most blatant shortcoming of earlier studies of decommissioning is that there is little information about public reactions, apprehensions, risk perceptions, expenses, disruptions or impressions related to decommissioning. Moreover, there is no official program to develop this information, and only a few individuals have identified significant gaps in the research.[5] In a recent evaluation of 10 major decommissioning studies, only one of them contained discussion of any substantive social component other than economics.[6]

In an earlier paper, I suggested that nuclear power could not have developed as it did if the public had not been willing to accept several contentions of the nuclear industry without convincing proof. These contentions, which I call the "seven leaps of faith," include: the low cost of electricity; the rapid and unceasing growth in demand for electricity; a harmless threshold limit for radiation hazard; the timely establishment of adequate waste disposal programs; an adequate and safe system of emergency preparedness; an adequate program for operator training; and the virtual impossibility of a major nuclear accident.[7] I believe decommissioning policy is being developed on a similar premise of public acceptance that all requirements and information will be developed and available by the time they are needed. Decommissioning, then, is the "eighth leap of faith".

The Eight Policy Issues of Decommissioning

At least eight interrelated policy issues emerge from examination of decommissioning as a social rather than as a technical issue.

The Objectives Issue

Despite the publication of several documents on decommissioning, including the decommissioning rule and the Generic Environmental Impact Statement, there is little formal public policy on the objectives of decommissioning.[8] The few announced objectives of decommissioning allude broadly to completing the process safely and releasing power plant sites for unrestricted use. Other objectives amount to inferences in the literature and include (along with their general topic in parenthesis):

- Minimizing radiological hazards for workers (health and safety);
- Minimizing radiological hazards for the general public (health and safety);
- Leaving a cleared and decontaminated site for future non-nuclear purposes (land use, health and safety);
- Ensuring that decommissioning costs are as low as reasonable and practicable (economics);
- Maximizing economic benefits of operations, including those to stockholders, by operating power plants as long as possible (economics);
- Securing sufficient decommissioning funding (economics, ethics); and
- Meeting legal requirements (law).

It is still unclear whether the policy is to continue operating the power plants or shut them down, keep them on site or get rid of them, dismantlement them promptly or hold them in safe-storage, rely on present technological developments or look to the future, give primary decommissioning responsibilities to present populations or defer responsibilities to future generations, declare the bulk of dismantlement debris below regulatory concern or plan to dispose of everything as radioactive waste, etc.

More precise guidance is needed on the objectives of decommissioning policy, because these objectives influence decommissioning decisions.

The Options Issue

Of the unresolved objectives listed, one has the most direct impact on waste handling, waste volumes, and waste hazards: how long will a retired plant remain on-site before it is totally dismantled? The principal health benefit of waiting (up to 135 years) is the reduction of hazards of Cobalt-60, a fission by-product with the relatively short half-life of 5.3 years.[9]

Usually, three broad alternatives are considered:[10]

- Prompt and complete dismantlement, with safe and permanent disposal of all wastes generated by the process;
- Delayed dismantlement, after a waiting period for radioactive decay; and
- Entombment (probably in concrete) for an indefinite period, possibly permanently.

These three options oversimplify and overstate the decommissioning choices. First, they imply that the nuclear industry is seriously considering all three options, when in reality the US nuclear industry has unofficially settled on delayed dismantlement (also referred to as SAFSTOR (safe-storage)). The industry argues that the prompt option is not viable, because there is no repository for permanent emplacement of long-lived commercial radioactive waste. The industry does not favor entombment, because there is a sense of irreversibility about it.

Second, delayed dismantlement is not just one option but actually a continuum of options. At one end of the continuum is on-site storage of high-level waste with some minimal decontamination of the power plant which remains. At the other end is dismantlement of everything but the reactor vessel and its nearby surrounding contaminated components. Either of these extremes, plus several variations and combinations in between, are possible across a wide time period.

Third, the present emphasis on revitalizing the nuclear industry (through, among other things, new reactor designs) and improving industry economics (through life extension and/or relicensing) is drawing attention away from decommissioning policy questions. The cynical expression of this trend is to ask: Why worry about decommissioning when the real profits are in jump-starting the industry into a new era of construction?

As Lough and White[11] pointed out, determining the appropriate decommissioning strategy for a nuclear plant requires site-specific decisions on a number of critical issues including:

- the policy options and technologies available for decommissioning;
- the impacts of alternative policy options;
- the levels of uncertainty associated with options and associated impacts; and
- the perceptions and acceptance of various interested parties concerning options, impacts, and uncertainties.

The question as to which decommissioning option is "best" is still being discussed. Each option has had its proponents. In the early days, several companies (e.g. Arkansas Power and Light Company, Consumers Power Company) favored prompt dismantlement.[12] Later, delayed decommissioning came into favor,[13] only to be countered with a renewed interest in prompt dismantlement.[14] A more recent study done for the Virginia State Corporation Commission favored life-extension.[15] In the United Kingdom the issue has gone full circle with prolonged safe-storage replaced by entombment,[16] reportedly in response to a proprietary survey of public opinion.[17]

Pasqualetti and Pijawka found that the highest public concern about decommissioning around the Humboldt Bay nuclear power plant is the disposition of its high-level wastes.[18] They further found that as long as the high-level wastes are secured off-site there would be little public pressure to remove the remaining facility entirely. The public may view dismantlement as an activity which would introduce an unnecessary additional risk. This has been the reaction to the proposed dismantlement of the small, experimental, Saxton nuclear facility in Pennsylvania, and it has also been discussed as a utility preference during the decommissioning planning of Yankee Rowe.[19]

The options issue is important because it is linked to a large number of other issues including economics, waste disposal, land use and siting, ethics, health and safety, and socioeconomics. Despite all the attention this issue has received, there are still no answers to any of the most fundamental questions: Which is the safest option? Which is the least costly? Which does the public prefer? Which has the lowest risk? Which has the least environmental impact? There are no answers to these questions because there has been no focused, data-based analysis of decommissioning options even though the type and timing of decommissioning is the most frequently raised issue in decommissioning policy.

Some would argue that the option question should be answered on a site-by-site basis. The problem with this approach is that it does not compel attention to questions such as those just listed.

The Economics Issue

Economic cost strongly influences most energy decisions and also plays a major role in nuclear decommissioning policy. Cost is the most frequently discussed topic and the subject for which there is the most concrete policy guidance.[20] Until the provision was dropped as part of the Energy Policy Act, the US decommissioning rule required that decommissioning funds be collected and set aside in secure, "Black Lung" investments. Despite the formality and scope of discussions, regulations, and interest in decommissioning economics, many questions persist which leave decommissioning economic policy largely incomplete:

Sufficiency. How much will decommissioning cost and when will adequate funds be available?[21] Although there is some experience on this issue from previous work such as the dismantlement of the Shippingport reactor, there are still many unknown costs.[22] Waste disposal costs, for example, largely reflect public demand for greater attention to health and safety issues, the most volatile part of the sufficiency debate.[23] In addition, it is difficult to estimate the effects of long periods of safe-storage on the final costs. Given that these and other uncertainties will drive up final decommissioning costs, the $105 million for a pressurized water reactor ($135 million for a boiling water reactor) stipulated by the decommissioning rule is low.[24]

Investment. Will the present conservative strategy toward decommissioning fund management and investment produce the necessary sums?[25]

Unexpected Events. Will funds be available in the event of premature decommissioning due to accident (e.g. Three Mile Island), political decisions (e.g. Rancho Seco, Trojan), mandatory refurbishment (e.g. Humboldt Bay), or unsuccessful attempts to meet revised emergency planning standards (e.g. Shoreham)?

Continued Operation. Is life extension an economically viable alternative to decommissioning? Some argue that it is not.[26]

Discount Rate. What is the most appropriate discount rate to use when calculating the ultimate 'real' cost of decommissioning and the economically optimum safe storage period?[27]

Utility Rates. How will estimates of decommissioning cost affect current utility rates and possibilities of life extension and relicensing?

These and other questions challenge current decommissioning economic policy. Postponing dismantlement decisions will likely increase the economic uncertainties involved.

The Waste Issue

Nuclear waste disposal has been a persistent and sensitive matter in the development of nuclear power contributing to public suspicions as to the wisdom of continuing to use the technology.[28] Although it was part of a bundle of topics attracting attention during the buildup of nuclear power, it did not attract sufficient attention until after most power plants were already constructed.

Waste disposal is a major factor in any decommissioning policy because of the problems with disposing of large amounts of nuclear waste resulting from the decommissioning process (although Shippingport and other reactors have been dismantled without them.)[29] The importance of waste disposal is reinforced by its strong influence on decommissioning costs.

Definitions are particularly important in determining the volume of waste requiring disposal. Under a policy of "Below Regulatory Concern", as long as it is shown that "the application or continuation of regulatory controls is not necessary to protect the public health and safety and the environment, and is not cost effective in further reducing risk", the volume of decommissioning waste would shrink substantially.[30] The proposed BRC policy statement was withdrawn after meeting substantial public protest, but its key element, removing official responsibility for waste hazards by regulatory fiat, is still being discussed.

The official lower limit of concern will strongly influence several decommissioning problems in addition to waste disposal itself, such as dismantlement timing, packaging, transportation, and final waste repository site selection and size. And the public perception of the risk of the waste will affect the level of regulatory concern.

Delaying final dismantlement removes some waste disposal problems. Delay can come in several forms, such as through safe-storage, entombment, or life extension. Under the first two forms, high-level waste would be stored on-site, either in pools or in dry casks. This approach would mean that each existing plant site would function like a Monitored-Retrieval-Storage (MRS) site.[31]

The third way to reduce some of the waste disposal problems is through life extension. As Bradbury recently pointed out, "The nuclear industry has found that a maximum effort should be given to keeping reactors operating, both to extract further revenue and also to allow time for the eventual appearance of waste disposal facilities to ease the thorny decommissioning questions."[32] The economic viability of such life extension, however, is questionable.[33]

The Land Use Issue

Present and future land uses also influence nuclear energy policy. The influence of land use arises from the impact of nuclear power facilities as competitors for space, from their effect on aesthetic and property values, and from the real and perceived public hazards of nuclear technology.

There are two principal connections between land use and decommissioning policy. The first is the influence surrounding land uses and property values can have on decommissioning choices, such as at Shearon Harris (NC), Indian Point (NY), and San Onofre (CA). In such locations, economic or safety concerns argue for a cleared site for near-term dismantlement. Dismantlement is linked to the establishment of an "unrestricted use" limit for radioactivity at cleared and decontaminated sites (a limit not yet established but presumably tied to BRC-like decisions) and likely public concern about future use of deactivated nuclear lands, regardless of how officially 'clean' the land is certified to be.

The second connection occurs as the options of near-term dismantlement, relicensing, or life extension reduce the required land commitments needed to establish fresh sites and infrastructure. The increasing difficulty in finding environmentally and politically acceptable nuclear power plant sites argues for near-term dismantlement, because it frees old sites for future nuclear use.[34]

Siting needs would play a limited role in stimulating earlier dismantlement if no new power plants were proposed, existing sites were not acceptable as future sites (for whatever technical, social, or political reason), or existing sites were large enough to accommodate new reactors without dismantling old ones.

Time also influences the use of power plant sites. The longer an active or inactive power plant is left on-site the greater the real and/or perceived chance of radioactive leaks. There is also a greater effect on land use and property values and a greater certainty that the public will never accept the property for unrestricted use.[35] Other linkages between land use and decommissioning include population densities and waste transportation routes and disposal sites. For example, a "safe-storage" delay, ostensibly for purposes of public and worker safety, would have impacts on site reuse, leak potential, and waste volume. An increased risk of leaks would limit future land use options, and a delay would reduce the size of the waste disposal site.

The Ethics Issue

The ethical issues of decommissioning are connected to the various decommissioning choices. Is delayed dismantlement a better option because it protects present-day workers? Which generation should bear the financial and safety responsibilities of decontamination and removal?

These and related questions are connected to an assessment of imminent versus future risks associated with retired power plants. The assessment of these risks is linked to new leaps of faith which the public will have to make, including:

- technological developments will make decommissioning easier in the future;
- no new legal requirements will increase the demands on decontamination, removal, and waste disposal;
- disposal routes and sites will be more readily available in the future;
- financial estimates are accurate and decommissioning funds will be available; and
- public health and safety risks will not increase during safe storage.

The history of nuclear development has witnessed an accumulation of public concerns. If this pattern continues, future generations may not appreciate the risks, the wastes, or the obligations the present generation leaves them. Is it safe to assume that future generations will be more adept at dealing with nuclear waste than the present generation? If not, then from an ethical viewpoint, as John Surrey recently suggested, "there is much to be said for the option of prompt dismantlement".[36] We cannot build a secure decommissioning policy on a foundation of presumed future innovation.

The Risk Perception Issue

In general, public acceptance of nuclear power is inversely proportional to its perceived risks. Over the past 15-20 years, a rising sense of risk contributed to the cancellation or indefinite postponement of 106 reactors in the US alone.[37] Such perceptions, coupled with a poor operating record and effective lobbying, have contributed to public initiatives to close several plants such as the Humboldt plant in Eureka, California; the Rancho Seco plant near Sacramento, California; the Trojan plant near Portland, Oregon; and the Rowe plant in Rowe, Massachusetts.

Even when public perceptions do not result directly in a decision to close a nuclear plant, they continue to influence nuclear policy. For example, several countries, including the US and United Kingdom, perceive nuclear power to be so risky that it has become virtually impossible to achieve public consensus on new nuclear power plant or waste disposal sites.[38] Public perceptions of the risks of nuclear power will influence collection and investment of decommissioning trust funds, the use of cleared nuclear sites, the mode and timing of decommissioning, and all other decommissioning policy decisions.

Despite the importance of risk perceptions on decommissioning decisions, virtually no empirical data exist on public views about decommissioning. This is partly the result of public ignorance and apathy about decommissioning, but more significantly it results from the lack of effort by the nuclear industry to engage citizen involvement in decommissioning decisions.[39] This failure is illustrated by the lack of opportunity for formal public comment on decommissioning in the US now that the decommissioning rule and the generic environmental impact statement on decommissioning have been approved.[40] A new approach, participatory rule making, being discussed at the NRC in the context of an unrestricted release limit for former nuclear sites, holds promise of bringing the public into decommissioning policy discussions.[41]

Until the public is brought more meaningfully into the decision-making process, private research must suffice in providing data and analysis on decommissioning risk perceptions. Recent surveys near the decommissioned Humboldt Bay nuclear station outside Eureka, California showed that if high-level waste were removed off-site, the public would prefer that the nuclear power plant not be dismantled (Table 11.2).[42] This finding differs fundamentally from the public opinion which the NRC and the managing utility company had assumed prior to the survey, and it illustrates the necessity of a pro-active program to involve the public in the decommissioning debate.

The Geosocial Issue

People live near nuclear power plants and waste disposal sites and share roads and railroads with nuclear waste transporters. Materials and personnel will converge on power plants at the beginning of the decommissioning process and then diverge from the plant when the process is complete. Decommissioning debris and waste will disperse

TABLE 11.2   Perceived Risks of Decommissioning Options at Humboldt Bay 3

Response Statement	Nuclear Facility Phase	Level of Perceived Risk (Percent)			Mean Score
		Low (1-3)	Mod (4-7)	High (8-10)	(1-10)
Continued Operation Of Humboldt	Operation	33.0	25.5	41.5	5.96
Decommissioned Plant with All Parts and Spent Fuel Removed	Complete Dismantlement	59.8	23.4	16.8	3.82
Plant with Spent Fuel Stored at the Facility	Safe Storage with Spent Fuel On-Site	26.1	28.8	45.1	6.29
Plant with Spent Fuel Stored in Casks at the Site	Cask Storage	21.2	34.7	44.1	6.51
Spent Fuel Removed and Remainder of Facility Left Standing	Safe Storage with Spent Fual Off-Site	55.6	26.3	18.1	4.08

from the plant to sites yet to be identified. These activities will be linked to social and spatial characteristics. These linkages, or "geosocial impacts", will influence decommissioning policy as they have influenced all forms of electrical generation.[43] For example, when a power plant such as Yankee Rowe is decommissioned without on-site replacement, those dependent upon its operation for their livelihood must turn elsewhere for employment, producing an economic "bust" condition. If dismantlement occurs after many idle years in "safe-storage", new jobs will be created later in the same area, producing a "boom" condition. This boom would then be followed by another "bust" condition once dismantlement was complete.

Although such a sequence is conceivable for non-nuclear facilities, radioactivity complicates the picture. In Saxton, Pennsylvania, for example, the utility company managing the Saxton nuclear plant has long wished to dismantle the facility completely, but the public has successfully resisted such overtures, because they believe dismantlement activities increase risk. Proposed dismantlement of Saxton has become a rallying cry and unifying theme for the small community. Similar sentiments against dismantlement have surfaced recently at the Yankee Rowe plant as well.

Nuclear decommissioning activities will affect people's lives and influence decommissioning policies. Recognizing some of our success in the potential geosocial impacts of decommissioning at this early stage suggests a broader and deeper range of such impacts will be discovered in the future.

Summary of Goals

The policy recommendations made below are based on an examination of decommissioning as directed toward five goals. The first goal was to identify unresolved and under-examined influences on decommissioning policy. The second goal was to provide evidence which would caution against becoming too assured about the existing technology involved with decommissioning and the influence of the public on decommissioning policy decisions. As with other areas of nuclear power, there is still much to learn about decommissioning and how the public reacts to the prospect of this activity affecting their lives. Policy will change with new information and reaction to the public will. The third goal was to highlight the ethics of shunting present decommissioning responsibilities onto future generations. (In the final analysis, this may be the key element in decommissioning policy.) The fourth goal was to stimulate discussion on some of the likely nuclear decommissioning policy issues, because the level of sophistication with these issues will depend on a greater public awareness of decommissioning processes and their implications. Public risk perceptions and future events, such as nuclear accidents, will stimulate these developments. The pursuit of these four goals leads to the fifth goal, to develop recommendations for decommissioning policy.

Policy Recommendations

The following policy recommendations include several in general form, because many of them require additional data prior to implementation. One plan for gathering such data is suggested in the closing section of this paper.

Recommendation #1. Develop clear nuclear power plant decommissioning objectives. These objectives should address, but not be limited to, the following topics: limitations on future site usage, timing of facility removal, time needed to carry out decommissioning activities, economic cost goals, and legal parameters.

Recommendation #2. Revisit the issues of nuclear decommissioning funds (with the possible exception of external fund formation and "Black Lung" investment requirements, both of which have received substantial attention already). Focus attention on the most appropriate discount rates to be used in cost estimates, the effect of decommissioning collections on current and future utility rates, and the influence of life extension and premature decommissioning on fund sufficiency.

Recommendation #3. Give the rights of future populations equal standing with the rights of current populations. This applies in particular to public hazards, waste disposal, land use, financial responsibility, and preparations for final dismantlement.

Recommendation #4. Require determination and disclosure of plans for decommissioning waste disposal (including sites and routes) as a prerequisite to obtaining a construction license.

Recommendation #5. For purposes of land use planning, consider nuclear power plants a permanently contaminating use. This recommendation reflects the difficulty in agreeing on unrestricted-use limits for site release and the unlikely public willingness to use such land for non-nuclear purposes.

Recommendation #6. Avoid using life extension and relicensing to delay decommissioning planning.

Recommendation #7. Develop a "default" policy of near-term dismantlement for each plant requiring all managing utility companies to develop decommissioning plans based on an assumption of near-term dismantlement. Such plans should include consideration of costs, ethics, present and future land use and property value, jobs, technological abilities, waste disposal routes and sites, occupational and public safety, future siting requirements, and air and water contamination.

In estimating the timing of decommissioning activities, consideration should be given the following advantages of near-term dismantlement:

- clears the land for subsequent use;
- demonstrates that decommissioning processes can be completed as intended, without trusting in undeveloped future abilities;
- assigns the associated risks of decommissioning to those who benefit from the generated electricity;

- assures adequate funds for decommissioning;
- reduces fluctuation in the local job base;
- increases the likelihood of full and accurate records, corporate memory and responsibility at the time of decommissioning; and
- stimulates development of waste facilities.

Adopting a default, near-term dismantlement approach would give a sense of urgency to resolving decommissioning problems. It would also help prevent later recrimination and finger-pointing. It need not, however, mean that dismantlement commence immediately after shut down at every plant. Dismantlement does not have to begin within five years, but it should not be postponed indefinitely. A 15-20 year waiting period is reasonable.

This recommendation is at odds with the opinions expressed by people living near Humboldt, North Anna, Saxton, and Rowe power plants, and I do not attempt to reconcile this difference here.[44] Instead, the recommendation rests on a personal opinion that these views will change with a fuller understanding of the implications and costs of long waiting periods.

There also has been no attempt to reconcile this recommendation with the industry claim that the absence of permanent high-level waste disposal sites makes dismantlement impossible. Elk River and Shippingport have been dismantled without such facilities, and efforts are under way to dismantle Shoreham and Rowe, again without permanent civilian waste dumps. The absence of these waste sites should not forestall the research and development requirements of dismantlement.

Recommendation #8. Develop an environmental data base for each nuclear power plant in the country. The current ad hoc assortment of plant-specific data now available is inadequate to identify, evaluate, and anticipate decommissioning trouble-spots. Instead, there should be a system which standardizes decommissioning data. This should have the benefit of reducing redundancy, saving money, and facilitating the sharing of mutually beneficial research.

Data should be collected in the eight policy categories identified above (objectives, options, economics, waste, land use, ethics, risk perceptions, and geosocial conditions), plus station size, operating characteristics, and environmental characteristics. Maps and photographs (especially aerial photographs) of power plant sites and situations should also be included.

The data should be stored in a geographic information system (GIS) to facilitate analytical evaluations of the impacts of decommissioning, and they should be updated regularly with the collective experience from decommissioning activities in the US and other countries.

Everyone should have equal access to this information, including the nuclear industry, power utilities, and anti-nuclear advocates.

The existence and use of such a data set, updated regularly, would help to standardize and facilitate decommissioning planning and exchange of experience and reduce the likelihood of costly errors and repetition. The costs would be small compared to the benefits achieved.

A Proposal for Consensus

Current decommissioning policy is incomplete in large part because it was developed with little input, consultation, education, or evaluation of public opinion. Periods for public comment on draft documents such as the US decommissioning rule and generic environmental impact statement have garnered inadequate public input. The participatory rule approach being implemented by the NRC is a step in the right direction, but there is not yet any data from this process, and it is currently focused on unrestricted-release limits only.

In view of the questions, issues, and information deficiencies raised in this paper, and the likelihood that these matters will return in the future, the next step in nuclear decommissioning policy should be *to develop a public consensus on the principal issues* mentioned above. This process should be initiated before the first major wave of decommissionings hits.

All attempts should be made to maintain objectivity while gathering this consensus. Accordingly, a university research team should develop the research methodology to achieve public consensus and sources of funds should be independent (e.g. The MacArthur Foundation). If independent funds are not available, they should come from a government agency through the National Science Foundation (NSF). As many of the questions have geosocial implications, the Geography and Regional Sciences Program is a suitable project-coordinating unit. Participants in the evaluation of research proposals should include a representative from each of the following organizations: the federal government (e.g. the US Environmental Protection Agency, the US Department of Energy, or the US Nuclear Regulatory Commission), environmental organizations (e.g. Public Citizen, the Nuclear Information and Resource Service, the Natural Resources Defense Council); as well as academic experts in physical, technical, and social sciences. In view of their demonstrated interest and past research, the Organization for Economic Cooperation and

Development, the International Atomic Energy Agency, and Nuclear Electric in the UK should also be reviewers.

The criteria should require that focus groups be formed near each of the power plants used in the initial evaluation. The power plants should have varied ages, site conditions, and locations. Ten to twelve power plants should be in the first round of study including the following: San Onofre, Trojan, Yankee Rowe, Maine Yankee, Shearon Harris, and Oyster Creek.

Several methods may be employed in developing the consensus. It will require an increased effort to identify and incorporate public reactions, influences, and impacts into the formation of decommissioning policy. It could also include the Nominal Group Technique (NGT) and the Delphi methods, as discussed in the decommissioning context by Lough and White.[45] NGT involves group idea-generation and consensus building and consists of three phases: an individual, silent, idea-generation phase; a clarification, discussion, and expansion phase; and a priority-selection phase.[46]

NGT could precede a Delphi survey. Delphi surveying is a method of consensus building where participants interact in an anonymous debate by responding to a series of questionnaires. It is an iterative procedure which continues until a satisfactory solution or consensus is reached. The purpose of both techniques would be to stimulate discussion and education in the development of decommissioning policy.

Replacing the currently passive, almost silent, solicitation of public opinion on decommissioning with an active effort to involve the public in decommissioning decisions may result in different decommissioning policy and conclusions than we now have. In the end, this approach will be cheaper and less contentious, and will produce policies with greater public support as we enter the 21st Century.

Notes

1. M.J. Pasqualetti, "Nuclear Decommissioning Impacts: Wastes and Land Use, Perceptions and Policy", *The Radiation Debate: At the Limits*, 7th International Standing Conference on Low Level Radiation & Health, June 22-23, 1991, Summary of Presentations.

2. "General Requirements for Decommissioning Nuclear Facilities," *Federal Register*, Vol. 53(123):24018-24056, 1988, ref. is to page 24,019.

3. Electric Power Research Institute. *Decommissioning U.S. Reactors: Current Status and Developing Issues*, EPRI NP-5494. Palo Alto, Calif. 1988.

4. Ibid.

5. As examples: Fred Barker, "Nuclear Power Station Decommissioning: The

Environmental Implications", paper presented to the Second Annual European Environment Conference, University of Nottingham, UK, September 1992; Fred Barker, *The Decommissioning of Nuclear Power Station*, prepared for the National Steering Committee of Nuclear Free Local Authorities, UK, January 1992; Robin Cantor, "Applying Construction Lessons to Decommissioning Estimates", in Pasqualetti and Rothwell, *op cit*, pp. 105-118; James Hewlett, "A Cost/Benefit Perspective of Extended Unit Service as a Decommissioning Alternative", in Pasqualetti and Rothwell, *op cit*, pp. 255-273; James Hewlett, "Financial Implications of Early Decommissioning", in Pasqualetti and Rothwell, *op cit*, pp. 279-291; W.T. Lough, *A Technology Assessment Methodology for Electric Utility Planning: with Application to Nuclear Power Plant Decommissioning*, report to the Commonwealth of Virginia, State Corporation Commission, Richmond VA, May, 1987; Pasqualetti, 1989, 1990, 1991, *op cit*; Pasqualetti and Rothwell, *op cit*; C.P. Pollock, *Decommissioning: Nuclear Power's Missing Link*, Worldwatch Paper 69, Washington, D.C: Worldwatch Institute, 1986; Seth Shulman, "Nuclear Power: The Dilemma of Decommissioning", *The Smithsonian* 20(7):56-69, 1989; John Surrey, "Ethics of Nuclear Decommissioning", *Energy Policy* 20:632-640; 1992.

6. W.T. Lough and K. Preston White, Jr. "A Critical Review of Nuclear Power Plant Decommissioning Planning Studies." *Energy Policy*, 1990, 18(5):471-479.

7. M.J. Pasqualetti, "Nuclear Decommissioning at Ground Level: Sizewell and the Uncertainties of Faith." *Land Use Policy*, 18(4): 415-431, 1988; see also Pasqualetti, 1990, *op. cit.*

8. US NRC, "General Requirements for Decommissioning Nuclear Facilities", *Federal Register* 54 (123): 24018-24056. Washington, D.C.: U.S. Nuclear Regulatory Commission, 1988; US NRC, *Final Generic Environmental Impact Statement on Decommissioning of Nuclear Facilities*, NUREG-0586. Washington, D.C.: U.S. Nuclear Regulatory Commission, 1988. Other examples include: Arkansas Power and Light Company, *Analysis of Decommissioning Arkansas Nuclear One*, Little Rock AR, 1977; Consumers Power Company, *A Nuclear Power Plant Decommissioning Study*, report by the Nuclear Plant Decommissioning Task Force, Jackson MI, 1978; T.S. LaGuardia, *Decommissioning Cost Estimate for the North Anna Nuclear Power Station* and *Decommissioning Cost Estimate for the Surrey Nuclear Power Station*, report by TLG Engineering Inc for Virginia Electric and Power Company, Brookfield CT, 1978; W.J. Manion and T.S. LaGuardia, *An Engineering Evaluation of Nuclear Power Reactor Decommissioning Alternatives*, Nuclear Energy Services for the Atomic Industrial Forum, report AIF/NESP-009, Bethesda MD, 1983. In addition, there is a series of generic decommissioning studies written by Richard I. Smith and others at Battelle Pacific Northwest Laboratory in Richland, Washington.

9. Paul B. Woollam, "The Potential Radiological Consequences of Deferring the Final Dismantling of a Magnox Nuclear Power Station." In K. Pflugrad, R. Bisci, B. Huber and E. Skupinski, eds, *Decommissioning of Nuclear Installations*, pp. 76-84. London and New York: Elsevier Applied Science, 1990.

10. IAEA, *op cit*; US NRC, *op cit*.

11. Lough and White, *op cit*, p. 472.

12. Arkansas Power and Light Company, *op cit*; Consumers Power Company, *op cit*.

13. Manion and LaGuardia, *op cit*.

14. T.S. LaGuardia, *op cit*.

15. Lough, 1987, *op cit*.

16. A. Holmes, "Take it Away, Kids!", *Energy Economics: An International Analysis*, July, 1991, pp. 17-18; F. Passant, "In-Situ Decommissioning - You Can Take It or Leave It", paper prepared for presentation at the Waste Management '91 Symposium, February 24-28, 1991, Tucson, Arizona; F. Passant, "Power Plant Decommissioning—U.K. Strategy", paper prepared for presentation at British Nuclear Forum, Nuclear Forum '91, London, 25-26 June 1991.

17. Fred Passant, Nuclear Electric, England, personal interview, 1991, referring to the document "Report on Public Attitudes Towards Nuclear Power Issues Particularly the Decommissioning of Nuclear Power Stations in the United Kingdom", proprietary report prepared for Nuclear Electric plc, Gloucester, UK, by The Harris Research Centre, Richmond, Surrey, October 1990.

18. M.J. Pasqualetti and K.D. Pijawka, "The Risks of Dormancy: The Perceived Risks of Nuclear Power Plant Decommissioning".

19. Burns and Roe, *"Project Plan" for Dismantling of the Saxton Nuclear Experimental Facility*, Burns and Roe Industrial Services Corporation, Paramus, NJ, 1981; personal discussion with William J. McGee, Yankee Atomic Electric Co, Dec. 1992.

20. See Pasqualetti and Rothwell, *op cit*, for a review.

21. Duane Chapman, "Decommissioning and Nuclear Waste Policy: Comprehensive or Separable?, in Pasqualetti and Rothwell, *op cit*, pp. 247-254; Gene R. Heinze Fry, "The Cost of Decommissioning U.S. Reactors: Estimates and Experience", in Pasqualetti and Rothwell, *op cit*, pp. 87-104.

22. William Murphie, "Greenfield Decommissioning at the Shippingport Nuclear Power Station", in Pasqualetti and Rothwell, *op cit*, pp. 119-132.

23. Duane Chapman, "Decommissioning and Nuclear Waste Policy: Comprehensive or Separable?" in Pasqualetti and Rothwell, *op. cit.*, pp. 247-254.

24. Robert S. Wood, "Federal Regulation of Decommissioning Economics", in Pasqualetti and Rothwell, *op cit*.

25. Howard Hiller, "Managing Qualified Nuclear Decommissioning Trust", in Pasqualetti and Rothwell, *op cit*, pp. 191-204; M. Didi Weinblatt, "Historical Lessons for Nuclear Decommissioning Trust Fund Investment", in Pasqualetti and Rothwell, *op cit*, pp. 205-216; Thomas R. Tuschen, "Investment Strategies for Externalized Nuclear Decommissioning Trusts", in Pasqualetti and Rothwell, *op cit*, pp. 217-229.

26. Cantor, *op cit*; Hewlett, *op cit*.

27. J. Jeffreys, "Who Pays for the Long-Term Costs of Nuclear Power?", *Energy Policy*, vol 15, 1987, pp. 376-378.

28. G. Jacob, *Site Unseen: The Politics of Siting a Nuclear Waste Repository*, University of Pittsburgh Press, Pittsburgh, 1992.

29. Frans Berkhout, "The Management and Regulation of Decommissioning Wastes", in Pasqualetti, *op. cit., Nuclear Decommissioning and Society*, pp. 59-84.

30. The policy statement suggested an individual dose criterion of between 1 and 10 mrem per year (0.01 and 0.1 millisievert per year) and a collective dose criterion of 1000 person-rem per year (10 person-sievert per year). For reference, see U.S. Nuclear Regulatory Commission, "Below Regulatory Concern; Policy Statement", effective data July 3, 1990, 23 pages. The quotation is from page 1.

31. Fred Passant in Holmes, *op cit*.

32. D. Bradbury, "Decommissioning of Civil Nuclear Facilities: a World Review", *Energy Policy*, 20(8)755-760, 1992, quotation is from page 757.

33. James Hewlett, "A Cost/Benefit Perspective of Extended Unit Service as a Decommissioning Alternative", in Pasqualetti and Rothwell, *op. cit.*, pp. 255-272.

34. Pasqualetti, *op cit*, all.

35. Woollam, *op cit*.

36. Surrey, *op cit*.

37. Peter Mounfield, *World Nuclear Power*, Routledge, London and New York.

38. Stan Openshaw, "Nuclear Archaeology: The Influence of Decommissioning on Future Reactor Siting in the UK", in Pasqualetti, 1990, *op cit*, pp. 143-158; Andrew Blowers, "Generations of Decay: The Political Geography of Decommissioning", in Pasqualetti, 1990, *op cit*, pp. 161-173.

39. Lough, 1987, *op cit*; and Lough and White, *op cit*.

40. Pasqualetti, 1991, *op cit*; US NRC, Generic Environmental Impact Statement, 1988, *op cit*; US NRC, 1988, Decommissioning Rule, 1988, *op cit*.

41. See, for example, US Nuclear Regulatory Commission, "Radiological Criteria for Decommissioning of NRC-licensed Facilities; Workshops"; and "Proposed Rulemaking to Establish Radiological Criteria for Decommissioning; Issues for Discussion at Workshops", 1992.

42. Burns and Roe, *op cit*; Pasqualetti and Pijawka, 1993, *op cit*.

43. Brian S. John, "Decommissioning and Jobs", in Pasqualetti, 1990, *op cit*; and Pamela M. Lewis, "The Economic Impact of the Operation and Closure of a Nuclear Power Station", *Regional Studies*, 1986, 20(5):425-432.

44. Burns and Roe, *op. cit.*; Lough and White, *op. cit.* McGee, *op. cit.*; Pasqualetti and Pijawka, *op cit*.

45. Lough and White, *op cit*.

46. *Ibid*.

12

The Disposal of
High-Level Nuclear Waste

Terry R. Lash

This paper focuses almost entirely on the U.S. Department of Energy's (DOE) programs for the storage and deep geologic disposal of spent nuclear fuel from commercial nuclear power reactors. Other important issues, such as the management of defense high-level radioactive waste and the transportation of spent nuclear fuel, are treated peripherally. Also, the regulatory programs concerning high-level radioactive waste at the U.S. Environmental Protection Agency and the U.S. Nuclear Regulatory Commission are not addressed, although they too play an important role in DOE's planning for the storage and disposal of spent nuclear fuel.

The assessment that follows may seem unduly bleak. My pessimism regarding the prospects of the current program is not universally shared. Several participants in the Yucca Mountain Project, who can point to substantial progress in recent years, have told me that they believe the program has momentum and that success at Yucca Mountain is very likely. Site characterization is, in fact, proceeding at Yucca Mountain notwithstanding the opposition of the State of Nevada and the concerns of others. Also, preparations are underway for initiating construction of a large exploratory tunnel in March, 1994. Most importantly, there are many scientists, including independent ones, who believe the Yucca Mountain site is very promising and should be carefully studied.

Nonetheless, the history of high-level radioactive waste management, and my own experience with siting a low-level radioactive waste disposal facility in Illinois, lead me to believe that DOE's optimism and confidence is unjustified. Radioactive waste issues are exceptionally complex and controversial. Proponents, such as DOE and its contractors, usually underestimate the challenges they face by a wide margin. Unless DOE more openly acknowledges the problems it faces and develops an improved program to solve them, a suitable geologic repository may not become available for the foreseeable future.

Historical Overview

Until about 1970, the former Atomic Energy Commission (AEC) focused on reactor development to the detriment of the radioactive waste management program. In particular, the AEC devoted very little effort to developing a disposal facility for high-level radioactive waste.[1]

In the 1970s, the problem of radioactive waste disposal received increasing attention. But as the size of the effort grew, a series of abrupt changes occurred in policy and organizational structure. Although the AEC and its successor, the Energy Research and Development Administration (ERDA), allocated growing amounts of resources and management time to waste issues, they achieved little progress or even continuity toward developing a geologic repository. One observer explained the lack of progress as follows:

> The early developers of nuclear power had three failings—they knew too much about radioactivity, not enough about geology, and almost nothing about dealing with the public and its reactions.[2]

The continued absence of a disposal solution combined with visible failures, such as leaks from the high-level waste tanks at Hanford and the need to abandon the bedded salt deposits near Lyons, Kansas, as a possible repository site, heightened public concern about the ongoing generation of high-level radioactive waste at commercial nuclear power plants. By the time of President Carter's election in 1976, the controversy had reached the level of The White House. President Carter first directed an internal review of ERDA's waste management program, and then appointed an Interagency Review Group on Nuclear Waste Management (IRG). Following review of waste management issues within the Administration and extensive public review, President Carter issued a statement on nuclear waste policy in February, 1980.

Of particular interest was the IRG's emphasis on investigating multiple potential repository sites in a variety of rock types. This approach, in contrast to the earlier focus on bedded salt as the geologic medium of choice, was selected because the IRG found an incomplete scientific foundation for believing that bedded salt was the best type of geologic formation. Technical uncertainties also convinced the IRG that there should be multiple engineered and natural features to reduce the potential release of radioactive waste in the long term. The IRG, nonetheless, basically supported DOE's focus on deep geologic burial as the preferred means for permanently disposing of high-level radioactive waste. And, unfortunately, the IRG did not point out that DOE's expectations for how quickly a repository could be built were wholly unrealistic.

In December 1982, Congress adopted the Nuclear Waste Policy Act (NWPA). President Carter's 1980 policy provided some of the basis for the Act, although Congress made significant changes in the President's proposal. The NWPA provided DOE with needed direction and guidance for locating a site for building a deep geologic repository for high-level radioactive waste. Congress, however, set tight deadlines for development of a repository that did not realistically consider the challenges facing DOE. At the time, no major organization publicly recognized the impossibility of meeting the legislated deadlines that had been suggested by DOE.

The IRG's caution about the scientific uncertainties in geologic disposal and the recommendation of using both engineered and natural features to assure safety were not given adequate attention by Congress or DOE in implementing NWPA. Part of the reason DOE did not adequately study important geologic issues, such as whether a repository should be located in the unsaturated or saturated zone, was the short period of time allowed by NWPA for finding a site and building an operational repository. DOE's emphasis was on quickly finding a site and building a repository that satisfied U.S. Environmental Protection Agency (EPA) and U.S. Nuclear Regulatory Commission (NRC) regulations and no more. In other words, the job was defined in relatively straightforward project management terms. Scientific research and engineering analysis on the geologic disposal concept, including repository design and engineered features, did not—and apparently still do not—have a high priority.

DOE's missteps and difficulties following passage of the Nuclear Waste Policy Act of 1982 received a great deal of attention and publicity. The public uproar caused by DOE's search for potential repository sites resulted in Presidential and Congressional actions to reorient the program dramatically in 1987. As a formal matter, the Secretary of Energy stopped the investigation of granite as a possible host rock for a second repository. This action probably was taken with Presidential approval in response to the protests of governors and members of Congress from several states in the Midwest, Southeast and Northeast.

At about the same time, the State of Tennessee disapproved the proposed siting of a Monitored Retrievable Storage facility (MRS) near Oak Ridge. Under the NWPA, this meant an end to the project unless Congress overrode the State, which it was unwilling to do.

Cancellation of the "Second Round" of site investigations focused political pressure on the governors and Congressional delegations of Texas, Washington and Nevada, which had the three remaining potential sites for the first geologic repository. The potential sites in Texas and Washington had particularly challenging problems. One major problem was that both were associated with valuable water resources: the Ogallala aquifer in Texas and the Columbia River in Washington. Locating a repository near these major water resources proved to be politically unacceptable. DOE's technical analyses to support site selection were not adequate to reassure a concerned public about technical uncertainties and the level of protection that could be assured.

Thus, by 1987 the repository and MRS siting efforts were in crisis. Resolution of the controversy seemed well beyond DOE's capabilities. Congress stepped in by passing major changes to the Nuclear Waste Policy Act in late 1987. The 1987 amendments focused DOE's investigation of potential repository sites exclusively on Yucca Mountain near the Nevada Test Site.[3] Congress also redirected the Monitored Retrievable Storage (MRS) siting process and tied construction of an MRS to success in receiving NRC permission to begin construction of a geologic repository.

The Current Situation

Geologic Repository. Today, more than five years after enactment of the NWPA amendments, DOE's high-level radioactive waste management program is once again facing a crisis, and it appears that the President and Congress will have to focus on the problem in the near future. The context of this attention initially will be the level of funding that should be provided for the Yucca Mountain Project and other civilian waste programs. DOE's Office of Civilian Radioactive Waste Management (OCRWM) is planning to seek hundreds of millions of dollars per year more than Congress appears willing to appropriate. The new Administration and Congress are likely to scrutinize the program carefully to see how annual costs can be kept much lower than OCRWM has planned, while still providing enough for continued evaluation of the suitability of Yucca Mountain. In this regard, the United States General Accounting Office has advised the new Administration and Congress that,

Although a decade has passed since the Congress established a program for disposing of nuclear waste from electric utilities and several billion dollars have been invested, siting a nuclear waste repository seems as distant as it did 10 years ago. . . .In view of the dim prospects for completing a repository by 2010 and the uncertain availability of a temporary storage facility, a reassessment is needed. It is time to reconsider the alternatives for storing nuclear waste and to ensure that funding levels and time frames realistically accord with the selected alternatives.[4]

Public opinion surveys continue to show that the great majority of Nevadans do not want a high-level radioactive waste "dump" in their state.[5] This lack of public support is viewed by some analysts to result from fundamental flaws in DOE's approach to solving the disposal problem and from DOE's past mistakes and behavior that have generally and irrevocably undermined the public's trust in its programs. These analysts, therefore, argue that an organization other than DOE should be responsible for the high-level radioactive disposal problem, and that a much different approach should be adopted in locating a new site for study.[6]

Ever since Yucca Mountain was selected by Congress in 1987 as the sole site for study for a geologic repository, the State of Nevada, reflecting public opinion, has tried vigorously to stop DOE's studies and progress toward building a repository. Under current circumstances, the State's political leadership appears committed to opposing the Yucca Mountain site for the foreseeable future. The state's efforts to date, however, have not been effective in delaying the project's progress significantly.

At least some within DOE recognize the seriousness of the public trust and confidence issue. In 1991, the Secretary of Energy created a special task force to study how DOE could improve public trust and confidence in its radioactive waste management program.[7] The task force released a discussion paper on December 8, 1992,[8] and a draft final report in early January, 1993.[9] Among the findings in the draft final report are the following:

- "Although OCRWM has recently placed more emphasis on building public trust and confidence, the program has a relatively constricted view of what is required to restore it."
- "Notwithstanding its public statements, OCRWM has not implemented any consistent approach to building public trust and confidence."
- "Many critical decisions about siting, policy, and technical design have been made in an arena open to few stakeholders. The broader public participated in those choices only formally and with little impact."

- "In making decisions, the implications of a program action for public trust and confidence have generally not been considered explicitly."[10]

In the last few years, there have been major objections to DOE's repository program by technical oversight bodies. For instance, the Board on Radioactive Waste Management of the National Academy of Sciences—National Research Council has concluded that,

> There are scientific reasons to think that a satisfactory HLW repository can be built and licensed. But...the current U.S. program seems unlikely to achieve that desirable goal.[11]

The Board went on to recommend a "more flexible and experimental" approach in the development of a repository. The proffered approach was seen to "use science in the proper fashion," whereas the current DOE approach was deemed to "justify decisions that have already been made on the basis of limited knowledge."

Another oversight body created by the 1987 NWPA amendments, the independent Nuclear Waste Technical Review Board, has also made recommendations for substantial changes in the technical approach to investigating Yucca Mountain. The Review Board's suggestions have covered a variety of major issues, such as alternative thermal-loading strategies for the repository, engineered barrier systems, and use of system-wide analyses in making decisions. DOE's official responses seem generally to have been receptive, but limited by "...the goal of meeting the two primary [and equally important] programmatic milestones: to begin receipt of waste in 1998 and to begin disposal of waste in 2010."[12]

Monitored Retrievable Storage Facility (MRS). After a period of inaction following the State of Tennessee's rejection of the Oak Ridge site, the MRS siting project relied on the efforts of the United States Nuclear Waste Negotiator to identify an Indian Tribe or a State that would volunteer to host the facility. The Office of the Nuclear Waste Negotiator, which was established by the 1987 amendments to NWPA, has reported that initial study grants were awarded to two counties and 10 Indian Tribes between October 17, 1991, and October 29, 1992.[13] But the search is not progressing well and seems doomed to failure. In South Dakota after county supervisors accepted a DOE grant to study the MRS, they were voted out of office in a recall election. Perhaps the most significant development in this regard was Wyoming Governor Sullivan's decision to disapprove Fremont County's acceptance of a second DOE grant for further study of the MRS. In his letter explaining the basis for disapproval, Governor

Sullivan listed five questions that he believes cannot be satisfactorily answered:

1. "Does the national policy (on MRS)...make sense?"
2. "Can we and are we willing to trust the federal government's assurances that the MRS site will be temporary?"
3. "Can we take comfort from the DOE record of nuclear facilities in the West?"
4. "Can we trust the federal government or the assurance of negotiation to protect our citizens' interests?"
5. "Who can assure us what risks we would accept that new businesses may choose not to locate in Wyoming or what the alteration of our image as a state, our environment or our tourism industry may be from our willingness to embrace this nuclear waste?"[14]

At the heart of Governor Sullivan's concerns, and others' calls for fundamental organizational change, is the belief that DOE cannot be trusted.

Early interest by Indian Tribes in potentially hosting an MRS seems also to have waned. As of October 29, 1992, only the Mescalero Apache Tribe in New Mexico had been awarded a partial second phase study grant. But the New Mexico Governor and Congressional delegation have expressed opposition to an MRS within the borders of New Mexico. The Negotiator apparently has indicated that he will not negotiate a deal with the Indian Tribe over the objections of the governor.

In a recent assessment of the Negotiator's program, his Chief of Staff observed that, among other concerns, DOE's credibility was still at issue:

- "Trust and confidence in the Federal government on this and a myriad of environmentally sensitive issues is largely non-existent."
- Trust and confidence in DOE is likewise significantly compromised."[15]

The outgoing Secretary of Energy belatedly recognized serious problems with both the MRS and repository programs. On December 17, 1992, he informed Senator J. Bennett Johnston, Chairman of the Committee on Energy and Natural Resources, that the Office of the Nuclear Waste Negotiator ". . . has not been able to identify a viable candidate site . . . that will permit spent fuel receipt by January 1998 as planned. Thus, alternative actions are required." On January 12, 1993, he wrote again to Senator Johnston to describe ". . . recent initiatives to minimize disposal program costs and to build confidence as the program proceeds that substantive progress is being made and safe disposal can be accomplished."

Thus, there appears to be little prospect of siting an MRS in the foreseeable future, and the investigation into the suitability of Yucca Mountain seems seriously troubled. In sum, as an astute observer of the program concluded, "The current solutions are not working."[16]

Discussion

Since the early 1970s the nation has developed substantial experience in the management of high-level radioactive waste. To a surprising degree, however, the lessons learned from this experience do not seem to inform the current federal program. One purpose of the following discussion is to draw on the federal high-level waste experience and some similar ones (e.g., the siting of low-level radioactive waste disposal facilities in several states) for lessons that can be applied to the current situation. The discussion is intended to provide support for the suggestions at the end of this paper.

General Observations

The most fundamental lesson from the past 20 years is that the disposal of radioactive waste is an exceptionally difficult problem, a problem much tougher to solve than virtually anyone has previously imagined. Often technical and managerial people involved in waste programs have blamed an overly emotional and ill-informed public— allegedly aided and abetted by a news media eager to publicize radioactive waste controversies—for the lack of new storage and disposal facilities.[17] Such opinions are overly simplistic and often result in counterproductive actions by those who hold them. Most importantly, such attitudes ignore more fundamental deficiencies within the federal program that need correcting.

Many examples exist of technical challenges associated with radioactive waste management that have exceeded their original estimates. For instance, for a long time there has been a broad scientific consensus that deep geologic disposal of high-level radioactive waste is technically feasible and desirable. This scientific consensus is fundamental to the current national policy to establish a mined geologic repository. But, what is not widely perceived outside of the scientific community, is that there is not a scientific consensus about how specifically to achieve safe, geologic disposal in practice. This lack of agreement is due in large measure to uncertainty about how best to address the unique issues of geologic disposal. The National Academy of Sciences - National Research Council's Board on Radioactive Waste Management has only recently observed that the technical challenges are "formidable."[18] The implications of this important understanding have not yet been incorporated into the nation's program for developing a geologic repository.

In the past, this lack of technical consensus on detailed aspects of geologic disposal resulted in a failed search for bedded salt deposits that might host a repository. Throughout the 1970s, the belief within the federal program was that bedded salt was the geologic medium of choice for the repository. As the federal program progressed toward finding a suitable salt deposit, however, scientists who concluded that there was inadequate information to support the use of bedded salt spoke out. This realization that not enough was known about the suitability of bedded salt came more than a decade after the AEC had established the goal of using bedded salt for the disposal of high-level waste.

Eventually, during the 1980s, the country embarked on a program to identify potentially suitable sites in a variety of rock types, including bedded salt. Most of the time, however, this search assumed that the repository would be located in the saturated zone. It was not until recently, with the focus on Yucca Mountain, that much consideration was given to the unsaturated zone.[19] Now the advantages of the unsaturated zone are more widely appreciated, and most serious consideration is being given to a repository at Yucca Mountain in the unsaturated zone. Thus, more than two decades were needed to reach a broad agreement within the technical community that a hard rock formation in the unsaturated zone was the most promising for a repository.

There are currently important technical disagreements about key aspects of a repository that might be located at Yucca Mountain. What type of waste package should be used? What other engineered barriers should be used? What emplacement configuration should be used? How easy should it be to retrieve the waste packages? These are just some of the major questions for which there is currently no consensus within the technical community. A repository at Yucca Mountain should not be finally designed until these and other key questions are openly discussed and resolved within the technical community.

Ultimately, the technical community's judgment will be evaluated by the public, and it may not be accepted. This is not bad; in a democracy the public has the right to review expert judgment and decide whether to accept it. Rejection by the public is most likely if a broad scientific consensus has not been developed or if the consensus was formed without adequate public input. DOE's current approach, however, seems too often to address key technical issues implicitly, not openly. Under these circumstances it should not be surprising that there is widespread concern about DOE's rush to submit a license application to the NRC.

A major step to address public concern and anxiety, therefore, is to take the time required to address important safety and environmental issues thoroughly and publicly. Leaving these questions to the future, after a commitment to develop the repository at Yucca Mountain is made, will not be satisfactory, because the public will believe that it is being asked to accept a project with too much uncertainty. The Nuclear Waste Technical Review Board made this point recently:

> DOE's current lack of emphasis on developing and testing long-lived packages and other elements of the engineered barrier system may prove to be counterproductive to the goal of building public trust and confidence.[20]

> [P]ublic confidence considerations require that the waste package design should substantially exceed minimal requirements.[21]

Recent experience in trying to establish new low-level radioactive waste disposal facilities in several states highlights the importance of technical questions in the public debate about radioactive waste management. In Illinois, for instance, the Department of Nuclear Safety's staff tried initially to develop a detailed technical methodology for progressively narrowing the search for a specific site for the disposal facility. Within the Department, however, it did not take long to realize that the screening process often recommended by geologists was not as practical or defensible from a scientific perspective as had been initially thought.[22] Instead of the traditional approach recommended by geologists, the Illinois Department of Nuclear Safety publicly proposed a site selection process emphasizing professional judgment, public involvement, and political acceptability. The Department did not use multi-attribute utility analysis or any other complicated quantitative technique for evaluating potential sites, as was attempted during DOE's search for potential high-level radioactive waste disposal sites. Up front, the Department publicly recognized that there was no satisfactory quantitative methodology for picking the "best" site or even numerically ranking potentially suitable sites during the selection process.

Explaining this approach to both lay and technical audiences resulted in mixed reactions. At the beginning of the site selection process, for reasons probably related to the openness and technical quality of the program, there were no serious challenges to the reliance on a combination of professional judgment and political acceptability as the method for site selection. No lawsuits were filed to stop the process; and no legislation was introduced to force a change in approach. When the process narrowed the field of potential sites to one, however, the earlier quiet acceptance changed dramatically, but not unexpectedly. The identified site, near Martinsville in Clark County, was vigorously attacked and eventually found unacceptable by an independent, three-person siting commission.[23] The commission members had many negative comments about the siting process and the site, but essentially they believed that better sites could be found elsewhere in the state based upon an approach in the technical literature that had been rejected explicitly by the Department of Nuclear Safety.

It is interesting to note that the community of Martinsville fully supported the process leading to selection of a site within its jurisdiction; and the City of Martinsville still supports building a disposal facility at the site. The City's support is based in part on its own extensive technical evaluation of the site.[24] The Illinois Department of Nuclear Safety, relying on its technical assessment, also publicly disagreed with the siting commission. Nonetheless, the Governor, citing a campaign pledge, accepted the Commission's decision without reservation, and the Department has stopped considering the Martinsville site.

A change in law abolished the siting commission in late 1992. A new siting process passed the legislature in early 1993, but the governor's position is uncertain. This new process proposed by the Illinois General Assembly focuses primarily on traditional, technical evaluation of potential sites, but it does give special consideration to potential sites that are voluntarily nominated by landowners or local governments. Another feature of the new process is to reduce dramatically the capability of opponents to stop selection of a proposed site. The process would also seem to allow reconsideration of the Martinsville site.

The subject of radioactive waste is one that arouses exceptionally strong feelings among all those involved, proponents and opponents alike. The issues tend to be viewed in simplistic, stark black and white terms, and positions are often argued with ideological zeal. Questions about the motives of individuals and organizations, and challenges to individuals' honesty and integrity are prevalent among all categories of participants. Therefore, generally acceptable compromises are extremely difficult to achieve. It is this prevalence of strong feelings that makes development of a consensus within the technical community extraordinarily difficult. The scientists and engineers have their own strong feelings about the problem, and they are as concerned about the reactions of others to their opinions as everyone else.

When these emotions are combined with the inherent technical challenges in picking a site and building a facility, it is easy to see how extremely difficult it is for managers to make progress toward programmatic milestones. Key decisions almost always strongly alienate some stakeholders, resulting in the program manager's loss of substantial credibility with them. Compounding this problem is that program managers seem to be given little, if any, credit for making technically sound or politically correct decisions. The list of mistakes or "negatives" is the only one kept. It is not balanced by a comparison with a list of good decisions.

Another aspect of the program manager's difficulties is that usually there are no outspoken constituents in favor of a specific radioactive waste disposal facility. Even the prospective users of a facility rarely stand up in public to support an agency's program or individual decisions. In essence, everyone is a critic of the program's leadership, albeit with different concerns.

Monitored Retrievable Storage Facility (MRS)

For about 20 years the commercial nuclear power industry has wanted the federal government to build an interim surface storage facility for spent fuel from nuclear power plants. With no permanent disposal facility in view, the industry wants some place to send spent fuel so that long term storage at reactors, particularly those that are no longer operating, will not be necessary.

The federal government agreed to this request to assume responsibility for spent fuel to relieve utilities of an obligation to provide long term storage. Neither the nuclear industry nor the federal government, however, has adequately appreciated the difficulty in siting an away-from-reactor spent fuel storage facility. In addition to all of the typical problems associated with such a radioactive waste facility, there is the major challenge of giving adequate assurance that a Monitored Retrievable Storage facility (MRS) will not become *de facto* a permanent storage facility. Furthermore, there is no compelling physical or safety justification for it.[25]

The task of siting the MRS proposed by DOE is at least as difficult as siting a geological repository. Moreover, DOE does not appear capable of siting an MRS while simultaneously conducting the Yucca Mountain Project. Continuing the MRS effort, therefore, seems to jeopardize the geological disposal program. In sum, the effort required to site DOE's proposed MRS is grossly disproportionate to any benefit that might be obtained.

In any event, the simple fact is that under the conditions of the NWPA, an MRS cannot be built as has been planned by DOE. In the past, DOE has acknowledged that the linkage established in NWPA between the start of construction of an MRS and the receipt of a construction permit for a geologic repository meant that an MRS could not be available to receive spent fuel in 1998. DOE therefore has hoped that Congress would remove the linkage.

DOE's difficulties in siting an MRS were recognized on December 17, 1992, when the former Secretary of Energy released a "new strategy." This strategy recommended that DOE "...be authorized and required by the Congress to select candidate Federal sites by December 31, 1993."[26] Until December 17, DOE had stated that it was relying on the U.S. Nuclear Waste Negotiator to obtain a site for the MRS through a voluntary approach.

The Negotiator's 1991 request for expressions of interest resulted in several communities and Indian Tribes requesting study grants from DOE. After this initial enthusiasm there seem to be only a few Indian Tribes left that wish to consider further the possibility of volunteering. The chances of the voluntary process working out favorably appear very small, because the state governors involved are unlikely to accept having a spent fuel storage facility within their states' borders.[27]

The successful opposition of the State of Tennessee to the MRS proposed near Oak Ridge, even though the community supported it, is strong evidence that governors are unlikely to approve of an MRS. The Wyoming governor's more recent action to stop further study by Fremont County also suggests that gubernatorial support is unlikely in the future. But gubernatorial acceptance apparently is a precondition for the Negotiator even to enter into serious discussions with Indian Tribes.

Despite two decades of effort and the expenditures of many millions of dollars, DOE and its predecessor organizations have not been able to make progress toward establishing an independent spent fuel storage facility. The outgoing Secretary of Energy's last-ditch effort to save the program seems unlikely to succeed. Specifically, there appears to be little chance that one of the states with an existing DOE facility would welcome hosting an MRS.[28]

But not only is the former Secretary's proposal unlikely to be politically acceptable, it has further undermined trust and confidence in DOE's waste programs. This new MRS initiative was undertaken with very little, if any, consultation outside of the Secretary's office.[29] Not even the senior staff within the Office of Civilian Radioactive Waste Management were consulted during the formulation of this proposed abrupt departure from recent policy. This type of sudden, seemingly arbitrary change in direction is what has significantly contributed to feelings of distrust in the past. The irony is that the very Secretary who established a special task force to advise on how to build the public's trust and confidence in DOE's waste programs is the same one who in his last hours as Secretary took action that will lower public opinion about the trustworthiness of DOE.

The Secretary's statement on the MRS understandably upset the U.S. Nuclear Waste Negotiator, who was surprised and disappointed by the announcement. In an unusual "Media Statement" issued following the Secretary's release of his "new strategy" for spent fuel management, the U.S. Nuclear Waste Negotiator ". . . expressed his extreme displeasure in the Department's handling of this announcement. . . ."[30] Subsequently, at a public meeting, held by the Nuclear Waste Technical Review Board, the Negotiator's chief of staff is reported to have ". . . dismissed the recent proposal by DOE to license federal sites for interim high-level nuclear waste storage as being part of the `policy of the month club.'"[31] In a year-end assessment of the Negotiator's program, the chief of staff also observed that:

> The most significant impediment to success is the public's lack of trust and confidence in the Federal government, and a concern about the consistency and commitment to follow through. I would caution that any significant changes in this program at present, might well destroy this process and the credibility and integrity it earned.[32]

In sum, the MRS program has been a failure for years and it is not on a path leading to success. The establishment of an independent spent fuel storage facility cannot be achieved in the foreseeable future. The nation should cut its losses and formulate a different approach to the interim storage of spent fuel that will be broadly accepted, including by nuclear utilities.

There may be an acceptable purpose for a federal surface storage facility, if it is conceived as part of a sound waste management system.[33] A surface storage facility built in conjunction with the development of a geologic repository could serve three important purposes:

1. A surface facility would allow extended storage for the purpose of allowing short-lived radionuclides to decay. Such decay

would result in the waste generating a relatively stable amount of heat for a long period of time. Stable heat generation by the waste emplaced in the geologic repository is desirable from a safety perspective.

2. A surface facility that could repackage waste is desirable, because there probably will be improved techniques for placing waste in a geologic repository that would require such repackaging.
3. A surface facility would serve as a backup to the geologic repository in case waste had to be retrieved because of unexpected problems

Yucca Mountain Project

In 1987, Congress short-circuited DOE's technical process for selecting a potential site for development for the nation's first high-level radioactive waste repository. Congress picked the Yucca Mountain site for characterization and stopped consideration of any other potential site until DOE can determine whether Yucca Mountain is suitable for a mined geologic repository. This Congressional decision has been criticized for putting politics above science. In the vernacular, this has been called "dump on Nevada" legislation. But, in fact, the technical process circumvented by Congress probably would have selected Yucca Mountain over the other potential sites DOE had under consideration anyway. Moreover, Congress had to intervene because DOE had caused unbearable political controversy in searching for potential repository sites.

Several earth scientists, both inside and outside DOE's program, have spoken approvingly of the Yucca Mountain site as a possible location for a mined geologic repository. They have stressed that they know of no better place to conduct site suitability investigations. One senior earth scientist who has been involved in the federal high-level radioactive waste management program for many years recently summarized his view of the Yucca Mountain site as follows:

The Yucca Mountain site is widely believed among technical people to be an excellent site. The potential that waste could be kept dry for tens of thousands of year is unequalled in other rock media. If an understanding of the site and the concepts derived from that understanding are correct, then it is possible to aim for total containment of the radionuclides, not just controlled release.[34]

Site Suitability Studies. Even though the natural characteristics of Yucca Mountain continue to look favorable, there appears to be strong and growing dissatisfaction with the current investigation of Yucca Mountain. The level of criticism and unhappiness has risen to the point that programmatic failure seems likely unless fundamental changes are made soon. Congress is not appropriating sufficient funds to implement the investigation of Yucca Mountain as currently proposed by OCRWM. As time goes on the disparity between current plans and accomplishments will grow to embarrassing proportions.

DOE's current narrow focus of trying to meet the 2001 deadline for completing a license application is biasing the determination of the suitability of Yucca Mountain and prematurely forcing final decisions on the design of a repository. Moreover, DOE's site suitability investigation is fundamentally flawed. There are no priorities for technical studies; there is no meaningful description of how to judge the suitability of Yucca Mountain; there is no serious consideration of repository design alternatives and the implications of those alternative designs on the suitability of Yucca Mountain. The Project also suffers from poor management, due in large part to the inherent structural problems of DOE. And, there is very little effective public involvement.

There are uncertainties about the suitability of Yucca Mountain as a location for the geologic repository that must be carefully studied. But DOE has not articulated a process for investigating those uncertainties in a manner that resolves them politically. As a result, DOE is risking an adverse decision by regulatory bodies, the courts or even Congress that would reorient the program in deleterious ways. In order to stabilize the program so that it will not be so vulnerable to undesirable change in the next few years, DOE should adopt several improvements to the program for investigating Yucca Mountain.

Nonetheless, many on DOE's and its contractors' staffs are enthusiastic about the progress being made by the Yucca Mountain Project. There seems to be the sense that "momentum" is picking up, making development of the site very likely or even "inevitable." Some DOE representatives have said that they would like the project to move even faster than the current budget allows.

But the present rapid pace, let alone a faster one, is opposed by key technical oversight bodies. For instance, the Nuclear Waste Technical Review Board has repeatedly addressed this issue:

> The Board understands and supports the need for schedules with target deadlines to maintain program momentum. However, there may be some disadvantages associated with basing program priorities so heavily on the current schedule. For example, (1) the DOE's current plans allow a

relatively short time period for the collection and analysis of underground data prior to license application; (2) the short time frame does not allow for resolving *unanticipated* [emphasis in the original] technical problems involved with constructing the exploratory studies facility, nor with obtaining adequate, consistent data for site characterization; (3) it leaves little time to resolve questions about unpredictable conditions important to the repository's performance; and (4) there is little opportunity to evaluate repository design and waste management system alternatives (such as long-lived waste packages or alternative thermal-loading strategies for the repository).[35]

To ensure the safe performance of the waste management system, the program should not be overly motivated by the need to meet a tight schedule driven by target dates. Instead, the Board urges DOE to ground all major technical decisions in sound scientific analysis that includes the careful evaluation of alternatives.[36]

The Board on Radioactive Waste Management also believes that DOE's schedule for studying Yucca Mountain is too rigid. This view was recently re-emphasized by the National Research Council's Commission on Geosciences, Environment, and Resources: "The inherent variability of the geologic environment . . . necessitates allowing flexibility and interaction in the design, construction, and scheduling of a repository."[37] Moreover, an ad hoc panel of scientists convened by the Board on Radioactive Waste Management to evaluate a specific ground water issue at Yucca Mountain independently arrived at a similar position. The panel's observation in favor of flexibility reads, in part, as follows:

[P]lans requiring adherence to a minutely scheduled sequence of observations and a rigid constraint as to analytical methods risk the loss of the use of one of scientists' most valuable tools, their intuition. Moreover, common in scientific investigations is the element of surprise, the unanticipated findings, that may be critical in developing new insights or understanding. The detailed study plans [prepared by DOE] apparently leave little room for possible changes in direction of a study. Such an inflexible approach inhibits scientific progress in achieving the objectives of the studies. *The panel, therefore, wishes to register a plea for greater flexibility in allowing the scientists room to exercise their disciplines as they have been trained and as they know their expertise will be most effective.*" [emphasis in original][38]

Individual scientists have also said that DOE's tight schedule does not allow enough time to conduct important studies and analyses. For instance, an eminent scientist with the U.S. Geological Survey, who is not involved in the Yucca Mountain Project, made an important suggestion for a study that has not been incorporated into DOE's rigid plans. Specifically, Dr. Winograd has suggested that, ". . . if we really want to get a handle on percolation amounts and on the potential role of [the Paint Brush] nonwelded unit as a capillary barrier to the flow into the Tonopah Spring Member, we need to be able to study it in great detail in three dimensions within an instrumented drift."[39] A consultant to Nevada's Nuclear Waste Project Office has also stressed the importance of the Paint Brush nonwelded unit.[40] Her concern about lateral flow through the Paint Brush unit could be addressed by the investigation recommended by Dr. Winograd. DOE's current schedule, however, appears unable to accommodate suggestions for such new studies.

Dr. Winograd found two other "major technical weaknesses" in what he saw as "an otherwise very impressive program":

(1)   "a lack of synthesis and prioritization of studies"; and
(2)   "an imbalance between earth science and engineering approaches to the HLW program."[41]

Others who have more recently reviewed DOE's efforts to investigate Yucca Mountain have also found that studies have neither been prioritized nor integrated effectively. For instance, the ad hoc panel convened under the auspices of the Board on Radioactive Waste Management concluded,

> that there was a significant lack of communication among project scientists in different disciplines, especially between those of the hydrologic and solid earth sciences, and among the different scientific organizations involved in the study, such as governmental agencies and national laboratories. Moreover, even among the geologists and geophysicists there seemed to be little integration of their individual spheres of knowledge and data. *Because this important site characterization program is large and complex, strong scientific leadership must be provided to the participants and adequate attention must be paid to the continuing coordination and syntheses of scientific results...[Therefore] the panel strongly recommends that DOE appoint a scientist as site characterization project coordinator. Such a person should not be currently associated with any of the participating organizations.* [emphasis in original][42]

A similar conclusion was made independently by a panel of fourteen "nationally recognized technical experts" established by a contractor to the Yucca Mountain Project. A "consensus position" developed by the geotechnical subpanel members concluded as follows:

Tasks to evaluate the site need to be prioritized. The objective would be to unambiguously identify tests designed to determine if the site were unsuitable. Prioritization should be based on determining which tests have a high probability of answering potential concerns, and a low probability of giving false alarms. It should be decided before characterization of the potential significance of the result. This approach would reduce uncertainty by focusing the data collection toward testing hypotheses in a prioritized order of importance.[43]

The "Consensus Statement" also states that "there needs to be closer integration of the program on all levels."[44]

The Nuclear Waste Technical Review Board also has recently stressed that ". . . DOE should provide a *timely* reassessment of its priorities among the numerous studies that are part of site-characterization plans. Of critical importance is the definition of those data most needed for assessing site suitability."[45] Related to this finding that characterization tests are not prioritized or integrated, the General Accounting Office concluded that "DOE has not yet implemented the [Energy] Secretary's strategy of conducting early surface-based tests to identify unsuitable site conditions."[46]

Recently, an internal dispute has become public that adds support to the criticisms of the independent oversight bodies. Brigadier General (Ret), U.S. Air Force, Joel T. Hall was hired in December, 1991, by the Technical and Management Support Services contractor to the Yucca Mountain Project. He states that he was asked ". . . to review the test and evaluation plans for Yucca Mountain to identify areas where the quality and credibility of the characterization program could be enhanced."[47] Based on his experience within the project, he observed that,

> The Site Characterization Plan (required by law and published for public comment) is not being implemented. ...Instead, the program is being worked by numerous sequential ad hoc task groups whose primary purpose is to sift through existing information and data used as a basis for selecting Yucca Mountain for characterization; establishing that information/data as the factual baseline, and then selecting from the tests, experiments, and studies outlined in the Site Characterization Plan those that are needed to support a conclusion that the site is suitable. Or, stated another way, those that are needed to support a license application——they are one and the same."[48]

General Hall went on to conclude that, "The current management and focus of the Yucca Mountain Project is a disgrace."[49] In explaining this strong condemnation, he said,

What is happening here is the development of tailored data, data files, computer models, and analysis to support and validate the selected conclusion that Yucca Mountain is suitable for a repository. What is happening here...is the pervasive focusing of all activities on "licensing issues/strategies" which completely refutes any claim to scientific objectivity and integrity regarding the study of Yucca Mountain.[50]

One of General Hall's most important recommendations for correcting the situation is to separate the site suitability investigation from the licensing process:

Licensing activity should be separated physically and organizationally from characterization activities. Moreover, expenditure of funds on licensing activities should be held in abeyance until sufficient results are in from the characterization program to warrant such activity...(I)t will take at least five years before any significant scientific basis might be available to support preliminary licensing activity...All Project documentation should be revised to eliminate pervasive reference to licensing as the Project goal. The first goal of the Project should be to conduct an honest evaluation of Yucca Mountain to determine if it is suitable for a repository.[51]

General Hall also made numerous observations and recommendations about the management of the Yucca Mountain Project. For instance, he believes that, "The absence of reasonable progress in the Yucca Mountain Project is directly attributable to the diffusion of responsibility, accountability, and authority."[52] In addition to clarifying the roles of OCRWM headquarters and the Yucca Mountain Project office, General Hall recommended a series of management improvements, including the following:

- "Establish a clear, prioritized, scheduled process for the completion of study plans which are specified in the Site Characterization Plan. Develop an analytical method to close the output of studies and supporting activities into reports that support a determination of whether or not the site is suitable in terms of the primary criteria required by the law."
- "Establish a prioritized and integrated set of tests and evaluations required to complete the studies."
- "Committees, conferences, and seminars with no decision authority, obligation, or responsibility should be eliminated."[53]

Thus, there seems to be a strong opinion among independent technical oversight organizations, as well as some involved in the project, that the current process for studying the suitability of Yucca

Mountain is fundamentally flawed. The recommendations to foster technical flexibility, adopt priorities for studies, and assure coordination and integration of scientific investigations are essential for success. They cannot be ignored by DOE, as now appears to be the case, without causing severe problems for the program later on. The Yucca Mountain Project undoubtedly will come under increasing political and public criticism if these recommendations are not adopted soon.

The threat to DOE's investigation of Yucca Mountain, due to not taking adequate time, is highlighted by Illinois' experience with trying to select a potential site for a new low-level radioactive waste disposal facility. The federal law for establishing new low-level radioactive waste disposal facilities, like NWPA, has firm deadlines that are supposed to be met by state governments and compacts of states. Through a series of rewards and punishments, states are given substantial incentives to meet the federal milestones.

As the Director of the Illinois Department of Nuclear Safety for five and a half years, I took the federally imposed deadlines seriously. I was determined to meet them if possible without jeopardizing public health and safety. Both the Governor and the Illinois legislature supported compliance with the federal requirements, as indicated by their consistent support for a substantial budget for the program.

One key federal deadline was December 31, 1989. By that date, states that were finding disposal sites had to either submit a complete license application for a disposal facility or issue a "Governor's Certification" that future milestones would be met and the state would be able to develop new disposal capacity as required by federal law.

But January, 1991, was the month when former Governor Jim Thompson would leave office, after an unprecedented four terms and fourteen years in office. In early 1989, the Governor's Chief of Staff instructed me to have a completed license application submitted as the means for satisfying the federal deadline, because he believed that Governor Thompson should not make promises in a certification that could be kept only by a future governor. Because the private contractor preparing a license application for the disposal facility would need time to finish it after a site was selected, I set June, 1989, as the date for selecting the site under the Illinois Low-Level Radioactive Waste Management Act. That announcement caused turmoil reminiscent of the current situation regarding Yucca Mountain.

Most significantly, the Illinois State Geological and Water Surveys publicly attacked the decision to proceed with site selection prior to completing tests and analyzing data that they believed were necessary for "complete characterization." They wanted further studies concerning ground water that had not been previously proposed by Departmental staff, the Department's characterization contractor or the Surveys. And there had been ample formal and informal opportunities for these recommendations to have been made over the previous three years.

Although my technical judgment was that these newly identified studies did not have to be undertaken prior to site selection for the purpose of initiating preparation of a license application, the political judgment in the end was that all characterization studies recommended by the Surveys had to be completed before a site could be formally selected. Under the guidance of the Governor's Office, a written agreement between the Department of Nuclear Safety and the Surveys eventually confirmed that the specific tests identified by the Surveys would be completed and analyzed prior to site selection. The public turmoil and interagency squabbles leading to this agreement significantly undermined the Department's credibility. In practice, the tests and analyses could not be completed in time for a license application to be submitted by December 31, 1989. Thus, for no practical benefit to the State of Illinois, the Department of Nuclear Safety suffered a substantial drop in public trust and confidence. This controversy, in fact, undoubtedly was a major contributor to the decision in October, 1992, to abandon the Martinsville site.

This experience with the politics of site characterization in Illinois provides lessons for DOE to consider. Most immediately relevant to DOE, the Illinois experience clearly shows the potential seriousness of political problems caused by trying to meet arbitrary deadlines that do not allow enough time to work with experts who believe that more studies are necessary. For such a controversial project as siting a radioactive waste disposal facility, the eventual political judgment is likely to be not to proceed in the face of disputes among experts about whether enough information is available for a decision. By trying to force a decision that seems premature to credible experts, project managers run a high risk of failure and the consequent loss of public trust and confidence.

One of the reasons for the technical dispute over characterization in Illinois is the absence of a clear definition of "characterization." Characterization is generally defined as a process of study, but it is left to individual scientists to determine what type of tests should be conducted.

Almost none of the scientists involved in Illinois were knowledgeable about risk or performance assessments for radioactive waste disposal facilities. As a consequence, decisions about what *should* be done more often became decisions about what *could* be done. This approach reached its highest form with the State Geological and Water Surveys, which were not responsible for other programmatic goals such as staying within budget and meeting federal milestones. DOE, therefore, needs to keep in mind that defining characterization is an ongoing process of consensus development. In trying to develop an effective technical consensus, simply publishing reports for review and comment is not nearly adequate. DOE needs to be aware that in the political arena it is likely to lose any argument over whether enough has been done to study a site, if credible experts say more has to be done before suitability can be determined. DOE does not seem to have paid enough attention to these issues.

In sum, the current schedule for investigating the suitability of Yucca Mountain, and completing a license application if it proves suitable, is far too accelerated given the recognized uncertainties in a project of this complexity and difficulty. Site suitability studies should proceed using a sound scientific approach that includes developing an effective consensus with technical oversight bodies and independent scientists. Such an approach needs to be flexible and to allow adequate time for data to be analyzed through peer review and public processes.

Design and Development Issues. The suitability of Yucca Mountain cannot be determined in the abstract. The question, "suitable for what?," has to be answered. In other words, Yucca Mountain might be a safe location for one type of repository, but not another. Therefore, in parallel with the characterization of Yucca Mountain, DOE needs to evaluate a range of design concepts in relation to the conditions at Yucca Mountain. The system of the natural conditions combined with the engineered facility must be evaluated for safety. In developing a systems approach to safety, DOE should consider the "monitored-decision process" described by Elio D'Appolonia as follows:

> The monitored-decision process...is a planned approach to decision making over time that draws on long-term field measurements for input, with planned analysis of the measurements and appropriate contingent action. . . . Its framework is one of recognizing uncertainties in the design process and making design decisions with the knowledge that planned long-term observations and their interpretation will provide information to decrease the uncertainties, plus providing contingencies for all envisioned outcomes of the monitoring program. The process enables us to make meaningful detailed predictions of facility performance and compare these predictions with measured field performance.[54]

DOE should aim to design a system that far exceeds existing regulatory requirements. For instance, a canister with an expected lifetime of at least 10,000 years should be developed. This development effort has been repeatedly urged by the Nuclear Waste Technical Review Board: "As evidenced by its past recommendations, the Board is very concerned that full consideration be given to robust, long-lived waste package concepts."[55] In connection with recently repeating this concern, the Board noted that,

> One family of the [waste package] concepts that appears in danger of being omitted consists of waste packages that are both high-capacity and self-shielded. Such waste packages could have diameters greater than seven feet and gross weights greater than 120 tons. ...If DOE were to omit high-capacity, self-shielded waste packages now, the option of a true multipurpose cask would effectively be foreclosed.
>
> Thus, the Board strongly recommends that high-capacity, self-shielded waste package designs—including designs compatible with multipurpose cask concepts - be included in the set of waste package conceptual designs now being developed.[56]

Related to canister designs are two important issues: Thermal loading of the repository and retrievability of the waste packages. If the waste is emplaced at a thermal loading of about 60 kilowatts per acre, the rock temperature near the waste would remain above the boiling temperature of water for 1,000 to 10,000 years.[57] The waste packages, therefore, would not be expected to come into direct contact with ground water for that same period of time. As a consequence, there could be no release of radionuclides to ground water due to leaching for 1,000 to 10,000 years. This could be a very positive benefit of having the repository located in the unsaturated zone.[58] Predictions of dryness and then monitoring of performance, potentially for hundreds of years, could be an important design element that would be consistent with the monitored-decision process recommended by D'Appolonia.

Using self-shielded casks that were kept dry because of temperatures above the boiling point of water could also facilitate retrieval far into the future. Easy retrievability of waste packages seems like a good way to compensate, at least partially, for residual uncertainties in performance of the repository system in the distant future. The capability to inspect and if desirable remove waste packages would be a significant improvement over the current plan of permanently closing the repository within a few decades after it begins to receive waste for disposal. The capability to retrieve waste easily should not, however, be used to compensate for fundamental problems with the natural characteristics of the site. In other words, no matter what design is finally proposed for Yucca Mountain, the suitability of the site should be judged under the assumption of not being able to retrieve waste by 50 years after operations begin.

Collaborative Decision Making

As one astute observer of the federal program said, "[T]he high level waste problem is a combination of a hard technical problem and a volatile political problem."[59] The technical problem has not been adequately addressed by the Yucca Mountain Project, as indicated in the previous section. But neither has the political problem, because there is an ". . . almost absolute disenfranchisement of the parties at risk."[60] Thus, in addition to correcting the technical flaws in the program, DOE needs to address the institutional issues in a more thorough and meaningful way.

The Office of Civilian Radioactive Waste Management's public involvement program is inadequate. With perhaps a few exceptions, there is no predecisional involvement of the public or its representatives. Essentially, the Office only provides information about the commercial high-level radioactive waste management program. Little effort is made to involve others in analyzing policy and programmatic alternatives, and decisions are jealously guarded as DOE's sole responsibility.

Although there are statements about the need for "public acceptance," the Office of Civilian Radioactive Waste Management evinces almost no understanding of how to develop support for its efforts and the Office devotes very few resources to trying to involve stakeholders. Suggestions for improving the program that come from the outside do not seem to be treated seriously. An indication of the low priority given to public input is the long time the Office takes to respond to comments submitted on draft documents. More fundamentally, such comments, if sought at all, appear to be solicited after decisions have been made, as indicated by the defensive manner in which suggestions are rejected.

Almost three years ago a knowledgeable analyst made a cogent observation that is at least as valid today. He noted that "The history of the Federal waste management program shows clearly that lack of consensus leads to damaging policy instability...[and] we do not now enjoy a broad social consensus about waste management policy." He then concluded that this situation should be rectified by developing "an effective consensus among the interested parties—if that's possible."[61] DOE should develop new programs that could help to build such a working consensus. Otherwise, the program appears doomed to repeat its history of political failure.

Representatives of the OCRWM Director's Office and the Yucca Mountain Project Office have made statements that public involvement and cooperatively working with state and local government are important. But the reality has not matched the rhetoric.[62] Many observers have noted the deficiencies in DOE's responsiveness to public input. For instance, one key affected local government in Nevada recently stated,

> USDOE has established a track record, from the perspective of Clark County [Nevada], that it (along with OCRWM) will do nothing in response to affected public's concerns that go beyond the narrowest interpretations of the NWPA. This has fundamental implications for the establishment of trust, as it is a very different thing to respond to a request, or a letter of inquiry, in a superficial or perfunctory manner, than it is to provide a thoroughgoing response. Complicating this minimal level of responsiveness is that from an outsider's perspective it would appear that USDOE is made up of a labyrinth of semi-autonomous structures, making communication and responsiveness all the more difficult.[63]

Effective public participation is often said to be necessary for the successful implementation of controversial projects such as the Yucca Mountain Project. But there is not a clear roadmap that can be followed for success. Indeed, a problem with DOE's past public participation efforts has been that implementation was seen in relatively straight-forward mechanistic terms, e.g., circulate draft documents for comment, hold public hearings, and set up advisory committees. To be effective, however, the substance of programs has to change in response to input. Fundamentally, there has to be an implicit sharing of decision-making authority, through a process of active collaboration.

One important success at collaborative decision making appears to have been achieved by the federal Bonneville Power Administration (BPA), which has its headquarters in Portland, Oregon. BPA is primarily responsible for the wholesale transmission of electricity from federal dams and some other generating facilities in the Pacific Northwest. When Peter Johnson became BPA Administrator in 1981, he confronted a lot of hostility and opposition to BPA's programs. But rather than trying to overpower that opposition he successfully worked with stakeholders to achieve a positive end. He has recently written about this experience as follows:

> We found that by inviting the public to participate in our decision-making process, our adversaries helped us make better decisions. When I say we

included outsiders in decision making, I'm referring to real involvement, with real changes in decisions based on what we heard. By listening to people's concerns and soliciting their advice on how to reconcile vast differences of opinion and conflicting needs, our operations did not come to a screeching halt. On the contrary, by involving the public in the decision-making process itself, we gained authority and legitimacy, avoided costly lawsuits and political challenges, and arrived at creative solutions to seemingly intractable problems. Overall, our policy-making improved.[64]

BPA's experience since Peter Johnson instituted changes should serve as a model for DOE in developing a new approach to public participation in radioactive waste management decisionmaking.

The Office of Civilian Radioactive Waste Management could begin much as BPA did. Peter Johnson hired a highly-regarded expert, Jim Creighton, to investigate and evaluate the existing situation. In 1984, Dr. Creighton submitted a publicly available report on his findings.[65] Many of his findings are probably similar to ones that would result from such a review of DOE's high-level radioactive waste program today. For example, Dr. Creighton found that

"BPA is generally viewed as arrogant, insensitive, and uncaring."[66]

And he identified key negative public perceptions:

- "BPA's public involvement process and decision-making process are not seen as well-integrated, and many customers and groups do not believe that their participation has any impact on decision-making. They suspect that BPA is simply doing public involvement to fulfill legal requirements."
- "BPA's reports and documents are seen as unnecessarily lengthy, unduly complex, and badly written. In addition, people feel overwhelmed by the sheer bulk of the materials which BPA puts out."[67]

To improve how BPA makes decisions, Dr. Creighton offered numerous suggestions, many of which undoubtedly could apply equally well to DOE's waste program. For instance, Dr. Creighton made the following recommendations:

- "Public involvement programs should rely more on smaller, less formal, kinds of meetings and interactions with the public, rather than large formal public meetings."
- "Develop substantive minimal standards for all BPA public involvement, and issue this in the form of an overall BPA public involvement policy."
- "Publish a public involvement manual."[68]

BPA's open publication of Dr. Creighton's first report on BPA, in Peter Johnson's words, was a "bold step" that ". . . began the hard work of restoring public confidence."[69] One of Administrator Johnson's first steps to improve BPA's program was to add "...public involvement to the performance requirements of every management position. There was to be no mistaking its importance. Those who did an excellent job of consulting with the public were recognized in the BPA newsletter and received cash awards."[70] This and the other initiatives resulted in much praise and recognition for BPA. The Natural Resources Defense Council even gave BPA an award as an "outstanding utility in North America."[71]

Peter Johnson believes that the experience at BPA can and should be applied to other organizations. He has summarized his view as follows:

> I am more convinced than ever that public involvement is a tool that today's managers in both public and private institutions must understand. With external stakeholders now exerting substantial influence on organizations in every sector, conflict is inevitable. The only choice is whether to dodge the controversy or learn to harness it.
>
> Those who harness it by including third parties rather than trying to vanquish them will find that they set the opportunity to consider new possibilities and to test out new ideas in the heat of dialogue. While others are mired in disputes and litigation, astute practitioners of public involvement will have hammered out an agreement and gotten on with the project. In short, they will have made better decisions. . . .[72]

A recent follow-up report to BPA by Dr. Creighton supports Peter Johnson's conclusions.[73] However, this new report also reveals that the process of evaluation and improvement cannot stop with the initial steps; it must be continuous. For instance, Dr. Creighton found that BPA had erred in recent years in stopping its public involvement training. Due to the lack of an ongoing training program, ". . . it is no longer safe to assume that people responsible for implementing public involvement have received training, and there has been little sharpening or reinforcement skills."[74]

The warning contained in Dr. Creighton's latest report to BPA is emphasized by a letter sent to the new Secretary of Energy by a variety of environmental organizations, including the Natural Resources Defense Council. The letter asks that the current BPA Administrator be put on "probation" and that he be judged by whether BPA practices maximum cost-effective conservation and gives higher priority to improving fish flows in the Columbia River Basin.[75] Thus, the relationship between the Administrator and some key stake-holders has sadly deteriorated in just a few years.

Reorganization

DOE's commercial high-level radioactive waste management program is poorly organized and managed.[76] As a result, substantial amounts of money are wasted, and public trust and confidence is decreased.

Notwithstanding its management problems, the program is planning on an increase in its budget to much higher annual levels than necessary to evaluate the suitability of Yucca Mountain as a possible repository site. The DOE budget used for planning purposes is also much higher than the amount Congress is likely to appropriate annually in the next few years. At the same time important studies and analyses concerning site suitability will not be conducted in time to affect the decision of whether to submit a license application to NRC.

There are numerous reasons for the management breakdown within the high-level radioactive waste program. Some key problems are endemic to DOE. Specifically, the extent to which DOE relies on private contractors virtually assures excessive costs. Unless the Office of Civilian Radioactive Waste Management is allowed to adopt a different approach to organizing and managing contractors, the program will continue to waste money and fail to make satisfactory progress toward determining whether the Yucca Mountain site is suitable.

Luther Carter, in a follow-up article to publication of his seminal book on high-level radioactive waste, concluded:

> Altogether, the difficult scientific issues presented, the planning gridlock, and the potential for much bungling and unintended mischief by a heavily layered bureaucracy would seem to suggest that the entire policy and management strategy for the geologic disposal program needs to be changed to ensure early progress.[77]

Since that observation was made in 1989, the management structure has not improved; it has only gotten larger and more cumbersome.

The radioactive waste program is hampered by being subject to internal influences within DOE. For instance, the Office of the Assistant Secretary for Environmental Restoration and Waste Management and the Office of General Counsel have had significant impacts on the program. Often their concern is that the OCRWM should not adopt positions that would set precedents for other DOE programs, rather than on the substantive merits of the issue.

The top level administrators of the program are presidential appointees with historically short tenures. The position of OCRWM Director has been unfilled for about half the time since it was created by the NWPA in 1982. The Secretary of Energy, the Deputy Secretary and the Under Secretary can be expected to serve no longer than four years and usually less than that. Their replacements typically come from outside the program so that at the beginning of their short terms they have to become familiar with the program before they can exert effective leadership. This frequent turnover in the top officials has clearly made management of the program less effective. The recent arbitrary initiatives by the outgoing Secretary and Undersecretary (see the discussion of MRS above) are examples of this problem.

DOE relies on a complex web of field offices, national laboratories, and a variety of private contractors to manage the high-level radioactive waste program. The number of employees in the consulting firms is significantly greater than the number of DOE employees in OCRWM. The large consulting firm staff is parcelled out to various DOE offices within the program. These contractor employees essentially act as staff to the lower level DOE officials within OCRWM. This fragmentation slows decision making and often leads to failure to address key issues in an effective manner. This system also fails to give the contractors clear, specific responsibilities for which they can be held accountable by the OCRWM Director.

The DOE employees in the field offices and national laboratories can have divided loyalties that interfere with effective management of the program. For example, some difficulties may be traced to the fact that employees responsible for project personnel and accounting are bureaucratically housed within the Nevada Field Office, which reports to DOE Headquarters separately from OCRWM. Although specifics are hard to document, there appears often to be inadequate cooperation among the different parts of DOE in addressing radioactive waste issues.

These underlying structural problems are important. They prevent DOE from having a cost-effective and technically sound program for studying the suitability of Yucca Mountain. Moreover, the organizational problems substantially reduce the capability of DOE to involve the public and state and local government in the decision making about Yucca Mountain. The managerial problems, therefore, indirectly contribute to a loss of public trust and confidence in the program.

Occasional discussion over the past 15 years has questioned whether DOE is inherently incapable of solving the country's high-level radioactive waste disposal problem. One analyst, who concluded that DOE cannot solve the problem, recommended that, a new structure must be established which provides adequate due process and public scrutiny while not sacrificing flexibility and responsiveness. A new structure must be *designed* [emphasis in original] drawing on the advantages of federal agencies and private corporations but which overcomes their built-in deficiencies. One candidate is a federally chartered public corporation."[78]

The report of the Advisory Panel on Alternative Means of Financing and Managing Radioactive Waste Facilities, which was mandated by NWPA, independently made a similar recommendation:

it is our principal recommendation that investigation of the specific steps necessary to implement, for example, a dedicated federally chartered corporation (the first choice of the Panel voting on organizational tests), should be undertaken immediately so that Congress can have a precise understanding of the legislative changes required to bring about such an organization.[79]

Although there was a commitment in the National Energy Strategy to follow up the Panel's recommendation,[80] the subsequent amendment to the waste program's Mission Statement reversed this commitment and no follow-up analysis has been undertaken by OCRWM.[81]

It is important to stress that the basic reason for considering the creation of a new dedicated, independent organization to manage the high-level radioactive waste program is to improve the management of the program. It is not to create enhanced public trust and confidence in some superficial manner. If the management of the program is improved and new approaches to involving the public are adopted, public trust and confidence should increase substantially as a result. This improved approach is more likely to be adopted under an independent, dedicated organization than under DOE.

The new Administration and Congress should consider whether to establish a new, dedicated, independent governmental organization (WASTEORG) to be responsible for management of the nation's commercial high-level radioactive waste. WASTEORG must have flexibility in hiring staff, conducting studies, working with federal, state and local governmental jurisdictions, and incorporating the views of the concerned public. This flexibility is essential for the effective management of such a controversial and challenging program.

WASTEORG also must be constituted so that it has support from those who have been most concerned about past delays and increasing costs. WASTEORG in other words must be a practical organization that will establish a reasonable waste management system. In addition, WASTEORG must be expected to use its resources cost-effectively and responsibly. This means that there must be sound financial reporting requirements, and WASTEORG must be fully accountable for its actions.

Most importantly, WASTEORG must be created in a manner that allows the disposal problem to be solved as a national problem, not exclusively as a federal government problem. WASTEORG must be expected to engage in collaborative decision making so that all of the stakeholders are fairly and effectively involved in defining solutions. This can occur most easily if decisions are distanced from Congressional and Presidential politics.[82] Such insulation has been achieved by organizations such as the Federal Reserve Board and the Interstate Commerce Commission. They may serve as useful models in this regard in setting up WASTEORG.[83] The federally chartered corporation should also be considered, as recommended in earlier years.

An independent, dedicated governmental organization, however, must not be established simply to implement the currently flawed program. Only changing organizational labels without addressing underlying problems would not achieve significant benefits in the long term. The Administration and Congress must first agree on an improved program, and then establish the new organization to implement it.

Fred Morris, who assisted the 1984 advisory panel on alternative financing and management, recently capsulized what should be done, as follows:

> The choice and design of an organization should support the strategic objectives of the program that the program is charged with implementing. Ideally, the Administration would build a consensus on technical/management strategy and then tailor the organization to the task, in light of a careful assessment of the alternatives and stakeholder buy-in.[84]

Suggestions for Change

The problem of radioactive waste management has proven to be extraordinarily difficult and complex. It is not even clear that we understand all of the reasons making the problem so intractable. Therefore, suggestions for change should be made modestly. There simply is no assurance that any set of initiatives will, in fact, finally lead to solving the problem.

Nonetheless, it is clear that there are correctable flaws in the existing federal program for managing civilian high-level radioactive waste. By making major improvements, based to a large degree on experience, the odds of developing a politically acceptable and technically sound program would be greatly increased.

In order to make the necessary changes, there needs to be a wider recognition that the problem is inherently very tough. The lack of accepted solutions today is not due to the incompetence of managers. Simply changing the people in charge will not make the situation dramatically different. We should also recognize that the waste management program will not be solved using standard project management techniques. In particular, the waste program should not be deadline controlled, as is the case now, because (1) the development of a geologic repository is a unique undertaking that requires flexibility in conducting scientific investigations, and (2) it is politically unacceptable to appear to be rushing to resolve technical uncertainties associated with a potential repository. Basically, what is needed is a slow-paced, flexible program that provides ample opportunity for achieving a practical consensus of stakeholders at each stage in the development of a repository system.

The following suggestions are made in the context of this ongoing need for a practical working consensus.[85] These and other suggestions should be fully considered in a variety of public forums in order to determine how to develop such a consensus. All efforts to correct existing problems should not wait for consensus, however. Clearly, some initiatives, such as improving the internal management of the program and reducing annual costs, should begin immediately, while consensus development efforts are undertaken simultaneously.

The federal civilian high-level radioactive waste management program can be substantially improved only with the support and cooperation of Congress. In fact, the following major suggestions for change would require amendments to existing law. In the past, Congress has had to step in to solve an impasse among stakeholders or to handle a major controversy. A different approach should be attempted this time. The new Administration, perhaps using the auspices of the U.S. Nuclear Waste Negotiator, should try to build a consensus among stakeholders on a package of desirable changes to the current law. The outcome of the legislative process probably would be more beneficial if an agreement, even a partial one, among stakeholders could be developed before Congress had to act. Even if such an agreement is not achievable, however, Congress will have to pass new legislation in order for necessary improvements to be made.

Surface Storage

1. As currently planned an MRS cannot be available by 1998, and the proposal should be dropped. The basic difficulty with the MRS is the lack of a clear and convincing need for it. Nuclear utilities continue to adopt satisfactory measures for long-term storage of spent fuel at

reactor sites. At-reactor storage, in air-cooled casks or vaults, should be available and safe until a suitable location is identified for the geologic repository.

The most significant problem with abandoning the MRS is that it does not satisfy the nuclear utilities' desire to begin to move spent fuel away from reactor sites by 1998. There are practical problems associated with longer-term storage at reactors, such as increased costs in order to maintain an operation at a closed reactor. In addition, there may be economic regulatory problems for some utilities in planning for longer-term storage at reactor sites. But there is no realistic alternative. DOE will not be able to satisfy the utilities' wish. Therefore, longer-term storage at reactor sites can either be planned or unplanned at the federal level. Federal acknowledgment of reality seems preferable.

DOE is more likely to satisfy its fundamental obligations to nuclear utilities by achieving programmatic stability through a series of improvements in the geologic program than by persisting in the current, impractical policy. A politically acceptable geologic repository program will probably result in the federal government taking physical possession of the spent fuel sooner than would occur under the current program to develop an MRS.

Until a suitable site for a geologic repository is identified, DOE should, as was recently suggested by the outgoing Secretary, develop a universal cask as soon as possible. Such a cask should be made available to utilities for at-reactor storage.

2. DOE should evaluate the alternative of a surface storage facility collocated with the geologic repository. This facility would store, and if desirable repackage, waste for disposal. In particular, DOE should consider locating a surface storage facility near Yucca Mountain if that site is found to be suitable. A process for determining suitability, however, must be developed that is technically sound and politically acceptable. Such a process does not now exist.

During the future operation of the geologic repository the surface storage facility would also be available to repair packages that did not meet design goals and to serve as backup in case the geologic repository did not perform acceptably. Thus, the surface storage facility should be viewed as an integral, important safety component of the disposal system.

Repository Development

1. The country would make a serious mistake if it rejected Yucca Mountain now and then simply started anew with another national screening for potential sites. There undoubtedly would be the same

political uproar and stalemate as before if DOE or any other organization began a new search. Many knowledgeable earth scientists believe that Yucca Mountain is a very good site to investigate, and no one can point to an obviously superior site for study. Thus, the investigations of the suitability of Yucca Mountain should continue, but the process for determining suitability needs to be improved.

There also must be official recognition that Yucca Mountain may not prove to be technically suitable or that it may not become available for other reasons. Therefore, there should be studies aimed at trying to locate other potential sites, particularly in the Great Basin. The United States Geological Survey should take the lead in conducting these studies, which should be based on existing information. Drilling and other intrusive field work should take place only if a community expresses interest in studying the possibility of having a repository.

2. The current overriding emphasis on meeting the unrealistic and undesirable 2001 deadline for submitting a completed license application to the NRC should be changed. Instead, the date for submitting a license application should be a dependent variable that is determined as a result of a very thorough investigation into the suitability of Yucca Mountain. In other words, this critical date should not be set in the abstract without the completion of a detailed assessment of the suitability of Yucca Mountain. Moreover, the suitability of Yucca Mountain should be ascertained formally and separately from work to prepare a license application. The determination should be conducted in collaboration with the State of Nevada, affected local governments and other stakeholders.

Each study essential to determining site suitability that is recommended by the National Academy of Sciences—National Research Council's Board on Radioactive Waste Management, the U.S. Nuclear Waste Technical Review Board, the Nuclear Regulatory Commission's Advisory Committee on Nuclear Waste, and the United States Geological Survey should be completed and carefully evaluated publicly before DOE decides whether Yucca Mountain is suitable. Their recommendations should not be postponed or incorporated only to the extent that they do not interfere with meeting the 2001 deadline, as is now the case in some instances.

During these comprehensive studies information may be gathered that shows Yucca Mountain is unsuitable. This realistic possibility must always be openly acknowledged and planned for. In conducting the Yucca Mountain studies DOE should not take actions that bias a decision in favor of suitability and rapid development of a repository. For instance, DOE should not, as is now planned, make the tunnels for the exploratory studies facility twenty-five or more feet in diameter, which is the tunnel size needed for the current repository design. More flexibility in designing the repository would be maintained with smaller (e.g., eighteen foot) diameter tunnels, as suggested by the Nuclear Waste Technical Review Board in its reports to Congress and the Secretary of Energy.

Conducting more extensive studies prior to a determination of suitability might add a decade to the current, but in any event unachievable, schedule. This additional time would allow other important work, such as development of long-lived waste packages to catch up with the repository investigation. Moreover, this longer period of time would allow for meaningful opportunities for public input and for collaborative decision making with state and local government.

3. In conjunction with developing a more thorough approach to studying the suitability of Yucca Mountain, DOE should stop conducting all studies that are not essential to a determination of suitability. The current "bottoms up" approach formulated by contractors is unnecessary and unduly expensive. If a future decision is reached that Yucca Mountain is indeed suitable, then information gathering focused on preparation of a license application should be initiated. Moreover, the excessive overhead associated with the current program should be cut back dramatically. The program is sized now more for building a repository than it is for conducting an appropriately designed site suitability study.

4. Recent reviews have found the current site suitability investigation to be without clearly defined priorities and lacking needed integration of specialized studies. This situation is shocking after so much effort has already been dedicated to studying Yucca Mountain. The Office of Civilian Radioactive Waste Management needs to establish its technical priorities as soon as possible. This task should be conducted and controlled from headquarters rather than by the Project Office as is the case currently. These priorities should be established in conjunction with development of an improved set of criteria for judging suitability. Both the suitability criteria and the study priorities should be finally adopted only after full public input. The Project Office should be delegated the full authority and responsibility for conducting the studies in conformance with the priorities, but responsibility for the determination of suitability should be retained by headquarters.

The Yucca Mountain Project Office should establish a government position of Project Scientist. This position should not be filled by a private contractor employee, although he or she might be detailed from a national laboratory or another federal agency. The Project

Scientist would be responsible for assuring that the most appropriate investigative techniques were being used and that the results of studies were being fully integrated. One prominent objective of the Project Scientist ought to be reducing the total cost of the site suitability investigation by avoiding redundant or unnecessary tests and by using the least costly techniques to obtain needed information. To date, there has not been an effective focus on cost.

5. DOE needs to develop a more secure waste package that will allow waste to be readily retrieved far into the future and that would likely provide complete containment for at least 10,000 years. One of the biggest deficiencies with the current plan for a geologic repository is how it deals with technical uncertainty. Even under an improved program, there will not be complete agreement among scientists about how much uncertainty remains at the beginning of repository operations. This lack of agreement will cause regulatory and public concern about long-term safety. A waste package durable for 10,000 years could appropriately provide partial compensation for this inevitable residual technical uncertainty.

6. The Nuclear Waste Technical Review Board, as well as individual scientists and engineers, have raised major repository design questions. For example, the alternative of providing a relatively stable thermal load in the repository for a long period of time needs more thorough examination. In addition, repository design alternatives that might keep water away from the emplaced waste for a very long period of time need to be carefully and publicly reviewed. DOE and the public need time to give these and other suggestions adequate consideration. Therefore, DOE should not finalize the repository design for its license application until technical oversight bodies, such as the Nuclear Waste Technical Review Board, concur that all reasonable design alternatives have been adequately considered. In addition, there should be ample time for the State of Nevada, affected local governments and the public to review and advise on these design alternatives.

7. Substantial confidence remains within the scientific community that a mined deep geologic repository is a viable approach to the disposal of long-lived radioactive waste. But as demonstrated during the past two decades, there are significant technical and political obstacles to implementing the concept. Even today, complete confidence in the practicality of a mined deep geologic repository is not yet warranted. Moreover, there may be preferable approaches developed in the future. For these reasons, DOE should increase and broaden its research and development program on alternatives. An aggressive R&D program should be implemented that ranges from

improved waste forms to technologies for transmutation of the long-lived radionuclides in waste.

Techniques, such as subseabed disposal and disposal into the sun, which have international implications, should also be thoughtfully reviewed in conjunction with other countries. International cooperation generally should be increased, including in current areas of research and development, such as deep mined geologic disposal.

Collaborative Decision Making

Taking adequate time to conduct scientific studies and to consider alternative repository designs carefully as part of a comprehensive waste management system would allow the public and its representatives a much better opportunity to participate in decision making than is currently the case. DOE's deadline-driven approach clearly does not allow state and local governments, concerned groups and citizens as much time as they need to get answers and provide meaningful input. But more time alone would not be enough to address the public trust and confidence question.

There is a significant chance that the State of Nevada eventually will be able to kill the Yucca Mountain Project if its opposition remains unabated during the coming decades. On the other hand, there is also the possibility that the State of Nevada may not be able to stop the Yucca Mountain Project. To date, notwithstanding its efforts, the State has not delayed the project much, and Congress continues to pass legislation affecting the project over the objections of the State's senators. If DOE's program is improved, the State may realize that there would be a better opportunity for protecting the interests of Nevada through collaborative decision making. But establishing a working relationship with the State may be beyond DOE's own capability, particularly in the near term. Perhaps the Office of the U.S. Nuclear Waste Negotiator could make arrangements that would allow more meaningful and productive exchanges of views between the State and the federal government.

Eventually, taking a more deliberate, methodical approach to the technical investigation of Yucca Mountain should help. Engaging in more and better public involvement efforts undoubtedly also would help create a less adversarial atmosphere with the State. There needs to be a process established that gives the State of Nevada and affected local governments an enhanced role in the Project's decision making. The Negotiator might be able to identify the basis for developing this process.[86]

New decision-making mechanisms should be created so that a wide range of citizens and outside organizations could effectively participate. The specifics of a new approach could be decided after an independent review and assessment, as was done by the Bonneville Power Administration in the early 1980s.

While this comprehensive review is taking place, others, not just DOE, should make stronger efforts to work with the public, and state and local governments in Nevada. For instance, the meetings of the National Academy of Sciences - National Research Council's Board on Radioactive Waste Management, the Nuclear Regulatory Commission's Advisory Committee on Nuclear Wastes, and the Nuclear Waste Technical Review Board, should be conducted as openly and with as much public involvement as possible. To the greatest degree practicable, their meetings should be held in Nevada. The public should be encouraged through word and deed to participate in these groups' meetings and activities.

Additionally, in contrast with past practice, meetings on regulatory matters between NRC and DOE staff about Yucca Mountain should be held in the Las Vegas area. These meetings are important and should be easily accessed by the public, the State of Nevada, and the affected local governments.

Reorganization

1. The Office of Civilian Radioactive Waste Management needs to rethink the way it uses contractors. The contractor system today appears to be based on an inappropriate model, namely, the historical structure for running DOE's national laboratories and defense facilities. Under this system, contractor employees are in effect DOE employees. In other words, contractors are essentially "body shops." A different approach should be instituted that more clearly assigns specific, time-limited tasks to contractors for which they can be held responsible. Moreover, the lines of responsibility between contractors and DOE employees need to be sharpened. This is particularly true of the responsibilities assigned to the Management and Operating contractor, which generally reports to headquarters, and the Technical and Management Support Service contractor, which generally reports to the Yucca Mountain Project Office. Their current relationship is overly cumbersome, complex and redundant. As soon as possible, the role of a Management and Operating contractor should be eliminated.

When the repository program became focused on only the Yucca Mountain site in Nevada, additional managerial difficulties began to occur. Today, the relations between headquarters in Washington, D.C., and the Yucca Mountain Project in Las Vegas do not appear to be productive. Representatives from both locations have negative views of the other. Headquarters needs more of a presence at the Yucca Mountain Project Office to foster better communication and cooperation. At the same time, headquarters should delegate greater decision making authority to the Project Office in order to improve the quality of the site suitability investigation.

If Yucca Mountain is found, through a technically sound and politically acceptable process, to be suitable for a repository, DOE should transfer the OCRWM Director to Las Vegas. In addition, the Director should be given the maximum possible amount of independence from DOE headquarters so that he or she could give the repository program the greatest possible degree of attention. Such a change would streamline program management and would likely improve relations with the State of Nevada, affected local governments and the public.

2. Because of the inherent managerial problems at DOE, the OCRWM may not be able to reorganize so that it is adequately effective. Therefore, the new Administration and Congress should seriously consider establishing an independent waste organization. Fundamental reorganization would be particularly appropriate to consider, if Congress decides to take the program off-budget. A dedicated, independent governmental organization appears to be the best approach to solving the managerial problems inherent to DOE, while at the same time fulfilling the government's responsibilities and involving all stakeholders.

Due to the controversial nature of the waste program, and its large cost, the various stakeholders have not agreed either that there should be a change to an independent waste organization, or that, if there were, what would be the best new organizational structure. An agreement among the stakeholders might be an appropriate goal of the U.S. Nuclear Waste Negotiator.

Notes

1. *See*, Luther J. Carter, *Nuclear Imperatives and Public Trust*, Resources for the Future (1987); Arjun Makhijani and Scott Saleska, *High Level Dollars, Low Level Sense*, Institute for Energy and Environmental Research (1992); and E.W. Colglazier and R.B. Langum, "Policy Conflicts in the Process for Siting Nuclear Waste Repositories," *Annual Review of Energy 13*, pp. 317-357 (1988). These materials were consulted frequently in preparing this brief historical overview.

2. R. Philip Hammond, "Nuclear Wastes and Public Acceptance," *American Scientist 67*, p. 146 (March-April 1979).

3. Luther Carter's book stops before passage of the 1987 amendments. In

addition to the Colglazier and Langum article, two good sources for this period are James A. Thurber, "Congress and the Executive: Improving the Management and Implementation of Public Policy, Case Summary of Nuclear Waste Policy", The American University (September 16, 1990); and John F. Ahearne, "Nuclear Waste Disposal: Can There Be A Resolution?" MIT International Conference on the Next Generation of Nuclear Power Technology (October 5, 1990).

4. United States General Accounting Office, *GAO Transition Series—Energy Issues*, pp. 19, 21 (December 1992).

5. *See*, for instance, Howard Kunreuther, Douglas Easterling, William Desvousges, and Paul Slovic, "Public Attitudes Toward Siting a High-Level Nuclear Waste Repository in Nevada," *Risk Analysis 10*(4), pp. 469-484 (1990); and K. David Pijawka and Alvin H. Mushkatel, "Public Opposition to the Siting of the High-Level Nuclear Waste Repository: The Importance of Trust," *Policy Studies Review 10*(4), pp. 180-194 (Winter 1991/92).

6. *See* James Flynn, Roger Kasperson, Howard Kunreuther and Paul Solvic, "Time to Rethink Nuclear Waste Storage", *Issues in Science and Technology*, pp. 41-48 (Summer 1992), and Arjun Makhijani and Scott Saleska, *High-Level Dollars, Low-Level Sense*, Institute for Energy and Environmental Research (1992). *See* also the eight part series about the Yucca Mountain Project in the *Las Vegas Review Journal*, October 21-28, 1990.

7. Secretary of Energy Advisory Board announcement, April 26, 1991.

8. *Draft Working Paper for Discussion by the SEAB Task Force on Radioactive Waste Management, December 10-11, 1992, in San Diego, California.*

9. *Draft Final Report of the Secretary of Energy Advisory Board Task Force on Radioactive Waste Management* (December 1992).

10. *Id.* pp. 30-31.

11. A Position Statement of the Board on Radioactive Waste Management, *Rethinking High-Level Radioactive Waste Disposal*, National Academy Press, p.7 (1990). (This report was recently republished with other pertinent materials following a symposium sponsored by the Board: *Radioactive Waste Repository Licensing*, National Academy Press (1992).)

12. "DOE Response to the Recommendations of the Nuclear Waste Technical Review Board in Its Fourth Report to the U.S. Congress and the U.S. Secretary of Energy, December 1991", March 31, 1992, in Nuclear Waste Technical Review Board, *Fifth Report to the U.S. Congress and The U.S. Secretary of Energy*, p.E-5 (June 1992). DOE's response dated September 30, 1992, to the Board's Fifth Report is general and does not seem to take the Board's suggestions to heart. For instance, in discussing the Board's recommendations concerning thermal loading, DOE says nothing about trying to optimize for safety. The focus is much more on the programmatic objective of ensuring "a defensible licensing basis."

13. Office of the United States Nuclear Waste Negotiator, *1992 Annual Report to Congress*, pp. 11-13 (January, 1993).

14. Letter, dated August 21, 1992, from Governor Mike Sullivan, State of Wyoming, to Fremont County Commissioners.

15. Memorandum from Charles Lempesis to David H. Leroy, "Abbreviated Program Assessment and Forecast," p. 5 (December 14, 1992). (The memorandum,

however, ended on a decidedly upbeat note by concluding: "The voluntary process is working...There is every reason to believe that within the short term, an agreement or agreements for an MRS will be available for Congressional consideration." This conclusion does not appear to be well supported by the body of the memorandum or the Negotiator's 1992 report to Congress, however.)

16. John F. Ahearne, "Nuclear Waste Disposal: Can There Be A Resolution?" MIT International Conference on the Next Generation of Nuclear Power Technology, p. 23 (October 5, 1990).

17. The news media often do take a sensationalistic approach to reporting on radiological issues, and this does make implementation of radioactive waste programs more difficult. For instance, an investigator into the Goiania, Brazil, accidental release of radioactive material made the following pertinent observation: "The role of the media in agitating and exaggerating the level of anxiety and fear was indeed profound." (John S. Petterson, "Perception vs. Reality of Radiological Impact: The Goiania Model," *Nuclear News 31* (14), p. 89 (November, 1988).)

18. *Rethinking High-Level Radioactive Waste Disposal*, p. 2.

19. Perhaps the first published suggestion that the unsaturated zone looks attractive for radioactive waste disposal was Isaac J. Winograd, "Radioactive Waste Storage in the Arid Zone, *EOS, Transactions of the American Geophysical Union 55* (10), pp. 884-94 (October 1974). *See* also, "Commentary on "Radioactive Waste Storage in the Arid Zone," in *EOS 57* (4) (April 1976). More recent publications are Eugene H. Roseboom, Jr., *Disposal of High-Level Nuclear Waste Above the Water Table in Arid Regions*, Geological Survey Circular 903, U.S. Geological Survey (1983); and Isaac J. Winograd, *Archaeology and Public Perception of a Transcientific Problem - Disposal of Toxic Wastes in the Unsaturated Zone*, U.S. Geological Survey Circular 990, U.S. Geological Survey (1986).

20. Nuclear Waste Technical Review Board, *Fifth Report to the U.S. Congress and the U.S. Secretary of Energy*, p. 19 (June, 1992).

21. Nuclear Waste Technical Review Board, *Sixth Report to the U.S. Congress and the U.S. Secretary of Energy*, p. 26 (December, 1992).

22. For descriptions of typical technical siting processes, *see* Richard C. Berg, H. Allen Waterman, and John M. Shafer, *Geological and Hydrological Factors for Siting Hazardous on Low-Level Radioactive Waste Disposal Facilities*, Circular 546, Illinois State Geological Survey (1989); and D. Siefken, G. Pangburn, R. Pennifill, and R.J. Starmer, *Site Suitability, Selection and Characterization*, NUREG-902, U.S. Nuclear Regulatory Commission (April 1982).

23. Seymour Simon, William J. Hall, Carolyn Raffensperger, *Martinsville, Report of the Illinois Low-Level Radioactive Waste Disposal Facility Siting Commission on its Inquiry into the Martinsville Alternative Site*, transmitted to Governor Jim Edgar on December 18, 1992.

24. Following the Siting Commission's disapproval of the site, the geologist advising the city stated that, "The Martinsville Alternative Site and the proposed facility together provide a technically acceptable and reasonable site for the disposal of LLRW in Illinois. Potential risk to the local population and

environment is minimal, certainly much less than many of the risks we all voluntarily accept every day of our lives." (Memorandum to Truman Dean, Mayor, from Robert H. Redman, dated October 26, 1992.)

25. See, Monitored Retrievable Storage Review Commission, *Nuclear Waste: Is there a Need for Federal Interim Storage?* (November 1, 1989).

26. "A New Strategy for Management of Commercial Spent Nuclear Fuel," transmitted by a letter from James D. Watkins, Secretary of Energy to Senator J. Bennett Johnston, Chairman, Committee on Energy and Natural Resources, dated December 17, 1992.

27. The Negotiator does not agree with this assessment. In a December 24, 1992, letter to Senator J. Bennett Johnston, he said, "...the voluntary process continues to mature and holds real promise for a solution that will be cooperative and long lasting." The Negotiator's Office also has indicated that there are communities interested in an MRS that have not made their interest public yet.

28. According to *Inside Energy* (January 11, 1993), "{S}ome utility and environmental sources are saying the "new" approach won't help the department with the real problem in siting a storage facility for nuclear waste: lack of public acceptance."

29. *Inside Energy* (January 11, 1993) reported that the Negotiator's chief of staff, when asked if the Negotiator had been informed about the Secretary's new process, said, "In no way. In no shape. In no form."

30. *Media Statement of U.S. Nuclear Waste Negotiator David H. Leroy, regarding the December 17, 1992, Announcement of a "New Strategy for Management of Commercial Nuclear Fuel",* p. 2 (December 23, 1992).

31. Ed Lane, "Insider Fault's DOE's Nuclear Waste Program," *The Energy Daily* 21(3) p. 1 (January 6, 1993).

32. Memorandum from Charles Lempesis to David H. Leroy, "Abbreviated Program Assessment and Forecast," p. 6 (December 14, 1992).

33. See, John S. Petterson, *Remedying Fundamental Flaws in the Nation's Civilian Radioactive Waste Management Program,* Impact Assessment, Inc., La Jolla, California (May, 1992).

34. Larry Ramspott, Lawrence Livermore Laboratory, personal communication (December 14, 1992).

35. *Fifth Report,* p.6. See also p. 47.

36. Nuclear Waste Technical Review Board, *Sixth Report to the U.S. Congress and the U.S. Secretary of Energy,* p. 15 (December, 1992).

37. Commission on Geosciences, Environment, and Resources, National Research Council, *Radioactive Waste Repository Licensing,* National Academy Press, p. 2 (1992).

38. Panel on Coupled Hydrolic/Tectonic/Hydrothermal Systems at Yucca Mountain, *Ground Water at Yucca Mountain, How High Can It Rise?,* National Academy Press, p. 143 (1992).

39. Isaac J. Winograd, *Yucca Mountain As A Nuclear Waste Repository—Neither Myth Nor Millennium,* U.S. Geological Survey Open-File Report 91-170, p. 5 (1991).

40. Linda L. Lehman, *Alternate Conceptual Model of Ground Water Flow at Yucca Mountain*, L. Lehman & Associates, Burnsville, Minnesota, p. 3 (December 17, 1991).

41. Winograd, op.cit., p. 4.

42. Panel, op. cit., pp. 141-142.

43. "Consensus Position", *Report of the Peer Review Panel on the Early Site Suitability Evaluation of the Potential Repository Site at Yucca Mountain, Nevada*, Science Applications International Corporation, p. B-1 (January 1992).

44. *Id.*

45. Nuclear Waste Technical Review Board, *Sixth Report to the U.S. Congress and the U.S. Secretary of Energy*, p. 38 (December 1992).

46. U.S. General Accounting Office, *DOE's Repository Site Investigations, a Long and Difficult Task*, GAO/RCED-92-73, p. 2 (May 1992).

47. Letter to James D. Watkins, Secretary of Energy, dated April 22, 1992, p. 1.

48. *Id.* at 3.

49. *Id.* at 5.

50. *Id.* at 6. In a subsequent letter, General Hall also observed that since 7 January 1983, "The Project has spent 1.2 billion dollars and accomplished very little of the characterization tasks outlined in the law...As of 8 May 1992 only 35 of the 109 required study plans have been submitted to the NRC for their review." (Letter to Tom A. Hendrickson, Acting Under Secretary of Energy, dated June 17, 1992, p. 2.)

51. *Id.* at 6.

52. Letter to Tom A. Hendrickson, Acting Under Secretary of Energy, dated June 17, 1992, p. 6.

53. *Id.* at 5.

54. Elio D'Appolonia, "Monitored Decisions," *Journal of Geotechnical Engineering 116*, American Society of Civil Engineering, p. 5 (January, 1990).

55. Nuclear Waste Technical Review Board, *Sixth Report to the U.S. Congress and the U.S. Secretary of Energy*, p. 26 (December, 1992).

56. *Id.*

57. *Id.* at 8.

58. *See*, Lawrence D. Ramspott, "The Constructive Use of Heat in an Unsaturated Tuff Repository," *Proceedings of the 1991 International High-Level Radioactive Waste Management Conference, Las Vegas, Nevada, April 28-May 3, 1991.* Volume 2, pp. 1602-1607.

59. Ahearne, *op. cit.*, p. 13.

60. Petterson, *op. cit.*, p. 5.

61. Thomas A. Cotton, "Current Social Systems Issues in the U.S. High Level Waste Management Program," presented at the 1990 High Level Radioactive Waste Management Conference in Las Vegas, Nevada, p. 2.

62. *See*, for instance, the discussion paper issued on December 8, 1992, by the Secretary of Energy Advisory Board Task Force on Radioactive Waste Management.

63. *Overview of the Clark County, Nevada, Nuclear Waste Repository Program,*

Yucca Mountain and Governmental Trust Issues: The Perspective from Clark County, presented before the Secretary of Energy Advisory Board Task Force on Civilian Radioactive Waste Management, November 6, 1991, p. 5.

64. Peter T. Johnson, "How I Turned A Critical Public Into Useful Consultants," *Harvard Business Review*, p. 4 (January-February 1993).

65. James L. Creighton, *Report on the Bonneville Power Administration Public Involvement Program*, Bonneville Power Administration, U.S. Department of Energy (August 1984). (A separate "Executive Summary" also was published.)

66. *Id* at 17 (emphasis in original)

67. *Id* at 20. (emphasis in original)

68. *Id* at 122-123.

69. Johnson, *op. cit*, p. 7.

70. Johnson, *op. cit.*, p. 8.

71. Johnson, *op. cit*, p. 8.

72. Johnson, *op. cit*, p. 12.

73. James L. Creighton, *Report on the Bonneville Power Administration Public Involvement Program*, Bonneville Power Administration, U.S. Department of Energy (March, 1991).

74. *Id.* at 34

75. "Conservationists Put Hardy on "Probation," *Northwest Conservation Act Report 12* (2), p. 7 (January 22, 1993).

76. One report assessing how to expedite the characterization of Yucca Mountain stated that "Following current procedures, it is estimated that more than 2 years are required to implement a new field test or analysis. In contrast, utility companies under NQA-1 [quality assurance] programs in reactor construction frequently begin new tests within several weeks of conception." The report explains that the DOE process takes so long, because "DOE uses an extensive review cycle and neither delegates authority for conducting tests nor designates the responsible participant to authorize work." (ATLAS Task Force, *Evaluation of Alternative Licensing Strategies for the Development of a High-Level Nuclear Waste Repository*, YMP/90-47, U.S. Department of Energy, p. B-4 (October 2, 1990).)

77. Luther J. Carter, "Nuclear Waste Policy and Politics," *Forum for Applied Research and Public Policy*, p. 14 (Fall 1989).

78. Jackie L. Braitman, *Nuclear Waste Disposal: Can Government Cope?* P-6942-RGI, The Rand Corporation, p. ix (December, 1983).

79. Advisory Panel on Alternative Means of Financing and Managing Radioactive Waste Facilities, *Managing Nuclear Waste—A Better Idea*, p. XII-2 (December 1984).

80. *National Energy Strategy*, First Edition, 1991/1992, p. 13 (February, 1991).

81. Office of Civilian Radioactive Waste Management, *Draft Mission Plan Amendment*, p. 169 (September 1991).

82. At a meeting convened by the U.S. Nuclear Waste Negotiator, he was advised to "(m)aintain a physical and bureaucratic distance from the `Washington Establishment' and federal agencies in which the public has little

confidence." (*Summary, Office of the Nuclear Waste Negotiator Panel Meeting, March 11, 1991*, Technical Resources, Inc., Rockville, Maryland.)

83. National Research Council, Division on Human Behavior and Performance, *Workshop on Establishing Institutional Credibility for SEAB Task Force on Radioactive Waste Management, Summary of Proceedings*, p. 10 (October 24-25, 1991).

84. Fred Morris, Senior Research Associate, Battelle Human Affairs Research Centers, Seattle, Washington, personal communication (December 2, 1992).

85. A similar set of recommendations by John S. Petterson was made independently to the Secretary of Energy Advisory Board Task Force on Civilian Radioactive Waste Management in May, 1992. Although the basic thrust of the two sets of recommendations is the same, there are significant differences in detail. Among the differences is Petterson's rejection of a new, independent organization to manage the high-level radioactive waste program and the specificity of his recommendation for a new, above-ground long-term storage facility for spent fuel.

86. A similar suggestion was made by an ad hoc contractor task force in the context of then-existing delays in obtaining environmental permits: "For example, the Nuclear Waste Negotiator [could] be called upon to help determine the terms and conditions under which the state may let portions of the site characterization program proceed." (ATLAS Task Force, *Evaluation of Alternative Licensing Strategies for the Development of a High-Level Nuclear Waste Repository*, U.S. Department of Energy, YMP/90-49, p. 3-7 (October 2, 1990).)

About the Book and Editors

Five decades after the first splitting of the atom, the military and civilian applications of nuclear energy have reached a critical juncture, providing an unprecedented opportunity to reexamine both the national and international mechanisms for controlling nuclear energy.

The disintegration of the Soviet Union has eliminated the need to maintain and modernize a large nuclear arsenal and sharpened the focus on horizontal proliferation problems, such as Iraq's clandestine nuclear weapons program, "civil" plutonium production, the potential loss of central Russian control over the former Soviet nuclear arsenal, and North Korea's threatened defection from the Nuclear Nonproliferation Treaty. In addition, both the United States and Russia are faced with the staggering environmental legacy of fifty years of nuclear weapons production.

On the civilian side, utilities have canceled or deferred plans to build more than 100 nuclear power plants since the early 1970s in response to nuclear safety concerns, limited on-site waste storage capacity, the absence of a permanent high-level nuclear waste repository, and high capital and operating costs as compared with other energy sources.

A reasoned reevaluation of military and civilian applications of nuclear energy is being thwarted by antiquated, undemocratic Cold War policies that polarize citizens, industry, and government into militant pro- and anti-nuclear camps, leading to gridlock in solving such key problems as the disposal of high-level nuclear waste. Written by a diverse group of experts, *Controlling the Atom in the 21st Century* offers an alternative problem-solving approach to these issues—one that seeks to minimize the environmental and security risks posed by nuclear energy while ensuring a more open, fair-minded assessment of its potential benefits as an energy source.

David P. O'Very, a Legal Fellow in the NRDC Nuclear Program during preparation of this book, is an attorney advisor to the Office of Radiation and Indoor Air, U.S. Environmental Protection Agency. **Christopher E. Paine** is a Senior Research Associate in the NRDC Nuclear Program. **Dan W. Reicher,** Senior Attorney in NRDC's Nuclear Program at the time this book was prepared, is Deputy Chief of Staff and Environmental Counsel to the Secretary, U.S. Department of Energy.

About the Contributors

Allan Robert Adler is a partner with the law firm of Cohn & Marks. Mr. Adler was formerly Legislative Counsel to the American Civil Liberties Union. He graduated from the National Law Center at George Washington University and received his undergraduate degree from the State University of New York.

Dan Berkovitz is Counsel for the U.S. Senate Committee on Environment and Public Works. From 1982-85, he worked as an attorney in the Office of General Council, U.S. Nuclear Regulatory Commission. Mr. Berkovitz is a graduate of Hastings College of Law and Princeton University.

Thomas B. Cochran is the Director of NRDC's Nuclear Project. Dr. Cochran co-authored NRDC's *Nuclear Weapons Databook* series and has served as a consultant to numerous non-governmental organizations and federal agencies, including the Department of Energy and the Nuclear Regulatory Commission. Dr. Cochran received a Ph.D. in Physics and an undergraduate degree from Vanderbilt University.

Diane Curran is a partner with the law firm of Harmon, Curran, Gallagher & Spielberg. Ms. Curran represents public interest organizations such as the Sierra Club and the Union of Concerned Scientists. Ms. Curran is a graduate of the University of Maryland School of Law and Yale University.

Eric Glitzenstein is a partner with the law firm of Meyer and Glitzenstein. Mr. Glitzenstein was formerly a partner with the law firm of Harmon, Curran, Gallagher & Spielberg and an attorney with the Public Citizen Litigation Group. Mr. Glitzenstein is a graduate of Georgetown University Law Center and Johns Hopkins University.

Kevin T. Knobloch was formerly Legislative Director for arms control at the Union of Concerned Scientists and Legislative Director for Senator Tim Wirth. Mr. Knobloch has a masters degree from the John F. Kennedy School of Government at Harvard University and received his undergraduate degree from the University of Massachusetts at Amherst.

Terry R. Lash is an independent consultant based in Springfield, Illinois. From 1984-90, Dr. Lash served as Director of the Illinois Department of Nuclear Safety and was a Senior Staff Scientist at NRDC in the 1970s. Dr. Lash received a

Ph.D. and M.Ph. in molecular biophysics and biochemistry from Yale University and a B.A. in Physics from Reed College.

Henry R. Myers worked as Chief Science Advisor to the Committee on Interior and Insular Affairs, U.S. House of Representatives from 1976-1991. Dr. Myers received his Ph.D. in Physics from the California Institute of Technology and is a graduate of the Massachusetts Institute of Technology.

David P. O'Very is an attorney advisor to the Office of Radiation and Indoor Air, U.S. Environmental Protection Agency. At the time this book was prepared, he was a Legal Fellow in the International and Nuclear Program at NRDC. Mr. O'Very is a graduate of the Willamette University College of Law and Pomona College.

Christopher E. Paine is a Senior Research Associate in the International and Nuclear Program at NRDC. Before joining NRDC in 1991, Mr. Paine worked as a legislative assistant for arms control to Senator Edward Kennedy and as a staff consultant for nuclear nonproliferation policy to the House Subcommittee on Energy and Power. He received his B.A. degree in Economics from Harvard University.

Paul Parshley is a Senior Vice-President of Lehman Brothers and head of electric utility fixed income research. Prior to joining Lehman Brothers, Mr. Parshley served as Senior Vice-President at Donaldson, Lufkin & Jenrette. He has an MBA from the Wharton School at the University of Pennsylvania, a Masters in Regional Planning from Harvard University, and received his undergraduate degree from Colgate University.

Martin J. Pasqualetti is a Professor of Geography at Arizona State University. Dr. Pasqualetti recently served as an advisor to the U.S. Congress' Office of Technology Assessment on nuclear power plant aging and decommissioning and as an advisor to the U.S. Department of Energy on inadvertent intrusion into the high-level nuclear waste facility in New Mexico (WIPP). Dr. Pasqualetti received a Ph.D. from the University of California at Riverside, a M.A. from Louisiana State University at Baton Rouge and a B.A from the University of California at Berkeley.

Dan W. Reicher is Deputy Chief of Staff and Environmental Counsel to the Secretary, U.S. Department of Energy. At the time this book was prepared he was a Senior Attorney in the International and Nuclear Program at NRDC, an Adjunct Professor at the University of Maryland Law School and a member of the National Academy of Sciences Board on Radioactive Waste Management. Previously, Mr. Reicher was an Assistant Attorney General in the Environmental Protection Division of the Massachusetts Attorney General's Office. He is a graduate of Stanford Law School and Dartmouth College.

Conference Participants

Professor Dean Abrahamson
Humphrey Institute of
  Public Affairs
University of Minnesota
301 19th Avenue, South
Minneapolis, MN 55455

Allan Robert Adler, Esq.
Cohn & Marks
Suite 600
1333 New Hampshire Ave., NW
Washington, D.C. 20036-1573

Dr. John Ahearne
Executive Director
Sigma Xi
P.O. Box 13975
Research Triangle Park, NC 27709

Robert Alvarez
Senate Committee on
  Governmental Affairs
340 Dirksen Senate Office Bldg.
Washington, DC 20510-6250

Dan Berkovitz, Esq.
Counsel
Senate Committee on Environment
  and Public Works
458 Dirksen Senate Office Bldg
Washington, DC 20510-6175

Dr. Robert Civiak
Office of Management & Budget
NEOB 8002
725 17th Street, NW
Washington, D.C. 20503

Dr. Benjamin S. Cooper
Staff Director
Senate Committee on Energy and
  Natural Resources
364 Dirksen Senate Office Bldg.
Washington, D.C. 20510-6150

Dr. Thomas Cotton
Vice President
JK Research Associates, Inc.
4303 N. 11th Street
Arlington, VA 22201

Madelyn Creedon, Esq.
Counsel
Senate Armed Services Committee
228 Russell Senate Office Bldg.
Washington, D.C. 20519-6050

David Culp
Plutonium Challenge
1350 New York Avenue, NW, Suite
300
Washington, D.C. 20005

Diane Curran, Esq.
Harmon, Curran, Gallagher &
  Spielberg
2001 S Street, NW, Suite 430
Washington, D.C. 20009-1125

James H. Davenport, Esq.
Suite 307
1110 S. Capital Way
Olympia, WA 95501

Robert DeGrasse
Professional Staff Member
House Armed Services Committee
2120 Rayburn House Office Bldg.
Washington, DC 20515-6035

Eric Glitzenstein, Esq.
Meyer & Glitzenstein
1601 Connecticut Ave., N.W.
Suite 450
Washington, DC 20009-1035

Sherri Goodman, Esq.
Goodwin, Procter & Hoar
Exchange Place
Boston, MA 02109

Emilia Govan, Esq.
Science, Information & Natural
  Resources Division
Oceans and Environment Programs
Office of Technology Assessment
600 Pennsylvania Ave., SE
Washington, DC 20510

Eldon Greenberg, Esq.
Garvey Schubert & Barer
1000 Potomac Street, NW, 5th Floor
Washington, DC 20007

William Lanouette
General Accounting Office
326 Fifth Street, S.E.
Washington, D.C. 20003

Dr. Terry R. Lash
1112 West Fayette Avenue
Springfield, IL 62704

Paul Leventhal
Nuclear Control Institute
1000 Connecticut Avenue, N.W.
Suite 704
Washington, DC   20036

Martin Malsch, Esq.
Office of General Counsel
Nuclear Regulatory Commission
Washington, D.C. 20555

William J. McGee
Director of Public Affairs
Yankee Atomic Electric
HC87, Box 160
Rowe, MA 01367

Dr. Daniel Metlay
Taskforce Director
Secretary of Energy Advisory Board
U.S. Department of Energy
Forrestal Bldg., Rm. 7B-198/AC-1
1000 Independence Ave., SW
Washington, D.C. 20585

Henry R. Myers
Former Chief Science Advisor
House Interior Committee
P.O. Box 88
Peaks Island, ME 04108

David P. O'Very, Esq.
U.S. Environmental Protection
Agency
Office of Radiation and Indoor Air
401 M Street, SW (6602J)
Washington, DC 20460

Christopher E. Paine
Natural Resources Defense Council
1350 New York Avenue, NW, Suite
300
Washington, DC 20005

Paul Parshley
Senior Vice President
Lehman Brothers
200 Vesey Street, 14th Floor
New York, NY 10285

Professor Martin J. Pasqualetti
Department of Geography
Arizona State University
Tempe, AZ 85287-0104

James Payne, Esq.
Assistant Attorney General
Environmental Enforcement Section
30 East Broad Street
25th Floor
Columbus, OH 43266-0410

Caroline Petti
U.S. Environmental Protection
Agency
401 M Street, SW, 6602J
Washington, D.C. 20460

Dan W. Reicher, Esq.
Office of the Secretary
U.S. Department of Energy
1000 Independence Avenue, SW
Washington, DC 20585

Victor S. Rezendes
Director
Energy Issues
General Accounting Office
441 G Street, NW, Rm. 1842
Washington, DC 20548

Jeff Seabright
Office of Senator Wirth
SR-380 Russell Senate Off. Bldg.
Washington, D.C. 20510-0603

Sue Sheridan, Esq.
Counsel
Subcommittee on Energy & Power
331 House Annex 2
Washington, D.C. 20515-6120

E. Gail Suchman, Esq.
Assistant Attorney General
State of New York
Department of Law
120 Broadway
New York, NY 10271

Dean Tousley, Esq.
Counsel
Subcommittee on Energy &
  Environment
House Committee on Interior
  and Insular Affairs
522 O'Neill House Office Bldg.
Washington, D.C. 20515-6202

Index